# JOAN OF ARC

*The truth is, since I was thirteen, I have been hearing unknown voices very often; they are beautiful and melodious voices... Sweet as it is, the nightingale's song is nothing compared to them.*

—Thérèse of Lisieux
From *The Plays of Saint Thérèse of Lisieux*
"The Mission of Joan of Arc"
January 21, 1894

# JOAN OF ARC

## AND

# HER TRIAL TRANSCRIPTS

LITTLE FLOWER PUBLISHING

Cover Design:  Tanja Grubisic/bookcoverworld.com

Cover Photo: Mazirama/bigstock.com

Published simultaneously in the United States of America, France, and other countries worldwide.

ISBN 978-0-9883230-1-8

RELIGION/Christianity/Catholic
REL010000

QC 0300.0513.0501.0929
Edition: CMG 032311210128

Little Flower Publishing
Dallas, TX

June 2016

*When asked why the angel came to her rather than to another person, she answered, "It pleased God to drive back the king's enemies through a simple virgin."*

—Trial Transcripts

# Contents – Trial Transcripts

## SOURCES

Guillaume Manchon, a notary, produced the original transcripts in Medieval/Middle French, with oversight and assistance from two other notaries, Guillaume Colles and Nicolas Taquel. Later, Manchon and one of the trial judges, Thomas de Courcelles, translated the Middle French into Latin and five handwritten copies were made. One copy was sent to Rome, three copies are in Paris, and one copy was destroyed ceremoniously in 1456 at the conclusion of a Rehabilitation Trial, which nullified the verdict of the Condemnation Trial. The first unabridged translations of those original Latin transcripts were published in modern French in 1841 by Jules Étienne Joseph Quicherat and in English in 1932 by W.P. Barrett. This abridged version produced by Emilia Philomena Sanguinetti was translated and edited using those two unabridged translations and Pierre Champion's *Procès de Condamnation de Jeanne d'Arc, Texte, Traduction et Notes,* published in 1921. Sanguinetti's Trial Transcripts were edited solely for readability in modern English, and no attempt was made to use language or the editing process as a means to support or refute various opinions about the sexuality and gender identity of Joan of Arc, the history of the Catholic Church, or the origin of Joan's "Voices."

# Contents – Epilogue

## PRE-TRIAL PHASE (JANUARY 9 - FEBRUARY 20)

### January 9, Experts Gather to Discuss Evidence

[Introductory statements are entered into the court's records, including the following.]

It has pleased divine Providence that a woman of the name of Joan, commonly known as the Maid [the Virgin], should be apprehended by military personnel within the boundaries and limits of our diocese and jurisdiction. The reputation of this woman has already been spread across many areas: how wholly forgetful of womanly honesty, and having thrown off the bonds of shame, careless of all the modesty of womankind, she wore with an astonishing and extreme brazenness immodest garments belonging to the male sex; and her audacity increased until she was not afraid to behave, speak and spread many ideas contrary to the Catholic faith and damaging to orthodox beliefs; and by doing so, in our diocese and in several other areas, she is said to be guilty of many offenses.

[A series of letters written by doctors and masters of theology from the University of Paris is introduced for discussion; among those letters is the following.]

Let this woman, commonly known as the Virgin, a prisoner, be sent to the king to be delivered to the Church so that she may be tried in court, being suspected of having committed numerous crimes such as sorcery, idolatry, the calling-up of evil spirits and many other activities opposed to our faith. Although she should not be considered a prisoner of war, nevertheless, to reward those who captured her, the king is pleased to grant them up to the sum of 6,000 francs, and to the individual who captured her, the king will grant a pension of 200 or 300 pounds for the upkeep of his estate.

Because this woman was captured in his diocese and under his spiritual jurisdiction, the Bishop requires that these individuals deliver her to him so that he may appropriately try her in court. This he is ready to do with the assistance of the Inquisitor of the Faith, and if need be, with the assistance of doctors of theology and other notable persons who are experts in judicial matters, as the legal case requires, in order that the trial may be carried out in a thorough, holy and proper manner, to the exaltation of the faith and to the instruction of many who have been deceived and abused through this woman's actions.

## January 13, Reading the Evidence against Joan

In the city of Rouen, we, with the Bishop of Beauvais, Pierre Cauchon, assembled a group of religious authorities and experts in canon law. All evidence that had been previously gathered was reviewed and members of the group asked each other for advice about the procedures that could be used in the forthcoming trial. Included in the group were Gilles, abbot of St. Trinite de Fecamp, Doctor of Theology; Nicolas de Venderes, licensed in canon law; William Haiton and Nicolas Couppequesne, bachelors of theology; Jean de La Fontaine, licensed in canon law; and Nicolas Loyseleur, Canon of the Cathedral of Rouen.

We read the specific evidence, collected both in the district where this woman was born and elsewhere, as well as documents prepared on items indicated in earlier reports. When all had been seen and heard, the lords and masters decided that specific articles should be prepared so that the case might appear to be more specific and better organized, so that officials could make decisions with greater certainty regarding whether there was sufficient evidence for a summons and a trial in matters of the faith.

In accordance with their advice, we decided to proceed to prepare the articles, and we appointed people who were known as authorities in canon and civil law to assist the notaries who would produce the documentation; and they, diligently complying with our command, proceeded to write the articles on the following Sunday, Monday and Tuesday.

## January 23, Decision on Preparatory Information

In the presence of the appointed experts the articles were read aloud, and we asked them for their most prudent opinions on the articles and the procedures that will be used in the forthcoming trial. We were advised that the articles were produced competently and that it was appropriate to proceed to interrogations corresponding to the articles. We declared that the Bishop of Beauvais, Pierre Cauchon, could and should proceed to produce the preparatory information regarding the behavior of the prisoner. Following this advice, we decided and commanded that the preparatory information be organized, but since we were otherwise engaged we appointed the esteemed and discreet Master Jean de La Fontaine, who is licensed in canon law, to conduct this task.

## February 13, Appointed Officers Take Oaths

Bishop Cauchon and other authorities required the court officials and notaries to take an oath to fulfill their offices faithfully. In obedience, they swore to fulfill and faithfully exercise their duties.

## February 14-16, Preparatory Information is Produced

Jean de La Fontaine, with assistance from two notaries, Guillaume Manchon and Guillaume Boisguillaume, produced the preparatory information.

## February 19, Decision to Summon the Inquisitor

Bishop Cauchon and other authorities informed the assembled officials that they had ordered a preparatory investigation into the words and behavior of this woman to discover if there was sufficient cause to begin proceedings against her and summon her in matters of the faith.

In their presence we read the articles and depositions contained in the preparatory evidence, which was followed by a lengthy and expert discussion of the evidence. We concluded that we had sufficient evidence to begin proceedings against this woman and summon her in matters of the faith, and we ruled that she should be cited and summoned to answer specific questions that would be addressed to her.

To benefit and facilitate carrying out the legal case, and with our respect for the apostolic Holy See [authority of the Catholic Church based in Rome], which has especially appointed lord Inquisitors of Heretical Error to correct evils that arise against orthodox faith, we decided at the advice of our experienced counselors to invite and summon the lord Inquisitor of Heretics for the kingdom of France to collaborate with us in this trial if it was his pleasure and interest. However, because the Inquisitor was then absent from the city of Rouen we commanded that his deputy, who was present in Rouen, be summoned and called in his place.

The same Monday at four in the afternoon we were visited in our house by the esteemed and discreet Master Jean Le Maistre of the Order of Preaching Brothers [Dominicans], deputy of the lord Inquisitor of the kingdom of France and appointed by him to the city and Diocese of Rouen. We summoned and required the deputy to join us so that we might proceed with the trial, and we offered to acquaint him with everything that had already been accomplished and what was being planned for the future.

The deputy answered that he was prepared to show us his commission, or letters of appointment, given to him by the lord Inquisitor, and he would gladly perform everything he was bound by duty to do on behalf of the holy Inquisition. But because he was especially appointed for the diocese and city of Rouen only, he doubted whether his commission could be interpreted to include the present trial, although the territory had been ceded to us because we had undertaken these proceedings in virtue of our jurisdiction in the Diocese of Beauvais. We answered that he should return to us tomorrow when we would be able to get additional counsel on the matter.

### February 20, Deputy of the Inquisitor Declines to Act

Jean Le Maistre replied that to ensure the serenity of his conscience and the safer conduct of the trial, he would not participate unless he received special authorization. Nevertheless, he indicated that we should proceed until he received additional counsel regarding the question of whether he could, by virtue of his commission, participate in the conduct of the trial. We then offered to acquaint him with our previous activities and future plans.

After receiving decisions by assessors of the evidence, which were documented in written letters, we ruled that this woman should be summoned to appear before us the following Wednesday.

## PREPARATORY TRIAL (FEBRUARY 21 - MARCH 17)

### February 21, First Session in a Public Venue

On Wednesday, February 21, at eight o'clock in the morning, Bishop Cauchon and others arrived at the royal chapel in the castle of Rouen, where they summoned the woman to appear before us at that hour and day.

In the presence of authorities and officials the first letters read were from the king regarding the surrender of this woman, and then the letters from Rouen granting us territorial authority.

Then Master Jean d'Estivet, appointed as Promoter in the trial, reported he had ordered Joan to be cited and summoned by our usher to appear at this place, on the day and hour prescribed, to answer questions that could be legally put to her, as is clearly shown in the usher's report affixed to our letters of citation:

Given at Rouen under our seal on Tuesday, February 20, 1431.

Pierre, by divine mercy the Bishop of Beauvais, being in possession of territory in the city and Diocese of Rouen, by the authority of the esteemed chapter of the cathedral of Rouen, in the vacancy of the arch-episcopal seat and for the purpose of conducting and concluding this matter, to the dean of the Christendom of Rouen, to all priests, whether curates or not, of this city and diocese, who will see these letters, I say to you, greetings in the name and consummator of our faith.

Because a woman commonly called Joan the Virgin was apprehended and captured within our Diocese of Beauvais, and because she surrendered and was dispatched, given and delivered to us by the most Christian and peaceful prince, the lord king of France and England, as a person overwhelmingly suspected of heresy so that we could begin proceedings against her in matters of the faith, and in view of the fact that rumors of her behavior and her words, which were wounding our faith, had notoriously spread not only throughout the kingdom of France but also throughout all Christendom, we, who desire to proceed authoritatively in these affairs, decided after a diligent inquiry and consultation with educated men, that Joan should be summoned, cited and heard to respond to the articles and questions that have

7

been made against her upon matters concerning the faith. Therefore, we require each and every one of you not to wait for another person if he is summoned by us, nor to excuse himself on account of another person.

Now, officially summon Joan, so overwhelmingly suspected of heresy, to appear before us in the royal chapel of the castle of Rouen at eight o'clock in the morning on Wednesday, February 21, to speak the truth about the articles, questions and other matters, and to be dealt with as we think just and reasonable, declaring to her that she will be excommunicated if she fails to appear before us on that day; give us a faithful account in writing, you who are to be present, to document the events.

## Usher's Statement

To the reverend father in Christ, the lord Pierre, by divine mercy Bishop of Beauvais, possessing territory in the city and Diocese of Rouen, in the vacancy of the arch-episcopal seat for the purpose of conducting and concluding this matter, and by the pleasure of the esteemed chapter of the cathedral of Rouen, your humble priest, Jean Massieu, dean of the Christendom of Rouen, offers prompt obedience to your orders in all reverence and honor. Let it be known to you, reverend father, that in virtue of the summons you addressed to me, I have authoritatively cited to appear before you at eight o'clock in the morning on Wednesday, February 21, in the royal chapel of the castle of Rouen, the woman commonly called the Virgin, whom I have imprisoned within the limits of this castle and whom you overwhelmingly suspect of heresy, to answer truthfully to the articles and questions that will be addressed to her upon matters of the faith and on other points which you consider her to be suspect, and to be dealt with according to law and reason, and the intention of your letters.

Joan replied that she would willingly appear before you and answer truthfully regarding the questions to which she will be subjected. Nevertheless, she requested for this trial that you summon clerics of the French side equal in number to those of the English side. Furthermore, she humbly begs you, reverend father, to permit her to attend Mass before she appears before you, and she asked that I inform you of these requests, which I have done. By these present letters sealed with my seal and signed with my signature, I testify to you, reverend father, that all this has been done by me. Given in the year of our Lord, 1431, on Tuesday, February 20.

After reading the letters submitted by the officials, the Promoter immediately requested that this woman be commanded to appear before us in judgment in accordance with the summons, to be examined upon certain articles concerning the faith.

But since this woman had requested to be allowed to attend Mass, we informed the assessors that we had consulted with notable lords and masters on this question; and in view of the crimes with which this woman has been accused, especially the impropriety of the men's clothing that she continues to wear, it was their opinion that we should properly defer permission for her to attend Mass and the Divine Office prayers.

**Joan is led in to the Courtroom**

While we were saying these things this woman was brought in by our usher. Since she was appearing in judgment before us, we began to explain how this Joan had been taken and apprehended within the boundaries and limits of our Diocese of Beauvais; how many of her actions, not only in our diocese but in many other regions, had harmed the orthodox faith, and how reports of her behavior had spread throughout all of Christendom; and how recently the most serene and Christian prince, our lord the king, had given and delivered this woman to us to be tried in matters of the faith according to law and reason.

Therefore, considering the public rumors and reports, and after expert consultation with men educated in canon and civil law, we ruled that Joan should be summoned and cited by letter to truthfully answer these questions in matters of the faith and other items, according to law and reason, as documented in the letters shown by the Promoter.

As it is our office to keep and exalt the Catholic faith, we first, with the gentle comfort of Jesus Christ whose issue this is, charitably admonished and required Joan, who is seated before us, that to quickly end this trial and unburden her own conscience, she should answer the whole truth regarding the questions to be put to her on these matters of faith, avoiding deception and other ploys that would hinder truthful confession.

Furthermore, in our official capacity, we lawfully required Joan to take the proper oath, with her hands on the holy Gospels, to speak the truth when answering the questions put to her.

Joan replied, "I do not know what you wish to examine me on. Perhaps you might ask me things that I would not be willing to discuss."

Then we said, "Will you swear to speak the truth about those things which are asked of you concerning the faith, which you know?"

Joan replied that concerning her father and her mother and what she had done since she had traveled through France, she would gladly swear; but concerning the revelations from God, these she had never told nor revealed to anyone, except only to King Charles; she said she would not discuss the revelations, even to save her life, because she had them in visions or by her secret counsel; however, she said that within a week she would know with certainty whether she might reveal them at a future date.

Then, repeatedly, we, with Bishop Cauchon, admonished and required her to take an oath to speak the truth in those things that concerned our faith.

Joan, kneeling, and with her two hands upon the book, namely the Catholic Missal, swore to answer truthfully whatever would be asked of her, which she knew, concerning matters of the faith, but she was silent regarding whether she would discuss or reveal to any person the content of the revelations made to her.

After she took the oath Joan was questioned by us about her name and her surname. She replied that in her own territory she was called Joanette, and after she came to France she was called Joan. Regarding her surname she said she didn't know it. As a result, she was questioned about the district from which she came. She replied that she was born in the village of Domremy, which is contiguous with the village of Greux.

Asked about the names of her father and mother, she replied that her father's name was Jacques d'Arc and her mother's Isabelle. Asked where she was baptized, she replied it was in the church of Domremy.

Asked who were her godfathers and godmothers, she said one of her godmothers was named Agnes, another was named Joan and another Sibylle; regarding her godfathers, one was named Jean Lingue and another was named Jean Barrey. She said she had several other godmothers according to what she had heard from her mother.

We asked her what priest had baptized her and she said it was Jean Minet. Asked if he was still living, she said she believed he was.

Asked how old she was, she said she thought she was nineteen years old.

She added that her mother taught her the Our Father prayer, the Hail Mary and the Creed, and that no one but her mother had taught her the Creed.

When we asked her to say the Our Father she said that if we would hear her in Confession then she would gladly say it for us. As we repeatedly demanded that she say the Our Father prayer for us, she replied that she would not say it unless we would hear her say it in the Sacrament of Confession. Then we told her that we would gladly send one or two distinguished men who spoke French to hear her say the Our Father prayer, to which Joan replied she would not say it to them, except in Confession.

At this point we forbade Joan to leave the prison cell assigned to her in the castle of Rouen without our authorization, under penalty of conviction of the crime of heresy. She answered that she did not accept this prohibition, adding that if she escaped nobody could accuse her of breaking or violating her oath because she had given this oath [of not escaping] to nobody.

She then complained that she was imprisoned with chains and restraints made of iron. We told her that she had tried elsewhere and on several occasions to escape from prison, and therefore, so that she might be more safely and securely guarded, an order had been given to bind her with iron chains.

She replied, "It is true that I wished, and I still wish, to escape, as is lawful for any captive or prisoner."

To safely guard Joan, we then commissioned John Grey, Squire of the bodyguard of our lord the king, and with him Jean Berwoit and William Talbot, directing them to guard her well and faithfully, and to permit nobody to speak with her without our consent. Then, with their hands on the Gospels, they solemnly swore to do so.

Finally, having completed all the preliminaries of the trial, we commanded Joan to appear before us the following day, Thursday, at eight o'clock in the morning, in the Robing Room at the end of the great hall of the castle of Rouen.

## February 22, Second Session

On Thursday, February 22, we entered the Robing Room at the end of the great hall of the castle of Rouen, where there were assembled the reverend fathers, lords and masters.

In their presence we saw Jean Le Maistre, deputy of the lord Inquisitor, who had been summoned and required by us to take part in the proceedings. We offered to discuss with him all that had been so far accomplished and what was being planned.

But the deputy said that he had been appointed and commissioned by the lord Inquisitor for the city and Diocese of Rouen only, whereas we were holding the trial, by reason of our jurisdiction in Beauvais, on ceded territory. Therefore, to avoid nullification of the trial and for the peace of his conscience, he put off his participation until he could receive further counsel and a more extended power or commission from the lord Inquisitor. In the meantime, the deputy said he would be pleased to have us continue our proceedings without interruption. When he heard our understanding of the situation, the deputy replied, "What you have said is true. I have been, and I am, as far as my capability allows me, satisfied that you should continue the trial."

Joan was then brought before us and we admonished and required her, under penalty of law, to take the oath she had taken the day before, and to swear to speak the truth, absolutely and simply, on everything which she was asked regarding the matters of which she was accused.

Her reply was that she had already taken an oath yesterday and that should be sufficient.

Then we required her to swear, because nobody, not even a prince, could refuse to take an oath when required in matters of the faith. She answered again, saying, "I swore yesterday and that should be quite enough. You over-burden me."

Finally she swore to speak the truth regarding that which concerned the faith. Then the distinguished professor of sacred theology, Master Jean Beaupere, at our order and command, questioned Joan as follows.

He first insisted that she answer truthfully, as she had sworn, to whatever he should ask her.

She replied, "You may well ask me some things that to some I shall answer truthfully and to others I shall not; if you were well informed about me, you would wish me to be out of your hands. I have done nothing except by revelation."

Asked how old she was when she left her father's house, she said she could not say with certainty.

Asked if in her youth she had learned any craft, she said yes, to sew and to spin, and in sewing and spinning she feared no woman in Rouen.

She admitted it was because of fear of the Burgundians [inhabitants of the region of Burgundy who were allied with the English against the French in the Hundred Years War] that she left her father's house and went to the town of Neufchateau, in Lorraine, to the house of a woman named La Rousse, where she stayed for about two weeks.

She said that as long as she was at home with her father she did ordinary domestic tasks and did not go into the fields to look after the sheep and other animals.

Asked if she confessed her sins once a year, she said yes, to her local priest, and when he wasn't available she confessed to another priest, with his permission. Sometimes, maybe two or three times, she said she confessed to mendicant friars, but that was in the town of Neufchateau. She said she received the Sacrament of the Eucharist at Easter.

When asked if, at feasts other than Easter, she received the Sacrament of the Eucharist, she said, "Go to the next question."

She said that at the age of 13 she first heard a Voice from God, to help her and to guide her. She said the first time she heard the Voice she was very frightened.

The first time the Voice came it occurred during the summer, around noon, when she was in her father's garden. She heard the Voice on her right side, coming from the direction of the church.

Whenever she heard the Voice it was almost always accompanied by a visible light, and the light came from the same side as the Voice, and generally the light was a very bright light.

Asked how she could see the light since it was at her side and not in front of her, she didn't reply and went on to describe other things. She said that if she was in a forest or a wooded area she easily heard the Voices coming to her.

She said that a characteristic of the Voice was that it was admirable, and she believed it was sent from God. When she heard the Voice for the third time she said she knew that it was the Voice of an angel; she also said this Voice always protected her well, and that she understood it well.

Asked what instructions this Voice gave to her regarding the salvation of her soul, she said it taught her to be good and to go to church often. The Voice also told her that she must travel to France. Joan added that Beaupere, the questioner, would not learn from her at this time in what form that Voice appeared to her.

She said this Voice told her once or twice a week that she should leave her house and come to France, and that her father wasn't aware that she was planning to leave. She said the Voice told her to come, and that she could no longer stay where she was.

The Voice told her that she should use military force to retake the city of Orleans [which was occupied by English soldiers]. To do this she said the Voice told her that she, Joan, should go to see Robert de Baudricourt in the town of Vaucouleurs, of which he was captain, and that he would provide an escort for her. Joan replied to the Voice saying she was a poor maid, and that she knew nothing about riding horses or fighting in military campaigns. After this conversation with her Voice she said she went to an uncle of hers and told him that she wanted to stay with him for some time. She stayed there about eight days and told her uncle that she must go to the town of Vaucouleurs, and so her uncle took her there.

When she reached Vaucouleurs she said she easily recognized Robert de Baudricourt even though she had never seen him before. She said she knew who he was through her Voice, because the Voice told her it was Robert de Baudricourt. Joan told Robert that she must go to France, but twice he refused to listen to her and disregarded her. The third time she spoke he listened to her and gave her an escort, and the Voice had told her that this would occur.

Then she said the Duke of Lorraine ordered that she should be taken to him, and she went to him and told him she wanted to go to France. The duke questioned her about the recovery of his health, but she replied she knew nothing about his illness and she spoke very little to him about her journey. Nevertheless, she told the duke to send his son and some men to escort her to France, and that she would pray to God for his health. She then returned to the town of Vaucouleurs.

She said when she departed from Vaucouleurs she wore men's clothes, and she carried a sword that Robert de Baudricourt had given her, but no other weapons. She was accompanied by a knight, a squire and four servants, and when she reached the town of Saint Urbain she slept there in an abbey.

She said that on her journey she passed through Auxerre and she attended Mass in the principal church there. From that time forward she said she frequently heard her Voices, including the one already mentioned.

When we required her to say by what counsel she decided to wear men's clothes, several times she refused to answer. Finally, she answered she could not say that anyone gave her the counsel to wear men's clothes, but several times she answered this question in various ways.

Regarding the men who accompanied her on her journey, she said that Robert de Baudricourt had made the men swear an oath that they would accompany her in a safe manner. Robert said to Joan, "Go," and as she departed, he said, "Go, and come what may."

Joan said she knows very well that God loves the Duke of Orleans, and because of this love, she has had more revelations concerning the Duke of Orleans than any man alive except King Charles. She also said that it was altogether necessary to exchange her women's clothes for men's clothes; she believed that her counsel instructed her well.

She said that she sent letters to the English military occupational force at Orleans telling them to depart. In the copies of these letters, which we read to her here in Rouen, she indicated there were discrepancies between these copies and the originals. In one copy, it reads "surrender to the Virgin," whereas she indicated it should read, "surrender to the King." There are also the words "body for body" and "commander-in-chief [Joan]," which she said were not in the original letters.

After this, Joan said she traveled to see the king without any interference or difficulties. She arrived at the town of St. Catherine de Fierbois and then reached Chinon around noon, where she lodged at an inn; after dinner she went to see the king, who was at the castle.

She said that when she entered a room at the castle, which was full of people, she was able to recognize the king [who was in disguise and mingling among the people] because her Voice told her which man was the king. She told the king she wanted to make war on the English.

Asked whether, when the Voice showed her the king, there was a light, she answered, "Go to the next question."

Asked if she saw an angel above the king, she answered, "Spare me that. Continue on."

She said that before the king put her to work he had experienced several apparitions and beautiful revelations. Asked what revelations and apparitions the king had, she answered, "I will not tell you. It is not now the time to tell you; but go to the king and he will tell you."

Joan said that her Voice had promised her that the king would receive her. She also said that other people accompanying her knew very well that the Voice was sent to Joan from God, and that they saw and knew this Voice. She further said that the king and several others heard and saw the Voices that came to Joan; among those were Charles de Bourbon and two or three others.

Then Joan said that there is not a day that goes by when she does not hear this Voice; and that she needs the Voice very much. She said she never asked the Voice for any final reward except only the salvation of her soul.

Her Voice told her to remain at the town of Saint-Denis in France, and although Joan wished to remain there, the lords took her away against her will. She added, however, that if she had not been wounded she would not have left Saint-Denis; she was wounded in the trenches on her way to Paris, but she recovered in five days.

She admitted that she was responsible for planning a military assault that was to be carried out on Paris; and when she was asked if that day was a Catholic feast day, she answered that she knew it certainly was. Asked if she thought it was a good thing to do, to attack Paris on a Catholic feast day, she answered, "Go to the next question."

At this point in the proceedings it appeared to us that we had covered sufficient ground for one day, so we postponed additional questioning until the following Saturday, at eight o'clock in the morning.

**February 24, Third Session**

On the following Saturday, February 24, we gathered in the same room in the castle of Rouen, where Joan appeared in judgment before us in the presence of many reverend fathers, doctors and masters. We first required Joan to speak the simple and absolute truth on the questions put to her, and to express no reservations regarding taking her oath; three times we admonished her to take the oath. Joan replied, "Just let me speak," and then said, "By my faith, you could ask me things that I would not answer."

She added, "Perhaps I shall not answer you truthfully in many things that you ask me concerning the revelations; and perhaps you would constrain me to tell you things that I have sworn not to speak about, and so I would be perjured, and you would not want that."

She added, "I tell you, be careful about what you say, because you are my judges and you assume a great responsibility, and you truly overburden me." She said that she thought it should be enough to have taken the oath twice already.

Then, when we asked if she would swear, simply and absolutely, she replied, "You may well do without it! I have sworn enough, twice!"

She added that all the clergy of Rouen and Paris could not condemn her except by law. She said that regarding her travels in France she would willingly speak the truth, but not the whole truth; and a week would not be enough for that.

But we, including the Bishop, told her to take the advice of the assessors regarding whether or not she should swear. To that she replied she would speak the truth about her coming to France, but nothing else, and that we must not speak to her about this anymore.

We said that she made herself open to suspicion if she would not swear to speak the truth. She replied in the same way as before.

Again, we required her to swear, precisely and absolutely. Then she replied that she would willingly say what she knew, but not everything. She also said that she came from God, and that there is nothing for her to do here, and she asked to be sent back to God, from whom she came.

Required and admonished to swear under threat of being accused of what was attributed to her, she answered, "Continue on."

A last time we required her to swear, and urgently admonished her to speak the truth in matters concerning the trial, telling her that she exposed herself to great danger by her refusal. She answered, "I am ready to swear to speak the truth of what I know concerning the trial," and it was in this manner that she took the oath.

Then, at our order, she was questioned by the distinguished Doctor Jean Beaupere, who first asked her when she last had anything to eat or drink. She answered that since yesterday noon she had not had anything to eat or drink.

Asked when she last heard the Voice come to her, she said, "I heard it yesterday and today."

Asked at what hour yesterday she heard the Voice, she said she heard it three times: once in the morning, once at Vespers [early evening prayers] and once when the Hail Mary [church bells] rung in the evening. Often she heard the Voice more frequently than that.

Asked what she was doing yesterday morning when the Voice came to her, she said she was sleeping and the Voice woke her up.

We asked if the Voice woke her up by touching her on the arm and she answered that it was without touching her.

We asked if the Voice was actually in her room and she replied that she didn't know, but that it was certainly in the castle.

When we asked if she thanked the Voice and knelt down, she answered that she did thank it, but she was sitting on the bed, and she put her hands together in prayer. Afterward she asked the Voice for advice and the Voice told her to answer our questions boldly.

We asked her what the Voice said when she was awakened. She said she asked the Voice to guide her in her replies to our questions, and she told the Voice to ask for the counsel of our Lord; the Voice told her to answer our questions boldly and that God would comfort her.

When we asked if the Voice had spoken to her before she questioned it, she replied that the Voice spoke certain words but she did not understand them all. However, when she was awakened from her sleep, the Voice told her to answer boldly.

Then she said to us and the Bishop, "You say that you are my judge; be very careful what you do, because in truth I am sent by God, and you put yourself in great danger."

Asked if the Voice sometimes varied in its advice, she answered that it never provided two contrary opinions. She also said that last night she heard the Voice tell her to answer our questions boldly.

We asked her whether the Voice had forbidden her to answer everything she was asked, and she said, "I will not answer you about that. I have revelations concerning the king which I shall not tell you."

Asked if the Voice had forbidden her to speak of the revelations, she replied, "I have not been advised about that, but give me two weeks and I will answer you."

She again asked us to delay our demands regarding the revelations and she added, "If the Voice forbids me, what would you say?"

We asked again if the Voice had forbidden her to speak about the revelations and she replied, "Believe me, it was not men who have forbidden me."

She said that she would not answer us today, and she does not know if she will reply or not until it has been revealed to her whether to do so. She said she firmly believes—as firmly as she believes in the Christian faith and that the Lord redeemed us from the pains of Hell—that the Voice comes from God and by His command.

Asked whether this Voice, which she says appears to her, comes as an angel or directly from God, or whether it is the Voice of one of the saints, she answered, "This Voice comes from God; I believe I will not tell you everything about it; and I am more afraid of failing the Voices by saying what is displeasing to them than of answering you. On this question, I beg you to grant me a delay."

Asked if she believed that God didn't like her to tell the truth, she answered, "My Voices told me to say certain things to the king, and not to you." That night she said the Voice told her many things that were good for the king, and that she would like the king to know these things even if it meant she had to go without drinking any wine until Easter! She said the king would be more comfortable at dinner if he knew these things.

We asked her if she could influence the Voice so that it would obey her and take the news to the king; she answered that she did not know whether the Voice would obey her unless it was God's will and God consented to it. She said, "And if it pleases God, He will be able to send the revelations to the king, and with this I shall be very well pleased."

Asked why this Voice no longer speaks with the king as it did when Joan was in the king's presence, she answered that she did not know if it was not the will of God. She added that, except for the will of God, she could do nothing.

When we asked if her Voice revealed to her that she would escape from prison, she answered, "Must I tell you that?" Then we asked whether the Voice had not counseled and advised her on how she should reply to this question, and she said that if the Voice revealed such things she did not understand them.

Asked whether during the last two days when she heard the Voices she had seen a light, she answered that "the light comes in the name of the Voice."

Asked if she saw anything else with the Voices, she replied, "I will not tell you everything, I do not have permission, nor does my oath touch on that. This Voice is good and worthy, and I am not required to answer you." She asked us to provide in writing any questions that she did not answer immediately.

When we asked whether the Voice could see and whether the Voice had eyes, she answered, "You will not learn that yet," and she added that there was a saying among little children that "men are sometimes hanged for telling the truth."

Asked if she knows whether she is in God's grace, she answered, "If I am not, may God put me there; and if I am, may God keep me there. I would be the saddest creature in the world if I knew I was not in His grace."

She said if she was in a state of sin she did not think the Voice would come to her. She said she wished everyone could hear the Voice as well as she did.

21

She thought she was about 13 years old when the Voice came to her for the first time. We asked her if in her youth she played in the fields with other children, and she answered that she certainly went to play sometimes but she did not know at what age.

Asked if the people of Domremy sided with the Burgundians or the other party, she answered that she knew only one Burgundian, and that she would have been quite willing for him to have his head cut off, that is, if it pleased God.

Asked if at the town of Maxey the people were Burgundians or enemies of the Burgundians, she answered they were Burgundians. We then asked her if the Voice told her in her youth to hate the Burgundians. She answered that since she knew the Voices were for the king of France, she did not like the Burgundians.

She said the Burgundians will continue to endure war unless they do as they should, and she knows it because of her Voice. Asked if it was revealed to her in her early years that the English would come to France, she answered that the English were already in France when the Voices began to come to her.

We asked her if she was ever with children who fought for her party, she answered no, as far as she remembered, but she sometimes saw certain children from Domremy who had fought against those from Maxey, and some returned wounded and bleeding.

Asked whether in her youth she had any great intention of defeating the Burgundians, she answered that she had a great desire and will for her king to have his kingdom.

Asked if she had wanted to be a man when it was necessary for her to travel to France, she said she had answered this question elsewhere [at Poitiers, where she was examined prior to being put in charge of the French army].

We asked if she took farm animals to the fields, and she said that she had answered this question elsewhere, but since she had grown up and had reached the age of understanding, she did not generally look after the animals, but she did help take them to the meadows and to a castle called the

Island, out of fear of the soldiers; however, she said she does not recall whether she tended to the animals in her youth.

Then we questioned her about a specific tree growing near her village. She answered that near Domremy there was a certain tree called the Ladies' Tree, and other people called it the Spirits' Tree, and that nearby the tree is a fountain spring. She said she heard that people who were sick of the fever would come to drink the water of this fountain and seek its water to restore their health, and that she has seen these people herself, but she does not know whether they are cured or not. She said she heard that the sick, when they can walk, go to the tree and walk around it; it is a large tree and it belongs, it is said, to a knight, Pierre de Bourlemont.

She said sometimes she would go playing with other young girls at the tree, making garlands for Our Lady of Domremy there. Often she heard the elderly people say, although not those of her family, that spirits frequently appeared near this tree. She heard a certain Joan—the wife of mayor Aubery of Domremy, her godmother—say that she had seen the spirits, but she herself doesn't know whether it is true or not. As far as she knew, she said, she never saw spirits at the tree. Asked if she saw them elsewhere, she said she does not know at all. She had seen young girls putting garlands on the branches of the tree, and she herself sometimes hung garlands there with the other girls; sometimes they took them away, and sometimes they left them there.

She said that since the time she learned that she must travel to France she had taken as little part as possible in playing games or dancing. She did not know whether she had danced near the tree since she had grown to the age of understanding; she said on occasions she may well have danced there with the children, although she more often sang than danced.

There is also a wooded area called the Oak-Wood, which can be seen from her father's door, less than two miles away. She does not know nor has she ever heard that spirits appear there, but she heard from her brother that it was in that area that she received her message at a tree; but she says she did not and she told him quite the contrary.

She added that when she came to see the king, several people had asked her if there was not in her part of the country a wooded area called the Oak-

Wood, because there was a prophecy that a young girl would come out of this wooded area and perform miracles. Joan said that she put no faith in that.

We asked if she wanted a woman's dress and she said, "Give me one, I will take it and go, otherwise I will not have it, and I am content with this because it pleases God that I wear it."

At this point we ended questioning for the day and scheduled the next session for the following Tuesday at the same hour and in the same place, where we would continue the questioning.

**February 27, Fourth Session**

On Tuesday, February 27, we assembled as on the previous days in a room in the castle of Rouen, where the trial has been taking place.

In the presence of all, we first required Joan to take an oath to speak the truth on whatever questions we asked during the trial, to which she replied that she would willingly swear to answer truthfully everything concerning her trial, but not everything she knows.

Then we required her to swear to answer truthfully everything she would be asked, and her reply was, "You should be satisfied, because I have sworn enough."

Then at our instruction, Master Jean Beaupere began to question her. He first asked how her health was since the preceding Saturday. She answered, "You see well enough how I have been as well as possible."

Asked if she would fast every day during this Lent, she answered us by stating a question, "Is that part your legal case?" Then she added, "Yes, truly, I have fasted the whole of Lent."

We asked her if since Saturday she heard her Voice, and she answered, "Yes, truly, many times."

We asked if on Saturday she had heard it in this room where she was being questioned, and she answered, "That is not in your legal case," but then she said she had heard the Voice.

Asked what the Voice said on Saturday, she answered, "I did not completely understand it until I went back to my room, and what I understood I could not repeat to you."

Asked what the Voice said to her in her room when she went back, she answered, "It told me to answer you boldly."

She said that she asked her Voice for advice regarding the questions we would be asking her, and then she said to us that she will gladly answer whatever she has our Lord's permission to reveal, but concerning revelations about the king of France, she will not say anything without permission from her Voice.

Asked if the Voice had forbidden her to tell everything, she answered she did not quite understand that was the case. Asked what the Voice said to her the last time she heard it, she said she asked the Voice to provide advice regarding specific points on our questioning.

We asked if the Voice had given her advice regarding these points, and she answered that on some she had received advice, and on others we might question her and she would not reply without permission. She added that if she replied without getting permission from the Voice, then perhaps she would not have a guarantee of support from the Voice; and that when she had permission from our Lord she would not be afraid to speak, because then she would have a good guarantee of support.

Asked whether the Voice that spoke to her was that of an angel or a saint, a male or a female, or straight from God, she replied that the Voices included the Voice of St. Catherine [of Alexandria] and the Voice of St. Margaret [of Antioch], and that their heads were crowned in a rich and precious fashion with beautiful crowns. She added, "I have God's permission to tell you this, and if you doubt it, then send someone to Poitiers where I was questioned before."

Asked how she knew that they were these two saints, and how she could distinguish between St. Catherine and St. Margaret, she said she knew very well who each one was, and that she could easily distinguish one from the other.

We asked how she knew one from the other and she answered she knew them by the greeting they gave her, that it had been seven years since they first began to guide her, and because the saints tell her their names.

Asked if the saints are dressed in the same clothes, she said, "I will tell you no more now; I do not have permission to reveal it. If you do not believe me, then send someone to Poitiers!"

She said there were some revelations made directly for the king of France, and not to us, those who question her.

Asked if the saints were the same age, she answered that she did not have permission to say.

Asked if the saints spoke at the same time, or one after another, she said, "I do not have permission to tell you, however, I have always received advice from both."

When we asked which saint appeared first, she said, "I did not recognize them immediately; I knew well enough once, but I have since forgotten; if I had permission I would gladly tell you; it is written down in the register at Poitiers." She added that she also received comfort from St. Michael [the archangel].

Asked which of the apparitions came to her first, she replied that St. Michael came first.

We asked her whether it was a long time ago that she first heard the Voice of St. Michael, and she said, "I do not speak of St. Michael's Voice, but of his great comfort."

We asked her which Voice came first to her when she was about 13 years old, and she said it was St. Michael who she first saw with her eyes, and that he was not alone, but was accompanied by many angels from Heaven. She added that she traveled to France only by way of instruction from God.

Asked if she saw St. Michael and these angels physically, in bodily form and in reality, she said, "I saw them with my bodily eyes as well as I see you, and when they left me I cried because I wanted them to take me with them too."

Asked in what form St. Michael appeared to her, she said, "There is, as yet, no reply for that because I do not have permission to answer."

When we asked what St. Michael said to her the first time, she said, "You will get no additional information today." She said the Voices instructed her to answer our questions boldly.

She said she once told the king everything that had been revealed to her because it concerned him; however, she did not yet have permission to reveal what St. Michael said. She said she wished her questioner had a copy of the record at Poitiers, provided that God desired it.

Asked if the Voices told her not to discuss her revelations without their permission, she said, "I will not answer you anymore about that; what I have permission to tell you, I will gladly answer. If the Voices prohibited me, I did not understand that."

Asked what sign she has that this revelation comes from God, and that it is St. Catherine and St. Margaret who speak to her, she said, "I have told you often enough already that it is St. Catherine and St. Margaret; believe me if you want to."

Asked if it is forbidden for her to say, she said, "I have not quite understood whether that is permitted or not."

We asked how she can distinguish between the points she will answer and the points she will not, and she said that on some points she had asked permission, and on some points she had received it. She added that she would rather be torn apart by wild horses than to have travelled to France without God's permission.

When we asked if God commanded her to wear men's clothes, she said that clothes are a trivial thing, the least thing. She said she did not wear men's clothes because of the advice of any man whatsoever, but that she put on men's clothes only by the command of God and the angels.

Asked whether it seemed to her that this command to wear men's clothes was lawful, she said, "Everything I have done is at God's command, and if He had ordered me to wear different clothes then I would have done it because it would have been His command."

Asked if she wore men's clothes at the order of Robert de Baudricourt, she said no.

We then asked if she thought she had done well to begin wearing men's clothes, and she answered that everything she did at God's command she thought was done well, and she hoped for good support and comfort in wearing men's clothes.

Asked if, in this particular case, by wearing men's clothes she thought she had done well, she said that she had done nothing in the world except according to God's commands.

We then asked whether, when she saw the Voice coming to her, there was a light. She answered that there was a great deal of light on all sides, as was most appropriate. She added, speaking to the questioner, not all the light came to him alone!

Asked whether there was an angel over the king's head when she saw the king for the first time, she said, "By Our Lady! If there was, I do not know and did not see it."

Asked if there was a light, she said, "There were three hundred knights and fifty torches [in the room], without counting the spiritual light; I rarely have revelations that are not accompanied by a visible light."

We asked how the king gave credibility to her words, and she answered that he received good signs and he knew through the clergy.

Asked what revelations the king had, she said, "You will not learn them from me this year."

She said that she was questioned by the clergy for three weeks at Chinon and Poitiers; and the king received a sign regarding her mission before he believed in her. The clergy of her party said that there was nothing except good in her mission.

Asked if she had been to the town of St. Catherine de Fierbois, she said yes; and there she attended Mass three times on the same day; and then she went to the town of Chinon. She said she sent letters to the king to ask if she should enter the town where the king was, that she had travelled more than 500 miles to come to his aid, and that she knew many things that would be to his advantage.

She said she had a sword which she took from the town of Vaucouleurs. She added that when she was at Tours or Chinon, she sent someone to get a sword that was hidden underground behind the altar in the church at St. Catherine de Fierbois. Upon arriving at the church the sword was immediately found but it was full of rust.

Asked how she knew the sword was there, she said she knew through her Voices that the sword was hidden in the ground, rusted over, and on it were five crosses. She said she had never seen the man who fetched it.

She had a letter taken to the clergy of St. Catherine de Fierbois asking if they would approve of her having the sword, and they sent the sword to her. She said it wasn't buried deep behind the altar, but she believed the letter indicated it would be behind the altar. She said that as soon as the sword was found the priests cleaned it and the rust fell off immediately, without effort. The man who fetched the sword was a merchant, a maker of armor from the town of Tours. Local priests gave her two scabbards [sheaths for holding a sword]; one was made of crimson velvet and the other a cloth of gold. She herself had another scabbard made out of very strong leather.

She said that when she was captured she did not have the sword with her, but that she carried it continuously from the time she received it until her departure from Saint-Denis, after the military assault on Paris.

Asked what blessing she said, or asked to be said, over the sword, she said that she neither blessed it herself nor had it blessed, and that she did not know how to do it. She said she loved that sword because it was found in the church of St. Catherine, whom she loved.

Asked if she had been to the area of Coulanges-la-Vineuse, she said she did not know.

We asked if she ever put her sword on the altar, and if she did, whether it was to bring the sword better fortune; she said no, as far as she knew.

Asked if she ever prayed for her sword to have better fortune, she said, "It is very good to know that I could have wished for my armor to have good fortune."

Asked if she had that sword when she was captured, she said no, but she had a different sword that had been taken from a Burgundian.

When we asked her where this sword was, and in what town, she said that she left a sword and armor at the church of St. Denis, but not this sword. She said she had this sword at Lagny, and from Lagny to Compiegne she had carried the Burgundian's sword, which was a good weapon for fighting, excellent for giving hard hits and blows to enemy fighters. But she added, to say where she had lost it was irrelevant to these legal proceedings and that she would not answer now. She added that her brothers have her belongings, her horses and swords, as far as she knows, and other things worth more than 12,000 crowns.

We asked her if, when she went to the battle of the city of Orleans, she had a military banner [a cloth flag with emblems or insignia], and what color it was. She replied she did have a banner, and it depicted the world with two angels, one angel on each side, on a background of a field sown with lilies; the cloth was made of white linen, fringed with silk, and on the banner were written, she thought, the names Jesus and Mary.

Asked if these names, Jesus and Mary, were written above, below, or at the side, she said at the side, she believed.

Asked which she preferred, her military banner or her sword, she said she much preferred her banner to her sword.

Asked who persuaded her to have these images on her banner, she replied, "I have told you often enough that I have done nothing except by God's command."

She said that she herself carried the banner when attacking the enemy so as not to kill anyone; she said she has never killed anyone.

When asked what military force the king gave to her when he sent her into battle, she said that he gave her 10,000 or 12,000 men, and that she first went to Orleans, then to the fortress of Saint-Loup, and then to the fortress of the Bridge.

Asked to which fortress she ordered her men to go, she said she does not remember. She added that she was confident of retaking Orleans [from English forces] because it had been revealed to her, and she had told the king about this revelation before going there.

We asked her if, when the assault was to be made, she told her men that she would receive arrows, crossbolts and stones hurled by catapults or cannons, she answered no, but that there were at least one hundred soldiers who were wounded. However, she had indeed told her men not to fear because they would successfully retake the city.

She said during the assault on the fortress of the Bridge she was wounded in the neck by an arrow or crossbolt, but that she received great comfort from St. Margaret and was better within two weeks. However, she did not give up her riding or military activities as a result of her injury.

Asked if she knew beforehand that she would be wounded, she said that she definitely did know in advance, and that she had told the king it would be so; however, regardless of the injury, she would not give up her work. She said the advance knowledge of her injury was revealed to her by the Voices of the two saints, blessed Catherine and Margaret. She said that she herself was the first to plant the ladder against the fortress of the Bridge, and as she was climbing the ladder she was wounded in the neck with a crossbolt.

Asked why she did not negotiate a treaty with the captain of Jargeau, she answered that the lords of her party replied to the English that they would not get the delay of two weeks that they had asked for, but that they must leave immediately with their horses, without delay. She added that for her own part, she told the people of Jargeau to leave if they wished, with their coats or tunics and their lives safe; otherwise they would then be taken by assault.

We asked if she had any conversation with her Voices regarding whether or not to grant the delay of two weeks, and she said she did not remember.

At this point the questioning was postponed to a later date; we scheduled the following Thursday to continue the inquiry and subsequent interrogations.

**March 1, Fifth Session**

On Thursday, March 1, we gathered in the castle of Rouen where Joan appeared before us in the presence of the reverend fathers, lords and masters. In their presence we summoned and required Joan to swear to speak the truth, the simple and absolute truth, in response to what she was asked. She answered that she was ready to swear to answer truthfully everything she knew related to the trial, as she said before. However, she said she knows many things which do not concern the trial and there is no need to discuss them. Then she said, "Everything I know regarding the trial I will truthfully and gladly tell."

When asked again to swear, she said, "What I can answer truthfully I will willingly say regarding the trial." It was in this manner that she took the oath with her hands on the holy Gospels; she said, "Of what I know regarding the trial I will willingly tell the truth, and I will completely tell you as much as if I was before the Pope of Rome."

Asked about what she said regarding our lord the Pope, and whom she believed to be the true Pope, she answered by asking us if there were two Popes.

[Pope Martin V died several days earlier, on February 20, and previously there had been ongoing disputes about the office of the Papacy, with arguments about whether "the true Pope" resided in Rome or in Avignon, France. As an example of the complexity of the 40-year period known as the Western Schism, Pope Martin V (legitimate Pope from 1417 to 1431) previously had deserted Gregory XII (legitimate Pope from 1406 to 1415). At one point, three individuals claimed to be Pope.]

We asked Joan if she had received letters from count d'Armagnac asking her which of the three pontiffs he should obey. She said that count d'Armagnac did write a certain letter to this effect, to which she replied, among other things, that she would give him an answer when she was in Paris or anywhere else she could be at rest; she was mounting her horse when she gave this answer [to a scribe, the count's messenger].

At this time we read in court a copy of the letters from the count and from Joan. We asked whether this was a copy of her actual reply. She said that she thought she had made this reply in part, but not all of it.

Asked if she had professed to know, on the advice of the King of Kings, what the count should believe in this matter, she answered that she knew nothing about it.

Asked if she had any doubts about which of the pontiffs the count should obey, she answered that she did not know how to instruct him to obey, since the count asked whom God wanted him to obey; but as for herself, Joan thought we should obey our Holy Father the Pope at Rome.

She added that she said other things to the count's messenger that are not in the copy of the letter. She also said that if the messenger had not departed at once he would have been thrown into the water, but not because of her. Regarding the count's inquiry about whom God wanted him to obey, she said that she did not know, but she sent him several verbal messages that were not put into writing. As for herself, she said she believed in our Holy Father the Pope at Rome.

Asked why she had a scribe write that she would give an answer at some other time if she believed in the Pope at Rome, she said that her answer was in reference to another matter, other than the matter involving the three pontiffs.

We asked if she said that she would have some advice on the question of the three pontiffs, and she answered that she had never written or caused to be written anything concerning the three pontiffs. This, she swore by her oath, that she had never written or caused to be written.

Asked if she was in the habit of putting in her letters the names of Jesus and Mary with a cross, she answered that in some letters she did and in others she did not. She added that sometimes she put a cross to warn someone of her party not to do as her letters said.

We then read letters that Joan addressed to our lord the king, to the Duke of Bedford and to others.

We asked if she recognized these letters and she answered yes, except for three words; where it was written "surrender to the Virgin" it should read "surrender to the King." Also, she said the words "commander-in-chief" [referring to Joan] and "body for body" were not in the letters she sent. She added that none of the lords ever dictated these letters, but that she herself dictated the letters before they were sent; however, she said that they were definitely shown to certain people of her party.

She said within the next seven years the English would lose a greater claim of French territory than they did at Orleans because they will lose everything in France. She added that the English would suffer greater losses than they ever did in France, and that it will be a great victory that God will give to the French.

Asked how she knew this, she said, "I know by a revelation made to me that within seven years it will happen, and I am very displeased that it would be postponed for so long." She said she knew this by revelation as clearly as she saw us standing in front of her at this moment.

Asked when it will happen, she said she knew neither the day nor the hour. Asked in what year it will happen, she answered, "You will not learn that from me; however, I wholeheartedly wish it would be before St. John's Day."

Asked whether she said it would happen before Martinmas in winter [Feast of St. Martin of Tours, which celebrates the end of the farming year and the beginning of the harvest], she answered that many things would be seen before Martinmas in winter, and it might be that the English would be over-thrown.

We asked her what she told John Grey, her guard, about Martinmas, and she answered, "I have already told you."

We asked through which Voice she knew that this would come to pass, and she answered that she knew it through St. Catherine and St. Margaret.

Asked if St. Gabriel [the archangel] was with St. Michael when he came to her, she answered she did not remember.

We asked her if since last Tuesday she had spoken with St. Catherine and St. Margaret, and she answered yes, but she does not remember at what time. Asked on what day, she said, yesterday and today, adding, "I hear them every day."

We asked her if she always saw them in the same clothing, and she said she always sees them in the same form, and their heads are richly crowned. Regarding their other clothing she doesn't say; regarding their robes she knows nothing.

Asked how she knew whether her apparition was a man or a woman, she said she knew for certain because she recognized them by their Voices and they revealed themselves to her. She added that she did not know anything except by revelation and God's command.

When asked what part of them she saw, she said the face. Asked if the saints that appear to her have hair, she said, "Yes, it is very good to know that they have hair."

Asked if there was anything between their crowns and their hair, she answered no.

We asked whether their hair was long and flowing down, and she answered, "I do not know." She added that she didn't know whether they appeared to have arms or other body parts. She said that they spoke very well and beautifully, and she understood them very well.

35

Then we asked how they spoke if they had no other body parts, and she answered, "I leave that to God." She added that the Voice was gentle, soft and low, and spoke in French.

When asked if St. Margaret spoke in the English language, she answered, "Why would she speak English when she is not on the English side?"

When asked whether on their crowned heads there were rings of gold or other materials, she said, "I do not know."

We then asked if she had some rings, and she replied, to the Bishop, "You have one of my rings; give it back to me."

She said the Burgundians have another ring, and she asked us if we had her ring, to show it to her.

Asked who gave her the ring that the Burgundians had, she answered her father or her mother; and she thought the names Jesus and Mary were inscribed on the rings, but she did not know who inscribed Jesus and Mary on the rings. She did not think there were any gemstones in the rings, and she said she was given a ring at Domremy. She said her brother gave her the other ring that we had, and she told us to give it to the Church.

She said she never cured anyone with any of her rings.

We asked if St. Catherine and St. Margaret spoke to her under the tree she described earlier and she answered, "I do not know."

Asked if the saints spoke to her at the fountain spring near the tree, she answered yes, she heard them there, but what they said to her there she did not remember.

Asked what the saints promised her, there or elsewhere, she answered that they made no promises to her except by God's permission.

We asked her what promises they made, and she answered, "That is not in your legal case at all." However, among other things, the saints said how the king would be reestablished in his kingdom regardless of whether his enemies wished it or not. She then said the saints also promised they would accompany her to Heaven, and that she had asked the saints to do so. Asked if she had received any other promises, she answered that she had, but she will not tell us because it does not concern the trial. She added that in three months she will reveal another promise.

Asked if the Voices had told her that within three months she would be delivered from prison, she said, "That is not relevant to your legal case, however, I do not know when I shall be delivered." She added that those who wish to get her out of the world might well precede her.

We asked if her Voices told her whether she would be delivered out of the prison where she currently is, and she replied, "Ask me in three months' time, then I will tell you." She added, "Ask the assessors, on their oath, if that question is related to my trial."

After the assessors had deliberated and unanimously concurred that the question was relevant to the trial, she said, "I have already told you that you cannot know everything. One day I must be delivered, but I want to get permission before I can tell you; that is why I ask for a delay."

Asked if the Voices had forbidden her to speak the truth, she said, "Do you want me to tell you what is the sole concern of the king of France? There are many things that are not relevant to this trial."

She said she knows for certain the king will regain the kingdom of France as certainly as she knows that we are seated before her in judgment. She added, except for the revelations she receives, which comfort her daily, she would be dead.

Asked what she had done with her mandrake, she answered that she has no mandrake and she never had one; however, she had heard that near her village there was one, although she never saw it. She said she had heard that mandrake was a dangerous and evil thing to keep, and she does not know its purpose or how to use it.

[Mandrake is a plant that was perceived to have magical powers. It is also an ancient folk remedy used to help infertile women conceive a child. Except for the fruit, the plant is poisonous, and it contains chemicals that are hallucinogenic. Mandrake plants have large roots that appear to have a human-like form. Mandrakes are referenced in witchcraft as well as in the Bible. In Genesis 30:14-16, Jacob's infertile second wife, Rachel, barters with her sister Leah for mandrake; in Song of Songs 7:13, mandrake is referenced for its fragrance.]

We asked Joan where the mandrake grows, the mandrake she mentioned, and she said it grows in the ground near the tree, but she does not know the exact spot. She said she heard that a hazel plant grows over the mandrake.

Asked what she has heard about the mandrake, she replied that she heard it attracts wealth but she does not believe it. She added that the Voices have never told her anything about this.

Asked in what form St. Michael appeared, she answered that she did not see his crown and she knows nothing of his clothing. Asked if St. Michael was naked, she answered, "Do you think God has not the ability to clothe him?"

Asked if he has any hair, she said, "Why would it be cut off?" She added that she had not seen St. Michael since she left the castle in the town of Crotoy, and she does not often see him, and she does not know whether he has any hair.

We asked Joan whether St. Michael had his scales, and she answered, "I do not know."

[St. Michael the Archangel is often depicted carrying a set of measuring scales and a sword to vanquish Satan.]

She said she was filled with great joy when she saw St. Michael, and she felt when she saw him that she was not in mortal sin. She said that St. Catherine and St. Margaret gladly heard her in confession from time to time, and each heard her in confession at alternate times. She said that if she was in mortal sin she was not aware of it.

Asked if, when she made her confession, she felt she was in a state of mortal sin, she said that she did not know whether she was in mortal sin, but she believed that she had not committed such sins. She added, "May it please God, I never was in mortal sin, and if it pleases Him, I shall never commit, nor have I committed, such sins that burden my soul."

Asked what sign she gave the king to indicate she came from God, she said, "I have always told you that you will not drag this from my lips. Go and ask him."

We asked if she had sworn not to reveal what was asked regarding the trial, and she answered, "I have already said that I will not tell you what concerns or involves our king; what concerns our king, I shall not tell you."

Asked if she did not know the sign she gave the king, she said, "You will not learn it from me." We told her this matter was relevant to the trial, but she answered, "What I have promised to keep secret I shall not tell you; I promised, and I cannot tell you without perjury."

Asked to whom she made this promise, she said she made the promise to St. Catherine and St. Margaret, and it was shown to the king. She said she promised it without their asking, and she did so at her own desire because she thought too many people might be questioning her had she not made this promise to the saints.

Asked if anyone else was with them when she revealed the sign to the king, she answered that she thought there were not, although there were many people nearby.

We asked if she saw the crown on the king's head when she revealed the sign to him, and she answered, "I cannot tell you without perjury."

Asked whether the king had a crown when he was at the city of Reims, she answered that she thought the king accepted with pleasure the crown he found at Reims, although a much richer crown was brought later; and he did so in order to quickly complete his coronation at the request of the people of Reims and to avoid burdening the men-at-arms. She said if the king would have waited he would have had a crown a thousand times richer.

Asked if she saw this richer crown, she said, "I cannot tell you without committing perjury; and if I have not seen it myself, I have heard that it is very rich and precious."

At this point we ended the proceedings for the day and scheduled the next session to begin on Saturday at eight o'clock in the morning, requiring those present to assemble together in the same place at that hour and day.

### Saturday, March 3, Sixth Session

On the following Saturday, March 3, Joan appeared before us in the presence of the reverend fathers, lords and masters; and in their presence we required Joan to answer the simple and absolute truth to the questions we asked her, to which she replied, "As I did before, I am ready to swear," and she swore saying this with her hands on the holy Gospels.

Because she had said that St. Michael had wings but said nothing else about his body or the bodies of St. Catherine and St. Margaret, we asked her what else she wanted to say about their bodies. She replied, "I have told you what I know, and I will not answer you further." She said that she had seen St. Michael and the saints so clearly that she certainly knew they were saints from Heaven.

Asked if she saw anything of them besides their faces, she said, "I have told you all that I know about that, and I would rather have you cut my throat than tell you all I know." She said that she would willingly discuss everything she knew concerning her trial.

We asked her if St. Michael and St. Gabriel had natural heads, and she replied, "I saw them with my two eyes, and I believe it was St. Michael and St. Gabriel that I saw as firmly as I believe in the existence of God."

Asked if she believed that God created them in the form and fashion that she saw, she answered, "Yes."

We asked her if she believed that God, from the very beginning, created them in that form and fashion, and she replied, "At this time you will learn nothing more from me other than what I have already told you."

Asked if she had known by revelation whether she would escape from prison, she answered, "That is not part of your legal case. Do you want me to speak against myself?"

We asked if her Voices told her anything about escaping and she replied, "That is not relevant to your legal case. If you ask me about matters related to the legal case, and if everything concerns the case, then I will tell you everything." She added that, by her faith, she does not know at what hour or day she will escape.

Asked if the Voices had told her anything about escaping in a general way, she answered, "Yes, definitely, they told me that I shall be delivered, but I do not know the day or the hour, and I must boldly show a cheerful expression in front of you."

We asked her, regarding the first time she spoke with the king, whether the king asked her if it was by revelation that she had changed her attire from wearing women's clothes to men's clothes. She replied, "I have answered this before; I do not recall whether I was asked this specific question, but my reply was written down at Poitiers."

Asked whether officials of her own party who examined her—some over the course of a month and others over the course of three weeks—had questioned her about changing her attire from wearing women's clothes to men's clothes, she replied, "I do not recall, but they asked me where it was that I began to wear men's clothes and I told them it was at Vaucouleurs."

We asked if the officials of her own party who examined her had asked her whether it was because of her Voices that she began to wear men's clothes, and she answered, "I do not recall."

Asked if, during her first visit with the queen, whether the queen asked her about wearing men's clothes, she answered, "I do not recall."

Asked if the king or queen or other people of her party did not sometimes ask her to stop wearing men's clothes, she replied, "That is not relevant to your legal case."

We asked her whether she was requested to stop wearing men's clothes at the castle of Beaurevoir, and she replied, "Yes, that is true, and I answered I would not stop wearing men's clothes without getting God's permission."

She said the Demoiselle of Luxembourg and the Lady of Beaurevoir offered her a woman's dress, or the cloth to make one, and they told her to wear it, however, Joan replied that she did not have God's permission and it was not yet time.

When asked if Messire Jean de Pressy and others at Arras did not offer her women's clothes, she said that he and many others had often asked her to wear a woman's dress.

Asked if she believed she would have done wrong or committed a mortal sin by wearing women's clothes, she replied that she did better to obey and serve her sovereign Lord, namely God. However, she said that if she had to wear a woman's dress, she would rather have done so at the request of those two ladies than of any other ladies in France, except the queen.

We asked her whether—when God revealed to her that she should change from wearing women's clothes to men's clothes—it was by the Voice of St. Michael, or by the Voice of St. Catherine or St. Margaret. She replied, "You will learn no more at the present time."

We asked her whether—when the king first sent her to do battle and she had her military banner made—the men-at-arms and others had flags made in the style of her military banner, and she answered, "It is good to know that the lords kept their own arms; some of my companions in arms had flags made at their pleasure, while others did not."

Asked what kind of material the flags were made of, linen or other cloth, she said, "It was white satin, and on some there were fleurs-de-lis." She had only two or three lances in her company, but her companions-at-arms some-times had flags made like hers, and did so merely to distinguish their men from others. Asked if the flags were often repaired, she said, "I do not know; when the lances were broken, new ones were made."

Asked whether sometimes she said that flags made like hers resulted in greater success, she said that sometimes she said to her followers, "Go boldly among the English," as she herself would do.

Asked if she told them to fly the flags boldly and then they would have greater success, she said that she had indeed told them that what had happened in the past would happen again.

We asked if she sprinkled Holy Water on the flags or requested others to sprinkle Holy Water on the flags when the flags were first taken into battle, and she answered "I do not know anything about that, and if it was done, it was not at my instruction."

When asked if she ever saw Holy Water sprinkled on the flags, she replied, "That is not in your legal case, and if I had seen it done I am not now advised to answer you."

When asked if her companions-at-arms did not have written on their flags the names Jesus and Mary, she answered, "By my faith, I do not know."

Asked if she herself had carried, or whether she made others to carry in procession around an altar or a church, cloth that was to be made into flags, she answered no, nor had she ever seen it done.

We asked her what she wore at the back of her helmet when she went to the town of Jargeau, and if it was something round, she answered, "By my faith, there was nothing."

When asked if she knew Brother Richard, she replied, "I had never seen him before I came to Troyes."

We asked her about the manner in which Brother Richard greeted her. She said that the people of Troyes, she thought, sent Brother Richard to her because the townspeople were afraid she was not a thing sent from God; so as he came close to her, he made the Sign of the Cross and sprinkled Holy Water at her, and she said to him, "Come boldly, I shall not fly away."

Asked if she had seen, or had made any images or pictures of herself, or in her likeness, she replied that at Arras she saw a painting in the hands of a Scot and she was depicted in full armor presenting letters to the king with one knee on the ground. She said she had never seen nor had made any other image or picture in her likeness.

Asked whether at her host's residence in Orleans there was a painting of three women with these words, Justice, Peace and Union, and she replied that she knew nothing about that.

Asked whether she knew that certain people of her party had religious services, Mass or prayers offered in her honor, she answered that she knew nothing about it, and if any such services were held it was not at her instruction; however, if they prayed for her, she felt that they had not done poorly.

We asked her whether people of her own party firmly believed she was sent from God, and she replied, "I do not know whether they do, and I refer you to their own opinions; but if they do not, nevertheless I am sent from God."

Asked whether she believed that by deeming her to be sent from God they believed correctly, she said, "If they believe I am sent from God they are not deceived."

We asked if she knew the feelings of members of her party when they kissed her feet, her hands and her garments, and she answered that many people were happy when they came to see her, but they kissed her hands as little as she could prevent them from doing so. She said the poor people were happy to see her because they knew she helped them as much as she could and did nothing unkind to them.

Asked what honor the people of Troyes gave to her when she entered the town, she said they gave her none. She added that she thought Brother Richard may have had entered Troyes with her, but she does not remember seeing him enter the town with her.

Asked if Brother Richard preached a sermon when she arrived, she said that she only briefly stopped in the town and did not sleep there at all; and she knew nothing about the sermon.

Asked if she spent many days at Reims, she said, "I think we were there four or five days."

When we asked if she acted as godmother to a child at Reims, she answered that at Troyes she did, to one child, but at Reims she does not recall doing so, nor at Chateau-Thierry, but at Saint-Denis she was twice a godmother. She added that she gladly gave the name of Charles to the boys, in honor of her king, and to the girls she gave the name Joan, but at other times she named them as the parents wished.

Asked whether the good wives of the town did not touch her ring with their own rings, she said, "Many women touched my hands and my rings, but I do not know their thoughts or intentions for doing so."

Asked who it was in her company who caught butterflies in her military banner before arriving at Chateau-Thierry, she said that nobody in her party had ever done that, and the other side invented it.

We asked her what she did at Reims with the gloves with which the king was consecrated. She said that the gloves were given as a present to the knights and nobles who were there; and regarding the person who lost his gloves, she did not say she would find them. She added that her military banner was in the church at Reims, and she thought that during the consecration of the king the banner was fairly close to the altar, and that she herself held the banner for a short time. She does not know whether Brother Richard held the banner.

We asked whether, when she was going through the country, she often received the Sacraments of the Eucharist and Confession when she was in the good towns, and she said yes, from time to time. Asked whether she received the Sacraments while wearing men's clothes, she answered yes, but she does not remember receiving the Sacraments when she was wearing armor.

Asked why she took the horse belonging to the Bishop of Senlis, she said it was bought for two hundred saluts, but whether he received the payment or not, she does not know. She said there was an arrangement that he was to be paid. She also wrote to him stating that he could have the horse back if he wanted because she herself did not want it, because it was no good for carrying a load.

Asked how old the child was whom she raised from the dead at the town of Lagny, she replied that the child was three days old and was brought to Lagny with an image of Our Lady. Maidens of the town who were accompanying the image of Our Lady informed Joan so that she might pray to God and to the Blessed Virgin Mary to restore life to the baby. So Joan went and prayed with the other maidens, and finally the child came back to life, yawning three times. The baby was then baptized but immediately died and was buried in consecrated ground. Before praying for the baby three days had passed, they said, with no sign of life in the child, which was as black as her coat. While Joan was with the maidens who were on their knees praying in front of the image of Our Lady, the child then yawned and the color began to return to the baby's skin.

Asked whether it was said in the town that Joan had brought about the resurrection of the child and that it was due to her prayers, she answered that she did not ask about it.

We asked her whether she knew or had seen Catherine de La Rochelle, and she answered yes, at Jargeau and Montfaucon in Berry.

Asked whether this Catherine showed her a woman robed in white who Catherine said appeared to her, Joan answered no.

Asked what Catherine de La Rochelle said to her, Joan said Catherine told her that a certain lady-in-white came to her arrayed in golden clothes, telling her to go through the good towns with messengers and trumpets that the king would give to her, to proclaim that whoever possessed gold, silver or hidden money should immediately bring it forth; and that she would immediately know those who were hiding their money and did not bring it forth, and that she would be able to easily find what was being hidden; and that this gold, silver or hidden money should be used to pay for Joan's soldiers.

After hearing Catherine's story, Joan said to Catherine that she should go back to her husband, tend to her household and care for her children.

To be certain about Catherine de La Rochelle, Joan spoke about her to St. Catherine or St. Margaret, who said that Catherine's story was mere folly and amounted to nothing. Joan sent a message telling the king what he should do, and when Joan came to see the king she told the king that this question about Catherine was folly and nothing more. However, Brother

Richard wanted to get Joan's approval to carry out this work, so Brother Richard and Catherine were both unhappy with Joan's response.

When asked if she spoke to Catherine about going to La Charité-sur-Loire, Joan said Catherine did not advise her to go, and that the weather was too cold and she should not go.

Joan told Catherine, who wanted to go to the Duke of Burgundy and make peace, that peace, it seemed to her, would not be found except at the lance's point.

Joan asked this Catherine if the lady-in-white who appeared to her came every night, saying that she would, to see her, sleep in the same bed with Catherine; and she went to bed with her and stayed up until midnight, but saw nothing, and then went to sleep.

In the morning, Joan asked Catherine whether the lady-in-white had come to her. Catherine replied that she had, while Joan was sleeping, but that she had not been able to awaken Joan.

Then Joan asked if the lady might not come another night, and Catherine answered yes; so Joan slept during the day, so that she might stay awake the whole night.

That night she stayed in the bed with Catherine and watched all night, but saw nothing. Throughout the night Joan often asked Catherine whether the lady-in-white would come, and Catherine answered, "Yes, soon!"

We then asked Joan what she did in the trenches of La Charité, and she replied that she had ordered a military assault but that she neither threw nor sprinkled Holy Water.

Asked why she did not enter the town of La Charité since she had been commanded by God to do so, she replied, "Who told you I was commanded to enter the town of La Charité?"

Asked if she was advised by her Voice, she replied that she wanted to come to France but that the soldiers told her it was better to go first to La Charité.

We asked if she was held prisoner a long time in the tower at Beaurevoir, and she answered that she was there about four months. She said that when she learned the English were going to arrive and take her she was very angry. She said that even though her Voices had forbidden her to jump from the tower, after a lengthy period and because she feared the English, she jumped from the tower and commended herself to God and Our Lady. She said she was wounded as a result of her fall from the tower. However, she said when she jumped from the tower the Voice of St. Catherine told her not to worry because the people at Compiegne would come to her aid. She said she always prayed with her Voices for the people of Compiegne.

Asked what she said when she jumped from the tower, she replied that some people said she was dead; but as soon as the Burgundians saw that she was alive, they told her she had tried to escape.

Asked whether she said she would rather die than fall into the hands of the English, she said she would rather surrender her soul to God than fall into the hands of the English.

We asked whether she was very distraught about her situation, and whether she blasphemed [cursed] the name of God because of her circumstances. She replied that she never blasphemed the saints, and that it was not her custom to swear.

We asked her about Soissons and the captain who had surrendered the town, and whether she disobeyed God and said that she would have the captain drawn and quartered if she captured him. She replied that she never disobeyed the saints, and that those who said or reported that she had disobeyed the saints were mistaken.

[To be drawn and quartered was a punishment implemented in England during the 1300s for crimes of high treason or disloyalty to the state. Men convicted of high treason were dragged by horse to a place of execution, hanged but not to the point of death, then had their penis and testicles cut off, had their abdomen cut open to remove their intestines, and finally had their head chopped off; then their body parts were displayed in prominent places such as on the London Bridge. Women convicted of high treason were instead burned at the stake. During the early 1800s the penalty was changed so that only after death by hanging was the body cut into pieces and then the body parts displayed; the punishment was abolished in 1870.]

At this point in the questioning Joan was taken back to the place that had been assigned as her prison cell. Then we, with the Bishop, declared that we would continue the trial without interruption and that we would call certain doctors and men who were experts in canon law and civil law. Since Joan's answers had been set down in writing we would ask the experts to review her admissions, and then after their review inform us regarding any points upon which Joan should be questioned at greater length. She would then be interrogated by deputies appointed by us, but without changing the entire number of assessors. Furthermore, everything would be set down in writing so that whenever it was necessary, the officials could deliberate on certain points to provide their opinions and advice.

We then instructed the experts to carefully review and study in their homes the trial transcripts and the parts of the proceedings they had already heard to identify what, in their opinion, should occur next. After a complete review and thorough deliberation, we asked the officials to submit their conclusions either to us or our deputies, or to reserve their conclusions in order to present them to us at an appropriate time and place. Additionally, each and every assessor was forbidden to leave the city of Rouen before the end of the trial unless they received our permission.

End of the first phase of the public sessions.

### Sunday-Friday, March 4-9, Analysis of the Evidence

On Sunday, the fourth day of March, and on the following days, Monday, Tuesday, Wednesday, Thursday and Friday, in our residence at Rouen, we, including the Bishop, gathered together with many esteemed doctors and masters knowledgeable in divine and canon law. We collected all of the information that had been admitted to and answered by Joan during our questioning, and we made notes of the points where she had insufficiently answered our questions and where it appeared that she should be questioned further.

From these points, so diligently analyzed and noted, and on the advice and deliberation of these educated men, we concluded that we must proceed to further question Joan. However, because of our numerous occupations we cannot always attend the questioning sessions in person, and so we appointed the esteemed and discreet person, Jean de La Fontaine, Master of Arts and licensed in canon law, to pursue the legal questioning for us, and we appointed him to do this on Friday, March 9, in the presence of the doctors and masters, Jean Beaupere, Jacques de Touraine, Nicolas Midi, Pierre Maurice, Thomas de Courcelles, Nicolas Loyseleur and Guillaume Manchon.

**Saturday, March 10, First Session Held in the Prison**

On the following Saturday, the tenth day of March, we went to the room in the castle of Rouen that had been assigned as a prison cell for Joan. There, with the Master Jean de La Fontaine, our Commissary and Deputy, and the esteemed Doctors of Sacred Theology, Masters Nicolas Midi and Gerard Feuillet, and in the presence of the witnesses, Jean Secard, advocate, and Master Jean Massieu, priest, we summoned Joan to swear and to take an oath to answer truthfully in response to our questions. She answered, "I promise to answer you truthfully that which concerns your legal case, but the more you constrain me to swear, the longer I shall take to tell you."

Then Master Jean de La Fontaine, specifically appointed and deputized by us in this matter, began to question Joan. He asked her, by the oath she had taken, from where she had travelled when she last went to Compiegne. She answered that she had come from the town of Crespy-en-Valois.

Asked whether she spent several days at Compiegne before she made any incursion or military attack from that area, she answered that she arrived there secretly in the morning, and she thought she had entered the town unbeknownst to the enemy; and on that same day, toward evening, she led the military assault during which she was captured.

Asked whether the bells were rung when she started the attack, she said that if the bells were rung it was not at her order or with her knowledge. She did not think, or remember saying, the bells were rung.

Asked whether she made the military assault because she was instructed by her Voices, she said that during the last week of Easter, when she was in the trenches at Melun, she was told by her Voices, namely by St. Catherine and

St. Margaret, that she would be captured before St. John's Day. Her Voices said this had to happen, but that she should not be distressed, that she should see it as a good thing, and that God would assist her.

We asked her if, since her time in Melun, she had been told by her Voices that she would be captured, and she said yes, that several times her Voices said this to her, nearly every day.

Joan asked her Voices that she might die quickly when she was captured so that she would not suffer a long time in prison. Her Voices told her to be resigned to everything and that these events must happen; but they did not tell her when these things would happen because if she had known the hour, she would not have gone. She said she often asked her Voices at what hour she would be captured but they did not tell her.

Asked if her Voices had ordered her to make the military assault on Compiegne and had told her that during the assault she would be captured, would she have gone anyway, she answered that if she had known when she was going to be captured she would not have willingly gone. However, she said, in the end, she would have obeyed the requests of her Voices whatever it cost her.

Asked whether, when she made this attack on Compiegne she received any Voice or revelation to go forward with the assault, she answered that on that day she did not know she was going to be captured, and she received no other orders from her Voices to go forward with the assault. However, she said she had always been told by her Voices that she must be taken prisoner.

We asked her whether she crossed over the bridge of Compiegne during the military maneuvers. She answered that she went over the bridge and onto the boulevard accompanied by her soldiers, and that she attacked the followers of Jean de Luxembourg, and twice drove them as far as the camp of the Burgundians, and the third time to the middle of the highway.

Then the English blocked the road from her and her soldiers, and she was captured while she was retreating to some fields located on the Picardy side near the boulevard. She said between the place where she was captured and Compiegne, there was nothing but the river and the boulevard with its ditch.

We asked her about her military banner, whether the world was painted on the banner she carried, with two angels and other insignia, and she answered yes, she had only one banner. We then asked her what it signified to paint God holding the world, with two angels, and she answered that St. Catherine and St. Margaret told her to make the banner, to carry it boldly, and to have the King of Heaven painted on the banner. She told the king this, much against her will, and she said she knew nothing more regarding what this signified.

Asked whether she had a shield and arms, she answered that she never did, but that the king granted arms to her brothers, namely a blue shield that depicted two fleurs-de-lis and a sword in between. She said she described these arms—with two fleurs-de-lis and a sword in between—to a painter because he asked her what arms she bore. She said the king gave them to her brothers without her request and without any revelation.

We asked whether she had a horse when she was captured, either a charger or a hackney, and she answered that she was riding a half-charger.

[Chargers were all-around war horses; hackneys were bred beginning in the 1300s because the King of England wanted powerful running horses that were also attractive.]

When we asked Joan who had given her this horse, she replied the king, or the king's people using the king's money. She said she personally had five chargers from the king's money, not counting her hackneys, of which she had more than seven.

We asked her whether she had any other assets from the king besides these horses. She said that she asked the king for nothing except good arms, good horses and money to pay her people.

Asked whether she had any money, she replied that the ten or twelve thousand worth she had was not much to carry on a war with, very little indeed; however, she thought, her brothers did have other assets. She said what she has is from the king's own money.

Asked what sign she gave the king when she went to see him, she replied it was attractive and honorable, most credible, good, and the richest sign in the world.

We asked her why she refused to reveal and show us this sign, since she herself wanted to see the sign of Catherine de La Rochelle. She answered that she would not have asked to see the sign of Catherine de La Rochelle if it had been as clearly visible as her sign was to the notable ecclesiastics and others, archbishops and bishops, including the archbishop of Reims and others whose names she doesn't know; among those who saw her sign were Charles de Bourbon, the Sire de la Tremouille, the Duke d'Alencon and many other knights who saw her sign and heard it as distinctly as she saw those speaking and standing before her there. She said she already knew through St. Catherine and St. Margaret that the activities of this Catherine de La Rochelle amounted to nothing.

We asked whether the sign still exists, and she replied yes, certainly, and she said the sign will last for a thousand years and more. She said the sign is with the king's treasure.

Asked whether the sign was gold, silver, a precious stone or a crown, she answered, "I will not tell you; no man can describe a thing as rich as this sign; the sign you need is for God to deliver me out of your hands, and most certainly this is a sign He can show you."

Then she added that when she had to travel to see the king she was told by her Voices, "Go boldly; when you stand in front of the king he will receive a good sign to accept you and believe in you."

We asked her what reverence she showed the sign when it was revealed to the king and whether the sign came from God. She replied that she thanked our Lord for her deliverance from the trouble that was arising from the opposition of the clergy of her party; and she knelt down many times in reverence of the sign. She said that an angel from God, and from none other but Him, revealed the sign to the king, and she thanked God many times for this. She said the clergy stopped opposing her when they had recognized the sign.

Asked whether the clergy of her party saw the sign, she answered that when the king and those of his company had seen the sign and also the angel that revealed the sign, she asked the king if he was satisfied, and he replied yes. Then she left and went to a little chapel, and she heard that after her departure more than three hundred people saw the sign. She added that, for her sake, and to stop men from preaching to her, God willed that those of her party who were there would see the sign.

We asked whether she and the king expressed reverence to the angel when the angel brought the sign. She answered that she did; she knelt down and uncovered her head.

**Monday, March 12**

On the following Monday, March 12, those gathered in our residence at Rouen included the religious and discreet Brother Jean Le Maistre of the Order of Preaching Brothers; the deputy of the lord Inquisitor of Heretical Error in the kingdom of France; the esteemed and discreet lords and masters Thomas Fiesvet and Pasquier de Vaulx, Doctors of Canon Law; Nicolas de Hubent, Apostolic Secretary; and Brother Isambard de La Pierre of the Order of Preaching Brothers.

We, with the Bishop, reminded the deputy that at the beginning of these proceedings, which we had instituted in matters of faith against this woman commonly called the Virgin, we had required and summoned him to collaborate with us, and we offered to communicate to him all of the processes, testimonies and other things related to this matter and the trial; but that he had raised certain difficulties that prevented his collaboration in the trial because he was appointed for the city and Diocese of Rouen alone, whereas the trial was being held, by reason of our jurisdiction of Beauvais, in ceded territory. Therefore, to ensure greater certainty regarding these proceedings and to exercise extreme caution, we, on the advice of educated men, resolved to write to the lord Inquisitor himself, urging him to return to his city of Rouen or at least appoint his deputy to attend to this task, and to entrust the deputy with complete authority from the lord Inquisitor himself to undertake and conclude this trial as set forth according to all of the evidence and materials that have been gathered.

Now the lord Inquisitor, upon receipt of our letters, in benevolent compliance with our demand and for the honor and exaltation of the orthodox faith, has specifically appointed and deputized Brother Jean Le Maistre to conduct and conclude this trial according to his secured letters and confirmed by his seal.

This same Monday morning we went with the bishop to the room assigned as a prison cell for Joan, where there were assembled at the same time the esteemed and discreet lords and masters Jean de La Fontaine, our appointed commissary; Nicolas Midi and Gerard Feuillet, Doctors of Sacred Theology; witnesses Thomas Fiesvet and Pasquier de Vaulx, Doctors of Canon Law; and Nicolas de Hubent, Apostolic Secretary.

In their presence we required Joan to swear to answer truthfully in response to whatever questions we would ask her. She replied, as she said before, she would willingly speak the truth "on what pertains to your legal case," and in this manner she took the oath.

Then she was questioned at our command by Master Jean de La Fontaine.

First, he asked her whether the angel that brought the sign to the king spoke any words, and she replied, "Yes, he told the king to put me to work so that the country might be freed without further delay."

Asked whether the angel that brought the sign to the king was the same angel that first appeared to her or whether it was another angel, she answered, "It is always the same one, and he never fails me."

When asked whether the angel did not fail her regarding things of good fortune when she was captured, she said she thought that since it pleased God it was better for her to be taken prisoner.

Asked whether the angel did not fail her regarding good things of grace, she answered, "How could he fail me when he comforts me every day?" She added that she believes this comfort is from St. Catherine and St. Margaret.

Asked whether she calls St. Catherine or St. Margaret, or whether they come to her without being called, she said, "They often come without my calling."

She added that sometimes, if they did not come, she would pray to God to send them to her.

Asked if she sometimes called them without their coming, she answered that she had never needed them without having them.

We asked her if St. Denis sometimes appeared to her and she answered no, as far as she knew.

We asked whether she spoke to our Lord when she promised Him to keep her virginity, and she answered that it was quite enough to promise her virginity to those who were sent from Him, namely St. Catherine and St. Margaret.

Asked what persuaded her to summon a man from the town of Toul for breaking a promise of marriage, she answered, "I did not have him summoned, it was he who summoned me; and I swore before the judge to tell the truth." Moreover, she said, she had made no promise of marriage to this man. She added that the first time she heard her Voice she vowed to keep her virginity as long as it would please God, and that she was 13 years old or about 13 years old at the time. She said her Voices assured her that she would win her legal case at Toul.

Asked if she had spoken to her priest or any other churchman regarding the visions that she claimed to have, she answered no, except to Robert de Baudricourt and to the king. She added that her Voices did not require her to conceal them, but that she was afraid of revealing them, afraid that the Burgundians might hinder her journey, and in particular she feared that her father would stop her from leaving.

We asked if she believed it was right to leave her father and mother without permission when she should honor her father and mother; she answered that in all other things she was obedient to them except in this journey to France, but afterwards she wrote to them and they forgave her.

Asked whether she thought she had committed a sin when she left her father and mother, she answered that since God commanded her to leave it was the right thing to do. She added that since God commanded it, even if she had a hundred parents or had been the king's daughter, she would have gone anyway.

We asked her whether she asked her Voices if she should tell her father and mother about leaving, and she answered, regarding her father and mother, the Voices were very well pleased that she should tell her parents except for the difficulties that would have resulted if she had done so. She added that, as for herself, she would not have told her parents anything. She said the Voices left it to her whether to tell her father and mother or to be silent on the matter.

Asked whether she showed reverence to St. Michael and the angels when she saw them, she replied that she did, and she kissed the ground where they had stood after they had gone.

Asked whether the angels were with her for a long time, she said that angels often came when she was among other Christians but the angels were not seen, and that she often saw angels among Christian people.

We asked whether she had letters from St. Michael or from her Voices, and she replied, "I do not have permission to tell you; within a week from now I will gladly tell you what I know."

Asked if her Voices called her daughter of God, daughter of the Church, or daughter great-hearted, she said that prior to the military assault on the city of Orleans and every day since, when they have spoken to her, they have often called her "Joan the Virgin, Daughter of God."

Asked why, since she calls herself daughter of God, she will not willingly say the Our Father prayer for us, she answered that she would willingly do so, and that on other occasions, when she refused, it was with the intention that the Bishop would hear her in Confession.

**Afternoon Session in Prison**

On this day, Monday, in the afternoon, there were present in Joan's prison cell the lords and masters mentioned above, including Jean de La Fontaine, Nicolas Midi and Gerard Feuillet, Doctors of Sacred Theology; Thomas Fiesvet and Pasquier de Vaulx, Doctors of Canon Law; and Nicolas de Hubent, Apostolic Secretary.

First, Joan was questioned about the dreams she said her father had before she left his house. She said that while she was still with her father and mother, she was often told by her mother that her father spoke of having dreamed that Joan would go off with soldiers, so her father and mother took great care to keep her safe and were overly protective. She said she was obedient to her parents in all things except in the incident at Toul regarding the action for marriage. She said she heard her mother say how her father once said to her brothers, "In truth, if I thought this would happen which I have dreamed about my daughter, I would want you to drown her; and if you would not, I would drown her myself." She added that her father and mother almost lost their senses when she left to go to Vaucouleurs.

Asked whether these thoughts and dreams came to her father after she had her visions, she said yes, more than two years after she first heard the Voices.

Asked whether it was at the request of Robert de Baudricourt that she first started wearing men's clothes, she answered that it was by her own decision and not because of the request of any man alive.

We asked whether the Voice ordered her to wear men's clothes, and she answered, "Everything I have done I have done at the instruction of my Voices, and regarding my clothes, I will answer that another time; at the present time I am not advised, but tomorrow I will answer."

Asked whether she thought she was doing something wrong when she wore men's clothes, she answered no; and even at this moment, if she were back with her own party, it seemed to her that it would be to the great good of France for her to do as she did before her capture.

We asked her how she would have rescued the Duke of Orleans [who was being held prisoner in England]. She answered that she would have taken enough English prisoners to ransom him; but if she had not taken enough prisoners on this side of the sea, she would have crossed the sea and then rescued him from England by force.

We asked her whether St. Margaret and St. Catherine had told her absolutely and unconditionally that she would take enough prisoners to ransom the Duke of Orleans, or whether she would have to cross the sea to rescue him. She answered yes, and she told the king to let her have her way with the English lords who were their prisoners. She added that if she had been able to continue military operations for three years without being hindered, she would have rescued the Duke of Orleans from England. She said three years would have been more than enough time, but that one year would have been too little. However, she said that she does not remember if St. Margaret and St. Catherine told her absolutely and unconditionally that she would take enough prisoners to ransom the Duke of Orleans, or if she would have to cross the sea to rescue him.

We asked her what sign she gave to the king, and she answered that she would ask advice from St. Catherine regarding this question.

**Tuesday, March 13**

The following Tuesday, the thirteenth day of March, we gathered at the same hour in the prison cell with the esteemed and discreet Brother Jean Le Maistre and other esteemed and discreet lords and masters. We charitably informed Joan, exhorting her and warning her for the salvation of her soul, to speak the truth in response to everything she was asked.

First, at our command, Joan was questioned about the sign she gave to the king, to which she replied, "Would you be satisfied if I perjured myself?"

Asked whether she had sworn and promised to St. Catherine that she would not tell us about this sign, she answered, "I have sworn and promised not to discuss this sign by my own decision because I have been pressured too much to discuss it." She promised to herself not to speak of the sign further to any man; she said the sign was that an angel gave assurance to the king by bringing him the crown and saying he would possess the entire kingdom of France by the help of God and the work of Joan, and that the king was to put Joan to work by giving her soldiers or else he would not be so soon crowned and consecrated.

We asked her whether she had spoken with St. Catherine since yesterday, and she said she had heard St. Catherine since yesterday and was told many times to answer the judges boldly in response to what they would ask her concerning the legal case.

Asked how the angel brought the crown and whether he placed it on the king's head, she said it seemed to her that the crown was given to an archbishop, namely the archbishop of Reims, in the presence of the king. She said the archbishop received it and gave it to the king, and Joan herself was present, and the crown was put in the king's treasury.

Asked about the place where this crown was taken, she answered that it was taken to the king's chamber in the castle of Chinon. Asked on what day and at what hour, she answered that she did not remember the day, and as for the hour, it was late, and beyond that she could not recall the hour. She added that it was in the month of April or March, she thought. She said that in the present month of March or the following April, it would be two years ago, and it was after Easter.

We asked whether the first day she saw the sign, the king also saw it, and she answered yes, and he himself received it.

Asked what the crown was made of, she said it was good to know it was made of pure gold, and the crown was so rich and precious that she did not know how to describe or appreciate its riches; she said it signified that the king would gain the kingdom of France.

Asked whether there were precious stones in it, she said, "I have told you what I know about it."

Asked whether she had held or kissed the crown, she answered no.

We asked her whether the angel who had brought this crown had come from Heaven or from Earth. She replied, "He came from Heaven," and she understood that he came by our Lord's command, and he entered the room through the door.

Asked again if the angel who brought the crown came from the Earth, she answered that when the angel came to the king, he expressed reverence to the king by bowing before the king and pronouncing the words of the sign that Joan said previously, and that the angel recalled to the king the sweet patience that the king had shown throughout the many great tribulations that had befallen him.

She said the angel entered through the doorway, stepped and walked upon the ground and moved towards the king. Asked how much space there was between the door and the place where the king was standing, she answered that as far as she knew there was the space of a good lance's length. She added that the angel went out of the room the same way he had come in.

She said that when the angel came, she accompanied him and went with the angel up the stairs to the king's chamber; the angel went in first and then she herself went in, and Joan said to the king, "Sire, here is your sign, take it."

We asked her in what place this angel appeared to her, and she answered, "I was almost always praying that God would send the king's sign, and I was in my lodging, in the house of a good woman near the castle of Chinon, when the angel came to me; and afterwards we went together to the king; and the angel was accompanied by many other angels whom no one saw."

She said that out of love for her, and to unburden her from the distress she was experiencing as a result of people who were opposing her, she thought that many people present saw the angel, people who would not have otherwise seen the angel.

Asked if all who were there with the king saw the angel, she answered she thought the archbishop of Reims, and the Lords d'Alencon, de la Tremouille and Charles de Bourbon saw the angel, and many clerics and others saw the crown but did not see the angel.

Asked of what appearance and size the angel was, she said she did not have permission to tell us that, but that she would answer tomorrow.

We asked her if all the angels who were in the company of this angel were of the same appearance. She said that some of the other angels were similar to one another while others were not, as far as she could see. She said some of the angels had wings and some were crowned while others were not. She added that St. Catherine and St. Margaret were with the angels during the time when she went with the angels up the stairs to the king's chamber.

Asked how the angel left her, she said that he left her when she was in a little chapel, and she was very upset when he left her; she cried and would have gladly gone with him, that is, her soul would have gone with him.

Asked whether, at the angel's departure, she was happy or upset, she answered that she was not fearful or trembling because the angel left her, but that she was very upset when he left her.

We asked whether it was because of any merit on her part that God sent His angel to her. She answered that the angel came for a great purpose, in the hope that the king would believe the sign, that men would stop opposing her, and to help the good people of Orleans. She added that the angel also came because of the merits of the king and the good Duke of Orleans.

When asked why the angel came to her rather than to another person, she answered it pleased God to drive back the king's enemies through a simple virgin.

Asked whether she had been told where the angel had acquired the crown, she answered that the crown was brought from God, and that no goldsmith on Earth could have made a crown so rich and beautiful; regarding where or how the angel acquired the crown, she referred us to God and said she knew nothing else about it. Asked if the crown had a good color and if it sparkled, she said she did not recall but would try to remember; then she said that it had a good color and would always be that way, as long as it was well and dutifully guarded and it was in the form of a crown. Asked whether the angel had written her letters, she answered no.

When asked what persuaded the king and the people who were with him that it was an angel who brought the crown, she said the king believed it was an angel because of what he was instructed by the clergy who were there and witnessed it, and by the sign of the crown itself.

Asked how the clergy knew it was an angel, she said they knew it because of their high level of education and because they were officials of the Church.

Asked about a married priest and a lost cup that she was said to have pointed out, she replied that she knew nothing about it, nor had she ever heard anyone talk about it.

Asked whether, when she travelled to Paris, she had a revelation from her Voices requesting her to go there, she answered no, but that she went at the request of nobles who wanted to make a military assault on Paris. She added that she intended to go beyond Paris and cross the trenches of Paris.

We asked her whether she had any revelation about her travels to the town of La Charité, and she answered no, that she went at the request of the soldiers, as she had answered previously.

Asked whether she had any revelation about going to Pont l'Eveque, she answered that after it had been revealed to her in the trenches of Melun that she would be captured, she usually deferred to the captains regarding questions of war; however, she added, she did not tell them that it had been revealed to her that she would be captured.

Asked whether it was right to attack Paris on the Feast Day of the Birth of the Blessed Mary, she answered that it was good to observe the Feast Days of the Blessed Mary, and in her conscience she felt it was right to observe the Feast Days of the Blessed Mary from beginning to end.

Asked whether, from the outer edge of Paris, she said, "Surrender this town in Jesus' name!" She answered no, and that she said, "Surrender it to the king of France."

**Wednesday, March 14**

In the prison cell where Joan is kept in the castle of Rouen, we questioned her in the presence of Master Jean de La Fontaine, the commissary appointed by us and the Bishop; Brother Jean Le Maistre; the assessors, the esteemed and discreet lords and masters Nicolas Midi and Gerard Feuillet, Doctors of Theology; Nicolas de Hubent, Apostolic Secretary; Isambard de La Pierre; and other witnesses.

We first asked her why she jumped from the tower at Beaurevoir. She answered that she had heard that the people of Compiegne, all of them to the age of seven years, were to be put to fire and the sword, and she would have rather died than live after such a slaughter of good people. She said another reason she jumped from the tower was she knew that she had been sold to the English, and she would have rather died than fall into the hands of her enemies the English.

Asked whether she decided to jump from the tower because of advice she received from her Voices, she answered that St. Catherine had told her almost every day not to jump, and that God would help her and the people of Compiegne. But Joan told St. Catherine that since God was going to help the people of Compiegne, she wanted to be there. Then St. Catherine said, "You must be resigned and not falter; you will not be delivered until you have seen the king of the English." Joan answered, "Truly, I do not want to see the king of the English, and I would rather die than fall into the hands of the English."

We asked her whether she said to St. Catherine and St. Margaret these words: "Will God let the good people of Compiegne die so wretchedly?" Joan answered that she did not say "so wretchedly," but, "How can God let these good people of Compiegne die, these people who have been and who are so faithful to their Lord?"

She said that after falling from the tower she was without food for two or three days, and she was so injured by the leap that she could not eat or drink; however, she was comforted by St. Catherine who told her to confess and ask God to forgive her for having jumped out of the tower, and that the people of Compiegne would get relief before St. Martin's Day in winter, without a doubt. Then she began to get well and started to eat, and soon afterward she recovered.

Asked whether, when she jumped from the tower, she expected to kill herself, she answered no, because as she jumped she trusted herself to God and she hoped that by the leap she would escape and not be delivered to the English.

Asked whether, when she regained her speech after falling, she denied God and His saints, since this is stated in the evidence; she answered that she did not remember that she had ever denied God and His saints, blasphemed or cursed, there or anywhere.

Asked whether she wished to stand by the evidence, she answered, "I leave it to God and nobody else, and a good confession."

We asked if her Voices sometimes requested a delay before providing her with answers, and she said that St. Catherine sometimes answered her but that she, Joan, failed to understand because of the noise in the prison and the commotion made by her guards. She added that when she makes a request to St. Catherine, then St. Catherine and St. Margaret take the request to God and then by God's order they give the answer to Joan.

We asked if, when the saints come to her, they are accompanied by a visible light, and whether she sees the light when she hears the Voice in the castle prison, and whether she knows it is in her room. She answered that there is not a day that goes by when the Voices do not come to the castle, and they always come with a light; and regarding the Voice, she does not remember whether she sees St. Catherine. She says she asks three things of her Voices: first, for her deliverance; second, that God would help the French and keep the towns that are under French control; and third, for the salvation of her soul.

Joan requested that if she is taken to Paris she would like to have a copy of the records that show our questions and her answers, so that she may give them to the people at Paris and say to them, "Here is how I was questioned at Rouen and here are my replies," so that she will not have to worry again about having to answer so many questions.

Because she said that we and the Bishop were exposing ourselves to great danger by bringing her to trial, she was asked what that meant, and to what peril or danger we exposed ourselves, we and the others. She replied, "You say that you are my judge, I do not know if you are, but be very careful not to judge me poorly because you will put yourself in great danger; I warn you so that if God punishes you for it, I shall have done my duty in telling you."

Asked what the danger or peril was, she answered that St. Catherine told her she would get assistance, but she does not know whether this will be her deliverance from prison, or if, while she is being tried, some commotion might occur through which she can be delivered. She thinks it will be one or the other, and beyond this, the Voices told her she will be delivered by a great victory; and then the Voices told her, "Take everything peacefully; do not be concerned about your martyrdom; in the end you will enter Heaven." She said her Voices gave her this message simply and absolutely, that is, without any uncertainty. She calls the pain and adversity she suffers in prison her martyrdom, but she also said she does not know whether she will suffer greater adversity, but if that is the case, she commits herself to God.

Because her Voices told her that in the end she would go to Heaven, we asked her whether she felt assured of her salvation and of not being damned to Hell. She answered that she firmly believed what the Voices told her, namely that she will be saved, and she believes it as firmly as if she were already in Heaven. Asked whether after this revelation she believed that she could not commit a mortal sin, she said, "I do not know, but in everything I commit myself to God." When we told Joan that her answer to this question was perilous, she said she believed that knowing she would go to Heaven was a great treasure.

**Wednesday Afternoon Session in the Prison**

Joan's first words were related to the immediately preceding matter concerning the certainty that she felt regarding her salvation, upon which she had been questioned in the morning session; she said that she intended to reply this way: provided she kept her oath and promise to our Lord, that is, to keep safe her virginity, of body and of soul.

Asked whether she needed to confess her sins since she believed by the revelation of her Voices that she will be saved, she answered that she does not know of having committed mortal sin, but if she were in mortal sin, she thinks St. Catherine and St. Margaret would abandon her immediately. She added that she believes, with regard to the preceding statement, that one cannot cleanse one's conscience too much.

We asked her since the time she has been in this prison whether or not she denied God, blasphemed or cursed God. She said no, but sometimes when she said, "Good God's will!" or "Saint Joan!" or "Our Lady!" the people who reported her words may have misunderstood.

Asked whether it was a mortal sin to take a prisoner for use as ransom and then put him to death, she answered that she had not done that.

We cited the case to her about a person who was put to death at Lagny, a certain Franquet d'Arras. She replied that she agreed to his execution since he deserved it, because he had confessed himself to be a murderer, a thief and a traitor. She said his trial lasted two weeks, and that he had as his judges the Bailly de Senlis and a jury of the people of Lagny. She said that she asked to have the prisoner Franquet exchanged for a man from Paris, the landlord of the Bear Inn; but when she heard of the death of the landlord, and when the Bailly had told her she would be doing a great injustice by freeing Franquet, she said to the Bailly, "Since the man I wanted is dead, do with Franquet as justice demands."

Asked if she sent money, or had money sent, to the person who captured Franquet as a prisoner, she answered that she is not "Master of the Mint" or "Treasurer of France" that she would be in a position to pay out money.

We reminded Joan of the following: she attacked Paris on a Catholic feast day; she was in possession of the horse of the Bishop of Senlis; she jumped from the tower at Beaurevoir on her own accord; she wore men's clothes; and she consented to the execution of Franquet d'Arras. We then asked her whether she believed she had committed mortal sin.

She replied first concerning the attack on Paris, saying, "I do not think I am in mortal sin." She added that if she was in mortal sin, then it was a matter only for God and for the priest in confession to know about it.

Secondly, concerning the horse, she answered that she firmly believes she did not commit mortal sin against God because the horse was valued at 200 gold saluts and the Bishop of Senlis was supposed to receive that payment in exchange for the horse. Nevertheless, she said the horse was sent back to the Sire de la Tremouille to give it back to the Bishop of Senlis. She added that the horse was of no use to her for riding. Moreover, she said it was not she who took the horse from the bishop; and she added, for another thing, she did not wish to keep the horse since she heard that the bishop was displeased that his horse had been taken, and besides that, the horse was useless to soldiers. Finally, and in conclusion, Joan said she did not know whether the bishop was paid the money that was due to him, nor did she know whether his horse was returned to him; she thought not.

Thirdly, regarding her leap from the tower at Beaurevoir, she said, "I jumped from the tower not out of despair, but in the hope of saving my body and going to the aid of the many good people who were in need of assistance." She added that after she jumped from the tower she confessed herself and asked God to forgive her. She said she received this forgiveness from God, and that it was not good to have made the jump from the tower and it was wrong to do so. She added that she knew she had been forgiven because of a revelation from St. Catherine during her confession, on whose advice she confessed herself.

Asked whether she received any great penance as a result of her confession, she answered that a large part of her penance was the injury she suffered in falling.

Asked whether she thought jumping from the tower to be a mortal sin, she answered that she knows nothing about this and defers to God.

Fourthly, concerning wearing men's clothes, she said, "Because I do it by God's command and in His service, I do not think I am doing wrong; and as soon as it shall please God to command it, I will stop wearing men's clothes."

**Thursday, March 15**

Joan was charitably urged, admonished and required to be willing to accept the decision of our Holy Mother the Church, as she ought, in the event of her having done anything contrary to our faith. She answered that her replies should be seen and examined by the clergy, and then she should be told if there was anything contrary to the Christian faith. She said she will be able to tell us with certainty what is contrary to the faith, and she will tell us whatever she learns from the counsel of her Voices. Moreover, she said if there was any evil advanced against the Christian faith, advanced against our Lord, she would not want to tolerate it and she would be grieved to be in opposition.

Then the distinction between the Church Triumphant [members of the Church in Heaven] and the Church Militant [members of the Church on Earth] was explained to her, what the Church Triumphant was and what the Church Militant was, and she was required to submit to the decision of the

Church Militant regarding whatever she had said or done was either good or evil. She replied, "I will not give you any answer at the present time."

Joan was required, upon the oath she had sworn, to say how she expected to escape from the castle of Beaulieu using two pieces of wood. She replied that she would gladly escape from being a prisoner in any place, and that while in the castle of Beaulieu she would have successfully restrained her jailers in the tower had not the porter seen and prevented her from doing so. She said apparently it did not please God to allow her to escape on that occasion, and that she must see the English king, as her Voices had told her.

Asked if she had permission from God or from her Voices to escape from prisons whenever it pleased her, she answered, "I have often asked for it, but so far I have not received it."

Asked whether she would escape now if she saw the opportunity, she said that if she saw the door open she would go, and it would be by God's permission. She said she firmly believes that if she saw the door open and her jailers and the other Englishmen were unable to restrain her, she would interpret it as her permission to escape and that God had given her the assistance. She added that without permission she would not escape, but she would make a firm effort to discern whether God would be pleased by it according to the French proverb, *"Aide toy, Dieu te aidera."* ["Help yourself, and God will help you."]; and by this she said that if she escaped nobody could say that she did not have permission.

We asked her, since she wanted to attend Mass, whether it seemed to her more appropriate to be wearing women's clothes, and which would she prefer, to wear a woman's dress and be at Mass, or to wear men's clothes and not attend Mass. She answered, "If you promise me that I may attend Mass if I wear a woman's dress, then I will answer you."

Then the questioner said to her, "I promise that you may attend Mass if you are in a woman's dress."

She replied, "And what is your answer if I have sworn and promised to our King not to stop wearing men's clothes? However, I will tell you this: give me a long dress reaching down to the ground, but without a train, and give it to me so I can go to Mass, and then, after Mass, I will put on once again these other clothes."

Asked, once and for all, whether she would wear women's clothes and go to Mass, she replied, "I will get counsel from my Voices on this and then I will answer you." Moreover, she urged us, that for the honor of God and Our Lady, she be permitted to attend Mass in this good town.

Then she was told by the questioner she should accept wearing women's clothes, simply and absolutely. She then replied, "Give me a dress like the daughters of your officials wear, a long houppelande, and I will wear it to go attend Mass."

[A houppelande was an outer garment worn by both men and women in Europe during the late Middle Ages; it was typically worn by the profession-al classes and featured a long, full body covering with flared sleeves.]

As urgently as she could, she implored us to allow her to attend Mass in the clothes she wore, without any change.

Asked if, regarding all that she has said and done, she will submit and commit herself to the decision of the Church, she answered, "Everything I have said or done is in the hand of God, and I commit myself to Him. I certi-fy to you that I would do or say nothing against the Christian faith; and if I have said or done anything, or if anything is discovered about me that the clergy would declare to be against the Christian faith established by our Lord, then I would not uphold it, but would cast it out."

Asked if she would submit herself to the decree of the Church, she replied, "I will not answer you now, but on Saturday send me a priest if you do not wish to come, and I will answer to the priest, with God's help, and it shall be set down in writing."

We asked her, when her Voices came to her, whether she bowed down to them fully, as if bowing down to a saint, and she said yes. We asked if sometimes she had failed to bow down and then afterward asked for forgiveness; she said that she was unable to honor them with proper rever-ence because she firmly believes they are St. Catherine, St. Margaret and St. Michael.

We asked her, since candles are commonly offered to the saints in Heaven, whether she has lit candles or other things, in church or elsewhere, or had Masses said, to the saints who visit her. She answered no, except at Mass and in the priest's hand, and in honor of St. Catherine. She believes it to be St. Catherine and St. Margaret who appear to her. She added she has not lit as many candles to St. Catherine and St. Margaret as she would gladly like to do, firmly believing it is they who come to her.

Asked whether, when she puts candles in front of an image of St. Catherine, she does it in honor of her who appears to her, she said, "I do it in honor of God, of Our Lady, and of St. Catherine who is in Heaven, and I do not differentiate between St. Catherine who is in Heaven and St. Catherine who appears to me."

Asked if she always did or accomplished what her Voices instructed her to do, she replied that with all her might she accomplished the requests our Lord spoke through her Voices, as far as she could understand. She added, the Voices gave her no instructions without having the good pleasure of our Lord.

We asked if in battle she had done anything without the permission of her Voices. She replied, "You already have my answer to this question. Read your notes carefully and you will find the answer."

However, she said at the request of soldiers, she made an attack on Paris, and also at La Charité at the king's request. She said these attacks were neither against nor according to the command of her Voices. Asked if she ever did anything contrary to the command and will of her Voices, she said that she did what she could and she knew to the best of her abilities.

She added, regarding her leap from the tower at Beaurevoir, she did it against the request of her Voices, but she could not help herself; and when her Voices saw her need and that Joan could in no way hold herself back, they provided assistance to protect her life and prevented her from being killed. Moreover, she said whatever she did in her extraordinary endeavors, they comforted her, and that this is a sign they are good spirits.

Asked if she had any other sign that they were good spirits, she said, "St. Michael certified it before they came to me."

Asked how she knew it was St. Michael, she said, "By the angel's speech and language." She said she firmly believes they are angels.

Asked how she recognized that they were angels, she said she believed it quickly and had the desire to believe it; she said that St. Michael, when he came to her, told her that St. Catherine and St. Margaret would also come to her, that she should follow their advice, and that they were instructed to lead her and advise her regarding what she had to do; and that she should believe what they said because it was at our Lord's command.

We asked how she could tell if he was a good or a bad spirit if the Enemy put himself in the form and disguise of a Holy Angel. She replied that she would certainly know whether it was St. Michael or a counterfeit appearing in his likeness.

At first she said she had serious doubts about whether it was St. Michael, and that the first time she saw the angel she was afraid, and that she saw him many times before she knew it was St. Michael.

Asked how she knew then, rather than on the first occasion, that it was St. Michael who had appeared to her, she answered that the first time she saw St. Michael she was a young girl and was afraid; but since then, St. Michael taught her and showed her so many things that she firmly believed it was him.

Asked what doctrine he taught her, she answered that in all things he told her to be a good child and God would help her; and, among other things, he told her she should go to the aid of the king of France. She said a large part of what the angel taught her is in the book of sacred scriptures; and the angel told her about the pitiful state of the kingdom of France.

When we asked about the height and stature of this angel, she said she would reply on Saturday with the other matter, namely what shall please God.

We asked if she believes it to be a great sin to anger St. Catherine and St. Margaret who appear to her, and to do things contrary to their requests. She replied yes, but she knows how to atone for it. She added that she believed what angered them most of all was her leap from the tower at

Beaurevoir, but she said she asked for their forgiveness for that as well as for other offenses she had committed against them.

Asked if St. Catherine and St. Margaret would take bodily vengeance for this offense, she answered that she does not know, and she has not asked them.

We asked her why she previously said that people are sometimes hanged for telling the truth, and if she knew of any crime or fault in her through which she might or ought to die if she were to confess. She answered no.

**Saturday, March 17**

We asked her about the appearance of St. Michael, including his shape, his size and the clothes he wore. She said that when St. Michael came to her, "He had the appearance of a very honorable man," but regarding his clothes and the other things we asked, she would not answer. Regarding the angels, she said she saw them with her own eyes, but she said we would not get any additional information from her other than that.

She said that she believes in what St. Michael says and does as firmly as she believes that our Lord Jesus Christ suffered death and passion for us; and she said she was led to believe it because of the good advice, comfort and good teaching that St. Michael gave to her.

Asked if she wished to submit to the decision of Our Mother the Church regarding whether her words and deeds were either good or evil, she answered that she loved the Church and would support the Church with all her might for the Christian faith, but that she was not a person to be forbidden to go to church or attend Mass.

Regarding the good works she did and her military activities, she said she must commit herself to the King of Heaven, who sent her to Charles, son of King Charles of France, who would be king of France. She said, "And you will see that the people of France will soon win a great victory that God will provide, and which will shake almost the entire kingdom of France." She added that she said this to us so that when it did happen, that men would remember that she had foretold it. When required to give the date of this event, she said, "I defer to our Lord."

73

Asked if she would submit to the decision of the Church, she said, "I commit myself to our Lord, who sent me, to Our Lady, and to all the blessed Saints of Heaven." She added that she thought that our Lord and the Church were all one, and so we ought not to create difficulties for her; she said, "Why do you create difficulties when it is all one?"

Then she was told there is the Church Triumphant, where God is with the saints and the souls who are already saved, and also the Church Militant, which includes our Holy Father the Pope, Vicar of God on Earth, the Cardinals, Bishops of the Church, the Clergy, and all good Christians and Catholics, and that this Church, in good assembly, cannot err and is governed by the Holy Spirit.

Therefore, she was asked if she would submit to the Church Militant, namely the Church on Earth. She answered that she traveled to see the king of France in God's name, and in the names of the Blessed Virgin and of all the blessed saints of Heaven and the Church Triumphant above, and she is at their command; and it is to that Church which she has submitted all her good deeds and all that she has done or would do. But regarding her submission to the Church Militant, she would not answer.

Asked about the woman's dress that was offered to her so that she might attend Mass, she said that she would not put it on until it pleased our Lord. She added that if she must be brought to judgment and executed, she requests the lords of the Church to grant her the mercy of wearing a woman's dress and a hood for her head. She said she would rather die than turn her back on what our Lord has commanded her to do. She firmly believes that God would not let her be brought so low, or be at this time without His help or a miracle.

We asked why she requested women's clothes in the event of her execution if it is God who commands her to wear men's clothes. She answered, "It is enough for me that the clothing is long."

Asked if her godmother, who saw the spirits at the Spirits' Tree, was known to be a wise woman, she answered that her godmother was known to be an honest woman, and not a witch or a sorceress.

Then she said she would put on women's clothes if we let her go. So we asked her if wearing women's clothes under those circumstances would please God, since God commanded her to wear men's clothes. She answered that if we permitted her to go because she wore women's clothes, she would do so, but then would immediately put on men's clothes and do what our Lord asked her to do. She said to accomplish God's will nothing would make her swear not to take up arms or wear men's clothes.

When asked about the clothing worn by St. Catherine and St. Margaret, she answered, "You already have my answer on this matter, and you will get nothing else from me. I have answered you as best as I can."

Asked if she believes the spirits at the Spirits' Tree were evil spirits, she answered she did not know anything about that.

We asked her how she knew that St. Catherine and St. Margaret hated the English. She said, "They love those whom God loves, and hate those whom He hates."

Asked if God hated the English, she replied that regarding God's love or His hatred for the English, or of what He would do to their souls, she knew nothing; but she was certain that, except for those English who had already died on French territory, the English would be driven out of France, and God would send victory to the French.

Asked if God was for the English when they were prospering in France, she said she didn't know, but she believed it was His will to allow people to be chastised for their sins if they were in a state of sin.

We asked her what permission she received from God and what help she expected to have from God because she wore men's clothes. She replied that in this matter, as in other things, she only sought the salvation of her soul.

Asked about the military armor she offered in the church at the town of Saint-Denis, she answered that she offered a whole suit of white armor, fitting for a soldier, with the sword she won at Paris.

When asked why she offered these arms, she said it was out of devotion and it was according to the custom of soldiers when they were wounded. She said because she had been wounded at Paris she offered the military armor to St. Denis, because his name was the battle-cry of France.

[French armies began to use "St. Denis!" as a battle-cry in the 1100s. St. Denis, Bishop of Paris, was beheaded as a martyr in 258 at Montmartre (Mount of Martyrs) in Paris. The site of his grave north of Paris became a burial place for the kings of France (all but three French kings are buried there). A church built on the site in the 1100s is recognized as the first major structure designed using Gothic architecture.]

We asked Joan if she offered the suit of armor and sword at the church of St. Denis so that the armor and sword might be worshiped there. She said no.

We asked her what the purpose was of the five crosses on the sword she found at St. Catherine de Fierbois, and she answered she knew nothing about it.

Regarding her military banner, we asked who persuaded her to have angels with their arms, feet, legs and robes painted on it. She said, "You already have my answer." Again regarding her military banner, we asked if the angels depicted on the banner were the angels who came to her. She said she had them painted in the fashion in which they are painted in churches.

Asked if she ever saw angels in the manner in which they were painted on the banner, she answered, "I will not tell you anymore."

We asked why the light that accompanied the angels or her Voices was not painted on the banner, and she answered that it was not commanded to her to do so.

**Afternoon Session in Prison**

Joan was questioned if the two angels who were painted on her military banner were St. Michael and St. Gabriel. She said the representation of the two angels was there solely for the honor of our Lord, who was also painted on the banner holding the world.

Asked if the two angels on her banner were the two angels who guard the world, and why there were not more, seeing that she was requested to carry this military banner in the name of our Lord. She answered that the design of the entire banner was commanded by our Lord and by the Voices of St. Catherine and St. Margaret, who said to her, "Carry the banner in the name of the King of Heaven." She added that because they told her, "Carry the banner in the name of the King of Heaven," she had the image of our Lord and the angels painted in color on the banner, and she did all of this at God's command.

Asked if she questioned her saints whether, due to this banner, she would win all the military battles she fought and emerge victorious; she said they told her to carry the banner boldly and God would help her.

We asked her whether she was more helpful to the banner, or whether the banner was more helpful to her. She replied that regardless of whether the victory was hers or the banner's, it was all for our Lord. Asked if the hope of victory was based on the banner or on her, she answered, "It was based on our Lord, and nothing else."

We asked whether, if anyone else had carried the banner, he would have been as successful as she was herself. She answered, "I do not know, and I leave it to our Lord."

Asked if one of her party had sent her his banner to carry, and particularly if she had been sent the king's banner, and she had carried it, would she have had as firm a hope in that banner as in her own, which was given to her in God's name. She answered, "I more gladly carried that which was requested of me in God's name, however, in everything I commit myself to God."

We asked her what the purpose was of the symbol she put on her letters, and the names Jesus and Mary. She said that the clerics who wrote her letters put them there, and some clerics said it was proper to put the two words Jesus and Mary.

Asked whether it had been revealed to her that she would lose her good fortune if she lost her virginity, and that her Voices would no longer come to her if she lost her virginity, she said, "That has not been revealed to me."

77

Asked if she believed her Voices would come to her if she were married, she answered, "I do not know, and I commit myself to our Lord."

We asked if she thought and firmly believed that the king did the right thing to kill, or cause to be killed, the Duke of Burgundy. She answered that it was a great pity for the kingdom of France, however, whatever there had been between those two men, God had sent her to the aid of the king of France.

We asked her to explain her comment that she would provide answers to us, the Bishop and our government officials, in the same manner as she would provide answers to our Holy Father the Pope, but that there were several questions to which she would not reply, and whether she would not answer more fully for the Pope than she answered for us. She said that she has answered everything as faithfully as she could, and if she knew anything that came to her mind that she had not already said, she would willingly tell us.

When we asked whether it seemed to her that she was required to answer the whole truth to the Pope, the Vicar of God, concerning all that she would be asked on matters of faith and the state of her conscience, her reply was that she demanded to be taken to the Pope and then she would answer for him everything that was required.

We asked her what material one of her rings was made of, the ring on which the words Jesus and Mary were written. She answered that she did not properly know, but if it was made of gold it was not fine gold; and she did not know whether it was gold or brass; she thought there were three crosses, and to her knowledge, there were no other signs on the ring except the words Jesus and Mary.

Asked why she so happily looked at this ring when she was going into battle, she answered that it was out of pleasure and in honor of her father and mother, and because, having her ring on her finger and in her hand, she touched St. Catherine who appeared before her.

Asked what part of St. Catherine she had touched, she said, "You will get no answer from me."

Asked if she had ever kissed or touched St. Catherine or St. Margaret, she answered she had touched them both.

We asked if St. Catherine or St. Margaret had a fine fragrance, and she answered that it is good to know that they did.

Asked whether, when embracing St. Catherine or St. Margaret, she felt heat or anything else, she said that she could not embrace them without feeling and touching them.

Asked where she embraced them, whether at their head or their feet, she said, "It is more fitting to embrace their feet."

Asked if she had given St. Catherine or St. Margaret chaplets of flowers, she said that many times in their honor, in front of their images and pictures in churches, she had given them chaplets of flowers, but regarding when they appeared to her in person, she does not remember giving them flowers.

We asked whether, when she hung garlands on the Spirits' Tree, she put them there in honor of those who appeared to her. She answered no.

We asked whether she showed reverence to the saints when they came to her, by kneeling or by bowing down. She answered yes; she expressed reverence for them as often as she could because she knew very well that they were from the Kingdom of Heaven.

We asked if she knew anything about the people who gather together with spirits at the Spirits' Tree. She said she was never there when that occurred, nor did she know anything about it, but she had heard talk of these people, how they went on Thursdays, but she did not believe in it and thought it was witchcraft.

Asked whether her military banner was raised above the king's head when he was crowned at Reims, she answered no, as far as she knew.

We asked why her military banner was carried into the church at Reims during the consecration, but not the banners of other captains. She answered, "The banner was present during the perils of war, and that is reason enough for it to be honored."

### COURT TRANSCRIPTS ARE READ IN JOAN'S PRESENCE (MARCH 24)

Saturday, the twenty-fourth day of March, before reading the court transcripts, the Promoter appointed by us stated that the task was to verify the accuracy of the transcripts; that everything they contained, our questions as well as Joan's replies, had been truly said and done. After this, Joan took an oath to add nothing but the truth to her replies.

While the transcripts were being read to Joan, she said that her surname was d'Arc or Rommee, and that in her area the girls took their mother's surname. She also requested that we read the questions and answers to her consecutively. She said that anything that was read to her without contradiction on her part she acknowledged to be true and admitted as testimony.

She added these words to the statements regarding her wearing women's clothes: "Give me a woman's dress to go to my mother's house, and I will take it." She said she would do this to escape from prison, but when she was outside of the prison she would take counsel regarding what she should do.

Finally, after the content of the court transcripts had been read to her, Joan admitted that she believed she had spoken well according to what had been written in the register and read to her, and she did not contradict any other information contained the court transcripts.

### JOAN SAYS IT IS NOT "IN HER" TO WEAR WOMEN'S CLOTHES (MARCH 25)

The following Sunday morning, Palm Sunday, the twenty-fifth day of March, in Joan's prison cell in the castle of Rouen, we, with the Bishop, spoke with Joan in the presence of Jean Beaupere, Nicolas Midi and Pierre Maurice, Doctors of Sacred Theology, and Thomas de Courcelles, Bachelor of Sacred Theology.

We told Joan that she had asked us several times, especially yesterday, due to the solemnity of these past days and of this time, if it would be permitted for her to attend Mass on Palm Sunday. That is why we asked her, if we gave her permission, whether she would abandon wearing men's clothes and put on women's clothes, as she used to do in the area of her birthplace and as the women there were usually clothed.

Joan replied by asking us if she could attend Mass wearing men's clothes, as she was currently dressed, and if she could receive the Eucharist on Easter Sunday. So we told her that if she were to respond to our request, that is, to abandon men's clothes, permission would be given. But she replied that she did not have counsel on this matter from her Voices and therefore could not yet wear women's clothes.

Then we asked her if she would get advice from her saints regarding wearing women's clothes. She replied that it might well be permitted for her to attend Mass as she is currently dressed, which she truly desired, but with regard to changing from men's clothes to women's clothes, she could not do it and it was not in her.

After the court officials had urged her, according to all the goodness and piety which she seemed to have, to wear clothes appropriate for her sex, Joan answered that it was not in her to do it; but if it was to be, it would be done soon.

Then we told her to speak with her Voices to find out if she could once again wear women's clothes to receive the Eucharist at Easter. Joan replied that as far as it was in her ability, she could not receive the Eucharist by changing her clothes for women's clothes. She asked to be permitted to attend Mass in her men's clothes, adding that this attire did not burden her soul, and that wearing these clothes was not against the Church.

### ORDINARY TRIAL; 70 ACCUSATIONS PRESENTED (MARCH 26 – 28)

It was decided that in addition to the preparatory trial conducted up to this time by our office, further proceedings should be carried out within the context of an ordinary trial. Articles precisely defining the accusations against Joan were produced so that she could be questioned and heard to answer before us. The articles would be put forward by a solemn lawyer or by the Promoter himself, and if Joan refuses to answer the articles of accusation after she has been canonically admonished, then her refusal to answer will be construed as her confession to the aforementioned articles.

After we discussed other matters it was decided that on the next day the articles would be offered by the Promoter, and that Joan would be questioned and heard with regard to the accusations contained in the articles.

## March 27, Introduction to Articles of Accusations against Joan

The following Tuesday after Palm Sunday, March 27, in a room near the great hall of the castle of Rouen, the Promoter appointed by us in this trial appeared before us in our episcopal presence.

Joan was led into our presence so that the Promoter could present to Joan specific petitions and requests.

The Promoter began with the following statement:

My lords, reverend fathers in Christ, and you, Vicar, especially appointed to this office by the lord Inquisitor of those who stray from the Catholic faith, established and appointed throughout the whole kingdom of France, I, the Promoter, appointed, charged and ordained by you in this trial according to the specific information produced on your behalf, propose and declare that Joan should be brought before us now to answer the questions which I shall ask of her regarding the faith.

I undertake to prove, if need be, through the declarations and conclusions that are fully stated in these articles, all of the facts, rights and reasons that are contained in these articles, which I will present to you as judges in this trial.

I implore and request that Joan be made to affirm and swear that she will answer these articles, each one separately, according to whether she believes or does not believe their assertions; and in the event of her refusal to swear to tell the truth, or to decline or postpone it, then she shall be ruled to be deficient and willfully disobedient to the authorities assembled in her presence; and if her obstinacy necessitates it, that she shall be excommunicated for the evident offenses.

If she delays answering, you may determine a specific day as soon as possible for Joan to answer these articles, indicating to her that if she does not answer before the appointed day, you will assert that she has confessed to the articles on which she has not given an answer, according to law, style, use and the custom you wish and require.

When the request of the Promoter had been completed and the opinions of each assessor heard, we concluded that the articles displayed by the Promoter should be read and explained to Joan in French, and that she should answer what she knows according to each article, but if there were topics on which she asked for a delay to answer, a reasonable delay should be granted to her.

The Promoter then took an oath regarding the accusations, and when this was completed, we told Joan that all of the assessors were ecclesiastical and educated men, experienced in canon and civil law, who wished and intended to proceed with her in all piety and meekness, as they had always been disposed, seeking not vengeance or corporal punishment, but rather her instruction and her return to the ways of truth and salvation.

Also, because she was not educated and literate enough in such complex matters, we suggested that she could choose one or more of the assessors present to give her some counsel with regard to what she should do and how she should reply, provided that she wished to answer truthfully. We stated that we required her to swear to speak the truth.

Joan replied, "First, for admonishing me about my salvation and our faith, I thank you and all who are gathered here. Regarding the counsel you offer me, I thank you for that too, however, I have no intention of departing from the counsel of our Lord; the oath you wish me to take, I will willingly swear to answer truthfully on everything that concerns your trial." She took the oath with her hands on the Holy Scriptures.

Then, at our invitation and command, the articles which the Promoter had shown us were read to Joan, and the contents of the articles of accusation were explained to Joan in French.

# JOAN OF ARC

## ARTICLE 1

Before you, competent judges, is the woman commonly called Joan the Virgin, found, captured and taken within the jurisdiction of your territory and within the boundaries of your Diocese of Beauvais. She surrendered and has been entrusted, delivered and restored to you, her ecclesiastical and ordinary judges, by our lord the Christian king of France and England, to be dealt with by law and corrected as a person who is strongly suspected, denounced and defamed by honest and sober people.

She should be denounced and declared by you, her judges, as a witch, an enchantress and a false prophet; a caller-up of evil spirits; superstitious; implicated in and given to the magic arts; thinking evil in our Catholic faith; schismatic in the faith; a skeptic, devious and sacrilegious; idolatrous; an apostate of the faith; accursed and doing evil; blasphemous towards God and His saints; scandalous and seditious; disturbing and obstructing the peace; inciting people to war; cruelly thirsting for human blood; encouraging blood to be shed; and having completely and shamelessly abandoned the modesty befitting her sex, she is guilty of indecently wearing inappropriate clothes and the clothes of soldiers.

For these and other things abominable to God and to man, contrary to laws both divine and natural, and to ecclesiastical discipline: misleading princes and people; having, to the scorn of God, permitted and allowed herself to be adored and venerated, giving her hands to be kissed; heretical, or at the least, strongly suspected of heresy; and according to divine and canonical sanctions, she should be punished and corrected canonically and lawfully for these reasons and for all other proper ends.

According to divine as well as canon and civil law, it is proper for the ordinary judge and Inquisitor of the Faith to drive out, destroy and completely uproot from your diocese and the whole kingdom of France the heresies, sacrileges, superstitions and other crimes declared above; to punish, correct and restore heretics, those who propose, speak and say things contrary to our Catholic faith or act against it in any way; and all evil doers, criminals or their accomplices who are apprehended in this diocese and jurisdiction, even if part or all of their misdeeds have been committed elsewhere, as other competent judges in their own dioceses, limits and jurisdictions are empowered and bound to do; even with respect to a lay person of whatever status, sex, quality or preeminence, you must be held as esteemed, reputable and competent judges.

Joan's response:

To this first article Joan replies that she is well aware that our Holy Father the Pope at Rome, the bishops and other clergy exist for the protection of the Christian faith and the punishment of those who fall from it; however, for her part, with regard to her activities, she will submit only to the Church in Heaven, that is, to God, to the Blessed Virgin Mary, and to the Saints in Heaven. She firmly believes that she has not failed in the Catholic faith and would not fail it in the future.

## ARTICLE 2

The accused, not only in the current year but also from the time of her childhood, and not only in your diocese and jurisdiction but also in neighboring and other parts of this kingdom, has performed, composed, associated with and commanded many charms and superstitions; she has been idolized and has permitted herself to be adored and venerated; she has called up demons and evil spirits, and has consulted and visited them, and has entered into pacts and treaties with them; she has similarly given advice, assistance and favors to other people doing the same things, and she has induced them to do the same or similar things; likewise, saying, believing, maintaining and affirming that to do these things or believe in them—to use such charms, divinations and superstitious activities—was neither a sin nor a forbidden thing; and she has instead assured people that it is lawful, praiseworthy and appropriate, enticing into these evil ways and errors many people of different status and of either sex, and in whose heart she has imprinted these ideas and similar notions. In committing these crimes, she was captured and taken within the boundaries and limits of your Diocese of Beauvais.

Joan's response:

To this second article Joan answers that she denies the charms, superstitions and divinations; and regarding the adoration, if certain people have kissed her hands or garments it was not because of her or at her direction; she said she kept herself from that as much as it was within her power to do so. Regarding the rest of the accusations in the article, she denies them.

Promoter's comments:

On Saturday, March 3, of this same year, with regard to the contents of this article, when Joan was asked if she knew what was in the thoughts of the people of her party as they kissed her hands, her feet and her garments, she answered that many people gladly saw her, and with that, she said she told them to kiss her garments as little as possible; however, the poor people came to her, and she did not disappoint them and she helped them as much as she could.

On Saturday, March 10, we asked her about leading the military assault at Compiegne, where she was captured. She said she was told by revelation or by her Voice to carry out the assault. She said on that day her Voice had not foretold her capture, and she was not advised by her Voice to go there, however, she has often been told by her Voice that she must be captured. Asked if, when she made this assault she passed over the bridge of Compiegne, she replied yes, and using the boulevard, she went with the company of her men against the men of lord Jean de Luxembourg, and that she twice drove them to the camp of the Burgundians, and a third time to the middle of the highway; then the English cut off the road from her and her company, between her and the boulevard, so her men retreated; and she, falling back to the fields on the Picardy side, was captured; and the river, which was an impediment, was between Compiegne and the place where she was taken, and between Compiegne and where she was captured there was only the river and the boulevard with its ditch.

## ARTICLE 3

The accused has fallen into many different errors of the worst kind, infected with heretical evil. She has said, uttered, voiced, affirmed, published and imprinted on the hearts of simple people specific false and lying assertions infected with heresy and actually heretical, without faith and contrary to our Catholic faith, and against the statutes made and approved by the General Councils, as well as by divine, canon and civil laws. Also, she has given advice and favors to people who have said, uttered, affirmed and spread scandalous and sacrilegious assertions that are contrary to good custom and offensive to pious ears.

Joan's response:

This third article Joan denies, and she declares that to the best of her ability she has upheld the Church.

## ARTICLE 4

To better and more specifically inform you of the offenses, excesses, crimes and misdemeanors committed by the accused, and as has been reported in many parts of the territory, in this diocese and elsewhere, it is true that the accused was and is a native of the village of Greux, that her father is Jacques d'Arc and her mother is Isabelle, his wife; that she was brought up in her youth until the age of about 18 in the village of Domremy on the Meuse, in the Diocese of Toul, in the Bailly of Chaumont-en-Bassigny, in the area of Monteclaire and Andelot.

In her youth, Joan was not taught or instructed in the belief and principles of the faith, but was taught and initiated by certain elderly women in the use of spells, divinations and other superstitious works or magic arts. Many inhabitants of these villages are known from previous times to have practiced these evil arts, and from certain of these women, and especially from her godmother, Joan stated that she often heard talk of visions or apparitions of spirits or fairy spirits; and from other people she has been taught and filled with these evil and malevolent errors about the spirits, so much so that she admitted to you, in judgment, that until this day she does not know whether these spirits were evil spirits.

Joan's response:

To this article Joan replies that she agrees with the first part about her father and mother, and the place of her birth; but as for spirits or fairies, she does not understand. Regarding her instruction by the women, she said she learned to believe and was appropriately and suitably taught how to behave as a good child should. Regarding her godmother, she referred us to what she had stated previously. When asked about saying her Credo, Joan answered, "Ask the confessor to whom I said it."

## ARTICLE 5

Near the village of Domremy stands a certain large and ancient tree, commonly called The Charmed Spirits' Tree of Bourlemont, and near the tree is a fountain. It is said that in the vicinity of this tree there are evil spirits, called fairies, and at night people who practice magic spells are accustomed to dancing with the spirits as they move around the tree and the fountain.

Joan's response:

To this fifth article, regarding the tree and the fountain, Joan referred us to an answer she had given previously; the rest she denies.

Promoter's comments:

On Saturday, February 24, Joan answered that not far from Domremy there is a tree called the Ladies' Tree, which some call the Spirits' Tree, and near it is a fountain. She has heard that people who are ill drink water from this fountain, and she herself has drunk water from this fountain. She said that sick people seek restoration of their health from its water, but she does not know whether they are cured or not.

On Thursday, March 1, when asked if St. Catherine and St. Margaret spoke to her under the tree, she said, "I do not know." Then we asked if the saints spoke to her at the fountain, and she answered that they did, and that she heard them there; but what the saints said to her there she no longer remembers. When asked, on the same day, what the saints had promised her, there or elsewhere, she replied that they made no promises to her except by God's permission.

On Saturday, March 17, when asked if her godmother, who saw spirits at the Spirits' Tree, is believed to be a wise woman, she answered that she is known as a good, honest woman, and not a witch or a sorceress.

The same day, when asked if she had believed the spirits to be evil spirits, she answered that she did not know; and the same day, when asked if she knew anything about those people who associate with the spirits, she answered that she never went there and never knew anything about that, but she had heard that some people went to the Spirits' Tree on Thursdays. She said she does not believe in it, and she said it was witchcraft.

## ARTICLE 6

Joan frequently went to the fountain and the tree, mostly at night but sometimes during the day, particularly to be alone at times when the Divine Office prayers were being recited in the church. While dancing, Joan would move around the tree and the fountain, and then she would hang garlands on the tree limbs; the garlands were made by her own hand using different herbs and flowers; all the while, she danced and sang, before and afterward, certain songs, verses and invocations, spells and evil arts; the next morning the chaplets of flowers would no longer be found there.

Joan's response:

To this sixth article, Joan referred us to another reply she previously made. The remainder of the article she denies.

Promoter's comments:

On Saturday, February 24, Joan said that she heard how the sick, when they were able to walk, would go to the Spirits' Tree to walk around it. The tree is a very large beech tree and the property is said to belong to Pierre de Bourlemont. Sometimes she went to the tree playing with the other girls in summer, and she made garlands for Our Lady of Domremy there.

She often heard elderly people say, but not people of her family, that spirits frequently visited the tree. She heard her godmother, the wife of the mayor of Domremy, Aubrey, say that she had seen the spirits, but Joan herself does not know if it is true. She never, as far as she knows, saw the spirits, and she does not know if she saw any of these spirits elsewhere.

She has seen girls putting chaplets of flowers on the limbs of the tree, and she herself has hung chaplets of flowers with other girls there, sometimes carrying them away, sometimes leaving them there. She added that ever since she knew that she must travel to France she has spent little time playing games or dancing, as little as possible.

She does not remember whether she has danced near the tree since she has grown to the age of understanding; she added that on some occasions she may well have danced there with the children, but she more often sang than danced there.

She added that there is also a wooded area, called the Oak-Wood, which can be seen from her father's door, less than two miles away. She does not know nor has she ever heard that spirits visit there, but she has heard from her brothers that after she had left the area, it was said that she received her message at the Spirits' Tree. She says that she did not, and she told her brother so.

Also, she said that when she travelled to see the king, several people asked her if there was in her part of the country a wooded place called the Oak-Wood, because there were prophecies saying that a young girl would come out of the Oak-Wood and work miracles; however, she said she put no faith in that.

## ARTICLE 7

Joan was accustomed to wearing a mandrake in her bosom, hoping thereby to have good fortune in riches and things of this world; this mandrake, she affirmed, possessed these capabilities and potency.

Joan's response:

This seventh article, of the mandrake, Joan absolutely denies.

Promoter's comments:

On March 1, when we asked what she had done with her mandrake, Joan replied that she never had one; she heard people say there was a mandrake plant near her village but she never saw it. She had heard that it is an evil and dangerous thing to keep; however, she cannot say what its use is. Asked where this mandrake plant is, the one she heard about, she replied that she heard it was in the ground near the tree, but she cannot say exactly where; she has heard that a hazel tree grows over the mandrake plant.

Asked what benefits the mandrake provides, she replied that she has heard it attracts wealth, but she puts no faith in that, and her Voices never told her anything about the mandrake.

## ARTICLE 8

Joan, of her own will and without the permission of her father and mother, went to the town of Neufchateau in Lorraine, and while she was there for some time she served in the house of a woman, an innkeeper named La Rousse, where many young unguarded women stayed, and the lodgers were mostly soldiers. Therefore, dwelling at this inn, she would sometimes stay with these women, sometimes she would drive the sheep to the fields, and occasionally she would lead the horses to drink, or to the meadow or to pasture. She said it was there that she learned to ride a horse and became acquainted with the profession of being a soldier.

Joan's response:

To this eighth article Joan referred us to her other replies, and she denied the remainder.

Promoter's comments:

On February 22, Joan confessed that out of fear of the Burgundians she left her father's house and went to the town of Neufchateau in Lorraine, to the house of a certain woman named La Rousse, where she stayed for about two weeks performing the common duties of a household, but she did not go into the fields. On Saturday, the twenty-sixth of the same month, when asked if she took the farm animals to the fields, she said she had already replied; she also added that since the time she had grown up and reached the age of understanding she did not typically look after the cattle, but helped to take them to the meadows and to a castle called the Island, out of fear of the soldiers, but she does not remember whether or not she tended them in her youth.

## ARTICLE 9

Joan, while serving at the house of the woman named La Rousse, summoned a certain youth before the magistrate of Toul for breach of a promise to marry, and in the course of this legal case she frequently went to Toul, and pursuing the legal case she spent almost everything she had. This young man, knowing she had lived with the women at the house of La Rousse, refused to marry her, and he died while awaiting an outcome of the litigation. For this reason, out of spite, Joan left the house of La Rousse.

Joan's response:

To this ninth article Joan answers that she has replied elsewhere, and she refers us to that reply. She denies the remainder.

Promoter's comments:

On Monday, March 12, while answering a question regarding who had persuaded her to summon the man from Toul for breach of a promise to marry, Joan said, "I did not have him summoned; it was he who summoned me, and I swore before the judge to tell the truth."

Also, she swore that she had made no promise to marry this man. She added that her Voices assured her that she would win her legal case against this man.

## ARTICLE 10

After leaving the service of La Rousse, Joan claims for the past five years she has been having visions and apparitions of St. Michael, St. Catherine and St. Margaret, and that they have privately revealed to her that she should carry out the military assault on the city of Orleans and have Charles, whom she calls her king, crowned, and that she should drive out all the adversaries of the kingdom of France.

Against the wishes of her father and mother, she left them, and of her own initiative and decision she went to Robert de Baudricourt, captain of Vaucouleurs, to inform him—according to the commands of St. Michael, St. Catherine and St. Margaret—of the visions and revelations made to her by God, as she claims, and to ask Robert to help her accomplish the objectives of these revelations. Twice refused by Robert and after being sent home, she received once more by revelation the command to return to Robert de

Baudricourt, and it was during this third time that she was welcomed and received by Robert.

Joan's response:

To this tenth article, Joan answers that she will stand by her other replies on this matter.

Promoter's comments:

Joan previously stated that when she was about 13 years old, she heard a Voice from God to help her and guide her, and that the first time she heard the Voice she was very frightened. The Voice came around noon on a summer's day, in her father's garden, when she was not fasting, and she had not fasted on the previous day.

She heard the Voice on her right, towards the direction of the church, and she rarely heard the Voice without it being accompanied by a visible light. The light came from the same side as the Voice, and generally it was a bright light, and the first time she heard the Voice there was a light. When she traveled through France she often heard a great Voice; she added that if she was in a wooded area she heard the Voice well, and it seemed to her an admirable Voice, and she believed it was sent to her from God.

After she heard the Voice three times she knew it was the Voice of an angel. She said the Voice always protected her well, and she understood the Voice well. Asked what instruction this Voice gave to her regarding the salvation of her soul, she said it taught her to be good and to go to church often, and that she must travel through France. She added that the questioner would not learn from her at this time in what form the Voice appeared to her.

The Voice told her two or three times a week to leave her home and travel to France, and that her father was to know nothing about her leaving. The Voice told her to come and she could no longer stay where she was. The Voice told her she would carry out the military assault on Orleans.

When she reached Vaucouleurs she recognized Robert de Baudricourt even though she had never seen him before. She recognized Robert through her Voice, which told her it was Robert. She told Robert that through her Voices it had been revealed to her that she must travel to France. Twice he refused her, but the third time he received her and he gave her an escort, as her Voice had foretold.

On Saturday, February 24, when we asked at what time on the preceding day she had heard the Voice, she replied that she had heard the Voice three times in all; first in the morning, next at Vespers, and lastly when the Hail Mary [church bells] were rung in the evening. She often heard the Voice more frequently than this; and the previous morning, while she was asleep, the Voice woke her not by touching her, but by speaking to her. She did not know if the Voice was in the room but she was certain it was in the castle. She admitted that when the Voice came to her for the first time she was 13, or about 13 years old.

On Tuesday, February 27, she said that it had been at least seven years since St. Catherine and St. Margaret began for the first time to guide her. Asked if St. Michael appeared first, she said yes, and she received great comfort from him. She also said, "I do not speak of St. Michael's Voice, but of his great comfort."

Asked which Voice was the first to come to her about the age of 13, she answered that it was St. Michael who she first saw with her eyes, and that he was not alone but accompanied by many angels from Heaven. She said that she travelled through France only by the instruction of God. Asked if she saw St. Michael and the angels physically and in reality, she replied that she saw them with her bodily eyes in the same manner that she saw the assessors at the trial. When St. Michael and the angels left her, she cried and wished they had taken her with them. Asked on the same day if there was a light with the Voice, she answered there was a great deal of light on all sides, as was most appropriate.

On Thursday, March 1, we asked if, since the preceding Tuesday, she had spoken with St. Catherine and St. Margaret, and she answered yes, both, on that day and on the previous day, but she did not remember at what hour. She said that there is not a day that goes by without her hearing them.

On Monday, March 12, we asked if she inquired of her Voices whether she should tell her father and mother that she would be leaving them, and she answered that her Voices would have been glad for her to tell her parents except for the difficulties it would have caused if she had done so. If the decision regarding whether to tell her parents was up to her, she would not have told her parents anything; the Voices left it up to her to tell her parents or to be silent.

Asked about the dreams her father had of her going away, she said that her mother told her several times that while she was still at home her father said he had dreamt of Joan's going away with soldiers, so they took great care to keep her safe and were overly protective; and she obeyed them in all things except for the incident at Toul regarding the action for marriage. She had heard her mother say how her father said to her brothers, "If I thought what I dreamed was going to happen, I would want you to drown her, and if you would not, I would do it myself." Her father and mother almost lost their senses when she left for Vaucouleurs. Asked whether these thoughts came to her father after she had her visions and heard her Voices, she answered yes, more than two years after she first heard the Voices.

## ARTICLE 11

Joan, having entered into intimate relations with Robert de Baudricourt, boasted to have told him that after having accomplished everything revealed to her by God, that she would have three sons: the first would be Pope, the second emperor, and the third king.

After hearing this, the captain said to her, "Now then, I would like to give you a child since they're going to be such powerful men, because I'm worth as much or more and I would be better off." To which Joan replied, "Gentle Robert, no, no, this is not the time, the Holy Spirit will find a way!" Robert confirmed and repeated this conversation in many places, including in the presence of clerics, lawyers and notable persons.

Joan's response:

To this eleventh article, Joan answered by referring us to the answers she made elsewhere on this subject; and as for having three children, she never boasted about it.

[The Duchess of Bedford requested Anna Bavon and at least one other midwife to examine Joan's virginity, and Anna stated that Joan appeared to be a virgin. It is unclear if the trial judges believed the midwives. At the time, it was generally believed that virgins could not be under the influence of demonic forces, so the judges would have a motive to claim that Joan was not a virgin. When Joan was asked why she called herself "the Maid" (the Virgin) and whether she was a virgin in reality, she answered, "I may tell you that I am."]

Promoter's comments:

On Monday, March 12, we asked if her Voices called her daughter of God, or daughter great-hearted, and she answered that before the military assault on Orleans and since then, her Voices have spoken to her every day, often calling her Joan the Virgin, Daughter of God.

## ARTICLE 12

To better and more easily accomplish her plans, Joan required Captain Robert de Baudricourt to have a man's outfit made for her, with armaments to match, and he finally consented to her demands, which he did reluctantly and with great repugnance. After the garments and armaments were made, fitted and finished, Joan stopped wearing and entirely abandoned women's clothes; and with her hair cropped short and styled like a vain young man, she wore a shirt, riding pants, a man's close-fitting jacket, stockings fastened to her riding pants, long leggings laced on the outside, a short cape reaching to her knees or thereabout, a close-cut cap, tightfitting boots, long spurs, a sword, a dagger, breastplate, and a lance and other armaments in the style of a soldier, with which she performed the activities of war and affirmed she was fulfilling the commands of God as they had been revealed to her.

Joan's response:

To this twelfth article Joan referred us to her other replies on this matter. Importantly, when we asked her whether she put on this clothing and these armaments and other uniforms of war because of God's command, she answered, "I refer you, as before, to what I have already said in reply to this."

Promoter's comments:

On Thursday, February 22, Joan said that her Voice had told her to go to Robert, Captain of Vaucouleurs, and he would give her soldiers. She answered to her Voice by saying she was a poor maid who could neither ride a horse nor fight a war. She said that she had told an uncle that she had to go to Vaucouleurs, so he took her there. Also, she said that when she went to see the king she wore men's clothes.

Before she went to the king, the Duke of Lorraine sent for her; she went and told him she wanted to go to France. The Duke questioned her about recovering his health, but she told him she knew nothing of that and spoke little to him about her journey. She told the Duke to give her his son and his men, to take her to France, and she would pray for his health. She traveled to the Duke and returned to Vaucouleurs safely.

Upon leaving Vaucouleurs she wore men's clothes and carried a sword that Robert gave to her, but no other armaments, and she was accompanied by a knight, a squire and four servants. She went to the town of St. Urbain and slept in the abbey there. During this journey she passed through Auxerre, where she attended Mass in the great church, and she said she frequently heard her Voices during this time.

Robert made those who were escorting Joan swear to lead her safely and surely, and when she left he said to her, "Go, go and come what may." She said that she had to change to men's clothes because she believed the advice she received from her Voices in that respect was good. She said she travelled without any difficulty to see the king, to whom she sent letters for the first time when she was at the town of St. Catherine de Fierbois.

On Tuesday, February 27, asked if her Voice had instructed her to wear men's clothes, she said that clothes are a minor thing, the least of all things; but that she did not wear men's clothes on account of any person's advice; she said she wore men's clothes and did everything only at the command of our Lord and His angels.

She said she did not wear men's clothes at Robert's request. Asked if she had done the right thing to wear men's clothes, she answered that to her mind everything she did at God's request was done well, and she expects good support and help because of it. She also said that she had a sword that she acquired at Vaucouleurs.

On March 12, we asked if it was at Robert's request that she wore men's clothes, and if the Voice had given her any commands in connection with Robert, and she answered as previously. Regarding the Voices, she said that everything good that she had done had been at the request of her Voices; and with regard to her clothes, she would answer another time because at the present time she was not yet advised by her Voices, but would reply on the following day.

On Saturday, March 17, we asked what support or aid she expected from our Lord because she wears men's clothes, and she answered that in this, as in other matters, she wanted no reward other than the salvation of her soul.

## ARTICLE 13

Joan attributes to God, to His angels and to His Saints, instructions that are contrary to the honesty of womankind, forbidden by divine law, abominable to God and man, and prohibited under penalty of anathema [not only excommunication from the Church and separation from the Sacraments, but also social exclusion from the Christian community] by ecclesiastical decrees, such as the wearing of short, tight and immoral men's clothes, those clothes underneath her pants and top, as well as the rest. She often dressed in rich and luxurious clothes, lavish accessories made of gold, and clothing made of fur; and not only did she wear short upper garments, but she dressed herself in short coats and garments open at the sides. She was notoriously captured while she was wearing a loose outer garment made of gold-colored cloth, a cap on her head, and with her hair cropped in the style of a man's haircut. Casting aside all womanly decency, and not only scorning feminine modesty but also the modesty of well-instructed men, she wore the clothes and garments of vain, self-indulgent men, and in addition, she carried military weapons.

To attribute her behavior to requests made by God, His holy angels and virgin saints is blasphemous to our Lord and His saints; it sets aside divine decrees as if they were nothing, and it infringes on canon law; it is a scandal for women and womanly decency, and it is the perversion of all modesty in outward behavior. It also provides a sign of approval and encouragement to engage in the most degenerate examples of behavior.

Joan's response:

To this thirteenth article, Joan answered, "I have not blasphemed God or His saints."

Promoter's comments:

On Tuesday, February 27, when asked if she thought the instruction to wear men's clothes was lawful, Joan answered that everything she did was at God's command, and that, if He had asked her to wear different clothes she would have done so because it was at God's request. Asked whether she thought that in this particular instance she had done well, she replied that she did not wear men's clothes without God's command, and that no single action of hers was otherwise than at His command.

On the following Saturday, we asked her whether, when she went to see the king for the first time, the king asked her if she had changed her clothing after her revelations, and she said, "I replied to this question before; I do not remember the details but my reply was written down during the investigation at Poitiers."

On the same day, when asked if she believed that she would be in error or commit mortal sin by returning to women's clothes, she answered that she would do better to obey and serve her sovereign Lord, namely God.

## ARTICLE 14

Joan affirms that it is acceptable to wear clothing and other items worn by vain, self-indulgent men, and she says that she will persist in doing so, saying that she must not stop wearing men's clothes except in the case where she is given specific permission to do so by revelation from God; to do otherwise would grieve God, His angels and His saints.

Joan's response:

To this fourteenth article, Joan answered, "I do not do wrong to serve God; tomorrow you shall have a reply."

Asked by one of the assessors if she had received an instruction or revelation to wear men's clothes, she answered that her reply had already been given elsewhere and she leaves it at that; but then she said that she would provide an answer the following day. She added that she knows very well who instructed her to wear men's clothes, but she does not know how she should reveal it to us.

Promoter's comments:

On Saturday, February 24, when asked if she wanted a woman's dress, she said, "If you will give me permission to leave, then give me a woman's dress, I will take it and go; otherwise I do not want one; I am content with this, because it is God's will that I should wear it."

On Monday, March 12, when asked whether she did not think she was doing wrong to wear men's clothes, she answered no, and even at that moment, if she were back with her own party, it seemed to her that it would be to the great good of France for her to do as she did before her capture.

On Saturday, March 17, when asked why, since she declares her wearing of men's clothes to be at God's command, she asks for a woman's long garment in the event of her execution, she answered that any garment would be sufficient for her if it was a long garment.

## ARTICLE 15

Joan, having repeatedly asked permission to attend Mass, was admonished to stop wearing men's clothes and return to a woman's dress. Her judges gave her the hope that she would be allowed to attend Mass and receive Holy Communion if she would finally stop wearing men's clothes and wear women's clothes, as is appropriate for her sex. She would not agree, and she preferred not to take Communion and participate in holy prayers rather than give up wearing men's clothes, pretending that by doing so she would displease God; by this she revealed her obstinacy, her stubbornness in evil, her lack of charity, her disobedience to the Church, and her scorn for the Holy Sacraments.

Joan's response:

To this fifteenth article, on this Tuesday, March 27, Joan answers that she would much rather die than turn her back on our Lord's command.

On this same day, when asked if she would stop wearing men's clothes and attend Mass, she replied that she would not stop wearing men's clothes, and that the day she would stop wearing men's clothes is not up to her.

She said that if the judges refuse to let her attend Mass, then it is in God's power to allow her to attend Mass when it pleases Him, without them.

As for the remainder of the article, Joan said that she admits she has been admonished to wear women's clothes, but she denies the charge that she is irreverent, and she denies the other charges in the article.

Promoter's comments:

On Thursday, March 15, when we asked which she would prefer, to wear a woman's dress and attend Mass or keep wearing men's clothes and not attend Mass, she answered, "Promise me I can attend Mass if I am in women's clothes and I will answer you." Whereupon the questioner said he promised, and then Joan said, "What do you say if I have sworn and promised to our King not to stop wearing men's clothes? However, I will answer you; have a long dress reaching down to the ground with no train made for me, and give it to me to go to Mass, and then on my return I will once again put on the clothes I have."

When asked, once and for all, whether she would wear a woman's dress and go to Mass, she answered, "I will get advice on that and then I will answer you."

Also, in honor of God and Our Lady, she insisted that she should be allowed to attend Mass in this good town; and at this point we told her to take a woman's dress, simply and absolutely, and she replied, "Give me a dress such as the daughters of your officials wear, a long houppelande, and I will wear it to go attend Mass." Furthermore, speaking as urgently as she could, she pleaded with us to allow her to attend Mass in the clothes she wore, without any change.

On Saturday, March 17, questioned on the subject of the woman's dress offered to her so that she could attend Mass, she answered that she would not put it on until it would please our Lord; but she added that if she must be brought to judgment and stripped of her men's clothes, then she asks the lords of the Church to grant her the mercy of wearing a woman's dress and a hood for her head, because she said she would rather die than turn her back on what her Lord commanded her to do. She firmly believes that God would not permit her to be brought so low, or be at this time without His help or a miracle.

Because she said that she would put on women's clothes if we let her go [from prison], we asked her if wearing women's clothes under those circumstances would please God, since God commanded her to wear men's clothes. She answered that if we permitted her to leave because she wore women's clothes, she would do so, but she would then immediately put on men's clothes and do what our Lord asked her to do. She said to accomplish God's will nothing would make her swear not to take up arms or wear men's clothes.

## ARTICLE 16

Joan, after her capture at the castle of Beaurevoir and at Arras, was repeatedly and charitably admonished by noble and distinguished persons of both sexes to stop wearing men's clothes and to wear clothes decently appropriate for her sex. This she absolutely refused, and she still obstinately persists in her refusal to do so, as well as perform other duties appropriate for her sex; in all things she behaves more like a man than a woman.

Joan's response:

To this sixteenth article, Joan admits that she was admonished at Arras and Beaurevoir to wear women's clothes, and that she refused and still refuses to do so. As for the other womanly duties, she says there are enough other women to do them.

Promoter's comments:

On Saturday, March 3, when asked if she remembers whether the clerics of her own party who examined her, some for a month and others for three weeks, did not question her about changing from wearing women's clothes to men's clothes, she replied that she did not remember. However, they did ask her where she began wearing men's clothes and she told them it was at Vaucouleurs. When asked if she began wearing men's clothes because of her Voices, she said, "That is not relevant to your legal case."

When we questioned her if she was asked to change from men's to women's clothes at Beaurevoir, she replied, "Yes, truly," but she said she would not do so without God's permission. The Demoiselle of Luxembourg asked Jean de Luxembourg not to turn her over to the English, and the Lady of Beaurevoir offered her a woman's dress and told her to wear it. Joan replied that she did not have God's permission and it was not yet time. Joan added that Messire Jean de Pressy and others at Arras did not offer her any women's clothes, but others did ask her to change her clothes. Moreover, she said that if she had to change her clothes, she would rather have done so at the request of those two ladies than of any other ladies in France, except the queen.

We asked her, when God revealed to her that she should change to men's clothes, whether it was by the Voice of St. Michael, or by the Voice of St. Catherine or St. Margaret, and she answered, "You will learn no more at the present time."

## ARTICLE 17

When Joan came to see King Charles wearing men's clothes and carrying a weapon, she made three promises, among others, to him: first, that she would carry out the military assault at Orleans; second, that she would get him crowned at Reims [Charles was not yet officially crowned as king]; and third, that she would take vengeance on his enemies, that she would kill them all by her magic arts, drive them out of the kingdom, both the English and the Burgundians. She boasted publicly of these promises many times in different places; and to increase faith in what she was doing and saying, she made use of magic spells, and she revealed to people, individuals whom she had never seen or known, details about their habits, various aspects of their lives and their secret activities, and then she boasted that her knowledge came by revelation.

Joan's response:

To this seventeenth article Joan replied that she gave news to the king that she came from God, saying that our Lord would restore his kingdom, would have him crowned at Reims, and would expel his enemies. She said she was God's messenger to that effect, and she told him to permit her to go to work boldly and she would carry out the military assault on Orleans; she spoke, she said, of the whole kingdom, and if the lord Duke of Burgundy and other subjects of the realm did not come to obedience, the king would compel them by force. With regard to recognizing Robert and the king, she said, "I maintain what I said before."

Promoter's comments:

On Thursday, February 22, she admitted that when she came to Vaucouleurs she recognized Robert de Baudricourt although she had never seen him before, because her Voice told her it was Robert. She said that she saw the king at Chinon; she arrived around noon and lodged at an inn; then after dinner she went to the king at his castle, and when she entered the room she recognized him from among the others by her Voices. She told the king she wanted to fight the English. On March 13, when asked about a certain married priest and a lost cup, she said she knew nothing about it and that she had never heard anything about it.

## ARTICLE 18

Joan, as long as she remained with Charles, discouraged him and his men with all her power from negotiating any treaty of peace with his enemies. She continually incited her soldiers to murder and shed human blood, saying that there could be no peace except by the sword and the lance's point; and that this was ordained by God because the king's enemies would not otherwise yield the territory they held, and therefore to make war on them was to her mind the greatest benefit to all Christendom.

Joan's response:

To this eighteenth article Joan answered that she summoned the Duke of Burgundy both by letter and ambassadors to make peace with the king. As for the English, she said the only peace possible with them is by their return to their own country, to England. Regarding the rest of this article, she said she has already replied and she referred us to her previous answers.

Promoter's comments:

On Tuesday, February 27, when asked why she did not conclude a treaty with the captain of Jargeau, Joan replied the lords of her party answered to the English they would not get the delay of two weeks that they requested, but must leave immediately with their horses. For her own part, she said they could safely leave with their coats and their lives if they wished, but otherwise they would be taken by assault. Asked if she had any conversation with her counsel, or Voices, to find out whether or not to grant the requested two-week delay, she answered that she did not remember.

## ARTICLE 19

Joan, by consulting demons and using magic spells, sent someone to get a specific sword hidden in the church at the town of St. Catherine de Fierbois, which she had wickedly and deceitfully hid or had hidden in this church, so that by misleading princes, nobles, clergy and common people, she might more easily induce them to believe that it was by revelation that she knew the sword was there, and they might more readily put absolute faith in her sayings.

Joan's response:

To this nineteenth article, Joan referred us to her earlier answers regarding the sword; the rest of the article she denies.

Promoter's comments:

On Tuesday, February 27, we asked Joan if she had been to St. Catherine de Fierbois and she said yes, and that she went to Mass there three times on the same day, and then went on to Chinon. The same Tuesday she said she had a sword from the church of St. Catherine de Fierbois, the sword she sent for when she was at Tours or Chinon. She said the sword was buried in the ground behind the altar, but immediately the sword was found, and it was all rusted. When asked how she knew the sword was there, she replied that through her Voices she knew it was in the ground, was rusted over and had five crosses on it; and she said that she had never seen the man she sent to fetch it.

She wrote to the clergy asking if she could have the sword, and the clergy sent it to her. She thought it was not buried deep behind the altar, and she did not know exactly whether it was in front or behind the altar, but she thought it was behind. As soon as the sword was found, she added, the priests cleaned it and the rust fell off immediately, without any effort. An armorer of Tours fetched it.

The priests at St. Catherine's church and also at Tours gave her sheaths for holding the sword, one of crimson velvet and the other a cloth of gold. She herself had another made of very strong leather, and added that when she was captured she did not have the sword with her, although she had it continuously until she reached Saint-Denis. Asked how it was blessed, whether she said a blessing or asked for any benediction to be said over the sword, she answered she had never asked for a blessing and did not know how to do it. She said she loved the sword because it had been found in the church of St. Catherine, whom she loved.

When questioned on Saturday, March 17, about the significance of the five crosses on the sword, she answered that she did not know.

ARTICLE 20

Joan put a magic spell on her ring, her military banner and on linen flags, which she carried or had her men carry for her; and she did likewise on the sword she claims to have found by revelation at St. Catherine de Fierbois, affirming that these objects brought good fortune. She spoke many curses and incantations over these objects in different places, publicly declaring that with their aid she would do great things and overcome her enemies, and her men would not be defeated in their attacks or fighting, or suffer any misfortunes because they carried these flags. In particular, she publicly said and proclaimed this at Compiegne on the eve of her attack on the lord Duke of Burgundy, during the course of which she was captured and taken prisoner, and many of her men were wounded, killed and captured. She also made such declarations at the town of Saint-Denis, where she incited her soldiers to attack Paris.

Joan's response:

To this twentieth article, Joan, on Tuesday, March 27, answered that she stands by her earlier answers regarding this matter. Furthermore, she added that there was never any witchcraft or magic involved in anything she did. With regard to her military banner, she referred to the good fortune that our Lord brought it.

Promoter's comments:

On Tuesday, February 27, when asked if she had her sword when she was captured, Joan answered no, but that she had a sword that was taken from a Burgundian soldier.

On Thursday, March 1, when asked who gave her the ring now in the possession of the Burgundians, she replied her father and mother; she thought it had written on it the names of Jesus and Mary, but she did not know who inscribed the names. The ring had no gemstone, and it was given to her at Domremy. She said her brother gave her another ring, in addition to the one which the bishop has, and she requested that we give it to the Church. Never, she said, did she use the rings as a means to cure any person or restore their health.

On Saturday, March 3, we asked about the time when the king first sent her to do battle and she had her military banner made, whether the soldiers and others of her party had flags made like hers. She said, "It is good to know that the lords kept their own arms." She replied that some of the soldiers had these flags made at their pleasure, while others did not. When asked of what material they were made of, linen or another type of cloth, she replied it was white satin, and on some flags fleurs-de-lis were depicted. She had only two or three lances in her company, but her soldiers had flags made like hers, doing so merely to distinguish their men from others. Asked if the flags were often repaired, she answered that she did not know, but that when the lances were broken new flags were made. Asked if those flags made like hers brought good fortune, she answered that she did indeed sometimes say to her men, "Go boldly in the midst of the English" or "Go boldly among the English," then she herself would go.

When asked if she told them to carry the flags boldly and they would have good fortune, she answered that she certainly told them what had happened before would happen again. Asked if she sprinkled Holy Water or had others sprinkle Holy Water over the flags when they were first taken into battle, she answered that she did not know, but if it was done it was not at her instruction. Asked if she ever saw Holy Water sprinkled on them, she answered, "That is not relevant to your legal case," and if she did, she was not now advised to answer.

Asked if her soldiers had written on their flags the names Jesus and Mary, she said that by her faith she did not know. Asked if she had carried around the altar of the church, or had others carry, the cloth that was to be made into flags, she answered no, and she had never seen it done.

On Saturday, March 17, when asked what her ring, which had Jesus and Mary written on it, was made of, she replied she did not exactly know. She said if it was gold, it was not fine gold; and she does not know if it was gold or brass, but she thinks there were three crosses on it, and to her knowledge, no other insignia except the words Jesus and Mary. When we asked why she so happily looked at this ring when she was going into battle, she said it was out of pleasure and in honor of her father and mother, and because having her ring on her finger and in her hand, she touched St. Catherine who appeared before her.

Asked what part of St. Catherine she touched with her ring, she answered, "You will get nothing more about that."

## ARTICLE 21

Joan, motivated by her boldness and her presumption, had the names Jesus and Mary written on her letters, signed with a cross, and addressed them from herself to our lord the king, to my lord Duke of Bedford, then regent of France, and to lords at Orleans; letters which contained many evil things, malicious and contrary to the Catholic faith.

Joan's response:

To this article, on Tuesday, March 27, Joan answered that she did not send these letters out of pride or presumption, but at our Lord's request, and she admits to the content of the letters except for three words.

Promoter's comments:

On Thursday, February 22, Joan said she had letters sent to the English at Orleans telling them to leave according to the instructions in the letters, which were read to her [text is inserted below]. Regarding the letters, she said where it states, "surrender to the Virgin" it should read "surrender to the King," and likewise regarding the three words, "body for body" and "commander-in-chief." The letters begin with "King of England," and they are inscribed with + Jesus Mary +.

On Saturday, March 3, when asked if her own party firmly believed her to be sent from God, she said she didn't know whether they did, but referred us to their opinions; but if they did not believe she was sent from God, she was nonetheless sent from God. When asked if she thought they were wise to believe she was sent from God, she said, "If they believe I am sent from God, they are not deceived."

## ARTICLE 22

[Transcript of the letter from Joan to the English military at Orleans follows.]

+ Jesus Mary +

King of England, and you Duke of Bedford, calling yourself regent of France, you, William Pole, Count of Suffolk, John Talbot, and you Thomas Lord Scales, calling yourselves lieutenants of the said Duke of Bedford, do right in the King of Heaven's sight, surrender to the Virgin, who was sent here by God the King of Heaven, the keys of all the good towns you have taken and laid to waste in France. She comes in God's name to establish the Royal Blood, ready to make peace if you agree to leave France and repay what you have taken. And you, archers, comrades in arms, gentlemen and others who are in the town of Orleans, leave, in God's name, and go to your own country. If you do not, expect to hear from the Virgin who will soon attack you and inflict great suffering upon you. And to you, King of England, if you do not do this, I am commander in chief and wherever I meet your followers in France, I will drive them out; if they will not obey, I will put them all to death. I am sent here in God's name, the King of Heaven, to drive you body for body out of all France; if they obey, I will show them mercy; do not think otherwise; you will not keep the kingdom of France from God, the King of Kings and Blessed Mary's Son. King Charles, the true inheritor to the throne, will possess it because God wills it and has revealed it to him through the Virgin, and he will enter Paris with good company. If you do not believe these messages from God and the Virgin, wherever we find you we shall strike you and make a greater uproar than France has heard for a thousand years. Know well that the King of Heaven will send a greater force to the Virgin and her good soldiers than you in all your assaults can overcome; and by these defeats shall the favor of the God of Heaven be seen. You, Duke of Bedford, the Virgin prays and implores you not to bring destruction to yourself. If you obey her, you may join her company, where the French shall do the fairest deed ever done for Christendom. If you desire peace in the city of Orleans, then answer; if not, then start thinking about your impending great suffering. Written this Tuesday of Holy Week.

ARTICLE 23

From the content of this letter it is obvious that Joan has been deceived by evil spirits and that she has frequently consulted them in her actions, or, to mislead people, she has maliciously and falsely invented these fictions.

Joan's response:

To this article, Joan replies that she denies the last part of it as well as the part which declares she acted on the advice of evil spirits.

Promoter's comments:

On February 27, she said she would rather have been drawn by horses than to have journeyed to France without God's permission.

## ARTICLE 24

Joan misused the names of Jesus and Mary and the Sign of the Cross placed with them.

Joan's response:

To this article, on Tuesday, March 27, Joan replied by referring us to a previous answer she gave regarding this matter.

Promoter's comments:

On March 17, when asked what the purpose was of the sign she put in her letters and of the names Jesus and Mary, she said that the clerics who wrote her letters put them in there, and that some people said it was proper to put the two names, Jesus and Mary, in letters.

## ARTICLE 25

Joan, assuming the office of angels, said and affirmed that she was sent from God, even in things tending openly to violence and to the spilling of human blood, which is absolutely contrary to holiness, and horrible and abominable to all pious minds.

Joan's response:

To this article on Tuesday, March 27, Joan answered that she first asked for peace, but if peace was not agreed to, then she was quite prepared to fight.

Promoter's comments:

On Saturday, February 24, Joan said that she came from God and therefore had no business being in this trial, and she asked to be sent back to God from whom she came. On Saturday, March 17, she said that God sent her to help the kingdom of France.

## ARTICLE 26

On Thursday, March 1, when asked if she had received a letter from the Count d'Armagnac regarding which of the three claimants to the Papacy he should obey, she answered that the Count did write a letter to her asking about this, to which she replied, among other things, that when she got to Paris or anywhere else where she had the time to reply, she would answer at that time; she was about to mount her horse when she said this.

After the letters from the Count and from Joan were read [the text is included in the following Articles], she was asked whether that was her actual reply. She answered that she thought part of what we read was her reply, but not all of it. When asked if she had professed to know, according to her advice from the King of Kings, what the Count should believe in this matter, she said she did not know.

When asked if she had any doubts about which of the three claimants to the Papacy she should obey, she answered that she did not know how to instruct Count d'Armagnac regarding which of the three claimants to obey because the Count asked her to say whom God wanted him to obey; but as for Joan herself, she believed that we should obey our Holy Father the Pope at Rome. She added that she said other things to the Count's messenger that are not included in the copy of the letter we read; and if the Count's messenger had not left immediately he would have been thrown into the water, though not by her.

Regarding the Count's question about whom God wished him to obey, she replied that she did not know, but she sent several verbal messages to the Count by courier which were not put into writing. But, as for Joan herself, she believed in our Holy Father the Pope at Rome.

When asked why she had written that she would answer at a later time if she believed in the Pope at Rome, she said her answer was related to a different matter other than the question of the three popes.

When asked if she had stated that she would get advice on the question of the three popes, she said she swore by her oath that she had never written, nor caused to be written, anything concerning the three popes.

## ARTICLE 27

[Transcript of the letter from Count d'Armagnac to Joan follows.]

My very dear Lady, I commend myself humbly to you and implore you for God's sake, seeing the division that now exists in the Holy Church Universal regarding the question of the popes, I request you to ask our Lord Jesus Christ, that in His infinite mercy, He confirm to us through you which of the three is the true Pope, and which He would have us obey, him who is called Martin, him who is called Clement, or him who is called Benedict, and in whom we should believe, because we are all ready to do the will and desire of our Lord Jesus Christ. Entirely yours, Count d'Armagnac.

## ARTICLE 28

Joan gave an answer by letter, signed with her own hand, which follows.

## ARTICLE 29

Jesus + Mary

Count d'Armagnac, my good and very dear friend, Joan the Virgin informs you that your message has reached her, whereby you say that you have written to her to determine which of the three Popes mentioned in your letter you should believe. In truth, I cannot say at the present time, until I am in Paris or at rest elsewhere, because I am now too busy with the business of war; but when you hear that I am in Paris, send a message to me and I will tell you in whom you should rightfully believe and what I can find out regarding what you should do, as far as I can, according to the advice of my just and Sovereign Lord, the King of all the World. I speak well of you to God, may He keep you. Written at Compiegne, August 22.

## ARTICLE 30

When asked by the Count d'Armagnac to declare which of the three was the true Pope and in whom the Count d'Armagnac should believe, Joan not only cast doubt upon who it was, when there was only one true and authentic Pope, but also, being arrogant of her own position and maintaining the authority of the Church Universal to be of little weight, and preferring her own

113

word to the authority of the whole Church, she affirmed that within a certain timeframe she would inform the Count d'Armagnac about which Pope he should believe, which she would discover by God's advice, as her letter declares at great length.

Joan's response:

Regarding Article 27, Article 28, Article 29 and Article 30, which were explained to Joan word for word, she refers us to the answer she has made, which is stated in Article 26.

## Wednesday after Palm Sunday, March 28

### ARTICLE 31

Regarding her clothes, Joan said that she wore her clothes and armaments at the request of God, and that this was true both of the men's clothes and the weapons. When asked to stop wearing these clothes she answered that she would not stop without our Lord's permission, not even to save her life, but if it pleased God she would soon stop wearing men's clothes; she added that if she did not receive permission from our Lord, then she would not wear woman's clothes.

Joan, since the time of her youth, has boasted, and she now daily boasts, of having had many revelations and visions; and regarding these revelations and visions, in spite of being charitably admonished and lawfully and properly required upon legal oath to tell us the details of these revelations and visions, she will not tell us, and she will not swear an oath to do so.

She continues to refuse and to delay in telling us about the details of these revelations and visions; and while formally refusing to swear an oath on many occasions, she has said and affirmed, while being questioned here and elsewhere, that she would not reveal her visions and revelations even if her head was to be cut off or her body was to be dismembered; she said that we would not pry from her lips the signs which God has shown to her, the signs by which she knows that she comes from God.

Joan's response:

To this Article 31, Joan answers that concerning the sign and other things contained in this article, she may well have said that she would not reveal it, but she adds that her answer should contain the statement that she would not reveal the sign without first having God's permission to do so.

Promoter's comments:

On February 22, Joan said there was no day when she did not hear this Voice or when she did not need it. On the following day she said that on the previous night her Voice told her many things for the benefit of the king, and that she wanted the king to know this information immediately, even if she had to go without wine until Easter; she said the king would eat all the more merrily because of the messages.

On Tuesday, February 27, Joan said that she sent letters to the king to ask if she should enter the town where the king was; that she had travelled more than 500 miles to help him, and that she knew many things that would be to his advantage. She said she thought the letters stated how she would be able to recognize him among all the other people.

On Thursday, March 1, when asked in what form St. Michael appeared to her, she said that she did not see his crown and knew nothing about his clothes. Asked if St. Michael was naked, she answered, "Do you think God has not the ability to clothe him?"

On Tuesday, March 15, when required to say how she expected to escape from the castle of Beaulieu using two pieces of wood, she said that she would gladly escape from being a prisoner in any place, and that while in the castle of Beaulieu she would have successfully restrained her jailers in the tower had not the porter seen and prevented her from doing so. She said apparently it did not please God to allow her to escape on that occasion, and that she must see the English king, as her Voices had told her.

On this same day we asked her about the size and stature of the angel who appeared to her, and she said that she would answer on Saturday along with other matters, specifically, whatever would please God. The same day we asked if she had said that a person is sometimes hanged for telling the truth,

115

and if she knew of any fault or crime of hers for which she should fear her execution if she did not confess; she answered no.

On Saturday, March 17, we asked Joan about the age and clothing of St. Catherine and St. Margaret, and she said, "You already have my reply in this matter and will get no additional information from me; I have answered you the best I can."

## ARTICLE 32

Consequently, you can and you must conclude that these revelations and visions, if Joan ever had them, came from evil and deceitful spirits, not from good spirits, and you must presume that this is the case, especially in view of the cruelty, pride, manner, actions, lies and contradictions indicated in several of these articles, which may be said and held to be lawful and entirely legitimate presumptions.

Joan's response:

To this thirty-second article, Joan answered, on the Wednesday after Palm Sunday, March 28, that she denies it, and she declares that she has acted according to the revelations of St. Catherine and St. Margaret, and will maintain this assertion until her death.

On this same day she said that she was advised by a certain person of her party to put "Jesus + Mary" on her letters, and she did so on some letters but not on others. She added that where it is written, "All that she has done is at God's command," it should read, "All the good I have done is at God's command."

When asked on this same day whether she thought her expedition to La Charité was done well or done poorly, she answered, "If I have done wrong, I will admit it."

When asked if it was right for her to go to Paris for a military assault, she answered that the French noblemen wanted to go to Paris, and by doing so, she believes, they performed their duty of attacking their enemies.

## ARTICLE 33

Joan arrogantly and recklessly boasted, and currently boasts, of foreseeing the future and knowing things that have occurred in the past that were secret or hidden; and this attribute of God she attributes to herself, a simple and uneducated creature.

Joan's response:

To this thirty-third article, this Wednesday, March 28, Joan answers, "It is for God to decide to make such revelations known to whomever He pleases." Regarding the sword and other events that will happen in the future, she says that she knows them by revelation.

Promoter's comments:

On Saturday, February 24, she said the Burgundians would have a war if they did not do as they should, and she said that she knows this from her Voice.

On Tuesday, February 27, when asked whether, when the military assault was to be made at Orleans, she told her men that she would be hit with arrows, crossbolts and stones, she said no, but at least one hundred men were wounded, and she told them not to have any fear because their attack on Orleans would be successful. When asked on the same day which fortress she ordered her men to leave, she said she did not remember. She added that she was confident the attack on Orleans would be successful because it had been revealed to her, and she told the king this before going to Orleans.

She also said that during the assault on the fortress at the Bridge she was wounded in the neck by a crossbolt, but she received great comfort from St. Michael and was better in two weeks. When asked if she knew beforehand that she would be wounded, she answered that she did indeed, and she had told the king this; however, even though she knew she would be wounded she would not give up her work; and this was revealed to her by the Voices of St. Catherine and St. Margaret. She added that she herself was the first person to plant the ladder up against the fortress of the Bridge, and as she was climbing it, she was wounded in the neck with a crossbolt.

On Thursday, March 1, she said that within seven years the English would lose a greater prize than they did at Orleans; that the English would suffer a greater loss than they ever did in France, which would be the victory that God would give the French over the English. This she knows by revelation; it will happen within seven years and she is very upset that it would be postponed for such a long time. She said she knows this by revelation as clearly as she knows that we are standing in front of her; she said, "I know it as well as I know you are here." Asked in what year this will happen, she said, "You will not learn that; however, I wholeheartedly wish it would be before St. John's Day."

This same day, when asked if she said it would happen before Martinmas, she answered that she had said many things would be seen before then, and it might well be that the English would be overthrown and struck down to the ground. When asked what she told John Grey, her guard in prison, about Martinmas, she said, "I have already told you!" Asked through whom she knew it would happen before Martinmas, she answered that she knew it from St. Catherine and St. Margaret.

This same Thursday, March 1, when asked what promises St. Catherine and St. Margaret made to her, she answered, "That is not relevant to your legal case," but, among other things, St. Catherine and St. Margaret told her that the king would be reestablished in his kingdom regardless of whether his enemies wished it or not. On this same day she said she knew very well that the king would regain the kingdom of France as well as she knew we were standing in front of her.

On Saturday, March 3, when asked if the Voices told her anything in a general way, she answered, "Yes, definitely, they told me that I would be delivered, but I do not know the day or the hour, and they told me I must boldly show a cheerful expression on my face in front of you."

On Saturday, March 10, when asked if the military incursion at Compiegne was made at the instruction of her Voices, she answered that during the last week of Easter, when she was in the trenches at Melun, she was told by the Voices of St. Catherine and St. Margaret that she would be captured before St. John's Day; her Voices said it had to be so, but that she should not be afraid and take everything in good stride, and God would come to her aid.

On this same day, when asked if since Melun she had been told by her Voices she would be captured, she answered yes, and that several times, almost every day, her Voices said this to her.

She asked her Voices if, when she was captured, she might die quickly so that she would not suffer for a long time in prison. Her Voices told her to be resigned, that these events must happen, but they did not tell her when these things would happen because if she had known when she was to be captured she would not have gone. She often asked her Voices at what hour she would be captured, but they did not tell her.

On the same day she said that when she had to leave to see the king, she was told by her Voices, "Go boldly, when you are in the king's presence he will receive a good sign to receive you and believe in you."

On Monday, March 12, when asked how she would have rescued the Duke of Orleans, she said that she would have taken enough English prisoners in this district to ransom him; and if she had not taken enough English prisoners she would have crossed the sea to England to take him by force. Asked if St. Catherine and St. Margaret had told her absolutely and unconditionally that she would take enough prisoners to ransom the Duke, who was in England, or else she would cross the sea to take him and bring him back within three years, she answered yes, and she told the king to let her have her way with the prisoners. She added if she had gone on for three years unhindered she would have rescued him; she said that she needed less than three years but more than one year.

On Wednesday, March 14, when asked to what risk and danger we, the bishop and clerics, were in because we were trying her in court, she replied that St. Catherine told her she would receive help; she does not know whether this will be her deliverance from prison, or if, while she is being tried in court, some turmoil might arise through which she can be rescued. She thinks it will be one or the other; most often her Voices tell her that she will be delivered by a great victory, and they say, "Take everything peacefully, and do not be concerned about your martyrdom."

## ARTICLE 34

Joan, persisting in her rash and arrogant ways, has declared, has spread abroad, and has had written, that she is able to recognize and distinguish the Voices of God's archangels, angels and saints, affirming that she can distinguish them from human voices.

Joan's response:

To this thirty-fourth article on Wednesday, March 28, Joan replies she stands by her previous answers in this matter; and with respect to her rashness and arrogance, she refers herself to the judgment of our Lord.

Promoter's comments:

On Tuesday, February 27, when asked if it was the Voice of an angel or of a saint, or God Himself, which spoke to her, she replied that it was the Voice of St. Catherine or St. Margaret, and their heads were crowned in rich and precious style with beautiful crowns. She added, "I have God's permission to tell you this, and if you doubt it, then inquire to Poitiers, where I was questioned before."

The same day, when we asked how she knew one saint from the other, she answered that she knew them by the greeting they gave her and because they tell her their names.

On Thursday, March 1, we asked how she knew whether her apparition was a man or a woman, and she answered, "I know very well and I recognize the saints by their Voices," and because they reveal themselves to her. The same day, when asked what part of them she saw, she answered the face. When asked if they had hair, she said, "It is good to know they have hair." Asked if there was anything between their crowns and their hair, she answered no. Asked if their hair was long and draped down, she said, "I do not know."

She added that she did not know whether they appeared to have arms or other body parts. She said they spoke very well and beautifully, and she understood them very well. When asked how they spoke if they had no other body parts, she said, "I refer myself to God."

On March 15, when asked if she had no other sign, other than these apparitions, regarding whether or not they were good spirits, she answered, "St. Michael certified it before the Voices came to me." Asked how she knew it was St. Michael, she answered, "By the angel's speech and language," and she firmly believes they are angels.

Asked how she knew it was the speech of angels, she answered that she knew it immediately and had the desire to believe it. She added that St. Michael, when he came to her, told her that St. Catherine and St. Margaret would also come to her, that she should follow their advice, and that St. Catherine and St. Margaret were instructed to lead her and advise her about what she had to do, and that she should believe what they said because it was at our Lord's command.

When asked how she could determine if he was a good spirit or an evil spirit if the Enemy put himself in the form and disguise of a Holy Angel, she answered that she would certainly know whether it was St. Michael or a counterfeit in his likeness.

She said at first she had serious doubts about whether it was St. Michael, and that the first time she saw him she was afraid; and she saw him many times before she knew it was St. Michael.

Asked how she knew then, rather than on the first occasion, that it was St. Michael who had appeared to her, she replied that the first time she was a young girl and was afraid; but since then St. Michael had taught her and showed her so many things that she firmly believed it was him.

When asked what doctrine St. Michael taught her, she answered that in all things he told her to be a good child and God would help her; and among other things, he told her that she should go to the aid of the king of France. A great part of what the angel taught her is in this book [sacred scriptures]; and the angel told her about the pitiful state of the kingdom of France.

## ARTICLE 35

Joan has boasted and asserted that she is able to tell whom God loves and whom He hates.

Joan's response:

To this thirty-fifth article, on Wednesday, March 28, Joan answers, "I stand by what I have already answered with regard to the king and the Duke of Orleans." Regarding other persons, she says she does not know. She says she knows very well that God loves the king and the Duke of Orleans more than her, and she knows this by revelation.

Promoter's comments:

On Thursday, February 22, Joan said that she knows God greatly loves the Duke of Orleans, and that she has had more revelations about him than any man alive, except the king.

On Saturday, February 24, when asked if she could influence the Voice so that it would obey her and take news to the king, she answered that she did not know whether the Voice would obey her unless it was God's will and God consented to it. She said, "If it pleases God, He will be able to send revelations to the king, and with this I shall be very pleased."

When we asked why this Voice no longer speaks with the king as it did when Joan was in his presence, she answered that she does not know if it is God's will or not.

On Saturday, March 17, when we asked how she knows St. Margaret and St. Catherine hate the English, she answered, "St. Margaret and St. Catherine love those whom God loves, and hate whom He hates."

When asked if God hates the English, she answered that she knows nothing about God's love or hatred, or what God will do to their souls, but she is certain that with the exception of those who shall die on French territory, the English will be driven out of France, and that God will send victory to the French against the English.

Asked if God was for the English when they were prospering in France, she answered that she did not know whether God hated the French, but she believed it was His will to allow them to be chastised for their sins if they were in a state of sin.

## ARTICLE 36

Joan has declared, affirmed and boasted, and still does so day after day, that she knows and has truly known, and not only she, but also other men at her request have truly known and recognized, a certain Voice that she calls her Voice, which comes to her; although by its nature, this Voice, which she describes and has described, must have been, and is, invisible to every human being.

Joan's response:

To this thirty-sixth article, Joan states she stands by her previous answers.

Promoter's comments:

On Thursday, February 22, she said that those of her party knew very well that the Voice was sent from God, and that they saw it and knew it, and she knew this very well. Moreover, she said that the king and several others heard and saw the Voice that came to her, and that Charles de Bourbon and two or three others were present as witnesses.

## ARTICLE 37

Joan admits that she has often done the opposite of what the revelations have instructed and commanded her to do, although she boasts to receive these revelations from God; for example, when she left Saint-Denis after the military assault at Paris, when she jumped from the tower at Beaurevoir, and on other occasions. As a result, it is clear that either she has not received revelations from God or she has rejected these instructions and specific revelations by which she asserts that she is completely influenced and governed.

Moreover, she said when she was ordered not to jump from the tower and was tempted to do the opposite, she could not do otherwise. As a result, she appears to hold erroneous ideas about men's free will, and she stumbles into the error of people who put forth the idea that human behavior is determined by fate or is predetermined.

Joan's response:

To this thirty-seventh article, on Wednesday, March 28, she answers, "I refer you to my earlier answers." However, she added that she did receive permission for her departure from Saint-Denis. When asked whether, by acting against the instruction of her Voices, she believed herself to be in mortal sin, she replied, "I have already answered this, and I refer you to that answer." With respect to the rest of this article, she commits herself to God.

Promoter's comments:

On Thursday, February 22, Joan said that her Voice told her to remain at Saint-Denis in France, but against her will the lords took her away. Nevertheless, if she had not been wounded she would not have gone. She was wounded in the trenches before Paris and said that she recovered in five days.

On Saturday, March 10, when asked if her Voices had ordered her to make the attack at Compiegne and had also told her that she would be captured, whether she would have gone, she answered that if she had known when she was going to be captured she would not have gone willingly; however, she said that she would have ultimately followed the requests of her Voices, whatever it may have cost her.

On Thursday, March 15, when asked if she ever did anything against the instruction and will of her Voices, she answered that she performed with all her might whatever she could do and was able to do. Regarding her leap from the tower at Beaurevoir, which she did against the request of her Voices, she said she could not help herself; and when her Voices saw she was in need of assistance, and that she could in no way have held herself back from jumping from the tower, they provided assistance to protect her life and prevented her from being killed. Moreover, she said that whatever she did in her great endeavors her Voices comforted her, and that this is a sign they are good spirits.

On the same day we asked if she believed it was a great sin to anger St. Catherine and St. Margaret by behaving in a manner contrary to their requests. She answered yes, but that she knows how to atone for it; and what angered St. Catherine and St. Margaret the most of all, in her opinion, was her leap from the tower at Beaurevoir; however, she asked their forgiveness for this as well as for other offenses she had committed against them.

## ARTICLE 38

Joan, beginning from the time of her youth, has expressed, committed and perpetrated many sins, crimes, errors and faults, and shameful, cruel, scandalous and dishonorable actions unfitting to her sex; nevertheless, she proclaims and affirms that everything she has done is at God's request and according to His will, and that she has never done anything which does not proceed from Him, through the revelations of His holy saints, and through the blessed virgins Catherine and Margaret.

Joan's response:

To this thirty-eighth article, Joan refers us to her previous answers in this matter.

Promoter's comments:

On Saturday, February 24, Joan said that except for the grace of God she could do nothing. The same day, when asked if the people of Domremy were on the side of the Burgundians or the others, she answered that she knew only one Burgundian in the village, and she would have been quite willing for him to have his head cut off, if it pleased God.

Asked if in her youth her Voice told her to hate the Burgundians, she answered that since she knew the Voices were for the king of France, she did not like the Burgundians.

On Thursday, March 15, when asked if in battle she had done anything without the advice of her Voices, she answered, "You already have my answer to this. Read your transcripts carefully and you will find it."

Nevertheless, she said that at the request of soldiers she made an attack at Paris, and also at La Charité, at the king's request; and it was neither against nor according to the commands of her Voices. When asked if she ever did anything contrary to the command and will of her Voices, she referred us to her earlier replies in this matter.

## ARTICLE 39

Although the just man falls seven times a day [good people sin many times each day], Joan has declared that she has never committed, or at least to her knowledge has never committed, acts of mortal sin, notwithstanding that she has in reality engaged in all of the behaviors that are customarily performed by soldiers, as is documented in the preceding and the following articles.

Joan's response:

To this thirty-ninth article on Wednesday, March 28, she answers, "I have answered this already and I stand by my earlier answers."

Promoter's comments:

On Saturday, February 24, when asked if she knows if she is in God's grace, she answered, "If I am not, may God put me there, and if I am, may God keep me there."

She said she would be the saddest creature in the world if she were not in God's grace, and she added that if she were in a state of sin, she did not think the Voice would come to her, and she wished everyone could hear the Voice as well as she did.

On Thursday, March 1, she said she is very glad when she sees her Voice, and she thinks that when she sees her Voice she cannot be in mortal sin.

She says that St. Catherine and St. Margaret, alternately, at different times, gladly hear her confession, and if she is in mortal sin, she is not aware of it.

Asked if, when she confesses, she feels as if she is in mortal sin, she replied that she did not know whether she was in a state of mortal sin, but she does not think she has committed such sins. She said, "Please God, I never was in mortal sin, and if it pleases Him, I never shall commit nor have committed such sins that burden my soul."

On Wednesday, March 14, when asked whether it was not a mortal sin to take a man for ransom, a prisoner, and then put him to death, she answered that she had not done that; and with regard to a certain Franquet d'Arras who was sent to Lagny to be put to death, she answered that she consented to his death if he deserved it, because he had confessed himself to be a murderer, a thief and a traitor. His trial lasted for two weeks, she said, and he was tried by the Bailly of Senlis and a jury of the people of Lagny. She said she had asked to have Franquet exchanged for a man from Paris, the landlord of the Bear Inn; and when she heard of the death of the landlord and the Bailly told her she would be doing a great injustice by freeing this Franquet, she said to the Bailly, "Since the man I wanted is dead, do with Franquet as justice demands."

After Joan was reminded that she had attacked Paris on a Catholic feast day, and that she had the horse of the lord Bishop of Senlis, and that she had thrown herself from the tower at Beaurevoir, and that she wore men's clothes, she was then asked if she believed she had committed mortal sin. She answered, firstly, concerning the attack on Paris, she did not think she was in mortal sin, and if she was, it was a matter only for God and the priest in confession to know about it.

Secondly, concerning the bishop's horse, she replied that she firmly believes she did not commit a mortal sin because the lord Bishop of Senlis received a warrant for 200 gold saluts for the horse. Thirdly, regarding the tower of Beaurevoir, she replied that she did not jump out of despair, but in the hope of saving her body and of going to the aid of many good people in need, and after the leap she confessed herself and asked forgiveness of God, which she received, and she thinks it was wrong to have made the leap. She knows she received forgiveness after her confession because of a revelation from St. Catherine, on whose advice she confessed herself. Fourthly, concerning the men's clothes, she answered, "Because I do it by God's command and in His service, I do not think I do wrong, and as soon as it shall please God to command it, I will stop wearing men's clothes."

## ARTICLE 40

Joan, forgetful of her salvation and at the instigation of the devil, is not ashamed, and has not been ashamed, from time to time and in many various places, to receive Holy Communion while wearing men's clothes, a style of clothing that is forbidden and prohibited by the command of God and the Church.

Joan's response:

To this fortieth article, Joan replies, "I answered this before, and I refer you to my earlier answers." In conclusion, she submits herself to God.

Promoter's comments:

On Saturday, March 3, when asked if, when she was journeying through the country, she often received the Sacraments of Holy Communion and Confession when she came to the good towns, she replied yes, from time to time; furthermore, when we asked if she received the Sacraments while wearing men's clothes, she answered yes, but she does not remember receiving them in armor.

## ARTICLE 41

Joan, like a madwoman, out of hatred and scorn for the English, and also out of fear of the destruction of Compiegne, decided to jump from the top of a high tower at the instigation of a devil; planning, attempting and performing all she could to accomplish it. She jumped from the tower, incited or induced by a diabolical instinct, more worried about the welfare of her body than the salvation of her soul and of other souls; she boasted often that she would rather die than let herself be delivered into the hands of the English.

Joan's response:

To this forty-first article, Joan answers, "I refer you to the answers I have already made."

Promoter's comments:

On Saturday, March 3, when asked if she was in the town of Beaurevoir for a long time, she answered that she was there for about four months; and when she heard that the English were on their way she became very angry; and although her Voices had forbidden her to jump from the tower, finally, out of fear of the English, she jumped and commended herself to God and Our Lady. Asked if she had said that she would rather die than fall into the hands of the English, she answered that she would rather surrender her soul to God than fall into their hands.

On Wednesday, March 14, when asked why she jumped from the tower at Beaurevoir, she answered that she had heard that the people of Compiegne, all of them to the age of seven years, were to be put to the fire and sword; and that she would rather die than live after such a massacre of good people; that was one reason why she jumped; the other was that she knew she had been sold to the English and she would have rather died than fall into their hands.

Asked if her leap was made at the advice of her Voices, she answered that St. Catherine told her almost every day not to jump, and that God would aid her and the people of Compiegne too. But Joan told St. Catherine that since God was going to help the people of Compiegne she wanted to be there too. St. Catherine said, "You must be resigned and not falter; you will not be delivered until you have seen the king of the English." Joan answered, "Truly, I do not want to see him, and I would rather die than fall into the hands of the English."

She said that after her fall from the tower she went two or three days without any desire to eat, however, she was comforted by St. Catherine who told her to confess and ask God's forgiveness for having jumped from the tower, and the people of Compiegne would assuredly receive assistance before Martinmas in winter; it was then that she began to eat and drink, and soon after she recovered her health.

We asked her if, when she regained her speech after her fall, she denied God and His Saints, and she answered that she did not remember that she had ever denied God or His Saints.

When asked if she was willing to abide by the evidence collected, or to be collected, for this trial, she answered that she would leave that up to God, and nobody else.

## ARTICLE 42

Joan has said and publicly declared that St. Catherine, St. Margaret and St. Michael have body parts such as a head, eyes and face, and that she has also touched these saints with her own hands, and has embraced and kissed them.

Joan's response:

To this forty-second article, Joan replies, "I have answered this before, and with regard to this, I refer you to my earlier statements."

Promoter's comments:

On Saturday, March 17, when asked whether she ever kissed or embraced St. Catherine and St. Margaret, she answered that she had embraced them both and they had a fine fragrance. Asked if, when she embraced them, she felt heat or anything else, she answered that she could not embrace them without feeling or touching them. Asked what part of them she embraced, their head or their feet, she answered that it was more fitting to embrace their feet.

## ARTICLE 43

Joan has said and publicly declared that the saints, angels and archangels speak French and not English, and that the saints, angels and archangels are not on the side of the English but on the side of the French; and she affirmed their scorn: that the saints in glory look with hatred on a Catholic realm and a country given to the veneration of all the saints according to the instruction of the Church.

Joan's response:

To this forty-third article, which was explained to her word by word, Joan said nothing beyond, "I refer myself to our Lord and to my earlier answers."

Promoter's comments:

On Thursday, March 1, she said that the Voice is fair, soft and humble, and speaks French. When asked if this Voice, that is, St. Margaret, spoke English, she replied, "Why should she speak English? She is not on the English side."

## ARTICLE 44

Joan has boasted and proclaimed, and still does boast and proclaim, that St. Catherine and St. Margaret promised to accompany her to Heaven, that St. Catherine and St. Margaret assured Joan of her salvation if she kept her virginity, and that Joan is assured of her salvation.

Joan's response:

To this forty-fourth article, Joan answers, "I refer myself to our Lord and to my earlier answers."

Promoter's comments:

On Thursday, February 22, she said that she never asked the Voice for any other final reward than the salvation of her soul.

When asked, since her Voices told her she will eventually go to the Heaven, whether she feels assured of her salvation and safe from damnation in Hell, she answered that she firmly believes what her Voices told her, namely, that she will be saved, and she knows this as firmly as if she were already in Heaven. When we told her that this answer of hers was critical, she replied that she held this as a great treasure; and she meant, with regard to this article, provided that she kept her oath and promise to our Lord, that is, to maintain her virginity of body and soul.

Asked whether, after this revelation, she believes it is possible for her to commit mortal sin, she replied, "I do not know, but I commit myself to God in all things."

Asked if she needed to confess her sins since she believes from the revelation of her Voices that she will be saved, she answered that she does not know of having committed mortal sin; but if she were in mortal sin, she thinks St. Catherine and St. Margaret would immediately abandon her; and she believes that it is impossible for a person to cleanse their conscience too much.

She said on Thursday, March 1, that her saints promised to accompany her to Heaven, and that she had asked them to do so.

## ARTICLE 45

Although the judgments of God are completely unfathomable to us, Joan has said, declared and proclaimed that she has known, and knows, who are the saints, the angels, the archangels and the elect [saved] of God, and that she can distinguish them, one from another.

Joan's response:

To this forty-fifth article, Joan replies, "I refer you to my earlier answers."

Promoter's comments:

On Tuesday, February 27, when we asked how and why she knew it was St. Catherine and St. Margaret who appeared to her, and how she could discern one from the other, she answered that she knew very well who they were and easily recognized one from the other.

On Thursday, March 1, when asked if the saints always appeared to her in the same clothing, she answered that she always saw them in the same form, and that their heads were richly crowned; and of their other clothing she does not speak, nor knows anything of their robes.

On Saturday, March 3, she said she clearly saw St. Catherine, St. Margaret and her other apparitions, and that she knows they are saints of Heaven.

## ARTICLE 46

Joan says that she very affectionately interceded with St. Catherine and St. Margaret for the people of Compiegne before taking her leap from the tower, saying to them, among other things, in a manner of criticism, "And why does God allow the people of Compiegne to die so wretchedly, those who are so faithful to Him!" With this statement, Joan expresses impatience and irreverence towards God and His Saints."

Joan's response:

To this forty-sixth article, Joan replies, "I refer you to my earlier answers."

Promoter's comments:

On Saturday, March 3, she said that after she was wounded by leaping from the tower of Beaurevoir, the Voice of St. Catherine told her to be of good cheer and that she would recover, and that the people of Compiegne would receive assistance. She said that she often prayed with her Voices for the people of Compiegne.

## ARTICLE 47

Joan, displeased with the wounds she received from her fall or leap from the tower of Beaurevoir, and upset that she had not accomplished her plan of escape, blasphemed God and His Saints, shamefully denied them, and terribly scorned them to the horror of all who were present; and further, since she has been in the castle of Rouen, on many different days she has blasphemed and denied God, the Blessed Virgin and the Saints, behaving with impatience and protesting against the fact that she is being brought to trial before us and is to be judged by the clergy.

Joan's response:

To this forty-seventh article, Joan replies, "I refer myself to our Lord and to my previous answers in this matter."

Promoter's comments:

On Saturday, March 3, when asked whether she was not upset and angry after jumping from the tower and whether she blasphemed the Name of God, she answered that she never cursed the Saints, and it was not her custom to swear. Asked about the town of Soissons, where her captain had surrendered the town, and whether she denied God and said that if she captured the captain she would have him drawn and quartered, she replied that she never denied the Saints, and that those people who said so were mistaken.

On Wednesday, March 14, when asked since she had been in this prison if she had denied or blasphemed God, she answered no, but that sometimes when she said, "Good God's will!" or "Saint Joan!" or "Our Lady!" the people who reported her words may have misunderstood.

## ARTICLE 48

Joan declared that she believed and currently believes the spirits that have appeared to her are angels, archangels and saints of God, as firmly as she believes in the Christian faith and in the doctrines of this faith, however, she doesn't provide any signs sufficient to determine their identity. Moreover, regarding these activities, she has not consulted any bishop, priest or other prelate of the Church, or any other cleric, to determine whether she should give credibility to these spirits. She also declares that she was forbidden by her Voices to reveal these communications to anyone except a captain of soldiers, to the king, and to other purely secular persons. As a result, she is admitting that her trust in these spirits is reckless, and her opinions on the doctrines of the faith and their foundations are erroneous. In addition, she has had suspicious revelations that she has hid from priests and from other clergy, while at the same time she has made these revelations known, preferentially, to secular persons.

Joan's response:

To this forty-eighth article, Joan answers, "I have already given you my reply and I refer you to what is already written down." About Joan providing signs sufficient to determine the identity of these spirits, she said if those people who ask for these signs are not worthy, she cannot help that. She added that many times she has prayed to God that, if it pleased Him, to reveal these signs to some people of her party. She also added that, regarding her believing in her revelations, she did not ask the advice of any bishop, priest or other cleric.

She said that she believes it is St. Michael because of the good doctrines he taught her. When asked whether St. Michael said to her, "I am St. Michael," she said, "I have already answered that," and with respect to the rest of this article, she said, "I refer myself to our Lord." She said she believes, as firmly as she believes our Lord suffered death to redeem us from the pains of Hell, that it is St. Michael, St. Gabriel, St. Catherine and St. Margaret that our Lord sends to her to comfort her and advise her.

Promoter's comments:

On Saturday, February 24, Joan said that she firmly believes, as firmly as she believes in the Christian faith and that our Lord redeemed us from the pains of Hell, that this Voice comes from God and is at His command.

On Saturday, March 3, when asked if she believes that St. Michael and St. Gabriel have natural heads, she answered that she had seen them with her own eyes and she believes they are St. Michael and St. Gabriel as firmly as she believes in the existence of God. Asked if she believes God created them with the heads that she saw, she answered, "I have seen them with my own eyes and I will not tell you anymore!"

When asked whether she believes God created them in the shape and form that she saw them, she answered yes.

On Monday, March 13, when asked whether she had spoken of her visions to her priest or to any other cleric, she answered no, only to Robert de Baudricourt and to the king. She added that she was not restricted by the Voices to conceal them, but she was afraid to speak about them out of fear of the Burgundians, in case they would prevent her travels through France. The same day, when asked if she thought it was right to leave her childhood home without the permission of her father and mother, because one should honor one's father and mother, she answered that she obeyed them in all things except for this departure; but since that time, she had written to her father and mother and they have forgiven her.

135

## ARTICLE 49

Joan, for no other reason except by her imagination, has venerated these spirits, kissing the ground where she saw they had passed, kneeling before them, embracing them and kissing them, and performing other acts of reverence, including giving them thanks, putting her hands together in prayer to them, and entering into relationships with them; however, she did not know whether they were good spirits, and moreover, considering these circumstances, they must be judged by her to be clearly more evil than good; and by her reverence and veneration she seems to be engaging in idolatry as the result of a pact made with devils.

Joan's response:

To this forty-ninth article on Wednesday, March 28, Joan answers, regarding the first part of this article, "I have already answered this." Regarding the remainder of the article, she says, "I refer myself to our Lord."

Promoter's comments:

On Saturday, February 24, asked whether she did not thank the Voice that appeared to her and kneel down before it, she answered that she thanked it but was sitting on the bed, and so she put her hands together, and this was after she had asked advice from the Voice.

On Saturday, March 10, asked what reverence she showed the sign when it came to the king and whether it came from God, she answered that she thanked our Lord for her deliverance from the difficulties arising from the opposition of the clergy of her party; and she knelt down many times. The same day, when asked whether the king and Joan showed reverence to the angel when the angel revealed the sign, she answered that she did, she knelt down and uncovered her head.

On Monday, March 12, when asked whether she spoke to our Lord when she promised Him to keep her virginity, she answered that it ought to be quite enough to promise it to those who were sent from Him, namely St. Catherine and St. Margaret. She said that the first time she heard her Voice she vowed to keep her virginity as long as it would please God, and she was then about 13 years old. The same day we asked whether she showed reverence to St. Michael and the angels when she saw them, and she answered that she did, and she kissed the ground where they had passed after they were gone.

On Thursday, March 15, we asked if, when her Voices came to her, she bows down completely, as if to a saint, and she answered yes; and if sometimes she failed to do so she asked forgiveness afterwards; she said she could not properly reverence them because she fully believes them to be St. Catherine and St. Margaret. She said the same with respect to St. Michael. The same day we asked her whether she had made offerings to the saints who come to her, by burning candles or other things, in a church or elsewhere, or had Masses said, she answered no, except at Mass, in the priest's hands, and in honor of St. Catherine. She believes that St. Catherine is one of the Voices that appears to her, and she has not lit as many candles to St. Catherine and St. Margaret, who are in Heaven, as she would have liked to, because she fully believes it is St. Catherine and St. Margaret who come to her.

Asked the same day whether, when she puts these candles before images of St. Catherine, she does it in honor of the saint who appears to her, she answered, "I do it in honor of God, of Our Lady, and of St. Catherine who is in Heaven, and I do not differentiate between St. Catherine who is in Heaven and St. Catherine who appears to me."

Asked the same day if she always successfully accomplished the requests made by her Voices, she answered that with all her might she accomplished the requests that our Lord spoke through her Voices, as far as she could understand them, and they told her nothing except in accordance with the good pleasure of our Lord.

On Saturday, March 17, when asked if she gave chaplets of flowers to the saints who appeared to her, she answered that in honor of these saints she gave many chaplets to their images or representations in churches, but as far as she remembers she has not given any flowers to those saints when they appear to her. Asked whether, when she hung garlands on the Spirits' Tree, she did it in honor of the saints who appeared to her, she answered no. The same day, when asked if, when the saints came to her, she showed reverence to them by kneeling or bowing, she replied yes; and the more she could show them reverence the more she did because she knows very well they are saints of Heaven.

## ARTICLE 50

Joan frequently and daily invokes these spirits, consulting with them about her private activities, for example, with regard to the answers she should give during her trial as well as in other matters, and this appears to involve an invocation of demons.

Joan's response:

To this fiftieth article on Wednesday, March 28, she replies, "I have already answered this," and she says she will continue to call these Voices to come to her aid as long as she will live. Asked in what manner she calls to them, she answered, "I beg Our Lord and Our Lady to give me their advice and comfort, and then they send it to me."

When asked what words she uses when she begs Our Lord and Our Lady to give her their advice and comfort, she answered that she says, "Very sweet Lord, in honor of Your Holy Passion, I beg You, if You love me, to reveal to me how I am supposed to answer these church people. I know very well your command regarding the matter of my clothes and the command by which I began to wear these clothes, but I do not know how I am to stop wearing men's clothes. In this matter, may it please You to instruct me." And then the Voices come to her immediately.

Often, she said, she receives news through her Voices regarding the Bishop of Beauvais. When we asked Joan what the Voices say to her about us, she answered, "I will tell you separately," and on that very day the Voices had come to her three times.

Asked if the Voices were in her room, she replied, "I have already answered your question about this; nevertheless, I hear them very well." She says St. Catherine and St. Margaret told her in what way she should reply to us with regard to wearing men's clothes.

Promoter's comments:

On Saturday, February 24, she said the Voice told her to answer boldly; and that when she woke up from her sleep she asked advice from the Voice regarding what she should reply, telling the Voice to ask advice from our Lord; the Voice told her to answer boldly and God would comfort her. The same day, when asked whether, before she questioned the Voice, the Voice addressed certain words to her, she said the Voice did speak certain words to her but she did not understand them all. However, when she awoke, she understood the Voice telling her to answer us boldly; she said that night she had heard the Voice say, "Answer boldly."

On Tuesday, February 27, when asked what the Voice had told her, she said that since last Saturday she had asked for advice on certain points regarding our questions during the trial. Asked if the Voice had given her any advice on certain points, she answered yes, on some points, but that on other points she might be asked questions that she should not answer without their permission. If she replied without getting permission perhaps she would not have the approval of the Voices; but when she had permission from our Lord she would not be afraid to speak because then she would have good authorization. The same day, when asked how she could distinguish between the points on which she would answer and the points on which she would not answer, she replied that on some points she had asked permission and on some of those she had received the permission.

On Monday, March 12, when asked whether the angel deceived her with respect to things of good fortune when she was taken prisoner, she said she thought that since it pleased God, it was better for her to be taken prisoner. Asked whether the angel did not fail her with regard to the good effects of grace, she answered, "How could he fail me when he comforts me every day?" And she believes the comfort is from St. Catherine and St. Margaret. Asked if she calls them or if they come without being called, she answered that they often come without being called, and sometimes, if they did not come, she would pray to God to send them. Asked if she sometimes had called them without their coming to her, she answered that no matter how little she needed them they always came to her.

On Wednesday, March 13, when we asked whether she had spoken to St. Catherine since the previous day, she answered that she heard St. Catherine since then and was told many times to answer the judges boldly in response to whatever they would ask regarding the legal case.

On Wednesday, March 14, when asked whether her Voices required a delay before answering, she said that St. Catherine answers her sometimes and sometimes Joan falls to understand her because of some commotion in the prison and the noise made by her guards.

After she makes the request to St. Catherine, then St. Catherine and St. Margaret immediately take Joan's request to our Lord; and then, at our Lord's request, they give the answer to Joan. Asked if there is a visible light with the saints when they come to her, and whether she sees a light when she hears the Voice in the castle, and whether she knows if the Voice is in her room, she answered that no day passes by without her Voices coming to her in the castle of Rouen, and they come with a visible light; however, on this occasion when she heard the Voice she does not remember if she saw the light, nor if she saw St. Catherine. She said she asked three things of her Voices, namely first, her deliverance; second, that God should help the French keep those towns already in their control; and third, the salvation of her soul.

## ARTICLE 51

Joan has not feared to boast that St. Michael, God's archangel, came to her with a great multitude of angels in the castle of Chinon and in the house of a certain woman; that St. Michael walked with her, holding her by the hand, and together they climbed the castle steps and entered the king's chamber; that this archangel St. Michael showed reverence to the king, bowed before him, and was accompanied by other angels, some of who were crowned and others had wings. To say such things about archangels and other holy angels must be viewed as arrogant, rash and deceitful, especially since these things have not been written about by any man, however honorable, and not even Our Lady, the Mother of God, has received such reverence or greetings.

Joan often said that the archangels St. Gabriel and St. Michael, and sometimes a million angels came to her. Moreover, Joan boasts that by her prayer the angel brought with him, in the company of other angels, a most precious crown for her king, to put on his head, and that the crown was put into the king's treasury. According to Joan, the king would have been crowned with this crown at Reims if he had waited a few days, but because of the haste with which his coronation was carried out he used another crown. These are less divine revelations than lies, invented by Joan, suggested or shown to her by a demon in illusive apparitions in order to simulate things in her imagination, all while she meddled with things that are beyond her competencies and abilities.

Joan's response:

To this fifty-first article on Wednesday, March 28, Joan answers that she has already replied regarding the angel who brought the sign; and as for the Promoter's statement about millions of angels, she answers that she has no recollection of having spoken about such a number. She added that whenever she was harmed she always received great comfort and aid from Our Lord and St. Catherine and St. Margaret. Regarding the crown, she says that she has already answered our questions about it; and regarding the last part of the article, as well as where the crown was made, she refers us to God.

Promoter's comments:

When asked if there was an angel above the king's head when she saw the king for the first time, Joan answered, "By Our Lady, if there was, I do not know of it, and did not see it." Asked if there was a visible light, she said that there were more than 300 knights and more than fifty torches, not counting the spiritual light, in the room; and she seldom had revelations without a visible light. Asked why the king believed in what she said, she answered that he received good instructions on that from the clerics. She said that the clerics of her party were of the opinion that nothing but good results would come from her mission.

On Thursday, March 1, when asked whether her king had a crown at Reims, she answered that she believes he gladly used a crown he found at Reims, but a much richer one had been since brought; he did this to speed up his coronation at the request of the townspeople and to avoid burdening the soldiers; but if he had waited he would have been crowned with a crown a thousand times richer. Asked whether she saw this richer crown, Joan answered that she cannot discuss this without committing perjury, and that if she did not see it, she heard that it is of such wealth.

On Saturday, March 10, when asked what the sign was that appeared to the king, she answered that it was fair, honorable and most credible, rich and good, the richest in the world.

Asked why she will not discuss or reveal the sign, considering that Joan wanted to see Catherine de La Rochelle's sign, she answered that she would not have asked to see Catherine's sign if it had been as well visible as her own sign was before notable ecclesiastics, archbishops and bishops, and others whose names she does not know; she said Charles de Bourbon, the Sire de la Tremouille, the Duke d'Alencon and many other knights saw and heard the sign as plainly as she saw those speaking to her at that time.

Moreover, she knew very well through St. Catherine and St. Margaret that the affairs of this Catherine de La Rochelle amounted to nothing at all. Asked whether the sign still exists, she answered, "It is good to know that it does, and it will last a thousand years and more." She said the sign is with the king's treasure. When asked whether it was gold, silver, precious stone or a crown, she answered, "I will tell you no more. No man could describe a thing as rich as this sign."

She added, "The sign you need is for God to deliver me out of your hands, the most certain sign He could show you."

The same day she said that an angel from God, and from no other source, gave the sign to the king, and for this she thanked our Lord many times. She said the clergy of her party stopped opposing her when they had seen this sign. Asked whether the clergy of her party saw the sign, she answered that when the king and those who were with him saw the sign, and also the angel who had it, she asked the king if he was satisfied, and he replied yes. Then she left and went to a little chapel nearby, and she heard after her departure that more than 300 people saw the sign. She added, that for her sake and to stop men from preaching to her, God willed that the people of her party who were there would see the sign.

On Monday, March 12, when asked whether the angel who brought the sign spoke any words, she answered yes, the angel told the king to put her to work and the country would quickly be at peace. Asked whether the angel who brought the sign was the same angel that first appeared to her or whether it was another, she answered that it was always the same one, and he never failed her. The same day, when asked about the sign she gave the king, she said she would seek advice from St. Catherine about it.

On Tuesday, March 13, when questioned about the sign she gave the king and what the sign was, she answered, "Would you be satisfied if I perjured myself?"

Asked if she had vowed and promised to St. Catherine not to discuss this sign, she answered, "I swore and promised not to discuss this sign on my own decision because I was being pressured too much to discuss it." Then she said she would not speak about it to any man. The same day she said the sign was that an angel gave assurance to the king by bringing him the crown and saying he would possess the entire kingdom of France by God's help and the work of Joan; and the king was to put her to work, that is, give her the soldiers, or else he would not so soon be crowned and consecrated.

The same day, when asked how the angel brought the crown and whether he placed it on the king's head, she answered that the crown was given to an archbishop, namely the archbishop of Reims, in the king's presence, so it seemed to her, and the archbishop took it and gave it to the king, and Joan was present, and then it was put in the king's treasure.

Asked where the crown was brought, she answered that it was brought to the king's chamber, in the castle of Chinon. Asked on what day and at what hour, she answered that she did not remember the day, and as for the hour, it was late, and beyond that, she could not recall the hour. She added it was in the month of April or March, she thought. She said that in the present month of March or the following April, it would be two years ago, and it was after Easter.

Asked whether the first day she saw the sign the king also saw it, she replied yes, he himself received it. Asked what the crown was made of, she replied, "It is good to know that it is made of pure gold," and was so rich that she could not count its richness, and it signified that the king would reclaim the kingdom of France.

Asked if there were precious stones in it, she answered, "I have already told you what I know." Asked if she held it or kissed it, she said no. Asked if the angel who brought it came from Heaven or from the Earth, she answered that he came from Heaven, meaning that he came at our Lord's command, and he entered the room by way of the door. Asked whether the angel walked on the ground when moving from the door, she answered that he walked and came forward from the door while walking on the ground, moving towards the king; and when he came before the king he showed reverence to the king by bowing before him, pronouncing the words of the sign, and at this time the angel recalled to the king the sweet patience he had shown during the great difficulties that had befallen him.

We asked her how far it was from the door to the king, and she answered that she thought it was a good lance-length, and that the angel went out by the same way he came in. She said when the angel came she accompanied him, and went with him by way of the stairs to the king's chamber, and the angel went in first, and then she said to the king, "Sire, here is your sign, take it."

Asked where it was that the angel appeared to her, she answered that she was almost always praying to God to send the king a sign; she was in her lodging, in the house of a good woman near the castle of Chinon, when the angel came. Then they went together to see the king, and the angel was accompanied by many other angels whom no one saw; but for her sake, and to unburden her from the distress she was experiencing as a result of the people opposing her, Joan said she believed that many people saw the angel who would not have otherwise seen him.

Asked whether all who were with the king saw the angel, she answered that she thought the Archbishop of Reims, de la Tremouille, and Charles de Bourbon saw him, and many churchmen and others who did not see the angel saw the crown.

When we asked her of what appearance and size the angel was, she replied that she does not have permission to discuss that but will answer tomorrow. When asked if all who were in the company of the angel were of the same appearance, she answered that some were fairly similar, and some, as far as she could see, were not; some had wings and some had crowns, and others did not; and among them were St. Catherine and St. Margaret, who were with the angel and the other angels while going up the stairs to the very chamber of the king.

Asked how the angel left her, she said he left her in a little chapel, and she was very upset when he left and she cried; she said she would have gladly gone with him, that is, her soul would have gone with him. Asked whether, at the angel's departure, she remained happy or if she was afraid and had great anxiety, she answered that the angel did not leave her in fear, but she was upset because he departed.

Asked whether it was because of any merit of hers that God sent His angel to her, she said it was because of the merit of the king and the good Duke of Orleans, and that the angel came with a great purpose, in hope that the king would believe the sign and Joan would no longer have any opposition.

When asked why the angel came to her rather than to another person, she answered, "It pleased God to drive back the king's enemies through a simple virgin."

Asked if she had been told from where the angel had initially received the crown, she said the crown was brought from God, and that no goldsmith on Earth could make a crown so rich and fair; however, with respect to where the crown came from, in this matter she refers us to God and knows nothing more about it.

Asked if the crown had a good fragrance and whether it sparkled, she answered she did not remember and would think about it to try to remember; afterwards, she said that it had, and always would have, a good fragrance, but must be guarded very well and appropriately; and it was in the form of a crown.

When asked if the angel had written her letters, she said no. Asked what sign the king and the people who were with him and Joan received to convince them that it was an angel who appeared to them, she answered that the king believed it because of the instruction of the churchmen who were there, and by the sign of the crown. Asked how the churchmen knew it was an angel, she answered that they knew because of their high level of education and because they were clerics.

## ARTICLE 52

Joan has so misled the Catholic people by her activities that many people have adored her as a saint in her presence, and they even adore her in her absence, offering Masses and collections in church out of reverence for her; indeed, they declare her to be greater than all of God's saints after Our Lady.

They set up images of Joan on the altars of saints; they wear medals that depict her image, like those medals made for the anniversaries of saints that are canonized by the Church; and they preach in public that she is sent from God, an angel rather than a woman. These are very scandalous actions, hurtful to the Christian religion and dangerous to the salvation of souls.

Joan's response:

To this fifty-second article, on Wednesday, March 28, she answers that, with regard to the first part of this article, she has already given us her answer, and regarding the last part of the article she defers to our Lord.

Promoter's comments:

On Saturday, March 3, when asked whether she ever knew Brother Richard, she said, "I had never seen him before I came to Troyes." Asked what type of greeting he gave to her, she said that the people of Troyes, she thought, sent Brother Richard to her, saying they were afraid she was not a thing sent from God, and so when he came close to her, he made the Sign of the Cross and sprinkled Holy Water at her, and she said to him, "Come boldly, I shall not fly away."

Asked whether she saw or had any images or pictures made in her likeness, she answered that at Arras she saw a painting in the hands of a Scot where she was shown in full armor with one knee on the ground, presenting letters to the king. Asked about a certain painting at her host's house in Orleans showing three women, Justice, Peace and Union, she answered that she knew nothing about that. Asked whether she knows that certain people of her party had a religious service, a Mass or prayers said for her, she said she knows nothing about it, and if any religious service was held it was not at her instruction, although if people prayed for her, she feels they did nothing wrong.

On that Saturday, March 3, Joan was asked what honor the people of Troyes gave to her when she entered the town, and she answered, "They did me no honor." She added that she thought Brother Richard entered Troyes with her but she does not remember seeing him enter. Asked whether he preached a sermon when she arrived, she answered that when she came she briefly stopped at Troyes, and did not even sleep there, and as for the sermon, she knew nothing about it.

## ARTICLE 53

Joan, acting against the wishes of God and His Saints, arrogantly and proudly assumed domination over men; she appointed herself leader and captain of an army that increased at times to 16,000 men, in which there were princes, barons and other nobles, all of whom she made fight under herself as the principal captain.

Joan's response:

To this fifty-third article, on Wednesday, March 28, Joan answers that with regard to the matter of being a leader during war she has already given her answer to us, and if she was the leader, it was to conquer the English. With regard to the last part of the article she defers to our Lord.

Promoter's comments:

On Tuesday, February 27, when asked what forces the king gave to her when he put her to work, she replied he gave her 10,000 or 12,000 men, and that she went first to Orleans, to the fortress of St. Loup, and then to the fortress of the Bridge.

## ARTICLE 54

Joan unashamedly walked with men, refusing to have the company or care of women, and she wished to employ only men whom she made serve in the private offices of her room and in her secret affairs, a thing unseen and unheard of in a modest or devout woman.

Joan's response:

To this fifty-fourth article, Joan answers that her leadership of military personnel was through men. Regarding where she lodged or slept at night, she usually had a woman with her, and during times of military battles if there was no woman to be found, she would sleep fully dressed and armored. Regarding the last part of the article, she defers to God.

## ARTICLE 55

Joan misused the revelations and prophecies she claims to have come from God, turning them into worldly profit and advantage; for example, by means of these revelations and prophecies she has acquired a great deal of wealth, status and attire, and many officers, horses and adornments; in this respect she has imitated the false prophets, who for love of worldly goods and to gain the favor of high-status people of this world, are inclined to pretend that they have received revelations concerning these high-status people, and thereby hope to please the princes of this world; as a result they abuse the divine oracles and attribute their false lies to God.

Joan's response:

To this fifty-fifth article, Joan answers that she has already replied to this; and regarding the gifts made to her brothers, the king gave the gifts from his grace, without her seeking those gifts. Regarding the accusation that the Promoter makes at the end of this article, she defers to God.

Promoter's comments:

On Saturday, March 10, when asked if she ever had any other riches from the king other than her horses, she answered that she never asked for anything from the king except good weapons, good horses, and money to pay the people of her household. Asked whether she had any wealth, she answered that the ten thousand or twelve thousand worth she had was not much to carry on a war with, very little indeed, and she thinks her brothers have those assets. She says that what she has is the king's own money. She said when she was captured she was riding a half-charger. When asked who gave the horse to her, she answered that the king, or the king's people using the king's money, gave the horse to her. She said she had five chargers from the king's money, not counting the hackneys, which were more than seven.

## ARTICLE 56

Joan has often boasted of having two advisors, whom she calls her advisors of the fountain, who came to her after she was captured, and this has been proved by the confession of Catherine de La Rochelle in front of an official in Paris, where Catherine said that Joan would escape from her prison with the devil's aid if she wasn't well guarded.

Joan's response:

To this fifty-sixth article, Joan replies she stands by her previous answers. Regarding the advisors of the fountain, she does not know what that means, but she believes she once heard St. Catherine and St. Margaret there. With regard to the last part of the article, she denies this, and she declares on oath that she would not want the devil to drag her out of the prison.

Promoter's comments:

On Saturday, March 3, when asked if she saw or knew Catherine de La Rochelle, she answered yes, at Jargeau and at Montfaucon-en-Berry. Asked if this Catherine showed Joan a lady robed in white who Catherine de La Rochelle said sometimes appeared to her, she answered no. Asked on the same day what this Catherine said to her, she answered that Catherine told her she was visited by a lady-in-white robed in clothing of gold who told Catherine de La Rochelle to go through the good towns, that the king would give her heralds and trumpets and she should cry out that whoever had hidden gold, silver or other assets should immediately bring them out; and those who did not comply she would immediately know and would be able to find their hidden assets, and these assets would be used to pay Joan's soldiers. Joan's reply to Catherine de La Rochelle was that she should go home to her husband, do her work and look after her children. To ensure she was correct, Joan spoke to St. Catherine and St. Margaret, who told her that the mission of this Catherine de La Rochelle was all madness and nonsense. Joan wrote to the king about Catherine de La Rochelle and told him what he should do about her, and later when Joan saw the king she told him it was all madness and nonsense.

Nevertheless, Brother Richard wanted to put Catherine de La Rochelle to work, and he and Catherine were unhappy with Joan. Asked whether she spoke to Catherine de La Rochelle about going to La Charité, she answered that Catherine did not advise her to go there because the weather was too cold and she should not go.

Also on March 3, Joan admitted that she told Catherine de La Rochelle, who wanted to go to the Duke of Burgundy and make peace, that no peace would be found except at the lance's point. Joan also admitted to having asked Catherine if the lady-in-white came to her every night, and that she would sleep with her to see the lady-in-white, which she did, and watched until midnight but saw nothing, and then Joan fell asleep. In the morning she asked Catherine if the lady had come and Catherine answered that she had, while Joan was sleeping, but Catherine was unable to wake up Joan. Then Joan asked if the lady would come the following night and Catherine said she would, so Joan slept during the day so that she could watch at night. The next night Joan lay with Catherine and watched all night long, but saw nothing, although she asked Catherine if the lady would come, and Catherine answered, "Yes, soon!"

## ARTICLE 57

On the Feast Day of the Birth of Our Lady, Joan called together all the soldiers of the army to march and launch a military assault on Paris. She led the soldiers in an attack against Paris and assured them they should enter on that day because she knew it by revelation. She had every preparation made by which she could attack the city, and Joan was not afraid to deny this in judgment before us.

Likewise, in many other places, at La Charité-sur-Loire, at Pont l'Eveque and at Compiegne, when she attacked my lord the Duke of Burgundy's army, she made many promises and pronounced many prophecies that she claimed to know by revelation, which in no way came true and were altogether contradicted. In front of you, she denied having made such promises and prophecies because they did not turn out as she had said. However, many trustworthy people reported that these promises were proclaimed and published by Joan.

During the attack on Paris, Joan said that thousands of angels accompanied her, ready to carry her to Heaven if she would die. She was asked why her entry into Paris had not taken place according to her promise, and that many soldiers of her company, and she too, had instead been injured with serious wounds, and some even killed; she is said to have answered, "Jesus has failed in His promise."

Joan's response:

To this article, on Wednesday, March 28, Joan replies regarding the first part of this article she has already answered this, and added, "If I am advised further by my Voices I will gladly answer more." With regard to the last part of this article, that Jesus had failed her, she denies saying this.

Promoter's comments:

On Saturday, March 3, when we asked what she did in the trenches at La Charité, she answered that she made a military assault there but she did not throw or sprinkle Holy Water. Asked why she did not enter the town since she had received God's command to do so, she answered, "Who told you I was commanded to enter?"

Asked if she had the advice of her Voices on this matter, she answered that she wanted to travel to France but the soldiers told her it was better to first go to La Charité.

On Tuesday, March 13, asked if, when she went to Paris, it was revealed by her Voices that she should go there, she answered no, but it was at the request of noblemen who wanted to instigate a battle or an assault; and she really intended to go beyond and cross the trenches. Asked whether she had any revelation regarding going to La Charité, she said no, but she went there at the request of soldiers, as she previously said.

On this same Tuesday, when we asked if it was revealed to her that she should go to Pont l'Eveque, she replied that after it was revealed to her at Melun that she would be captured, she generally deferred to the will of the captains in questions of war, however, she did not tell them that it had been revealed to her that she would be captured. When asked if it was right to attack Paris on the Feast Day of Our Lady's Birth, she answered that, in her opinion and conscience, "It is good to celebrate the Feast Day of Our Lady" from beginning to end.

## ARTICLE 58

Joan had painted on her military banner two angels and God holding the world in His hand, with the words Jesus and Mary and other images, and this she says she did at God's command, who revealed it to her through His angels and saints. She placed this military banner in the cathedral of Reims near the altar when Charles was crowned, desiring out of arrogant pride that people should honor this banner in particular. She also had her coat-of-arms painted with two lilies in a blue field, and in the midst of the lilies a sword or dagger with the point topped by a crown; and this appears to reflect ostentation and vanity instead of piety or religion; and to attribute such vanities to God and the angels contradicts the reverence that is due to God and His Saints.

Joan's response:

To this fifty-eighth article, on March 28, Joan replies, "I have answered this already." Regarding the contradiction indicated by the Promoter, she says, "I defer to our Lord."

Promoter's comments:

On Tuesday, February 27, when asked if, when she went to Orleans, she had a military banner and what color it was, Joan answered yes, and its field was sown with lilies, and the world was pictured on it with two angels at the sides. It was white, made of white linen or boucassin. The names Jesus and Mary were written on it, and it was fringed with silk. Asked whether these names were written above or at the side or beneath, she said they were at the side. Asked if she liked her sword better than her banner, she answered that she liked her banner forty times better. Asked who made her paint her banner with this design, she answered, "I have told you often enough that I have done nothing except by God's command."

She said that she herself carried the banner when moving among enemy combatants to avoid killing anyone; she said she has never killed a man.

On Saturday, March 3, she said she thought her banner was in the church of Reims, fairly close to the altar, and she carried it there for a short time, but she did not know whether Brother Richard carried it.

On Saturday, March 10, when asked whether the world with two angels was painted on her banner, she answered yes, she had only one banner. Asked what it signified to show God holding the world with two angels, she answered that St. Catherine and St. Margaret had told her to paint on the banner an image of the King of Heaven, and to take this banner and carry it boldly. She told the king that was all she knew of its significance. Asked whether she had a shield and arms, she answered that she never had, but the king granted arms to her brothers, namely a blue shield with two fleurs-de-lis and a sword in between, which she described to a painter in Reims because he asked what arms she carried. She said the king gave them to her brothers, to their joy, and without her request and without a revelation.

On Saturday, March 17, when asked why she decided to have painted on her banner angels with arms, feet, legs and robes, she answered, "You already have my reply to that." Asked if she had the angels painted as they appeared to her, she answered that they were painted in the style in which they are represented in churches. Asked if she ever saw angels in the manner in which they were painted, she answered, "I will not tell you anything more."

Asked why the light that came along with the angels and her Voices was not painted on the banner, she said that she was not commanded to paint the light. The same day she was asked if the two angels painted on her banner were St. Michael and St. Gabriel, and she answered that the representations of the two angels were solely for the honor of our Lord, who was painted holding the world.

Asked if the two angels on her banner were the two angels who guard the world, and why there were not more angels considering that she was commanded in our Lord's name to carry the banner, she answered that the design of the entire banner was commanded by our Lord and by the Voices of St. Catherine and St. Margaret, who said to her, "Take the banner in the name of the King of Heaven." And because the saints told her, "Take the banner in the name of the King of Heaven," she had this image of Our Lord and the angels painted in color on it. All of this, including the colors, she did at God's command.

Asked if she questioned her saints whether, because of this military banner, she would win all the battles in which she fought, she answered that the saints told her to carry the banner boldly and God would assist her. When asked which was of more help, she to the banner or the banner to her, she replied that whether the victory was her victory or the banner's, it must all be attributed to God.

Asked whether the hope for victory was based on the banner or on her, she answered that it was based on Our Lord, and nothing else.

When asked if anyone else had carried the banner, whether he would have been as fortunate as she was, she answered, "I do not know and I leave it to God."

Asked if, whether one of her party had sent his banner to her to carry, and particularly if she had been given the king's banner and had carried it, she would have had as firm a hope in that banner as in her own banner, which she received in God's name, she answered, "I more gladly carried that which was requested of me in God's name, however, in all things I commit myself to God."

The same day, when asked if she made her banner wave above the king's head when it was unfurled, she said that she did not know it had been done. Asked why her banner was carried into the church at Reims during the consecration of the king rather than the banners of other captains, she replied, "The banner was present during the perils of war, and that is reason enough for it to be honored."

## ARTICLE 59

At the church in Saint-Denis in France, Joan offered, and positioned in a high place, the armor in which she had been wounded during the assault on Paris, so that it might be honored by the people as relics; and in the same town she had candles lit, from which she poured melted wax onto the heads of little children, foretelling their fortunes, and with these enchantments she made many divinations about the children.

Joan's response:

To this fifty-ninth article, on Wednesday, March 28, Joan replies, "I have answered this already." Regarding the armor and the lighted candles that were melted, she denies it.

Promoter's comments:

On Saturday, March 17, when asked what armor she offered at Saint-Denis, she replied that it was a whole suit of black armor for a man-at-arms, with a sword, which she had worn during the assault on Paris. When asked why she made an offering of this armor and arms, she answered that it was an act of devotion, such as soldiers perform when they are wounded; and since she had been wounded at Paris she offered them to St. Denis because "St. Denis!" was the battle-cry of France. When asked if she did it so that the armor might be worshiped, she said no.

## ARTICLE 60

Joan, scornful of the precepts and sanctions of the Church, many times refused to take an oath to speak the truth, exposing herself to the suspicion of having said or done certain things in matters of faith or revelation, which she dare not reveal to the judges, being fearful of a just punishment. She appears to know this when she makes statements such as, "Men are sometimes hanged for telling the truth," "You will not know everything," and, "I would rather have my head cut off than tell you everything."

Joan's response:

To this sixtieth article, Joan answers that she only asked for a delay so that she could more definitely answer the questions. Regarding the last part of this article, she said that she was afraid to answer and she asked for a delay to find out if she had permission to answer. She said that because the advice for the king did not concern this legal case she did not wish to discuss it; she discussed the sign given to the king because the clergy commanded her to disclose it.

Promoter's comments:

On Thursday, February 22, when asked whether there was a light when the Voice showed her who the king was among the crowd, she answered, "Go to the next question." Asked whether she saw an angel over the king's head, she answered, "Spare me, and continue to the next question." She said that before the king had set her to work he had many apparitions and beautiful revelations. When we asked what kind of apparitions and revelations these were, she answered, "I will not tell you this; you will get no further answer, but ask the king and he will tell you."

On Saturday, February 24, we explained to Joan that she must swear to speak the simple and absolute truth, with no conditions tied to her oath; and she was admonished three times to do this. She said, "Give me permission to speak," and she added, "By my faith, you could ask such things that I would not answer." She also said, "Perhaps I shall not answer you truthfully in many things you ask me concerning the revelations; perhaps you would pressure me to say things I have sworn not to discuss, and so I would be perjured, and you would not wish that." She also said, "I tell you, pay close attention to what you say, because you are my judge and you assume a great responsibility, and you overburden me."

Asked if she would swear simply and absolutely, she answered, "You should be content. I have sworn enough, twice." She added that all the clergy of Rouen and Paris could not condemn her, except by law. She said she could not tell us everything in one week. She said that regarding her coming to France she would gladly speak the truth, but not the whole truth.

Joan was told to take the advice of the assessors regarding whether or not she should swear, however, she answered that she would willingly speak the truth about her coming to France but not otherwise, and we must not speak to her about this anymore.

She was again warned that she made herself open to suspicion, but she answered the same way as previously. Then we, including the Bishop of Beauvais, summoned her to swear precisely; she answered, "I will willingly discuss what I know, but not everything." She was required to swear, and she was admonished under the penalty of being charged with what was attributed to her, but she replied, "I have sworn enough," and "Continue on." Then, required and admonished to speak the truth in all matters concerning the trial, and being told that she exposed herself to great danger, she answered, "I am ready to swear to speak the truth about what I know concerning the trial, but not everything I know," and it was in this manner that she took the oath.

The same day, February 24, when asked if the Voice prohibited her from telling us everything, she replied, "I will not answer you about that. I have revelations concerning the king which I shall not tell you."

When asked if the Voice prohibited her from discussing the revelations, she replied, "I have not been advised about that," and she asked for a two-week delay in which to answer. Regarding the delay she said, "If the Voice prohibited me, what would you say?" When we asked her again if the Voice prohibited her, she replied, "Believe me, it was not men who prohibited me." She said she would not answer that day, and she does not know if she would answer all that was revealed to her.

When asked if she thought it was displeasing to God for her to tell the truth, she replied that her Voices said she was to discuss certain things with the king but not with us. Asked if the Voices revealed to her that she should escape from prison, she answered, "Must I tell you that?"

Asked whether that night the Voice had advised her how she should reply to our questions, she said that if the Voice said it she did not understand it well. Asked whether a light was visible during the last two days when she heard the Voices, she answered that the light comes in the name of the Voice.

When we asked her whether she saw anything with this Voice, she replied, "I will not tell you everything, and I do not have permission to discuss that." She said her oath did not include that. She said the Voice is beautiful, good and worthy, and she is not required to answer whatever she is asked. Asked whether the Voice had sight or eyes, she answered, "You will not learn that yet." She said little children have a proverb, "Men are sometimes hanged for telling the truth."

On Tuesday, February 27, when we required Joan to take an oath and swear to speak the truth on questions concerning the trial, she answered that she would willingly swear with respect to the questions concerning her legal case, but not about everything she knew. Then we required her to answer truthfully about everything she would be asked, but she replied as she did previously, saying, "You ought to be satisfied, I have sworn enough."

She said she would willingly speak the truth regarding subjects for which she had permission from our Lord, but without the permission of her Voice she would not tell us about the revelations concerning the king.

The same day, when we asked whether St. Catherine and St. Margaret were dressed in the same clothing, she replied, "I will not tell you any more now," because she did not have permission to discuss it; but she added, "If you don't believe me, go to Poitiers."

She said that certain revelations came for the king but not for those who were questioning her. Asked if the saints who appeared to her were of the same age, she said she did not have permission to tell us. Asked whether they spoke at the same time, or one after another, she said she may not tell us, however, every day she receives advice from both St. Catherine and St. Margaret.

Asked which one appeared to her first, St. Catherine or St. Margaret, she replied, "I did not recognize them immediately." However, she said that she previously knew which one appeared to her first, but has now forgotten. If she is permitted, she said she will willingly discuss these matters, and she continued to refer us to previous transcripts of her answers, saying, "It is written down at Poitiers."

When asked in what form St. Michael appeared to her, she said, "There is as yet no answer for that because I do not have permission to answer." Asked what St. Michael said to her the first time, she answered, "You will get no additional information today." She said the Voices told her to answer boldly, and she added she does not yet have permission to discuss what St. Michael told her, but she wished that her questioner had a copy of the transcripts taken at Poitiers, if it was God's will.

Asked if St. Michael and the other saints told her she must not talk about them without their permission, she said, "I still may not answer, but what I have permission to discuss, I will gladly answer."

Asked what sign she has that this revelation comes from God, and that it is St. Catherine and St. Margaret who speak to her, she answered, "I have told you often enough that it is St. Catherine and St. Margaret," and "Believe me if you will." Asked what revelations the king had, she answered, "You will not learn that from me this year."

On Thursday, March 1, when we asked what the saints promised her, she answered, "That is not in your legal case at all." Asked if they promised her anything beyond that they would accompany her to Heaven, she answered that there were other promises, but she will not tell them to us because they do not concern this trial. She said within three months she will tell us the other promises. Asked if the saints said that within three months she would be delivered out of this prison, she answered, "That is not in your legal case." Nevertheless, she said she does not know when she will be delivered. She said that the people who want to get her out of this world may well go before she does.

Asked if her Voices had told her she would be delivered from prison, she answered, "Speak to me about it in three months' time and then I will answer you." She added that we should ask the assessors on their oath whether this question was relevant to her trial; and after the assessors had deliberated and unanimously decided that it was relevant, she said, "One day I must be delivered, and I want to get permission to tell you," and so she asked us for a delay.

When asked whether the saints prohibited her from speaking the truth, she answered, "Do you want me to tell you what concerns the king of France?" She said many things do not concern her legal case. The same day, when asked what sign she gave the king that she came from God, she said, "I have always told you that you will not drag this from my lips. Go and ask him."

Asked if she had sworn not to reveal what she was asked concerning the trial, she answered, "I have already told you that I will not tell you what concerns our king."

Asked if she did not know the sign, she answered, "You will not learn it from me." She was told that this was relevant to the trial and she replied, "What I have promised to keep secret I shall not tell you," and she added, "I have already said that I cannot tell you without committing perjury." Asked to whom she made the promise that would result in her committing perjury, she replied that she promised St. Catherine and St. Margaret, and this was made known to the king. She said she promised without their asking, by her own decision, and said that too many people would have asked her about her sign had she not made this promise to her saints.

When we asked her if anyone else was present when she showed the sign to the king, she said, "I think there was no one but him, although many people were quite near." Asked if she saw a crown on the king's head when she showed him the sign, she answered, "I cannot tell you without committing perjury."

On Saturday, March 3, when asked whether she believes God created St. Michael and St. Gabriel from the beginning in the form and fashion in which she saw them, she replied, "You will learn no more from me at the present time other than what I have already told you."

Asked whether she had seen or known by revelation that she would escape, she answered, "That does not concern your legal case; do you want me to speak against myself?"

Asked if the Voices told her anything about escaping, she said, "That is not in your legal case. I leave it up to our Lord, and if everything concerned you, I would tell you everything." She added, "By my faith, I do not know the hour."

Asked if, when God told her to change her clothing, it was through the Voice of St. Michael, St. Catherine or St. Margaret, she replied, "You will not learn anymore."

On Monday, March 12, when asked whether she had received letters from St. Michael or her Voices, she answered, "I do not have permission to tell you, but within a week I will gladly tell you what I know."

## ARTICLE 61

Joan, admonished to submit all her deeds and words to the decision of the Church Militant, and advised of the distinction between the Church Militant [Members of the Church on Earth] and the Church Triumphant [Members of the Church in Heaven], professed to submit to the Church Triumphant and refused to submit herself to the Church Militant, and so she declares herself to have an erroneous opinion with regard to *Unam Sanctam* [authoritative document establishing the Pope as supreme head of the Church], and in all this she shows herself to be at fault. She said it was for God alone, without an intermediary, to judge her, and she committed herself, her deeds and her words to Him and His Saints, and not to the judgment of the Church.

Joan's response:

To this sixty-first article, Joan answers that she would desire to bring to the Church Militant all the honor and reverence in her power, but with regard to submitting her actions to the Church Militant, she says, "I must submit them to the Lord God who commands me."

Asked whether she submits her actions to the Church Militant, she answers, "Send me a cleric next Saturday and I will tell you."

Promoter's comments:

On Thursday, March 15, Joan was told about the Church Triumphant and the Church Militant, and she was required to submit her words and her deeds, both good and bad, to the decision of the Church, and she answered, "I will not give you any further answer at the present time." After warnings were given to her that if she had done anything contrary to our faith she ought to refer it to the decision of the Church, she answered that her replies should be seen and examined by the clergy, and then she should be told if there was anything contrary to the Christian faith, and that she would certainly be able to tell that it was, and then she would say to us what she learned from her Voices.

She said if there was anything contrary to the Christian faith, the faith that our Lord ordained, she would not want to sustain it, and she would be grieved to be in opposition. The same day, when asked whether she would submit her deeds and words to the decision of the Church, she answered, "Everything I have said or done is in God's hands, and I commit myself to Him. I certify to you that I would do or say nothing contrary to the Christian faith, and if I had said or done anything, or if anything was found about me that the clerics would declare to be against the Christian faith established by Our Lord, then I would not uphold it, and I would cast it out."

Then asked whether she would submit herself to the decision of the Church, she answered, "I will not now answer you anymore, but next Saturday send me a cleric if you do not wish to come, and I will answer this question with God's assistance, and it shall be set down in writing."

On Saturday, March 17, when we asked if she thought she was required to answer the whole truth to our Holy Father the Pope, God's Vicar, regarding everything we asked her concerning the faith and state of her conscience, she replied that she required to be taken to the Pope, and then she would answer.

On Saturday, the last day of March, when asked whether she would submit to the decision of the Church on Earth regarding everything she had done, either good or evil, especially the questions, crimes and misdemeanors attributed to her, and all that concerns her legal case, she answered that with respect to what she was asked she would submit to the Church Militant provided we did not ask her to do what was impossible, meaning by impossible the revocation of her deeds and words put forth in these proceedings which concern the visions and revelations she claims to have from God; she would not revoke them for anything in the world. She said that what our Lord has requested of her she will not for any man alive cease to do; that, she could not revoke.

In the event of the Church wanting her to do otherwise, against the request of our Lord, she would not obey for anything. Asked whether she would submit to the Church if the Church Militant said that her revelations were false and devilish things, superstitious and evil, she replied that she would submit to our Lord, whose requests she will always fulfill, because she knows that the actions described in these proceedings were done at God's request; it would be impossible for her to do other than what she declares she has done at God's request. If the Church Militant told her to do otherwise, then she would submit to nobody other than our Lord, whose good requests she always fulfilled.

When asked if she believes she is subject to the Church on Earth, namely our Holy Father the Pope, to the cardinals, archbishops, bishops and other prelates of the Church, she answered yes, our Lord being served first. Asked whether her Voices requested her not to submit to the Church Militant on Earth or its judgment, she said that she does not merely answer us by saying anything that comes to her mind, but she answers according to the Voices' instructions, and they do not forbid her to obey the Church, our Lord being served first.

Because of her illness, Joan was told that the more fearful she was about her health the more necessary it was for her to reform, and that she would not receive the rites of the Church as a Catholic if she did not submit to the Church. She answered, "If my body dies in prison, I expect you to bury it in holy ground, and if you do not, I put my trust in our Lord."

The same day, when we asked—since she desired the Church to give her the Sacrament of the Eucharist—whether she would submit to the Church if she was promised the Eucharist, she replied that with respect to this question she would not answer other than what she had already answered, but she loves and serves God as a good Christian, and she would assist and sustain the Church with all her might.

## ARTICLE 62

Joan endeavors to scandalize the people, to induce them to believe all her words and prophecies, assuming the authority of God and His angels, lifting herself above all ecclesiastical power to lead men into error, as false prophets are wont to do when they introduce sects of error and damnation and separate from the unity of the body of the Church. This is malicious to the Christian religion, and unless the clerics of the Church take action, a subversion of the future ecclesiastical authority may arise; men and women pretending to have revelations from God and His angels will pour in from all sides and sow lies and errors, as has often occurred since this woman arose and began to scandalize the Christian people and propagate her inventions.

Joan's response:

To this sixty-second article on this Wednesday, March 28, Joan replies that she will answer on Saturday.

## ARTICLE 63

Joan has not been afraid to lie before the law, in violation of her oath, and she has continually affirmed numerous conflicting and contradictory things about her revelations; she has pronounced curses against nobles and distinguished people, and against a whole nation; she has without shame proclaimed falsehoods and contemptuous words that in no way are appropriate for a holy woman, showing thoroughly she has been directed and governed in her actions by evil spirits, and not by the advice of God and His angels, as she boasts. Christ said of false prophets, "By their fruits you will know them."

Joan's response:

To this sixty-third article, Joan this day answers, "I refer you to what I have already said," and regarding the accusation and conclusion of this article, she defers to Our Lord.

Promoter's comments:

On Tuesday, February 27, Joan said that she had a sword at Lagny, and from Lagny to Compiegne she carried the sword of a Burgundian that was a good fighting weapon, excellent for giving hard hits and blows; regarding where she lost the other sword, she said this is not in the legal case so she will not answer.

On Thursday, March 1, she said she would have died except for the daily revelations and comfort she received from her Voices. Asked whether St. Michael had any hair, she answered, "Why should it be cut off?" She has not seen St. Michael since the time she left the castle of Crotoy and did not often see him.

## ARTICLE 64

Joan boasts of knowing that she has obtained remission of the sins she committed when, due to a despairing heart and at the incitement of an evil spirit, she cast herself from the top of the tower at the castle of Beaurevoir. She says this even though Scripture teaches us that nobody knows if he is worthy of love or of hatred, and therefore if he is purged or freed from sin.

Joan's response:

To this sixty-fourth article on Wednesday, March 28, Joan answers, "I have answered this already and I refer you to my previous answer." Regarding the remainder of this article and its conclusion, she defers to our Lord.

## ARTICLE 65

Joan many times declared she has asked God to send her special revelations through St. Catherine and St. Margaret regarding her conduct, for example, whether she should answer truthfully in this trial certain questions and matters personal to her. This behavior tempts the Lord God, to ask Him needlessly for forbidden things, without having performed all inquiries and investigations possible to man. Especially with regard to her leap from the tower, it is clear that she tempted God.

Joan's response:

To this sixty-fifth article on this Wednesday, Joan says that she has already answered this; she will not speak about what has been revealed to her without permission from God. Furthermore, she says that she does not ask God needlessly, and she wishes He would continue to send other revelations so that it can be more clearly seen that she comes in His name, and that He has sent her.

## ARTICLE 66

Some of Joan's prophecies depart from divine, evangelic, canon and civil law, and are contrary to decisions approved by the Church Councils; they contain spells, enchantments and superstitions, some formally and others casually, and others pertain to heresy; many contain errors against the faith that encourage and incite people to heretical error; some are seditious, harmful and contrary to the peace; some encourage the spilling of human blood; some are nothing but curses and blasphemies against God and His saints; others offend the ears of pious men.

In all this the accused, with daring recklessness and at the instigation of the devil, offended God and His Holy Church, against which she has scandalously committed excesses and crimes, is notoriously defamed, and has appeared before you to be corrected and reformed.

Joan's response:

To this sixty-sixth article, Joan answers that she is a good Christian, and with respect to all of the accusations contained in this article she commits herself to God.

## ARTICLE 67

Each and every one of these activities the accused has committed, perpetrated, pronounced, produced, declared, published and accomplished, both in this and in other jurisdictions, and in many and diverse locations within the territory, not once, but repeatedly on many occasions, days and hours; she has persisted in these activities, and she has given her aid, counsel and favor to people who have committed them.

Joan's response:

This sixty-seventh article Joan denies.

## ARTICLE 68

Therefore—since the time you discovered by the insinuating sounds that struck your ears, not once but many times, and by public reports and the evidence collected—the accused is strongly suspected and defamed; and so you ruled that it was proper to hold an inquiry against her, and that you, or one of you, must initiate proceedings against her and call her to answer these questions, and this has been done.

Joan's response:

To this sixty-eighth article, Joan answers, "This article concerns the judges."

## ARTICLE 69

The accused, in everything, was and is strongly suspected, scandalous, and to the highest degree notoriously defamed in the eyes of honest and sober men, yet she in no way corrected her ways or reformed; on the contrary, she delayed and declined to correct and amend herself; and she continued and persisted in her errors, and she still does, although you and other notable clergy and other honest people have, charitably and otherwise, appropriately and sufficiently, asked and required her to do so.

Joan's response:

To this sixty-ninth article, Joan says that she has not committed the errors attributed to her by the Promoter; regarding the remainder of this article, she commits herself to God; regarding the crimes of which she is accused, she does not think she has done anything contrary to the Christian faith.

Asked whether, if she has done anything contrary to the Christian faith, she would be willing to submit to the Church and to those whose responsibility it is to administer corrections, she answered that she would give her reply after dinner on Saturday.

## ARTICLE 70

That each and every one of these propositions is true, known and clear, and that the public opinion and reports have reflected them, and the accused has acknowledged and confessed them as true on many and appropriate occasions, before trustworthy and honorable men, both in and out of court.

Joan's response:

This seventieth article Joan denies, except for that which she has previously admitted.

Promoter's comments:

On these points and on others that you will complete, correct and further inquire into, the Promoter requests and demands the accused be evaluated; and as he has sufficiently proved, wholly or in part, you should decide on and pronounce sentence on each and every one of the abovementioned articles, and make additional statements and judgments according to law and reason; thereby the Promoter appropriately and humbly implores you to carry out the responsibilities of your offices.

## JOAN IS INTERVIEWED ABOUT SUBMITTING TO THE CHURCH (MARCH 31)

The following Saturday, Easter Eve, the last day of March in the year of our Lord, 1431, we gathered in Joan's prison cell in the castle of Rouen.

First she was asked whether she would submit to the judgment of the Church that is on Earth regarding all of her actions and words, whether good or evil, and especially regarding the causes, crimes and errors of which she was accused, and in everything concerning her trial. She answered that in all these matters she would submit to the Church Militant provided that it did not command her to do the impossible; and by impossible it is understood that she means the revocation of the things she has said and done regarding the visions and revelations she claims to have from God. She said she will not deny them for anything in the world. What our Lord told her and will tell her to do she will not cease from doing for any man alive. She said it would be impossible for her to deny them, and in the event of the Church commanding her to do anything contrary to God's requests, she would not do it under any circumstances.

Asked whether she would submit to the Church if the Church Militant said that her revelations were illusions, diabolical, superstitious and evil things, she said she would submit to our Lord, whose will she would always do. She knows that what is written in these proceedings came at His requests, and what she claims to have done at God's command she could in no way have done otherwise. If the Church Militant commanded her to do otherwise she would not submit to it for any man in the world, except our Lord, whose good will she would always do.

Asked if she thought she was subject to the Church on Earth, namely to our Holy Father the Pope, the cardinals, archbishops, bishops and other prelates of the Church, she answered yes, our Lord being served first. Asked whether her Voices had requested her not to submit to the Church Militant on Earth or its judgments, she answered that she did not respond to our questions according to whatever happened to come into her mind, but she answered at our Lord's command. Her Voices did not tell her not to obey the Church, our Lord being served first in all things.

Asked whether documents had been found implicating her behavior in the castle at Beaurevoir or Arras or elsewhere, she answered "If any were found regarding me, I have nothing more to answer." At this point we then left her prison cell to continue the proceedings upon these matters of the faith.

### 70 ACCUSATIONS ARE SUMMARIZED INTO 12 ACCUSATIONS (APRIL 2 - APRIL 4)

The following Monday after Easter, April 2, and the following Tuesday and Wednesday, we, the judges, with several other lords and lawyers, gathered together and reviewed the seventy articles, both the questions and replies made by Joan. We then produced twelve articles based on these seventy, which comprehensively summarized all of the propositions and statements made by Joan. We decided to send these twelve articles to doctors and other men educated in canon and civil law, requesting their advice and consultation for the good of the faith.

### THE SUMMARY OF ACCUSATIONS IS SUBMITTED TO THE ASSESSORS (APRIL 5)

On Thursday, April 5, we took our schedule of requirements with the following 12 articles to all of the doctors who, to our knowledge, were in the town of Rouen.

### ARTICLE 1

Firstly, this woman says and affirms that in the thirteenth year of her age or thereabout, she saw with her bodily eyes St. Michael, who would console her, and at times St. Gabriel, and they appeared to her in bodily form. Sometimes she also saw a large number of angels. Since then, St. Catherine and St. Margaret have appeared to this woman and she saw them in the flesh. Every day she sees them and she hears them speak, and when she embraces and kisses them, she touches them and feels them physically.

She has seen not only the heads of these angels and the saints, but other parts of their bodies of which she has chosen not to speak. She said that St. Catherine and St. Margaret spoke to her at times by a certain fountain near a large tree commonly called the Spirits' Tree. With regard to the matter of the fountain and the tree, the common report is that it is the frequent gathering place of witches, and that many people who are sick go to this fountain and tree to recover their health, although these are located in an unholy place. There, and elsewhere on several occasions, Joan has adorned the tree with garlands and shown reverence to the tree and the fountain.

In addition, she has said that St. Catherine and St. Margaret appeared and revealed themselves to her crowned with rich and beautiful crowns; and from that moment, and taking up the matter again on many occasions, St. Catherine and St. Margaret said to Joan that God had commanded her to go to a certain prince of this world [the king of France, who the English did not recognize as king], promising that they would assist the efforts of Joan, and the king would recover by force of arms great worldly dominions and glory, and that he would overcome his enemies; also that the king would welcome her, and give her soldiers and weapons to fulfill her promises. Moreover, the so-called St. Catherine and St. Margaret instructed Joan, in the name of God, to take and wear men's clothes; and Joan has worn them, and still wears them, stubbornly obeying this command to such an extent that Joan has declared that she would rather die than abandon wearing these clothes. She has made this declaration to wear men's clothes simply and purely, adding at times, "except at our Lord's command."

She prefers to be absent from Mass if she has to wear women's clothes, and to be deprived of the Holy Sacrament of Communion, including at the times when the Church commands the faithful to receive the Sacrament. She does this instead of giving up wearing men's clothes.

The so-called St. Catherine and St. Margaret would seem to have shown similar favor to Joan when, unknown to and against the will of her parents, in the seventeenth year of her age or thereabout, she left her father's house and joined with a company of men following the profession of being a soldier, living with them day and night, and never, or rarely, having another woman with her.

Also, these saints have told and commanded her to do many other things; this is why Joan has claimed to be sent by the God of Heaven, and by the Church Triumphant of the saints already in Heaven, to whom she submits any good that she has done.

But she has postponed and declined to submit her actions and words to the Church Militant; and, having been questioned and admonished on this point more than once, she has answered that she could not do otherwise than

170

what she has claimed to have done in answering to the commands of God, because in these matters she did not refer herself to the consideration and decision of living men, but to the judgment of our Lord alone.

These saints have revealed to her that she will enter into the salvation and glory of the blessed in Heaven, and her soul will be saved if she preserves the virginity she has consecrated to the saints when she first saw and heard them; and since the time of this revelation she has asserted that she was as sure of her salvation as if she had suddenly found herself in reality in the Kingdom of Heaven.

## ARTICLE 2

Joan said the sign the king received that led him to trust in her revelations, to receive her, and to let her command the war efforts, was that St. Michael approached the king along with a multitude of angels, some of whom wore crowns and others who were winged, and with them were St. Catherine and St. Margaret.

The angel and Joan walked together by land and by highway, traveling long distances, climbing steps and crossing a hallway, and other angels and the saints were with them. One angel gave the king a precious crown of fine gold and bowed down before the king, giving honor to him. On one occasion Joan stated that when the king received this sign he seemed to be alone, although there were several men very near him; and on another occasion it seemed to her an archbishop also saw this sign with the crown and gave it to the king, all in the presence and view of several noblemen.

## ARTICLE 3

Joan recognizes and is certain that he who visits her is St. Michael. She is certain of this because of the good advice, consolation and wise doctrine that St. Michael brings to her; also because he names himself, saying that he is Michael. Similarly, she recognizes and distinguishes St. Catherine from St. Margaret because they name themselves when they greet her. This is why she believes that the St. Michael who visits her is St. Michael himself, and that his actions and words are good and true, as firmly as she believes that our Lord Jesus Christ suffered death to redeem us.

## ARTICLE 4

Joan says and affirms that she is certain of future and purely contingent events, and that these future events will occur as surely as she sees the reality in front of her. She boasts that she has knowledge of secret things through the verbal revelations of St. Catherine and St. Margaret; for example, that she will be delivered from prison, that the French will have more glorious success in her presence than all of Christendom has had up until now. In addition, she has, according to her own account, recognized by revelation people she had never seen before; and she has spoken and revealed the place where a certain sword was hidden in the ground.

## ARTICLE 5

Joan says and affirms that by the will and command of God she has taken to herself and has worn, and still wears, clothes like those of a man. Moreover, Joan has said that since she has received God's command to wear men's clothes, she must wear a cap and a tight jacket, pants and stockings with many details, and her hair cropped short above her ears; there is nothing about her that displays and announces her sex except nature's own distinctive marks.

In these clothes she has received the Sacrament of the Eucharist on several occasions; and she has declined and still declines to wear women's clothes, although many times she has been gently requested and admonished to do so; she says that she would rather die than give up wearing men's clothes; she has said this purely and simply, at times adding, "unless it is at our Lord's command."

She has said that if she found herself in these clothes among people of her party, for whom she previously took up arms, and if she could do as she did before her capture and captivity, it would be one of the greatest blessings that could come to the whole realm of France. She added that not for anything in the world would she swear to give up wearing men's clothes and carrying weapons. In all this she has declared that her acts were good, and are good, and that she has obeyed God and His commands.

## ARTICLE 6

Joan admits and affirms that she has caused certain letters to be written, and that on some of those letters were written the names Jesus and Mary, with the invocation of the Sign of the Cross, and sometimes she added a cross to show she did not wish to be done what she indicated in her letters. Moreover, in other letters she has caused to be written, she indicated that she would have those who disobeyed her letters and warnings killed, and that "by blows would the favor of the God of Heaven be seen." Often she has said that she has done nothing except by the revelation and command of God.

## ARTICLE 7

Joan says and admits that during or about her seventeenth year, according to her own account, she went and found, intuitively and by revelation, a certain squire whom she had never seen before, leaving her parents' house against their wishes. Her parents, when they discovered her departure, were almost stricken out of their senses. Joan requested this squire to lead her, or have her led, to the king. Then this squire, a captain, lent Joan, at her request, men's clothes and a sword. He told and instructed a knight, a squire and four soldiers to escort her. When they arrived at the king's castle, Joan said to the king that she wished to direct the war effort against his enemies, promising the king great dominion, that he would annihilate his foes, and that she had been sent for this purpose by the King of Heaven. In this matter she says that she has done very well according to the revelation and the command of God.

## ARTICLE 8

Joan says and admits that, without constraint or compulsion, she threw herself down from a high tower, preferring death to captivity in the hands of her enemies, or life after the destruction of the town of Compiegne. Moreover, she has said that she could not help throwing herself down in this fashion, although St. Catherine and St. Margaret had forbidden her to do so, and she says that to offend them was a serious sin. However, she claims to know that this sin was forgiven after she confessed it, and she says that she has had a revelation about this.

## ARTICLE 9

Joan says and affirms that St. Catherine and St. Margaret promised to lead her into Heaven if she preserved the virginity of her body and soul, which she consecrated to them; and she says that she is as certain of this as if she were already among the blessed in Heaven. She thinks that she has not committed any mortal sin, because, if she were in mortal sin, it seems to her that St. Catherine and St. Margaret would not visit her every day, as they do.

## ARTICLE 10

Joan says and affirms that God loves certain people whom she points out and names, who are still alive, and that He loves them more than He loves her; and that she is aware of this by the revelations of St. Catherine and St. Margaret, who often speak to her in the French language, and not in the English language, because they are not on the side of the English; and since she has known by revelation that they are on the side of her king, she has therefore disliked the Burgundians.

## ARTICLE 11

Joan says and admits that she has on several occasions shown reverence to the Voices and spirits whom she calls St. Michael, St. Gabriel, St. Catherine and St. Margaret, and that she has uncovered, knelt and kissed the ground where they walked; she consecrated her virginity to St. Catherine and St. Margaret when she embraced and acknowledged them; she has touched them bodily and felt them, asking their advice and consolation; and she has called upon them, although they often visited Joan without an invocation.

She has submitted to and obeyed their advice and commands, and she has done so from the beginning, without asking counsel from another person, for example, from her father or her mother, or from a priest or prelate, or from any other cleric. Nevertheless, she firmly believes that the Voices and revelations she has had, through saints both male and female, come from God and are ordained by Him; she believes it as solemnly as she believes the Christian faith and the fact that our Lord Jesus Christ suffered death for our sake.

She has said that if an evil spirit were to appear to her, pretending to be St. Michael, she would be able to tell whether he was St. Michael or not. Joan has also said that, of her own free will, without being in any way requested or constrained, she swore to St. Catherine and St. Margaret, who appeared to her, that she would not disclose the sign of the crown which she was to give to the king, adding "unless she was given permission to reveal it."

## ARTICLE 12

Joan says and admits that if the Church were to desire her to do anything contrary to the commands she claims to receive from God, she would not do it for any reason whatsoever. She affirms that she is quite certain that the things declared in her deposition were done in God's name, and that it would be impossible for her to do otherwise.

She does not submit herself to the judgment of the Church Militant, or to the judgment of any living men, but only to God, our Lord, whose commands she will always obey; she does this principally in all matters relating to these revelations, and what she claims to have performed according to the revelations.

She says she does not make this response and other responses by the power of her own mind alone, but she gives these responses as instructed by her Voices and by revelation; although the judges and others who were present often reminded her of that article of faith, *Unam Sanctam,* explaining to her that every faithful pilgrim in this life must obey it and must submit his words and deeds to the Church Militant, principally in matters of belief regarding all that is related to holy doctrine and ecclesiastical sanctions.

### Experts in Theology Give Their Opinions

The deliberations and opinions of experts in theology regarding the 12 articles were received over the course of several days. Sixteen doctors and six bachelors of theology gave their opinions on the 12 articles; with minor reservations, the doctors and masters gave their judgment as follows.

We declare, having conscientiously considered, discussed and weighed the quality of the person in question, her words and her actions, the character of her apparitions and revelations, their purpose, cause and circumstances, and all that is contained in the articles and proceedings, that there is reason to think that these apparitions and revelations, which she boasts and affirms she has received from God through His angels and His saints, do not come from God through His angels and His saints, but are rather the fictions of human imagination or proceeding from evil spirits.

Joan has not received sufficient evidence to believe and recognize them as holy; in these articles there are fabricated lies, certain improbabilities and beliefs that have been informally accepted on her part; superstitions and divinations; scandalous and irreligious acts; audacious, arrogant and boasting speech; blasphemies and curses toward God and His saints, St. Michael and St. Gabriel; disrespect towards parents; disregard of the command to love our neighbor; idolatry, or at least misleading fictions; schism directed against the unity, authority and power of the Church; and things that seem to be evil and are strongly suspected of heresy.

In proclaiming that these apparitions are St. Michael, St. Catherine and St. Margaret, and their actions and words are good as firmly as she believes the Christian faith, she is considered to be suspect of straying from the faith; because if she believes that articles of the faith have no more assurance than her own beliefs—her apparitions whom she names to be St. Michael, St. Catherine and St. Margaret, and her statement that their acts and words are good—then she strays from the faith.

Because to say, as contained in Article 5 and also in Article 1, that she has acted rightly by not receiving the Sacrament of the Eucharist at a time ordained by the Church, and that all she has done was done by God's command, then that is a blaspheme against God and strays from the faith.

**Statements by Notaries**

The doctors and masters asked us, as public notaries, for a deposition regarding the proceedings and requested us to forward it to the lord judges. This was done in the chapel of the archbishop's house at Rouen, in the presence of Master Jean de la Haye and Jean Barenton, priests of the Church at Rouen, called and requested to be witnesses to this.

I, Guillaume Manchon, priest of the Diocese of Rouen, notary public and sworn by the imperial and apostolic authority of the archbishop's court of Rouen, have been present at all that has been said, done and reported, with another notary and the above-signed witnesses, and have seen and heard it done; and for that reason I have affixed my usual signature together with my seal and subscription as a notary public, to this public document, faithfully written in my hand, as a witness and in good faith, at the request of the authorities listed above.

Signed: Guillaume Manchon

And I, Guillaume Colles, also known as Boisguillaume, priest of the Diocese of Rouen, public notary by apostolic authority and of the archbishop's court of Rouen, notary sworn in this case, have been present at all that has been said and done, with the witnesses and the notary named above, and have seen and heard it done; and so I have signed this public document, which is a faithful record written by Guillaume Manchon, with my usual signature and seal as called and sworn to do, in assurance and as a witness to these proceedings.

Signed: Guillaume Boisguillaume

### JOAN IS PRIVATELY ADMONISHED IN HER PRISON CELL (APRIL 18)

On Wednesday, April 18, we, the judges—knowing from the deliberations and opinions of many doctors of sacred theology and of canon law, and of individuals licensed in law and graduates of other faculties—are aware of the great number of serious errors contained in the answers and assertions made by Joan, and we know if she does not correct herself she is exposed to grave dangers.

For these reasons we have decided to urge her charitably and admonish her gently, and to have her admonished gently by many honest and educated men, doctors and others, in order to lead her back to the way of truth and a sincere profession of the faith. It is for this reason that we visited Joan in her prison cell, accompanied by Guillaume Le Boucher; Jacques de Touraine; Maurice du Quesnay; Nicolas Midi; Guillaume Adelie and Gerard Feuillet, both Doctors of Sacred Theology; and William Haiton, Bachelor of Sacred Theology.

In their presence we, with the bishop, addressed Joan, who said she was sick. We told her that the masters and doctors had come in all friendliness and charity to visit her in her illness, to comfort and console her. Then we reminded her that on many different days in the presence of many educated persons she had been questioned on grave and difficult questions concerning the faith, to which she had given varied and divergent answers that wise and educated men, evaluating and examining diligently, had found to contain words and admissions that from the point of view of the faith were dangerous; but because she was an uneducated and ignorant woman, we offered to provide her with wise and educated men, honest and kind, who would appropriately instruct her.

We urged the doctors and masters present to give helpful advice to Joan for the salvation of her body and her soul, and to conform to the duty of faithfulness that aligned her body and soul with the true doctrine of the faith. If Joan knew others who were appropriate for this we offered to send them to her so that they would also give her advice and instruction regarding what she should do, maintain and believe.

We added that we were clergy, and by our vocations, decisions and inclinations, we were prepared to seek the salvation of her soul and assure the saving of her body by all means possible, just as we would do for our closest relatives and for ourselves; that we would be happy each day to provide her with such men who would instruct her appropriately, and to do for her all the Church is accustomed to do in such circumstances, because the Church does not close the gate against the lamb who wants to return.

Finally, we told Joan to carefully consider our admonition and put it into effect, because if she should act in opposition, trusting her own mind and her inexperienced level of knowledge, we would be compelled to abandon her; and that she must therefore see the danger that would result to her if that was to be the case, which, with all our might and affection, we hoped to avoid.

Joan answered that she thanked us for what we said regarding her salvation, and she added, "It seems to me, seeing how sick I am, that I am in great danger of death; if it is so, that God desires to do with me as He sees fit, then I ask to receive the Sacrament of Confession and my Savior in Holy Communion, and for a burial in holy ground."

Joan was told that if she wished to receive the Sacraments of the Church she must do as good Catholics are in duty bound to do, and she must submit to the holy Church; and if she persisted in her intention not to submit to the Church, then she would not be allowed to receive the Sacraments she asked for, except the Sacrament of Penance, which we were always ready to administer. However, she answered, "I cannot now tell you anything more."

She was told that the more she feared for her life because of her illness, the more she ought to amend her life; that she would not enjoy the rites of the Church as a Catholic if she did not submit to the Church. She answered, "If my body dies in prison, I trust you will have it buried in holy ground; if you do not, then I put my trust in our Lord."

She was told that in her trial she had said that if she had done or said anything contrary to our Christian faith ordained by God, then she would not wish to sustain it. She replied, "I refer you to the answers I gave and I refer myself to our Lord."

Then, because Joan had professed to have many revelations from God through the mediums of St. Michael, St. Catherine and St. Margaret, she was asked this question: "If some good creature came to you and affirmed that he had received revelations from God concerning your mission, would you believe him?" She replied that no Christian in the world could come to her saying he had a revelation about her without her knowing whether he was speaking the truth or not; and that she would know this through St. Catherine and St. Margaret.

Asked whether she thought God could reveal something to a good creature that she would not know, she answered that she knew very well that He could. "But," she added "I would not believe any man or woman if I did not receive a sign."

Asked whether she believed that the Holy Scriptures were revealed by God, she answered, "You know it very well, and it is good to know that it was."

Then she was asked, urged and required to take the good advice of the clergy and notable doctors, and trust in their advice for the salvation of her soul. She was asked if she would submit her actions and words to the evaluation of the Church Militant, but she answered, "Whatever happens to me, I will do and say nothing except what I have already said in the trial."

At that point the venerable doctors who were present pressed her as urgently as they could to submit herself and her words to the Church Militant, citing in explanation to her many authorities and examples from the Holy Scriptures; and in particular one of the doctors, Nicolas Midi, in his exhortation, quoted this biblical passage from St. Matthew, Chapter 18, "If your brother shall trespass against you..." and also, "If he neglects to listen to the Church, let him be to you as a heathen man and a publican." This was explained to Joan in French, and she was told that if she would not submit to the Church and obey it, then she would be abandoned as unfaithful.

Joan replied that she was a good Christian, and that she had been properly baptized, and so she would die a good Christian.

Asked why, since she requested the Church to administer the Sacrament of Holy Communion to her, she would not submit to the Church Militant, because she was promised she could receive the Sacrament if she submitted to the Church Militant. She answered that she would not reply other than what she had already said previously on this question of submission to the Church Militant and Church Triumphant; she said she loved God, that she was a good Christian, and she desired to help and support the Holy Church with all her strength.

Asked if she wanted a fine and distinguished procession of ordained ministers to restore her to a good state if she were not currently in a good state, she replied that she very much wanted the Church and the Catholic people to pray for her.

### JOAN IS PUBLICLY ADMONISHED BY THE JUDGES ON SIX ITEMS (MAY 2)

On Wednesday, May 2, we, the judges, held a session in a room within the castle of Rouen near the great hall of the castle, assisted by the reverend fathers, lords and masters assembled at our command. After Joan had been thoroughly questioned, she then replied to the articles that were carefully prepared against her by the Promoter. Then we sent the summary of her admissions, which were in the form of twelve articles, to doctors and other persons who are educated in canon and civil law for the purpose of obtaining their advice.

Although her case has not finally been decided by us, we have already adequately perceived that in the opinion and decision of many people, Joan appears reprehensible with regard to many points. But before we come to a final judgment, many honest, conscientious and educated men thought it would be beneficial to try by every possible means to instruct this woman on the points in which she seems to be in error, and, as far as we are able, to bring her back to the way and knowledge of the truth. This is the objective we have always desired, and we still desire it with all our strength, and this is what we should seek, especially we who live in the Church and live for the administration of holy things. We ought to show her in all charity where her acts and sayings are out of harmony with the faith, truth and religion, and charitably warn her to consider her salvation.

It is for this objective that we first tried to lead her back by means of many notable doctors of theology, whom we sent to her on many different days; they gave of themselves with all possible zeal to do this work, but they did not coerce her.

However, the cunning of the devil prevailed, and these notable doctors of theology have not yet had any effect on her. When we perceived that our private admonitions bore no fruit, it appeared to us that it would be appropriate that Joan should, in a solemn assembly, be gently and charitably admonished to amend her ways; because perhaps the presence and exhortations of some of you gathered here will more easily induce her to humility and obedience, and dissuade her from having too much reliance on her own opinions, so that she will give credibility to the advice of these worthy and educated men who are knowledgeable in divine and human laws; therefore, she will not expose herself to perils so great that they endanger her body and soul.

To address this solemn admonition to Joan we have appointed an old and educated master of theology, one particularly understanding in these matters, namely Jean de Chatillon, arch-deacon of Evreux, who, if it so pleases him, will accept the present task of demonstrating to Joan why she is in error on specific points. According to the advice and consultations we have received from the authorities, he will persuade Joan to abandon her faults and errors, and he will show her the way of truth.

Now, therefore, this woman will be brought before you to be publically admonished. If any among you think that he can say or do anything to facilitate her return, or helpfully instruct her regarding the salvation of her body and soul, we ask him not to hesitate to speak to us or to the assembly.

After Joan was led in before us on this day, we, the judges, with the bishop, in our name and on behalf of the Vice-Inquisitor, her judge with us, counseled her to listen to the advice and warnings which the lord arch-deacon, professor of sacred theology, would address to her, because he was about to say many things profitable for the salvation of her body and her soul, to which she must agree; because if she did not, she made herself vulnerable to dangers of body and soul; and so we explained many things to Joan as described in the following statements.

We, the judges, then required the lord arch-deacon to proceed charitably and begin the admonitions. In obedience to our order, the lord arch-deacon, beginning to teach and instruct Joan, explained to her that all faithful Christians were compelled and obliged to believe and hold firmly the Christian faith and its teachings; and he warned her and required her in a general admonition to correct and reform herself, her words and her deeds, in accordance with the advice of the venerable doctors and masters who were educated in divine, canon and civil law.

In response to the arch-deacon's general admonition, Joan replied, "Read your book," referring to the document that the lord arch-deacon held in his hand, "and then I will answer you. I trust in God my creator for everything, and I love Him with my whole heart."

When she was asked if she had anything further to say in response to this initial general admonition, Joan said, "I trust in my Judge; He is the King of Heaven and of Earth."

Then the lord arch-deacon proceeded to the particular admonitions, which he addressed to Joan according to the following statements. He began:

## ITEM 1

In the first place, he reminded her that she had recently said that if anything evil were found in her actions and her words that the clergy pointed out to her, she would desire to correct herself in that respect. This was a good and laudable thing to say because every Christian must be meek and always be ready to obey people who are wiser than him, and to give greater credit to the judgment of good and educated men than to his own judgment.

Now, the actions and words of this woman had been diligently and moderately examined for many days by doctors and clergy, who had found many grave deficiencies in Joan's actions and words; and if she wished to reform herself, as a good devout Christian must, the clergy were always ready to act towards her in all mercy and charity to affect her salvation. If, however, out of arrogant and haughty pride she desired to persist in her own views, and imagine that she understood matters of the faith better than doctors and other educated men, then she would expose herself to grave danger.

## ITEM 2

The arch-deacon explained to her, regarding the revelations and visions she professed to have, that she would not submit to the Church Militant or to any living man, but intended to refer herself to God alone with respect to her actions and words. He explained to her on this point the nature of the Church Militant, the authority it derives from God, in Whom its power resides; how every Christian is bound to believe that the Holy Church is one and Catholic, that the Holy Spirit governs it, that it never errs or falls into error; that every Catholic is bound to obey it as a son obeys his mother, and they must submit all their actions and words to its judgment; that nobody, regardless of their apparitions or revelations, must on their own decision withdraw from the judgment of the Church, since the apostles themselves submitted their writings to the Church, and that the whole Scripture, which is revealed by God, is sent for our belief by our mother the Church as an infallible guide to which we ought to conform in all things, without schism or division of any kind, as St. Paul the apostle teaches in many passages.

Moreover, every revelation from God leads us to maintain meekness and obedience toward our superiors, and never otherwise, because our Lord never desired anyone to presume to call himself subject to God alone, or to refer himself with respect to his actions or words to Him alone.

Indeed, our Lord committed and gave into the hands of the clergy the authority and power to know and judge the deeds of the faithful, whether they were good or evil; those who scorned the clergy scorned God; those who listened to the clergy listened to God.

Finally, the arch-deacon warned her that she must believe that the Catholic Church is incapable of error or false judgment, because he who does not hold this belief infringes upon the teaching contained in *Unam Sanctam*, which had been explained to Joan in detail; and he who persists in denying it must be determined to be a heretic; he is schismatic and shows himself an evil thinker with respect to the holiness of the Church and the infallible direction of the Holy Spirit; and canon law lays down a heavy punishment that must be inflicted upon such wanderers.

## ITEM 3

Joan was shown how for a long time she persisted in wearing men's clothes in the style of soldiers, and she continually and needlessly still wears these clothes contrary to the honesty of her sex, which is scandalous and against decent living and customs; and she wore her hair cropped short and round. All these habits are contrary to the commandments of God declared in Deuteronomy, Chapter 22, "A woman shall not wear a man's apparel, nor shall a man put on a woman's garment; for whoever does such things is abhorrent to the Lord your God." Also, this is contrary to the instruction of the Apostle who says that women shall veil their heads, and contrary to the prohibitions of the Church proclaimed in the holy General Council, to the teaching of the saints and of the doctors in canon and civil law; and this is an evil example for other women.

Joan was especially in error when, out of a peculiar insistence on continuing to wear her disgraceful clothes, she preferred not to receive the Sacrament of Holy Communion at a time ordained by the Church; rather than abandoning these clothes and putting on other clothes in which she could receive the Sacrament reverently and decently, she scorned the command of the Church to satisfy her persistent desire to wear men's clothes; she did this even though she had been often warned on this point, particularly regarding

Easter, when she said she greatly desired to attend Mass and receive Holy Communion. At that time we told her to return to wearing women's clothes, which she had available, but she still refused to do so. In our opinion, she gravely erred in this matter. Therefore, she was admonished to change these desires and stop wearing men's clothes.

## ITEM 4

Joan, not content to wear women's clothes even under the aforementioned and aggravating circumstances, went further by maintaining that she was acting wisely and was not in error. To maintain that one is acting well when one goes against the teaching of the saints and against the commandments of God and His apostles, and to scorn the teachings of the Church out of mere obstinacy in wearing dishonest and indecent clothes, is to deviate from the faith, and he who maintains this falls into heresy.

Moreover, she wanted to attribute responsibility for her sins to God and His saints. She blasphemed God and His saints by attributing unseemly things to them; the saints wish all honesty to be preserved and all perversities and sins to be avoided, and so they would never have the commandments of the Church disdained for such things. Therefore, the arch-deacon admonished Joan to cease from pronouncing such blasphemies, from recklessly attributing such thoughts to God and His saints, and from maintaining them as lawful.

## ITEM 5

Many doctors and notable ecclesiastics have considered and examined with diligence the statements of Joan concerning her revelations and apparitions, and there are clear falsehoods; for example, regarding the crown brought to Charles and the coming of angels, which she has invented; these falsehoods and imaginations have been recognized as such by those who are of our party as well as by others.

Her statements regarding the kisses and embraces she gave to St. Catherine and St. Margaret, who, if she is believed, came to her every day, and even many times daily with no special intention or apparent reason; there was no reason why they should come so frequently, and there is no precedent of saints revealing themselves in such miraculous apparitions.

Joan said she knows nothing about their limbs or any other details about their bodies except for their heads, which is not in accordance with such frequent visions. Regarding the many commands she says that they gave to her, such as commands to wear men's clothes and commands to provide such answers as she did in the trial, these commands are not in accordance with God and His saints, and cannot be allowed to have originated from them.

Finally, in view of the numerous other points that the doctors and other educated men have closely evaluated in this matter, they see and recognize that such revelations and apparitions are not sent from God, as she boasts. Joan was shown how extremely dangerous it is to believe, so audaciously, that it is appropriate for a person to receive such apparitions and revelations, because she lied with respect to things that are in the domain of God, falsely prophesying and foretelling events that were going to occur in the future, and God did not grant her this power, but she discovered these in the imaginations of her heart, and from this prophesying and foretelling of future events nothing can follow except the seduction of people, the springing up of new sects, and many other ills that are inclined to the overthrow of the Church and the Catholic people.

It is grave and dangerous to search curiously into things that exceed our understanding, to put faith in what is new without consulting the opinion of the Church and its prelates, and even to invent new and unfamiliar things, because devils are accustomed to insinuate themselves into these kinds of strange activities, either by occult instigation or by visible apparitions in which they transform themselves into angels of light; using the appearance of piety or some other good, they lead a person into malevolent pacts and plunge a person into error, which is permitted by God in order to punish the presumption of those people who allow themselves to be carried away by such things. Therefore, Jean de Chatillon, arch-deacon of Evreux, admonished Joan to renounce her vain imaginations, to cease propagating these falsehoods, and to return to the way of truth.

## ITEM 6

These invented revelations are the primary reason why she was induced to commit so many other crimes; and as a result, usurping the office of God, she did not hesitate to announce and affirm future and contingent events, as well as the presence of hidden objects such as a sword buried in the ground. Additionally, she boasted of knowing with certainty that some people were loved by God; and for her own part, she said she knew that she would receive forgiveness for the sin she had committed by leaping from the tower of Beaurevoir, which was nothing but divination, presumption and rashness.

Joan also said that she adored these unusual apparitions that appeared to her, although she had no adequate proof to believe that they were good spirits. She said she did not ask for the counsel of priests or any other ecclesiastics regarding these apparitions, so she presumed too much on her own initiative with regard to a matter in which the danger of idolatry is always looming; she impulsively believed something that she should not have given the slightest credibility, even if there was a basis of reality in these apparitions (which, nevertheless, to our minds, are false).

Moreover, Joan dared to say that she believed these apparitions to be St. Catherine, St. Margaret and angels as firmly as she believed in the Catholic faith; in saying this, she not only exhibited a reckless naïveté, but she also appeared to indicate that there is no more or stronger reason to believe in the Christian faith and its doctrines, which the Church has handed down to us, than in certain apparitions of a new and unfamiliar kind. In this matter she received no judgment or consultation from the Church; additionally, Christ and His saints teach us that it is not appropriate to carelessly have faith in such apparitions, and she was told to consider these things carefully.

While the arch-deacon was explaining these matters to Joan in French according to the text of his document, Joan interjected comments regarding the first and second items of the arch-deacon's document. She said, "As I have answered you before, so I will answer you now."

Previously she had been advised about the nature of the Church Militant and was admonished to believe and uphold the teaching of *Unam Sanctam,* and that she must submit to the Church Militant as explained in Item 2. She now responded, "I indeed believe in the Church on Earth, but regarding my words and deeds, as I have already declared, I trust in God and refer myself to God. I believe that the Church Militant cannot err or fail, but with respect to my deeds and words, I submit them and refer everything to God, who caused me to do what I have done." She added that she submitted herself to

God, her Creator, who had caused her to do those things, and referred herself to Him and to her own self concerning her words and deeds.

Asked if she wished to say that she had no judge on Earth, and whether our Holy Father the Pope were not her judge, she answered, "I will not say anything more. I have a good master, Our Lord, to whom I refer everything, and to none other."

When Joan was told that if she would not believe in the Church and in the teaching of *Unam Sanctam* she would be a heretic, and that she would suffer the punishment of being burned at the stake by the sentence of the judges, she replied, "I will say no more to you, and if I saw the fire, I would say all that I do now to you, and nothing more."

Asked if the General Council, or our Holy Father the Pope, the cardinals and other ecclesiastics were present, she would submit and refer herself to the General Council, she answered, "You will get nothing further from me."

Asked if she would submit to our Holy Father the Pope, she replied, "Take me to him, and I will reply to him."

Regarding what was said in Item 3 and Item 4 about her clothing, she said she would willingly accept a long dress and a woman's head covering to go to Church and receive the Sacrament of the Eucharist, as she had previously said, provided that immediately after her return she might take it off and wear her current clothes. When it was explained to her that she was in no need of wearing this clothing, especially in prison, she said, "When I have completed what God sent me to do I will resume wearing women's clothes."

Asked if she thought she was doing well to wear men's clothes, she replied, "I refer myself to Our Lord."

After she was admonished and the other matters of Item 4 were explained to her, she said that she had neither blasphemed God nor His saints. Then, when she was admonished to stop wearing men's clothes and stop believing that it was good to wear men's clothes, and was advised to resume wearing women's clothes, she said she would not do otherwise.

Asked if, whenever St. Catherine or St. Margaret came to her, she made the Sign of the Cross, she answered that sometimes she did and sometimes she did not.

We asked Joan about what she had been told regarding her revelations in Item 5, and she answered that on that question she referred herself to her judge, namely God. She said her revelations came to her directly from God.

We asked her about the sign given to the king, whether she would defer to the archbishop of Reims, to the Sire de Boussac, to Charles de Bourbon, to the Sire de la Tremouille or to Etienne, called La Hire, to whom she said she had shown the crown, because they were present when the angel brought it to Charles; we asked her whether she would defer to these other people of her party, writing about this incident under their seal, and she answered, "Give me a messenger and I will write to them about this trial." Otherwise, she would not believe them or defer to them.

With regard to Item 6, we asked Joan about the audacity of her beliefs and her presumptions in prophesying future and contingent events; she replied, "I refer myself to my judge, who is God, and to my earlier answers written in this book."

Asked if she were sent three or four clergy of her own party she would refer herself to them concerning the apparitions and all that was contained in the trial, she replied that we should first let them come and then she would answer, otherwise she would not refer herself or submit to them in this trial.

Asked whether she would refer herself and submit to the church of Poitiers, where she was previously examined, she answered, "Do you think you will catch me that way and thereby persuade me to come to you?"

Then, in conclusion, she was admonished profusely to submit to the Church under the threat and pain of being abandoned by the Church; because if the Church abandoned her she would be in great danger concerning her body and soul; her soul would be in danger of eternal fire and her body in danger of temporal fire by the sentence of the judges. She said, "You will not do as you say against me without evil overtaking you, in body and soul."

Asked to give at least one reason why she would not refer herself to the Church, she would make no other reply.

Whereupon many doctors and other educated men of various estates and faculties admonished her and charitably guided her, urging her to submit to the Church Universal and Church Militant, to our Holy Father the Pope, and to the sacred General Council, explaining to her the dangers of body and soul to which she exposed herself by her refusal to submit her actions and words to the Church Militant. She answered as before.

Finally, we, with the bishop, told Joan to be sure to seriously consider our admonitions, our counsel and our charitable exhortations, and change her mind. She answered us by stating this question: "How long will you give me to think it over?" We told her that she must think it over immediately and answer as she wished. However, because she made no further reply, we departed and Joan was taken back to her prison cell.

### JOAN IS THREATENED WITH TORTURE AT THE ROUEN CASTLE (MAY 9)

On Wednesday, May 9, Joan was brought into the great tower of the castle of Rouen to appear before us, the judges.

She was required and admonished to speak the truth about many different items addressed to her in her trial, activities which she had either denied or responses she had given that were false, because we possessed specific information, evidence and strong beliefs regarding these items. Many of these points were read to her and explained to her, and she was told that if she did not confess them truthfully she would be tortured, and we showed her that these instruments of torture were all prepared to be used on her in this area of the castle. There were also present, by our command, men ready to torture her in order to restore her to the way and knowledge of the truth, and by this means to secure the salvation of her body and soul, which by her lying inventions she exposed to such grave perils.

Joan replied, "Truly, if you were to tear me limb from limb and separate my soul from my body, I would not tell you anything more, and if I did say anything, I would say afterwards and declare that you had coerced me to say it by force."

Joan said that on the previous Holy Cross Day she received comfort from St. Gabriel. She firmly believes that it was St. Gabriel, and she said it was by her Voices that she knew it was him. She said that she asked for advice from her Voices about whether she should submit to the Church since the clergy were pressing her hard to submit. Her Voices told her that if she desired Our Lord to help her she must wait upon Him in everything she does. She said that Our Lord has always been the master of everything that she does, and that the Enemy never had any power over what she did or said. She asked her Voices if she would be burned at the stake and they answered that she must wait for God, and He would help her.

When asked about the crown she had given to the archbishop of Reims, and whether she would refer herself to him, she answered, "Bring him here and then I will answer you; he dare not deny what I have already told you."

Seeing the hardness of her heart and the manner by which she answered our questions, the judges, fearing that the torments of torture would be of little profit to Joan, decided to postpone their use until we had received additional counsel on this matter.

### INDIVIDUAL ASSESSORS DECLARE WHETHER JOAN SHOULD BE TORTURED (MAY 12)

On the following Saturday, May 12, the judges gathered at our episcopal residence at Rouen. We, with the bishop, recalled what had taken place on the previous Wednesday. We asked for advice from the assessors regarding what remained to be done in Joan's trial, in particular, whether it would be useful to torture Joan.

First, Raoul Roussel said he thought it would not be useful because a trial so well conducted could be exposed to slanderous statements.

Master Nicolas de Venderes said he thought it was not yet useful to torture Joan.

Master Andre Marguerie said it was not useful at this time.

Master Guillaume Erart said it was unnecessary to torture her because we possessed sufficient evidence without it.

Master Robert Le Barbier gave a similar opinion, but he thought she should again be charitably admonished, once and for all, to submit to the Church; then, if she would not, then in God's name the proceedings should continue.

Master Denis Gastinel said it would not be useful.

Master Aubert Morel said he thought it would be useful to torture Joan in order to discover the truth about her lies.

Master Thomas de Courcelles said he thought it would be wise to torture Joan, and she should also be examined about whether she would submit to the judgment of the Church.

Master Nicolas Couppequesne said it would not be useful to torture her, but she should, once more, be charitably admonished about her need to submit to the decision of the Church.

Master Jean Le Doulx agreed.

Brother Isambard de La Pierre similarly agreed, saying that for the last time she should be admonished to submit to the Church Militant.

Master Nicolas Loyseleur said he thought it would be good for the health of Joan's soul to torture her, nevertheless, he deferred to the earlier opinions.

Master William Haiton, who arrived later, said there was no need to torture Joan.

Master Jean Le Maistre, Vice-Inquisitor, said Joan should be once more examined regarding the question of whether she would submit to the Church Militant.

After these opinions had been heard and we considered the answers that Joan had made on the previous Wednesday, and in light of her disposition and her will, and in light of the circumstances, we concluded that it was neither necessary nor useful to torture Joan, and that we should proceed further in the matter of her trial.

## STATEMENTS FROM THE UNIVERSITY OF PARIS ARE READ (MAY 19)

On the following Saturday, May 19, the judges met in the chapel of the archepiscopal manor at Rouen. In the presence of these judges, the bishop explained how we had recently received a significant number of opinions and evaluations made by notable doctors and masters concerning Joan's statements and confessions; and that based on these findings, which were undoubtedly sufficient, we thought we might be able to render a judgment on Joan's legal case.

However, to show our honor and reverence for our mother the University of Paris, and to obtain an even stronger and more detailed explanation of the matter before us, and for the great peace of our conscience and instruction of everyone gathered, we decided it was wise to send our statements and findings to the University of Paris, in particular to the Faculties of Theology and Canon Law, to ask for their advice and counsel.

The University, and particularly the members of these two Faculties, who were burning with extraordinary zeal for the faith, gave us their thorough, mature and solemn counsel regarding each of our statements; and they addressed their responses to us in the form of a public, formal document. So we ordered that the opinions contained in this document be read aloud, word for word, clearly and publicly, so that all of the doctors and masters gathered here could hear them.

After everyone had heard the reading of the opinions from the University and the two Faculties [the text is inserted after the following two letters], the masters gathered here explained how the opinions they had already developed, as well as the procedures that are being used in the trial, were in compliance with the opinions of the University and its Faculties of Theology and Canon Law.

We have included below a letter from the University of Paris addressed to the [English] king, a letter from the University addressed to the Bishop of Beauvais, and other documentation received from the University.

First, the letter from the University addressed to our lord the king.

To the most excellent, high and mighty prince, King of France and England, our most feared and sovereign lord:

Most excellent prince, our most feared and sovereign lord and father, your royal excellence should in all things carefully endeavor to keep whole the honor, reverence and glory of the divine Majesty and His Holy Catholic faith by exterminating errors, false doctrines and all other offenses hostile to God and the Church. By following through in these endeavors, your highness will receive help, comfort and prosperity by the grace of the Most High as well as receive a large increase in your notoriety.

To this end, your most noble highness, and with God's grace, there began a most excellent work regarding our holy faith, namely the legal proceedings against this woman known as the Virgin, against her scandals, errors and crimes, which are apparent across the entire territory and which have been communicated to you repeatedly in our letters and documents.

We are acquainted with the matter and procedures of this trial by way of letters we have received in your name from our agents, the very honorable and most reverend masters Jean Beaupere, Jacques de Touraine and Nicolas Midi, Masters of Theology, who have also provided answers to our questions on points to which they have been entrusted.

Truly, when we had heard and closely examined these reports, it appeared to us that in this woman's trial, which involves extremely grave matters, a holy and just procedure has been followed, which must be pleasing to all men. Therefore, we express our most humble gratitude, first to the sovereign Majesty, and then to your most high nobility, both with a humble and loyal affection; and finally we give our thanks to all those who, by their reverence for God, have endured many difficulties and have given their labors and energies to this matter for the good of our holy faith.

Furthermore, most feared and sovereign lord, after many meetings and wise deliberations among ourselves, we are providing our counsel and conclusions on the points, statements and articles that were delivered and explained to us, all in accordance with your instructions and demands received in letters; and we are always prepared to work wholeheartedly in such matters that so directly concern our faith, as our profession requires us to do, and as we have always demonstrated to the best of our ability.

If anything further remains to be said or explained by us, these honorable and reverend masters, who have now returned to your highness and who were present at our deliberations, will be able to declare and explain everything in accordance with our intentions. May it please your magnificence to have faith in all that they will say in our name and receive them with this special recommendation, because in truth they have shown great diligence in these matters, all stemming from their pure and holy affection, unsparing in their efforts and without regard to threatening dangers, especially while traveling on the roads. Undeniably, it is through their wisdom, methods and discreet judiciousness that this matter will be brought to its conclusion, if it pleases God, with wisdom, holiness and reason.

Finally, we humbly request that your excellent highness bring this matter to its conclusion as soon and as diligently as possible, because truly the length of these proceedings and any further delays are perilous; it is necessary to provide a great and noteworthy reparation for the people who have been so scandalized by this woman, to bring them back to the true holy doctrines and beliefs.

To the entire exaltation and integrity of our faith, and for the praise of the eternal God, who may in His grace maintain your excellency in prosperity until you reach eternal glory.

Written at Paris in our solemn assembly at St. Bernard on May 14, 1431.

Your most humble daughter, the University of Paris.

Signed: Michel Hébert

[Michel Hébert, Priest, Master of Arts, Notary and Secretary, University of Paris.]

Then follows the letter from the University of Paris addressed to the Bishop of Beauvais.

To the reverend father and lord in Christ, the Bishop of Beauvais:

My lord and most reverend father, your diligent work and pastoral vigilance are clearly motivated by an immense dedication to a most singular charity. Out of pious concern for the public safety you never cease to work on behalf of our holy faith with a firm righteousness and never-ending commitment.

Your strong and renowned combative spirit, your heroic and forceful sense of justice, and your most sincere fervor showed its true measure when this woman, commonly known as the Virgin, was brought into the hands of your diocese by an auspicious grace of Christ. Christians throughout most of the western world seem to have been infected by the poison she has widely spread. However, by your reverent watchfulness, which is always at pains to perform the duties of a true pastor, you did not fail to oppose this woman as a public menace.

In our general assembly various notable doctors of theology as well as our agents, the masters Jean Beaupere, Jacques de Touraine and Nicolas Midi, intelligently explained to us the evidence and how the trial procedures have been conducted, using specific assertions, accusations and letters from our lord the king, as well as documentation and commands issued by your reverence, to address the grave offenses of this treacherous woman.

After they completed their presentations, we resolved to express our most enthusiastic gratitude to his highness as well as to your reverence, who has never been indifferent with regard to the noble work of protecting the integrity and glory of the orthodox faith whenever the divine name is in question, and to the beneficial instruction of faithful people. We approved of this distinguished trial and its procedures, we considered it to be in compliance with the holy canons, and we see it is being conducted by the most eloquent and experienced minds.

Out of respect for our lord the king and our enduring devotion to your reverence, we granted all the requests which the doctors presented to us verbally or in writing, because we desired with all our strength and sincere affection to please you, reverend father.

On the principal question, we took care to conduct many very serious consultations and deliberations; and after the matter had been repeatedly discussed with all freedom and honesty, we decided to produce in writing the outcome of these consultations and deliberations, which, in the end, we unanimously agreed upon. These doctors, our agents, who have returned to your reverence, will faithfully show you this documentation. They will also carefully discuss certain other things that are more fittingly explained at great length, and which we more fully declare in our letter to our lord the king, a copy of which is included here.

May your reverence receive with special recommendation these eminent doctors who, unmindful of their labors and perils, have not spared their energies and have worked unceasingly on this matter of faith.

We give our ongoing support to your reverence's tireless zeal and perseverance with regard to completing this endeavor, which has not been carried out in vain, and which will continue until reason shall decide that the divine Majesty has been appeased by a reparation which is proportionate to the offense, that the truth of our orthodox faith remains stainless, and that this wicked and scandalous demoralization of the people has ended. Then, when the Prince of shepherds will appear, he will reward your reverence's pastoral fervor with a crown of eternal glory.

Written at Paris in our general assembly, solemnly held at St. Bernard on May 13, 1431.

The Rector, The University of Paris.

Signed: Michel Hébert

Then follows statements from the University of Paris.

In the name of the Lord, amen. Let it be known and obvious to all by the content of this public document that our mother the University of Paris was assembled and called together solemnly at St. Bernard with respect to two matters.

To address the first and principal of these matters, we heard the reading of letters and assertions from the most Christian prince, our lord the king, from his council, and from the lord judges involved in this trial in matters of faith against a certain woman named Joan, commonly called the Virgin, and then we deliberated upon these letters and assertions; the second matter concerned ordinary requests and criticisms.

These articles were explained to us by the venerable and prudent Master Pierre de Gouda, Master of Arts, Rector of the University and President of the Assembly.

After the letters had been opened and read and their credentials explained by one of the ambassadors from our lord the king—a member of his council and one of the judges sent to the University—the twelve articles inserted below were read.

My lord the rector identified, proposed and declared that the content of the articles was important and challenging to the orthodox faith, the Christian religion and holy laws. He said the task of evaluating and judging these articles was of particular concern to the venerable Faculties of Theology and Canon Law, in accordance with their professions. He also said the University could not deliberate and decide upon these matters and articles without the assistance of these two Faculties; so the decision and judgment of the two Faculties will be submitted to the University, together or separately.

After this explanation to the general assembly of all the masters and doctors here present, the rector opened a deliberation on each and every one of the items that had been set forth. Then each Faculty or authority met separately in the place where it customarily gathered to consider the most difficult matters and tasks. After thorough deliberations by the Faculties and authorities, the private decisions of each were made public according to custom and were reported to the University.

Finally, the University, through the offices of the lord rector and in conformance with the deliberations made by the Faculties and authorities, resolved to entrust the judging of the articles and the decisions on these matters to the Faculties of Theology and Canon Law, and that their final evaluations would be reported to the University.

In the end, each Faculty, after long and thorough deliberations, had doctrinally reached a decision according to the content of a specific document which Master Jean de Troies, vice-dean of the Faculty of Theology, held in his hands. In the presence of the University, he first displayed and then read the document in a clear and loud voice, with the articles already mentioned. The content of these articles, judgments and qualifications, contained in this document, are given below word for word.

Here follows the text of the deliberations and conclusions reached by the Holy Faculty of Theology at the University of Paris, which are judgments on the articles already transcribed concerning the words and deeds of Joan, commonly called the Virgin. The Faculty submits these entire deliberations and conclusions to the judgment of our Holy Father the Pope and the Holy Council General.

## ARTICLE 1

Regarding the first article [that Joan claimed to receive revelations from St. Catherine, St. Margaret, St. Michael and St. Gabriel], the Faculty declares doctrinally that in view of the purpose, manner and content of these revelations, the places they occurred and other circumstances, and the quality of Joan as a person, these revelations are either fictitious, malevolent and misleading lies, or they proceed from evil and diabolical spirits, such as Belial, Satan or Behemoth.

## ARTICLE 2

Regarding the second article [that Joan claimed to walk with St. Michael to the king's chamber when the sign was given to the king], it appears to be based on audacious, misleading, malicious and contrived lies, and it is disrespectful to the dignity of angels.

## ARTICLE 3

Regarding the third article [that Joan believes it is St. Michael himself who visits her, and she believes his actions and words as firmly as she believes that Christ suffered death to redeem humanity], there is no sufficient sign of its validity, and Joan believes lightly and affirms impulsively; moreover, in the comparison she made, her belief is evil and she wanders from the faith.

# JOAN OF ARC

## ARTICLE 4

Regarding the fourth article [that Joan is certain about future events that will occur as surely as she sees the reality in front of her], it is nothing but superstition, divination, arrogant affirmations and vain boasting.

## ARTICLE 5

Regarding the fifth article [that Joan wears men's clothes at the command of God, that she received the Eucharist wearing men's clothes, and that she would rather die than give up wearing men's clothes], Joan is blasphemous towards God, contemptuous of God in His Sacraments, unmindful of divine and sacred law and ecclesiastical sanctions, exhibits evil thinking, and she foolishly errs in the faith. She is boastful and must be suspected of idolatry, and by the malediction of herself and her clothing, she has imitated the rites of the heathen.

## ARTICLE 6

Regarding the sixth article [that Joan had letters written to English soldiers threatening them with being killed in battle and "by blows would the favor of the God of Heaven be seen"], the woman is treacherous, cunning, cruel, thirsty for the spilling of human blood, subversive, inciting to tyranny, and blasphemous of God in light of her commands and revelations.

## ARTICLE 7

Regarding the seventh article [that Joan left her parents' house against their wishes and told Robert de Baudricourt she would annihilate the king's enemies], Joan is impious towards her parents, contemptuous of the commandment to honor her father and mother, scandalous, and blasphemous towards God; also, she wanders from the faith and has made rash and presumptuous promises.

## ARTICLE 8

Regarding the eighth article [that Joan jumped from the tower where she was being held prisoner, that she could not resist jumping from the tower, and that she was forgiven of her sin after confessing to St. Catherine], we observe a fear that is bordering on despair and, by interpretation, a suicide attempt; she makes a rash and presumptuous assertion concerning the remission of her sin; and she has an erroneous opinion concerning free will.

## ARTICLE 9

Regarding the ninth article [that St. Catherine and St. Margaret promised to lead Joan into Heaven, and Joan's belief that she has not committed any mortal sin because she believes St. Catherine and St. Margaret would not visit her every day if she was in mortal sin], there appears to be an impulsive and presumptuous assertion and a wicked falsehood; also, she contradicts herself in the preceding article and holds evil opinions in matters of faith.

## ARTICLE 10

Regarding the tenth article [that God loves certain people whom Joan points out and names, and that St. Catherine and St. Margaret "are not on the side of the English"], we find impulsive and presumptuous pronouncements, superstitious divinations, blasphemy of St. Catherine and St. Margaret, and transgression of the commandment to love her neighbor.

## ARTICLE 11

Regarding the eleventh article [that Joan has shown reverence to the Voices and spirits whom she calls St. Michael, St. Gabriel, St. Catherine and St. Margaret, that she has uncovered, knelt and kissed the ground where they had walked, and that she consecrated her virginity to St. Catherine and St. Margaret when she embraced and acknowledged them], this woman, by assuming she has had the revelations and apparitions of which she boasts, and according to the circumstances in Article 1, is idolatrous, a conjurer of evil spirits, a wanderer from the faith, and makes impulsive affirmations and unlawful oaths.

## ARTICLE 12

Regarding the twelfth article [that Joan says and admits that if the Church were to desire her to do anything contrary to the commands she claims to receive from God, she would not do it for any reason whatsoever, and that she does not submit herself to the judgment of the Church Militant, or to the judgment of any living men, but only to God, whose commands she will always obey], Joan is schismatic, erroneous in her opinions of the unity and authority of the Church, and an apostate; also, she obstinately persists in her deviations from the faith.

Now, here follows the text of the deliberations and doctrinal judgments of the venerable Faculty of Canon Law at the University of Paris regarding the six items on which Joan was publically admonished by Jean de Chatillon, the arch-deacon of Evreux, to persuade her to abandon her faults and errors and show her the way of truth. The Faculty submits these deliberations and findings to the decision and judgment of the sovereign Pontiff of the apostolic Holy See and the Holy Council General.

## ITEM 1

This woman is schismatic because schism is an unlawful separation due to disobedience against the unity of the Church, and Joan separates herself from obedience to the Church Militant, as she has said.

## ITEM 2

This woman deviates from the faith and contradicts the teaching contained in *Unam Sanctam;* and, as St. Jerome wrote, he who contradicts the faith proves not only that he is ignorant, malicious and not Catholic, but also a heretic.

## ITEM 3

This woman is an apostate because the hair which God gave her for a veil she has cropped short, and with the same motivation she rejected women's clothes and put on the clothes of men.

## ITEM 4

This woman proves herself to be a liar and a witch when she says she has been sent by God and that she speaks with angels and saints because she is unable to defend these claims by way of any miracle or special evidence from the Scriptures. For example, when the Lord sent Moses into Egypt to the sons of Israel, Moses gave them a sign so that they could believe he was sent by God: Moses changed a rod into a serpent, and he changed a serpent into a rod. Likewise, when John the Baptist began his mission he delivered a special testimony and evidence from the Scriptures when he said: "I am the voice of one crying out in the wilderness; prepare the way for the Lord," as Isaiah had foretold.

## ITEM 5

This woman, by law and by presumption of law, deviates from the faith because, firstly, she persists in her behavior after she has been declared anathema by the authority of canon law; secondly, she declared that she preferred to wear men's clothes rather than receive the body of Christ in the Eucharist and go to Confession at a time ordained by the Church. Moreover, she is strongly suspected of heresy and should be thoroughly examined on articles of the faith.

## ITEM 6

This woman sins when she says she is certain of being received into Heaven and that she is already sharing in that blessed glory; on this earthly journey no pilgrim knows if he is worthy of glory or of punishment, which only the Sovereign Judge knows. Consequently, if this woman, being charitably exhorted and duly admonished by a competent judge, will not willingly return to the unity of the Catholic faith and publicly repudiate her errors to the good pleasure and satisfaction of this judge, then she must be abandoned to the discretion of the secular judge to receive the penalty proportionate to her crime.

After these articles and evaluations were read, the lord rector clearly and publicly demanded the venerable Faculties of Theology and Canon Law to state whether the deliberations and evaluations which had just been read from the book agreed with the deliberations and decisions of the Faculties, and each of the Faculties answered separately. Master Jean de Troies of the Faculty of Theology, and the venerable Master Guerould Boissel, dean of the Faculty of Canon Law, declared that these decisions and evaluations were exactly those which they had given and pronounced.

Then the lord rector reminded them and stated how the University of Paris had commissioned the Faculties of Theology and Canon Law to issue these decisions and evaluations; and that the University, as reported, had undertaken to accept and honor the decisions made by the Faculties of Canon Law and Theology as good, ratified and acceptable.

After this was declared in this general form, the lord rector then opened for discussion the particular points that had been set forth and declared to all the masters and doctors present in the general assembly.

After a long and thorough discussion by the Faculties and authorities, each assertion was made and repeated in public, and the University, through the person of the lord rector, stated that it accepted the decisions and evaluations of the Faculties of Theology and Canon Law as good, ratified and acceptable, and held them as their own.

In witness of these decisions, the prudent and venerable masters Jean Beaupere, Jacques de Touraine and Nicolas Midi, Professors of Sacred Theology, requested us to deliver and present to each of them one or more copies of the public documents signed by the following notaries:

I, Jean Bourrillet, called François, Priest, Master of Arts, licensed in Canon Law and Bachelor of Theology, Notary Public by imperial and apostolic authority, with the venerable Master Michel Hébert, Priest of the Diocese of Rouen, Master of Arts, Notary and Secretary of our mother the University of Paris by imperial and apostolic authority, declare that I was present at all which was said, explained, discussed, deliberated and resolved in the assemblies of the University. In witness of this I have put my official seal on this document, as I have been summoned and called to do, in testimony of its faith and truth.

Signed: Jean Bourrillet

And I, Michel Hébert, Priest of the Diocese of Rouen, Master of Arts, Notary and Secretary of the University of Paris by pontifical and imperial authority, having been present with Master Jean Bourrillet at all which was said, set forth and discussed at the University, and as has been declared above, certify that I have seen and heard these things. Therefore, I have put my official signature on this document, written with my own hand and signed below in witness of its faith and truth, as I have been summoned and called to do.

Signed: Michel Hébert

After this, the doctors and masters of Rouen stated that their opinions were in conformance with the opinions of the University of Paris. Then we, the judges at Rouen, thanked the reverend fathers, lords and masters, and we said that we should once more charitably admonish Joan to return to the way of truth for the salvation of her body and soul, and we would proceed to conclude the trial and set a date for pronouncing a sentence according to the deliberations and helpful counsel provided by the University.

### JOAN'S FAULTS ARE EXPLAINED TO HER AND THE TRIAL ENDS (MAY 23)

The following Wednesday, May 23, Joan was led to a room near her prison cell in the castle of Rouen and into our presence with the judges assembled in tribunal. In the presence of Joan we explained certain points on which she had been in error and strayed according to the conclusions of the Faculties of Theology and Canon Law from the University of Paris. The faults, crimes and errors contained in each of these points were explained to her, and we warned her to abandon these faults and errors, to correct and reform herself, and to submit to the correction and decision of our Holy Mother the Church, as is stated in the documentation transcribed below, which was explained to Joan in French by Master Pierre Maurice, Canon of Rouen and a distinguished Doctor of Theology.

### ITEM 1

Firstly, Joan, you have said that from the age of 13 years or thereabout, you have had revelations and apparitions of angels and of St. Catherine and St. Margaret, whom you have frequently seen with your bodily eyes, and they have often spoken with you and told you many things that were well documented in your trial.

On this point the clergy of the University of Paris and others have considered the manner of these revelations, their purpose, the content of the things revealed, and the quality of you as a person, and having evaluated everything that is relevant, they declare that these revelations are false, seductive and wicked, and that these revelations and apparitions are super-stitions and proceed from evil and diabolical spirits.

## ITEM 2

You have said that the king received a sign by which he knew that you were sent from God, and that this sign was St. Michael in the company of many other angels, some with crowns and others with wings, that St. Catherine and St. Margaret were among these angels when they came to you in the town and castle of Chinon. They all went up the stairs of the castle with you to the chamber of the king, and the angel who carried the crown bowed before the king. At another time you said this crown, which you call a sign, was given to the archbishop of Reims, who presented it to the king in front of many princes and lords whom you have named. The clergy declares that this is not likely to have happened, and that you have stated an audacious, misleading and wicked lie, which is offensive and insulting to the dignity of angels.

## ITEM 3

You have said that you recognized the angels and saints by the good advice, comfort and doctrine they gave you, and by the fact that they told you their names when the saints greeted you; you believe that their words and deeds are good; and you believe it was St. Michael who appeared to you as firmly as you believe and have faith in Jesus Christ. The clergy declares that these signs are not sufficient to truly recognize angels and saints, that you be-lieved it too easily and affirmed it impulsively; and in the comparison you make with faith in Jesus Christ you deviate from the faith.

## ITEM 4

You have said that you are sure about the occurrence of future and contin-gent events, that you have known where things were hidden, and that you have recognized men you had never previously seen because of revelations from the Voices of St. Catherine and St. Margaret. The clergy declares that this is based on superstition, divination, arrogant assertions and haughty boasting.

## ITEM 5

You have said that you wore and still wear men's clothes at God's command and to His good pleasure, and that you received instruction from God to wear this clothing; and so you have worn a short tunic, a sleeveless jacket, and stockings with many points; you wear your hair cut short above your ears; you do not maintain anything about you that would indicate your sex except what nature has given you; and you often received the Sacrament of the Eucharist while wearing these clothes. Although you have been admonished many times to stop wearing these clothes, you would not do so, saying that you would rather die than stop wearing these clothes, unless it was God's command to do so; and that if you maintained wearing men's clothes while in the company of the people of your party it would be for the great benefit of France. You also say that nothing would persuade you to take an oath not to wear these clothes and carry military weapons; and you say that all of this is by divine command.

Regarding these matters, the clergy declares that you blaspheme against God and scorn Him and His Sacraments; you transgress divine law, Holy Scripture and the canons of the Church; your thinking is evil and you err on matters of the faith; you are full of haughty boasting, and you have given in to the idolatry and worship of yourself and your clothes, as the heathen do.

## ITEM 6

You have often said that in your letters you have put the names Jesus Mary, and have put the sign of the cross in letters to warn those to whom you wrote not to do what was indicated in the letter. In other letters you boasted you would kill all those who did not obey you, and that by your blows the approval of the Lord would be seen. You have also often said that all of your deeds were done according to revelation and by divine command. With regard to such affirmations, the clergy declares you to be a traitor, disloyal, cruel, desiring human bloodshed, seditious, an instigator of tyranny, and a blasphemer of God's commandments and revelations.

## ITEM 7

You have said that according to revelations given to you at the age of 17, you left your parents' house against their will, driving them almost mad. You went to see Robert de Baudricourt, who, at your request, gave you men's clothes and a sword, as well as soldiers to take you to the king. When you met with the king you told him that his enemies would be driven away, and you promised to make the king victorious over his enemies and bring him into a great kingdom, and that it was for this purpose that God had sent you. You say that you accomplished these things in obedience to God and according to revelation.

Regarding these matters, the clergy declares that you have been disrespectful to your father and mother, thereby disobeying God's commandment; you have also given occasion for scandal, blasphemed, erred in the faith, and have made rash and presumptuous promises.

### ITEM 8

You have said that of your own will you threw yourself from the tower of Beaurevoir, preferring to die rather than be delivered into the hands of the English and remain alive after the destruction of Compiegne. Although St. Catherine and St. Margaret prohibited you from making the leap, you said you could not restrain yourself from jumping; and despite the great sin you have committed by offending these saints, you said you knew by your Voices that after your confession your sin was forgiven.

The clergy declares that you jumped from the tower out of cowardice, verging on despair, and you possibly attempted suicide. In this matter you also made a rash and presumptuous statement in asserting that your sin is forgiven. You also err in the faith regarding the teaching on free will.

### ITEM 9

You have said that St. Catherine and St. Margaret promised to accompany you to Heaven if you preserved the virginity which you vowed and promised to them, and you are as assured of entering Heaven as if you had already entered into the glory of the Blessed. You believe you have not committed mortal sin, and it seems to you that if you were in mortal sin the saints would not visit you daily as they do.

The clergy declares your assertion to be a wicked lie, and a presumptuous and rash statement; your assertion also includes a contradiction of what you had previously said, and your beliefs err from the true Christian faith.

## ITEM 10

You have said that you know very well that God loves certain living persons more than you, and you learned this by revelation from St. Catherine and St. Margaret. You also say that St. Catherine and St. Margaret speak French, not English, because they are not on the side of the English; and because you knew your Voices were for your king, you began to dislike the Burgundians.

The clergy declares these matters to be rash and presumptuous assertions, superstitious divinations, blasphemies uttered against St. Catherine and St. Margaret, and a transgression of the commandment to love our neighbors.

## ITEM 11

You have stated that to those whom you call St. Michael, St. Catherine and St. Margaret, you showed reverence by bending your knee, removing your cap, kissing the ground on which they walked, and vowing to them to keep your virginity; you believed the instruction given by these saints, whom you invoked, kissed and embraced as soon as they appeared to you, without seeking counsel from your priest or from any other ecclesiastic. You believe these Voices came from God as firmly as you believe in the Christian religion and the Passion of Our Lord Jesus Christ. Moreover, you said that if any evil spirit would appear to you in the form of St. Michael you would know such a spirit and be able to distinguish an evil spirit from a saint; and many times you have said that by your own decision you have sworn not to reveal the sign you gave to the king, adding "except by God's command."

The clergy declares that if you had these revelations and saw these apparitions, of which you boast in such a manner as you say, then you are an idolatress, an invoker of demons, an apostate from the faith, a maker of rash statements, and a swearer of an unlawful oath.

## ITEM 12

You have said that if the Church wanted you to disobey the orders you say God gave to you, nothing would induce you to do so; that you know all the deeds you have been accused of in your trial were done according to the command of God, and that it was impossible for you to do otherwise. Regarding these activities, you refuse to submit to the judgment of the Church on Earth or to any living man, and you will only submit to God; also, you declared that this statement itself was not made by your own decision but by God's command, despite the article of faith *Unam Sanctam* having been declared to you many times; nevertheless, it is appropriate for all Christians to submit their words and deeds to evaluation by the Church Militant, especially everything that concerns revelations and similar matters.

Therefore, the clergy declares you to be a schismatic, an unbeliever in the unity and authority of the Church, an apostate, and persistently erring in the faith.

Now, after these assertions and the evaluations of the University of Paris had been declared and explained to Joan, she was admonished in French by the same doctor and instructed to think very carefully about her words and deeds, especially in light of the last item.

He spoke to her thus:

Joan, dearest friend, it is now near the end of your trial and it is time for you to think very carefully about everything that has been said. For the honor and reverence of God, for the faith and the law of Jesus Christ, for the alleviation of the scandal you have caused, and for the salvation of your body and soul, you have been most diligently admonished four times by the Bishop of Beauvais, the lord Vicar of the Inquisitor, and by other doctors sent to you on their behalf and for the peace of their consciences.

Until now you have not wanted to listen to us, even though you have been shown the dangers to which you expose your body and soul if you do not reform yourself and your statements, and correct them by submitting your words and deeds to the Church and accepting her judgment.

Now, although many of your judges would have been satisfied with the evidence already collected against you, in their fear for the salvation of your body and soul, they submitted your statements to be evaluated by the University of Paris, the light of all knowledge and the eradicator of all errors.

When the trial judges received the evaluations of the University, they decided that you should once again be admonished and warned of your errors, scandals and other crimes, and that we should beg, urge and advise you—for the kind consideration of Our Lord Jesus Christ who suffered cruel death for the redemption of humanity—to correct your statements and submit them to the judgment of the Church, as every loyal Christian is required and obligated to do. Do not permit yourself to be separated from Our Lord Jesus Christ, who created you to be a partaker in His glory.

Do not choose the path of eternal damnation with the enemies of God, who daily attempt to distract people by fabricating the likeness of Christ and His angels and His saints, who they profess and affirm themselves to be, and as has been explained fully by the Church fathers and in the Scriptures.

Therefore, if such apparitions have appeared to you, do not believe them; more than that, put away the belief or imagination you had in such things, and believe instead in the words and opinions of the University of Paris and other doctors who, being well acquainted with canon law, God, and the Holy Scriptures, have concluded that no faith should be given to such apparitions, or in any extraordinary apparitions or forbidden novelties that are not supported by Holy Scripture, or by a sign or a miracle, none of which you have.

You have believed these apparitions carelessly instead of turning to God in devout prayer to grant you certainty; and you have not consulted clerics or educated ecclesiastics to enlighten you on these matters, although considering your situation and the simplicity of your knowledge, you should have done so.

Consider this example. Suppose the king appointed you to defend a fortress, forbidding you to let anyone enter. Would you admit anyone who claimed to come in the king's name but brought no official letter or authentic sign? Likewise, Our Lord Jesus Christ, when He ascended into Heaven, committed the government of His Church to the apostle St. Peter and his successors, forbidding them to receive in the future those who claimed to come in His name but provided no sign other than their own words. So you should not have put faith in those which you say came to you, and nor should we believe in you, since God commands the contrary.

Joan, you should consider this. If, when you were in the king's territory, a soldier or another person born in his territory had arrived and said, "I will not obey the king or submit to any of his officers," wouldn't you have said this man should be condemned?

So, what shall you say of yourself, who, brought up in the faith of Christ by the Sacrament of Baptism and have become the daughter of the Church and the spouse of Christ, if you do not obey Christ's officers, that is to say, the clerics of the Church? What judgment shall you deliver upon yourself?

Stop, I pray you, from saying these things if you love your Creator, your precious Spouse and your salvation. Obey the Church and submit to its judgment, and know that if you do not, if you persist in this error, your soul will be condemned to eternal punishment and perpetual torture; I do not doubt that you will go to Hell.

Don't let human pride and useless shame, which perhaps constrain you, or perhaps hold you back out of fear that if you do as I advise you to do you will lose the great honors you have accumulated, because the honor of God and the salvation of your body and your soul must come first. You will lose everything if you do not do as I say, because you will separate yourself from the Church and from the faith you swore in the Holy Sacrament of Baptism. You will cut yourself off from the authority of the Church, which is led, ruled and governed by Our Lord through His Spirit and authority, because He said to the ministers of the Church, "He that hears you hears Me, and he that despises you despises Me."

Therefore, if you will not submit to the Church you have in fact separated yourself; and if you will not submit to the Church you refuse to submit to God, and you err with respect to the teaching of *Unam Sanctam*. What the Church is, and her authority, has been sufficiently explained to you already in our previous admonishments to you.

In view of all these things and on behalf of your judges, the lord Bishop of Beauvais and the lord Vicar of the Inquisitor, I admonish, beg and urge you, by the sorrow you have for the Passion of your Creator, and by the love you have for the salvation of your body and your soul, correct and amend these errors, and return to the way of truth by obeying the Church and submitting everything to her judgment and decision. By doing so, you will save your soul and redeem, as I hope, your body from death; but if you do not, if you persist, know that your soul will be overcome by damnation, and I fear the destruction of your body. From these ills may Our Lord preserve you!

After Joan had been admonished in this manner and had heard these exhortations, she replied this way: "As for my words and deeds, which I declared in the trial, I refer you to them and maintain them."

Asked if she thinks she is not bound to submit her words and deeds to the Church Militant or to anyone other than God, she answered, "I maintain that manner of speech which I always said and believed during the trial."

Joan said that if she were condemned and saw the fire or the executioner ready to light the fire, and if she herself were in the fire, she would say nothing else and would maintain until death what she said in the trial.

Then we, her judges, asked the Promoter and Joan whether they had anything further to say. They answered they did not. Then we proceeded to conclude the trial according to the formula of a specific document that the bishop held in his hands, which stated the following:

We, competent judges in this trial, as we regard ourselves to be insofar as it is necessary, declare that by your refusal to say anything further, the trial has ended. With this conclusion pronounced, we assign tomorrow as the day on which you shall hear us deliver justice and pronounce sentence, which shall afterward be carried out according to law and reason.

In the presence of the witnesses Brother Isambard de La Pierre and Master Mathieu le Bateur, priests, and Louis Orsel, clerics of the dioceses of Rouen, London and Noyon.

## JOAN RENOUNCES HERESY ON A SCAFFOLD AT THE ROUEN CEMETERY (MAY 24)

On the morning of Thursday, May 24, the judges went to a public place, the cemetery of the Saint-Ouen abbey in Rouen, where Joan was present before us on a scaffold or platform. First, for the constructive admonition of Joan and for the benefit of the great multitude of people who were present, we had a solemn sermon delivered by Master Guillaume Erart, distinguished Doctor of Sacred Theology.

We had with us the very reverend father in Christ, Henry, Cardinal of the Holy Roman Church and commonly called Cardinal of England; the reverend fathers in Christ, the Bishops of Therouanne, Noyon and Norwich, individuals licensed in canon law, and many others.

Master Erart began his sermon, taking his text from the Scriptures in the fifteenth chapter of St. John, saying, "A branch cannot bear fruit by itself unless it remains in the vine."

He solemnly explained that all Catholics must remain in the true vine of Our Holy Mother Church, which Our Lord planted with His right hand. Master Erart also explained how Joan had cut herself off from the unity of our Holy Mother Church by her many errors and serious crimes, and how she had frequently scandalized the Christian people. Using suitable doctrines, he admonished and exhorted Joan and the multitude of people gathered.

When the sermon was over he spoke to Joan, saying, "Look at your judges, who have repeatedly summoned you and required you to submit all your words and deeds to Our Holy Mother Church, showing and pointing out to you that, in the opinion of the clergy, many things are found in your words and deeds which are neither good to affirm nor maintain."

To which Joan replied, "I will answer you. Regarding my submission to the Church, I have already answered the judges on this point. Let all that I have said and done be sent to Rome to our Holy Father the Pope, to whom, after God, I refer myself. As for my words and deeds, they were done at God's command."

Joan said that she charged nobody with her words and deeds, neither her king nor any other person; and that if there were any faults in her words and deeds, they were hers and no other person's.

Asked whether she would retract all her words and deeds that are disapproved of by the clergy, she replied, "I refer myself to God and to our Holy Father the Pope."

Then she was told that this would not be sufficient; that it was not possible to seek our Holy Father the Pope at such a great distance, and that the jurisdictional Ordinaries, each in his own diocese, were competent judges; and therefore she must necessarily submit to Our Holy Mother Church by holding as true all that the clergy and other authorities had said and decided concerning her words and deeds, at which point she was cautioned by three more admonitions.

Then, because Joan would say nothing more, the bishop began to read the final sentence.

When we had almost completed the reading of the sentence, Joan began to speak, saying she would hold all that the Church would command, and all that her judges would say and rule, and that she would obey our orders and will in all things. She said repeatedly that to the extent the clergy had declared her revelations and apparitions were not to be upheld or believed, she would not maintain them, and that she would defer in all things to her judges and our Holy Mother Church.

Then, in our presence and before a great multitude of people and clergy, she made and pronounced her recantation and abjuration according to the formula of a specific document written in French, which was then read and which she spoke with her own lips and signed with her own hand.

The content of Joan's recantation and abjuration follows:

All those who have erred and have been at fault in the Christian faith, and have by God's grace returned to the light of truth and unity in Our Holy Mother Church, should vigilantly prevent the Enemy in Hell from driving them back and causing their relapse into error and damnation.

Therefore, I, Joan, commonly called the Virgin, a miserable sinner, recognizing the snares of error in which I was held, and through God's grace have returned to Our Holy Mother Church, in order to show that my return is not a deception but made with a good heart and will, I confess that I have most grievously sinned in falsely pretending to have had revelations and apparitions from God, His angels, and St. Catherine and St. Margaret; seducing others; believing foolishly and impulsively; making superstitious divinations; blaspheming God and His Saints; breaking the divine law, Holy Scripture and canon law; wearing immoral, tight and immodest clothing, and hair cropped short like a man's, against all modesty of women and against the decency of nature; carrying weapons most inappropriately; cruelly desiring the shedding of human blood; declaring that I did all these things by the command of God, His angels and saints, and that to do so was good and not to err; being seditious and idolatrous; and adoring and calling up evil spirits. I also confess that I have been schismatic and have in many ways erred from the path.

Without deception and with a good heart, I abjure and recant, renouncing and cutting myself off from all these crimes and errors. By God's grace I have returned to the way of truth through holy doctrine and the good counsel of the doctors and masters whom you sent me.

I submit to the correction, disposition, amendment and the entire decision of Our Holy Mother Church and of your good justice regarding all of these errors; and I vow, swear and promise to you, to my lord Saint Peter, Prince of the Apostles, to our Holy Father the Pope of Rome, his Vicar and his successors, to you, my lords, to the lord Bishop of Beauvais and the religious Brother Jean Le Maistre, Vicar of the lord Inquisitor of the Faith, and my judges, that I will never, through incitement or by any other means, return to these errors from which it has pleased God to deliver and remove me; but will always dwell in the unity of Our Holy Mother Church and the obedience of our Holy Father the Pope of Rome.

This I say, affirm and swear by God almighty and the holy Gospels, and so I have signed this document with my mark.

Signed: Jehanne +

## Sentence after the Abjuration

After we, the judges, had received her recantation and abjuration as noted above, we, with the bishop, pronounced our definitive sentence in these terms:

In the name of the Lord, amen. When the treacherous sower of errors painstakingly attempts with great cunning to infect the flock of Christ with venomous poisons, all pastors of the Church who desire and work to faithfully lead the Lord's flock must pull together all their strength with greater and more urgent vigilance to combat the assaults of the Evil one.

This is particularly necessary in these dangerous times, which were declared in the words of the apostles, that many false prophets would come into the world and introduce sects of error and damnation, and by their various and foreign doctrines might seduce Christ's faithful people if our Holy Mother Church did not struggle to defeat these erroneous inventions with the support of strong doctrines and canonical sanctions.

Therefore, Joan, commonly called the Virgin, has been arraigned to account for many malicious crimes in matters of the faith, and she has been ordered to appear before us, your competent judges, namely Pierre, by divine mercy Bishop of Beauvais, and Brother Jean Le Maistre, especially appointed to officiate in this case by Jean Graverent, Inquisitor of Heretical Error in the kingdom of France.

Having seen and examined with diligence the procedure of Joan's trial and all that has occurred during the trial, principally the answers, admissions and affirmations which Joan made; and after having also considered the most notable decisions of the masters of the Faculties of Theology and Canon Law at the University of Paris, and that of the general assembly of the University; and of the clerics, doctors and men educated in theology and both canon and civil law, who gathered together in a great multitude in this town of Rouen and elsewhere for the deliberation and judgment of your statements, words and deeds; and having counsel and thorough deliberations with those zealots of the Christian faith; and having seen and weighed all there is to see and weigh in this matter, all that we and any man of judgment and law could and should observe; we, having the honor of the orthodox faith before our eyes so that our judgment may seem to emanate from the face of Our Lord, we state, rule and pronounce that Joan has gravely sinned by falsely simulating revelations and apparitions; by seducing others; by carelessly and impulsively believing; by pronouncing superstitious prophecies; by blaspheming God and His saints; by evading the law, the Holy Scripture, and the canonical sanctions; by despising God in His Sacraments; by provoking sedition; by apostasy; by falling into the crime of heresy; and by erring on many points in the Catholic faith.

After repeated charitable admonitions and by God's help, and after a long delay, you have returned into the bosom of Our Holy Mother Church with a contrite heart and without deception, as we would be pleased to believe; you have openly renounced your errors, upon which you were recently admonished in a public sermon, and you have with your own lips publicly abjured and renounced all heresy. According to the formula established by ecclesiastical sanctions, we therefore unbind you from the bonds of excommunication which enchained you, on the condition that you return to the Church with a true heart and a sincere faith, observing what is and shall be commanded by us.

But inasmuch as you have rashly sinned against God and the Holy Church, we finally and definitively, for your constructive penance, condemn you to perpetual imprisonment, with the bread of sorrow and water of affliction, so that you may cry over your faults and never from this day forward do anything to cause further weeping.

### JOAN ABANDONS MEN'S CLOTHES AND PUTS ON A WOMAN'S DRESS (MAY 24)

In the afternoon of the same day we went to Joan's prison cell with Brother Jean Le Maistre, the noble lords and masters Nicolas Midi, Nicolas Loyseleur, Thomas de Courcelles, Brother Isambard de La Pierre and several others. We, with our assessors, explained to Joan how God had on this day been most merciful to her, and how the clergy had shown her great mercy by receiving her into the grace and forgiveness of our Holy Mother Church; and how, therefore, it was right that she, Joan, should humbly submit to and obey the sentence and decree of the lord judges and ecclesiastics, and she should totally abandon her errors and her former fabrications, never to return to them; and how, if she did return to them, the Church would not receive her in clemency and she would be completely abandoned. Also, she was told she must stop wearing men's clothes and wear women's clothes, as the Church had commanded.

Joan replied that she would willingly wear women's clothes, and in all things she would obey and submit to the clergy. She was given a woman's dress, which she immediately put on after taking off the men's clothes; also, she desired and allowed her hair, which was cropped short around her ears, to be shaved off and removed.

### JOAN RESUMES WEARING MEN'S CLOTHES AND IS INTERVIEWED (MAY 28)

On the following Monday, the day after Holy Trinity Sunday, the judges went to Joan's prison cell to witness her appearance and disposition. We were accompanied by the lords and masters Nicolas de Venderes, William Haiton, Thomas de Courcelles, Brother Isambard de La Pierre, Jacques Le Camus, Nicolas Bertin, Julien Flosquet and John Grey.

Because Joan was wearing men's clothes, a short mantle, a cap, a man's close-fitting jacket and other garments used by men, we questioned her to find out when and for what reason she had resumed wearing men's clothes and rejected wearing women's clothes. Joan said that she had only recently resumed wearing men's clothes and rejected women's clothes.

Asked why she had resumed wearing men's clothes and who had compelled her to wear them, she answered that she had taken the men's clothes of her own will, under no compulsion, because she preferred men's clothes to women's clothes.

She was told that she had promised and sworn not to wear men's clothing again, but she answered that she never meant to take such an oath.

Asked for what reason she had resumed wearing men's clothes, she answered that it was more lawful and appropriate for her to wear men's clothes than women's clothes because she was among men. She said she had resumed wearing men's clothes because the promises made to her had not been kept, which were to allow her to go to Mass and receive her Savior in the Eucharist, and to take off her chains.

Asked whether she had not abjured and sworn in particular not to resume wearing men's clothes, she answered that she would rather die than be in chains, but if she were allowed to go to Mass, and if her chains were taken off and she were put in a women's prison, she would be good and obey the Church.

Because we, her judges, had heard from certain people that she had not yet cut herself off from her illusions and pretended revelations, which she had previously renounced, we asked her whether she had heard the Voices of St. Catherine and St. Margaret since Thursday. She answered yes.

Asked what they told her, she replied they told her that God had sent word to her through St. Catherine and St. Margaret of the great sorrow related to her disloyalty, by which she agreed to abjure and recant in order to save her life; that she had damned herself to save her life.

She said that before Thursday, St. Catherine and St. Margaret told her what to do and say, which she did. Also, her Voices told her, when she was on the scaffold or platform in front of the people, to answer the preacher boldly. Joan said he was a false preacher, and had accused her of many things she had not done. Joan said that if she declared God had not sent her, then she would damn herself, because, in truth, she was sent by God. She said that her Voices had since told her that she had done a great evil by declaring that what she had done was wrong. She said that what she had declared and recanted on Thursday was done only because she feared the fire.

Asked if she believed her Voices to be St. Catherine and St. Margaret, she replied, "Yes, and they come from God."

Asked to speak truthfully about the crown that had been discussed before, she answered, "In everything, I told you the truth about it in my trial, as well as I could."

When she was told that when she made her abjuration on the scaffold or platform before the judges and the people, she had admitted that she had falsely boasted that her Voices were St. Catherine and St. Margaret, she answered that she did not mean to do or say so.

Joan said that she did not deny, or intend to deny, her apparitions, that is, that they were St. Catherine and St. Margaret; she said that everything she said on the scaffold was due to her fear of the fire.

She said she would rather do her penance once and for all, that is, die, than endure any longer the suffering she experienced in her prison cell.

Joan said that whatever the judges made her deny, she had never done anything against God or the faith; furthermore, she said she did not understand what was in the formula of abjuration.

She said that she did not mean to recant or abjure anything, except at God's good pleasure.

She said if the judges wished, she would once again wear women's clothes, but regarding everything else, she would do nothing more.

After hearing these statements from Joan, we then left her to further discuss these matters according to law and reason.

### JUDGES DELIBERATE ON RELAPSE OF WEARING MEN'S CLOTHES (MAY 29)

The next day, Tuesday after Holy Trinity Sunday, May 29, the judges gathered together in the arch-episcopal chapel of Rouen to meet with doctors and other persons educated in theology as well as in canon and civil law.

In their presence, we, with the bishop established that we had, in unity with the counsel of the judges, produced a public admonition to be addressed to Joan on certain points that she was, in the opinion of the University of Paris, judged to have fallen short and erred, and that these were explained to her.

We urged Joan to reject these errors and return to the way of the truth. But because she in no way acquiesced, and as neither she nor the Promoter had anything further to say, we then pronounced the legal case concluded and ordered the parties to appear on the following Thursday to hear the reading of the sentence.

Then we reminded the judges about what happened on Thursday, how Joan, after hearing the solemn sermon and admonitions addressed to her, had recanted and abjured her errors, and with her own hand she signed the recantation and abjuration, as was documented; and how on Thursday after dinner, we, with the vicar of the Inquisitor and assessors, had charitably admonished Joan to persevere in her good intentions and keep herself from relapsing; and, obeying the orders of the Church, she had stopped wearing men's clothes and put on women's clothes.

But Joan, prompted by the devil, had again, in front of many witnesses, declared that the Voices and spirits which were accustomed to visiting her had again returned to her and told her many things; and that Joan had again rejected women's clothes in favor of men's clothes. When we were told about this, we visited Joan and examined her.

Then, in the presence of the lords and masters mentioned above, we ordered the confessions and statements made by Joan to be read aloud, specifically those statements that were made in front of us the previous day.

We then asked those present to provide their counsel and advice, and they provided their opinions as follows:

Master Nicolas de Venderes, licensed in canon law, arch-deacon of Eu, and Canon of the Cathedral of Rouen, said Joan should be considered a heretic, and when the sentence was to be pronounced she should be handed over to secular justice with a request to act toward her with gentleness.

The reverend father in Christ, Gilles, Doctor of Sacred Theology and Abbot of the monastery of St. Trinite de Fecamp, stated that Joan had relapsed. Nevertheless, he said it would be good to again read to Joan the formula she had recently heard, explain it to her, and preach the Word of God to her; then after that, the judges should declare her a heretic and abandon her to secular justice, praying that it act toward her with gentleness.

Master Pierre Pinchon, licensed in canon law, arch-deacon of Jouy, and Canon of the Churches of Paris and Rouen, thought that Joan had relapsed, but regarding what should happen next, he deferred to the masters of theology.

Master Guillaume Erart, Doctor of Sacred Theology, Sacristan and Canon of the Churches of Langres and of Laon, stated that Joan had relapsed and therefore should be abandoned to secular justice; regarding what should happen after that, he agreed with the opinion of Abbot Gilles.

Master Robert Ghillebert, Doctor of Sacred Theology and Dean of the Chapel of Our Lord the King, said he agreed with Master Guillaume Erart.

The reverend Father in Christ, Abbot of the monastery of St. Ouen of Rouen, agreed with the opinion of Abbot Gilles.

Master Jean de Chatillon, Doctor of Theology and Canon of the Church of Evreux, stated a similar opinion.

Master Guillaume Le Boucher, Doctor of Sacred Theology, declared that Joan had relapsed and should be condemned as a heretic; regarding what should happen next, he referred to the statement of Abbot Gilles.

The reverend Father Pierre, lord Prior of Longueville-Giffard and Doctor of Sacred Theology, stated that, if after the period of the passion this woman confessed this point contained in the formula, he agreed with the judgment of Abbot Gilles.

Master William Haiton, Bachelor of Sacred Theology, considered that in view of the articles which had been read, Joan had relapsed and should be condemned as a heretic; regarding what should happen next, he referred to the statement of Abbot Gilles.

Master Andre Marguerie, licensed in civil law, Bachelor of Canon Law, archdeacon of Petit-Caux and Canon of Rouen; Master Jean Alespee, licensed in civil law and Canon of Rouen; and Master Jean Garin, Doctor of Canon Law and Canon of the Church of Rouen, all gave opinions that agreed with the statement of Abbot Gilles.

Master Denis Gastinel, licensed in canon and civil law, and Canon of the Churches of Paris and Rouen, declared that Joan was a relapsed heretic and should be abandoned to the secular authority, with no prayer for mercy.

Master Pasquier de Vaulx, Doctor of Canon Law and Canon of the Churches of Paris and Rouen, agreed with the opinion of Abbot Gilles.

Master Pierre Houdenc, Doctor of Sacred Theology, stated that, based on Joan's behavior and the decisions she made, she had always been a heretic and was, in fact, relapsed, and therefore she should be abandoned to the violence of secular justice in line with the decision of Abbot Gilles.

Master Jean de Nibat, Doctor of Sacred Theology, said Joan had relapsed, was unrepentant, and should be viewed as a heretic, and that this is also the opinion of Abbot Gilles, who has been so frequently mentioned.

Master Jean Le Fevre, Doctor of Sacred Theology, declared Joan to be obstinate and willfully disobedient to authority, and with regard to what should be done next, he referred to the decision of Abbot Gilles.

The reverend Father in Christ, Guillaume, Abbot of Mortemer and Doctor of Sacred Theology, held to the opinion of Abbot Gilles.

Master Jacques Guesdon, Doctor of Theology, agreed with the opinion of Abbot Gilles.

Master Nicolas Couppequesne, Bachelor of Sacred Theology and Canon of the Cathedral of Rouen, agreed with the opinion of Abbot Gilles.

Master Guillaume du Desert, Canon of the Church of Rouen, gave an opinion in agreement with Abbot Gilles.

Master Pierre Maurice, Doctor of Sacred Theology and Canon of Rouen, considered that Joan should be evaluated and judged to be a relapsed heretic, and he agreed with the decision of Abbot Gilles.

Master Guillaume de Baudribosc, Bachelor of Sacred Theology; Master Nicolas Caval, licensed in civil law; Master Nicolas Loyseleur, Master of Arts; and Master Guillaume Desjardins, Doctor of Medicine and Canon of the Church of Rouen, all agreed with the opinion of Abbot Gilles.

Master Jean Tiphaine, Doctor of Medicine; Master Guillaume de Livet, licensed in civil law; Master Geoffrey du Crotay and Master Pierre Carel, individuals licensed in civil law, all gave opinions that agreed with the decision of Abbot Gilles.

Master Jean Le Doulx, licensed in canon and civil law; Master Jean Colombel, licensed in canon law; Master Aubert Morel, licensed in canon law; Brother Martin Ladvenu of the Order of Preaching Brothers; Master Richard de Grouchet, Bachelor of Theology; Master Jean Pigache, Bachelor of Theology; and Master Guillaume de La Chambre, licensed in medicine, all gave opinions in accordance with that of Abbot Gilles.

Master Thomas de Courcelles, Bachelor of Theology, Canon of the Churches of Therouanne and of Laon, and Brother Isambard de La Pierre of the Order of Preaching Brothers, gave opinions in alignment with the decision of Abbot Gilles, who has so frequently been mentioned; they added that Joan should once more be charitably admonished for the salvation of her soul and be told that she had no further hope of remaining alive in this world.

Master Jean Maugier, licensed in canon law and Canon of the Church of Rouen, agreed with the opinion of Abbot Gilles.

Finally, when we had heard the opinions of everyone, we thanked those present and concluded that Joan, according to law and reason, should be treated as a relapsed heretic.

Tomorrow, Joan was to be summoned to appear before us to hear the lawful sentence pronounced by the usher appointed to this legal case; further details explaining the sentence would be contained in our letters and read tomorrow by the usher.

The following declaration was given in the chapel of the arch-episcopal manor of Rouen, on Tuesday, May 29, in the year of Our Lord, 1431:

Pierre, by divine mercy Bishop of Beauvais, and Jean Le Maistre, Vicar of the distinguished Doctor Jean Graverent, appointed by the apostolic Holy See as Inquisitor of the Faith and Heretical Error within the kingdom of France; to all public priests, rectors of churches established in this town of Rouen or elsewhere in this diocese, to each and every one, greetings in the name of Our Lord.

For specific causes and reasons more completely documented elsewhere, a certain woman, commonly called Joan the Virgin, has relapsed into many errors against the orthodox faith after a public abjuration of those errors in the presence of the Church; she has fallen into error again, which has been sufficiently proven by her statements, assertions and behavior.

Therefore, we explicitly command and order each of you who is required, without waiting or excusing yourself because of something or someone, to appear in person with us at eight o'clock tomorrow morning in the Old Market Place of Rouen to summon Joan; the order is to hear us declare Joan to be relapsed, excommunicated, and a heretic, along with the customary warnings that are given in such cases.

Signed: Guillaume Manchon; Guillaume Boisguillaume

### JOAN IS BURNED AT THE STAKE IN THE OLD MARKET PLACE OF ROUEN (MAY 30)

The following statement was given on this Wednesday, at seven o'clock in the morning, in the year of Our Lord, 1431:

To the reverend father and lord in Christ, the lord Pierre, by divine mercy Bishop of Beauvais, and to Brother Jean Le Maistre, Vicar of the distinguished Doctor Jean Graverent, appointed by the apostolic Holy See as Inquisitor of the Faith and Heretical Error in the kingdom of France.

With all due reverence, obedience and respect, I, your humble priest, Jean Massieu, dean of the Christendom of Rouen, inform your reverend fathers that according to your mandate addressed to me, to which these letters are attached, I have summoned this woman, commonly called the Virgin, to appear before you this Wednesday after Holy Trinity Sunday at eight o'clock in the morning at the Old Market Place of Rouen, according to the procedure and content of your mandate and instructions.

By these letters signed with my seal, I signify to your reverend fathers that I have done these things that you have requested.

Afterwards, toward nine o'clock in the morning of the same day, the judges went to the Old Market of Rouen, which is near the church of St. Sauveur, in the presence of, and assisted by, the reverend fathers in Christ the lord

Bishops of Therouanne and of Noyon, Masters Jean de Chatillon, Andre Marguerie, Nicolas de Venderes, Raoul Roussel, Denis Gastinel, Guillaume Le Boucher, Jean Alespee, Pierre Houdenc, William Haiton, the superior of Longueville, Pierre Maurice, and many other lords, masters and clergy.

Joan was led before us in view of a great multitude of people gathered in this place, and she was placed upon a scaffold or platform. For her constructive admonition and for the edification of all the people gathered here, a solemn sermon was delivered by the distinguished Doctor of Theology, Master Nicolas Midi. For his text he took the words of the Apostle in the twelfth chapter of the first epistle to the Corinthians, "Where one member suffers, all the members suffer with it."

When this sermon was over, we once more admonished Joan to seek the salvation of her soul, to reflect on her errors, and to repent and show true contrition for her errors. We urged her to believe the counsel of the clergy and of the notable people who had instructed and taught her about many things concerning her salvation, especially the words of the two venerable Preaching Brothers who were then standing near her, and whom we had appointed to instruct her continuously and zealously in order to address her with constructive admonitions and valuable advice.

Then the Bishop and Vicar stated what had occurred; that it was clear that Joan, in her obstinate foolishness, never truly abandoned her errors and horrible crimes; but instead she had shown herself infinitely more damnable by the diabolical nature and malice of her false imitation of contrition, penitence and correction; by falsely using God's holy name; and by the blasphemy of His saints. By doing so, she has declared herself to be obstinate, incorrigible, a heretic, relapsed in heresy, completely unworthy of grace, and altogether unworthy of the communion that we had mercifully offered to her in our previous sentence.

In view of everything that has been considered in this matter, and after thorough deliberations and counsel with many educated people, we proceeded to the final sentence in these terms:

In the name of the Lord, amen. Whenever the poisonous virus of heresy obstinately attaches itself to a member of the Church and transforms him into a limb of Satan, very diligent care must be taken to prevent the filthy contamination of this wicked leprosy from spreading to other members of the Mystical Body of Christ. The decrees of the holy fathers have mandated that hardened heretics must be separated from the midst of the just, rather than permit these malicious vipers to lodge themselves in the bosom of Our Holy Mother Church, which then puts other members of the Church in great danger.

Therefore, we, Pierre, by divine mercy Bishop of Beauvais, and Brother Jean Le Maistre, Vicar of the distinguished Doctor Jean Graverent, the Inquisitor of heretical Error and especially appointed by him in this case, both competent judges in this trial, have declared by an objective judgment that you, Joan, commonly called the Virgin, have fallen into many errors and crimes of schism, idolatry, invocation of demons and many other misdeeds.

But the Church never closes her bosom to the wanderer who returns. We thought that with a pure spirit and genuine faith you had cut yourself off from these errors and crimes, because on a specific day you renounced them, you swore in public, and you vowed and promised never to return to these errors or heresy under any inspiration or in any manner whatsoever. You chose to remain inextricably within the unity of the Catholic Church and the communion of the Roman Pontiff, and this was indicated in great detail by the formula you signed with your own hand.

However, subsequently, after this abjuration of your errors, the author of schism and heresy has arisen in your heart, he has seduced you and you have fallen again. How sorrowful! You have returned to these errors and crimes just like a dog that returns to his vomit, and this is sufficiently and completely clear by your willing confessions and statements. We have concluded in our most distinguished deliberations that your previous denial of these errors and fabrications was simply speech and not heartfelt.

Therefore, we declare that you have fallen again into your former errors, and under the sentence of excommunication which you originally incurred, we now decree that you are a relapsed heretic. By this sentence, which we deliver in writing and pronounce at this tribunal, we denounce you as a rotten member, and so that you will not infect other members of Christ, we must cast you out of the unity of the Church, cut you off from the body of the Church, and we must hand you over to the secular powers for judgment and penalty; we cast you off, separate you, and abandon you, praying that this same secular power, prior to your death and mutilation of your body, will moderate its judgment toward you: if true signs of repentance appear in you, that they may permit you to receive the Sacrament of Penance prior to your death.

Attestations by the notaries appointed in this trial:

I, Guillaume Colles, otherwise called Boisguillaume, Priest of the Diocese of Rouen, by apostolic authority a sworn notary in the arch-episcopal court of Rouen and in this trial, I attest that the documentation of this trial has been correctly made with the original minutes, and therefore I have signed this copy of the proceedings with my seal at the bottom of each document; in witness of this, I have signed with my own hand, followed by the two other notaries.

Signed: Guillaume Boisguillaume

And I, Guillaume Manchon, Priest of the Diocese of Rouen, apostolic notary by imperial and pontifical authority, and sworn notary of the arch-episcopal court of Rouen, and with others in this process, I confirm that I was present with the other notaries during the documentation of this trial and that the documentation was correctly made with the original register of the trial. I have transcribed the trial with my own hand and therefore, with the other notaries, I have affixed my signature as I was required.

Signed: Guillaume Manchon

And I, Nicolas Taquel, Priest of the Diocese of Rouen, notary public by apostolic authority, sworn notary of the arch-episcopal court of Rouen and called to participate in this process, I attest that, with the other notaries, I heard and saw the documentation of these proceedings with the original register of the trial, and that the documentation has been properly made. With the other notaries, I have transcribed this trial with my own hand and therefore I have affixed my signature as I was required.

Signed: Nicolas Taquel

Attached are the seals of the Bishop of Beauvais and the Inquisitor.

# Epilogue

By February 1450, about twenty years after Joan's death, Guillaume Bouille, an advisor to King Charles VII and dean of the Faculty of Theology at the University of Paris, began conducting a formal inquiry into her trial. Both men recognized that because Joan had been condemned as a heretic and sorceress, her reputation was not only a potential source of dishonor for the king, but could create problems for his monarchy. Joan had not only played a decisive role in securing the victory of France over England, but she was also directly responsible for the king's coronation and consecration in 1429 at the Reims Cathedral.

Investigations into what occurred during Joan's trial initially began with depositions taken in 1450, which were followed by two sets of depositions taken in 1452. Then, in 1455 and 1456, over one hundred people provided testimony in the Rehabilitation Trial (or Nullification Trial) of Joan of Arc.

On March 5, 1450, Bouille interviewed one of the Dominican judges in Joan's Condemnation Trial, Isambard de La Pierre. A notary made a record of his statement, which included the following:

After Joan had made her abjuration and resumed wearing men's clothes, he and several others were present when she defended herself for having returned to wearing men's clothes, stating and affirming that the English guards had committed, or enabled to be committed, much wrongdoing and [sexual] outrage against her in prison when she was wearing women's clothes; also, he saw Joan crying, her face covered in tears, contorted and distressed in such a manner that he felt pity and compassion for her. He said that in front of all those who were present, when Joan was labeled an obstinate and relapsed heretic, she stated, "If you, my lords of the Church, had brought me to, and had kept me in your own prisons [Church prison facilities that employed nuns as guards for women prisoners], perhaps it would not be this way for me." Furthermore, he states and testifies that, after the end of this session with Joan, the Bishop of Beauvais then remarked to the Englishmen who were waiting outside, "Farewell, be of good cheer, it is done!" [1]

Also on March 5, 1450, Bouille interviewed Jean Massieu, who served as one of the bailiffs during the trial:

On that day [of Joan's abjuration], after dinner, in the presence of the ecclesiastical council, she gave up the men's clothes and put on women's clothes, as she had been ordered to do; it was then Thursday or Friday after Pentecost, and the men's clothing was put into a sack and placed in the same room where she had been held as a prisoner. She remained under guard in that location under the custody of five Englishmen, three of whom stayed inside the room during the night and two of them stayed outside. ... Then, when the following Sunday morning came, which was Trinity Sunday, and she had to get out of bed, she said to the Englishmen, her guards, "Unchain me, so I can get up." Then one of these Englishmen took away the women's clothing she had and they emptied the sack that contained the men's clothing, and they tossed this clothing upon her while saying to her, "Get up." Then they put away the women's clothing in the same sack, and as she put on the men's clothes they had given to her, she said, "Sirs, you know that this is forbidden for me, and without fail, I will not accept it." But they would not give her anything else to wear, and she continued arguing with them until the noon hour, and finally, because she was compelled by necessity of the body to leave the room, she wore this clothing. After she returned to her cell, the guards would still not give her anything else to wear, regardless of any appeal or request that she made of them. [2]

On May 2, 1452, Jean Bréhal, who was the Inquisitor-General of France from 1452 until 1474, interviewed the primary notary at the trial, Guillaume Manchon, who stated that Joan was:

Dressed in men's clothes and was complaining that she could not give it up out of fear that during the night her guards would inflict some [sexual] outrage upon her; and she had complained once or twice to the Bishop of Beauvais, the Vice-Inquisitor and Master Nicholas Loyseleur that one of the guards tried to violate her. [3]

The Rehabilitation Trial officially opened at Notre Dame Cathedral in Paris on November 7, 1455, when Joan's mother, Isabelle, accompanied by officials from the city of Orleans, arrived at the Cathedral with a document that contained a mandate from Pope Callixtus III, which Isabelle read aloud. The document detailed the fundamental legal errors of Joan's trial, including falsifying evidence used against her by embellishing it, charging her with crimes the judges knew that she did not commit, using deceptive tactics in attempts to mislead her into making statements deemed to be heretical, not providing adequate defense counsel, and using tactics of harassment and violence in the pursuit to condemn her.

On December 20, 1455, the new trial's promoter issued a declaration to call witnesses under threat of contempt of court if they did not appear. The witnesses included soldiers who fought under Joan's leadership, citizens from Orleans who were acquainted with Joan after she ended the siege of the city, childhood friends and family members from Domremy, as well as individuals who were present during the Condemnation Trial.

Jean Moreau, Joan's godfather, was present at her baptism and knew Joan throughout her childhood. He testified on May 10, 1456, and provided detailed accounts of Joan's life in Domremy. Joan's childhood friend, "Little Mengette," also testified during the Rehabilitation Trial about events that occurred during Joan's early childhood. Moreau's testimony included a report that described what he witnessed while in the crowd on May 24, 1431, near the scaffold where the preacher Guillaume Erart was delivering his admonishing sermon to Joan. Moreau stated that during Erart's sermon, Joan responded to him, saying:

[She] began wearing men's clothes because she had to live among soldiers, and among whom it was safer and more appropriate for her to be in men's clothes rather than women's clothes, and that what she was doing, and had done, she had done properly. [4]

Manchon testified on May 12, 1456, saying:

[I] heard Joan complain to the Bishop and Earl of Warwick, when she was asked why she wasn't wearing women's clothes, and they said it wasn't proper for a woman to wear men's clothes, and that she wore stockings firmly tied together with many cords; Joan said that she didn't dare give up the stockings nor keep them not firmly tied up because they, the Bishop and Earl, knew very well, as they themselves had said, that her guards had attempted to rape her a number of times, and that on one occasion when she had cried out, the Earl himself came to her assistance at the sound of her cries, and if he hadn't arrived the guards would have raped her, and she complained about this. [5]

Also on May 12, 1456, Manchon recalled the interview with Joan on May 28, 1431, regarding why she resumed wearing men's clothes after the first sentence:

She was asked why she had resumed wearing men's clothes, and Joan replied that she had done it for the protection of her virginity, because she did not feel safe while wearing female clothing with her guards present, who had tried to rape her, and which she had complained about many times to the Bishop and Earl; and that the judges had promised her that she would be placed in the custody of nuns in the Church's prisons, that she would have a woman with her, also saying that if the judges would be pleased to place her in such a safe location where she would not be afraid, then she was prepared to resume wearing women's clothes. [6]

After his initial testimony six years earlier, Massieu was again interviewed on May 12, 1456, and he stated:

When Joan was accused of having relapsed, she replied that, as she was lying in bed, her guards removed the women's clothing from the bed in which she was lying, and they gave her the men's clothes; and although she asked the guards to return the women's clothing so that she could leave her bed to go relieve herself, they refused to give it back to her, saying that she would not receive anything to wear but the men's clothes. She said the guards knew perfectly well that the judges had prohibited her from wearing this clothing, but they nevertheless refused to give her the women's clothing they had taken; finally, induced by bodily necessity, she put on the men's clothes; nor was she able to obtain any other clothing from the guards during all the rest of the day, and so she was then seen in these men's clothes by many people. [7]

On the day of Joan's death, Martin Ladvenu, a Dominican friar, heard Joan in the sacrament of Confession and administered the sacrament of the Eucharist to her. Ladvenu testified on May 13, 1456, he "heard from Joan that a certain high-ranking English lord visited her in prison and attempted to violate her by force" and "this was the reason she had resumed wearing men's clothing after the first sentence." [8]

The final verdict of the Rehabilitation Trial was pronounced on July 7, 1456. Among other statements that were included in the official verdict is the following: "We, in session of our court and having only God before our eyes, say, pronounce, decree and declare that the [Condemnation] trial and sentence were tainted with fraud, slander, injustice, contradictions and many obvious errors involving facts and laws, including the abjuration, the execution and all their consequences; the trial is ruled to be null, invalid, worthless, without effect and annihilated."

The entire final ruling was read aloud, and then one of the five original handwritten copies of the trial transcripts was ceremoniously torn up. Celebrations were held throughout all of France, but particularly in Orleans, where Joan's victory, which ended the siege of the city, proved to be the turning point in the Hundred Years War.

Documentation about Joan's military achievements during the Hundred Years War and the transcripts of her trials provide an extraordinary level of detail about her life, particularly for a historical figure of the fifteenth century. Various and sometimes opposing conclusions about Joan's gender identity, sexual orientation, and the origin of her Voices can be reached based on the available information. Also, in literature and film, Joan of Arc is often depicted as a Christ-figure due to parallels involving her life, suffering, and execution, however, imagery from her trial transcripts clearly presents Joan the Maid (the Virgin) as an icon of the Blessed Virgin Mary.

## Joan of Arc: Transgender?

Many Catholics, including those in the hierarchy of the Church, believe that becoming a transgender person is a *sin against nature* because they believe inherited chromosomes are the only biological variables at work in determining or influencing gender identity. Scientific evidence increasingly gives credibility to the notion that *not* becoming a transgender person may, in fact, be the sin against nature. Concepts regarding the difference between sex (female and male) and gender identity (a person's perception of whether they are female or male—or neither or both) have evolved over the last thirty years. A predisposition for gender identity may be initially encoded in inherited DNA at the moment of conception, but other factors, including acquired memories and epigenetic processes, can influence a person's perception of their identity. Epigenetic processes involve variances in gene expressions that occur over the course of life. The inherited DNA—females have XX chromosomes and males have XY chromosomes—does not change, but the genes contained in inherited DNA may be variably expressed or activated due to external factors that include a person's inter-action with the environment as well as the processes of biological matu-ration, such as when specific hormones are released into the bloodstream during puberty.

An individual's genome is their complete set of DNA molecules, which contain the instructions needed to assemble all of the other molecules that make each member of the species unique. The individual's epigenome (the word is derived from Greek, meaning "above the genome") includes the non-DNA molecules that can provide instructions to the genome regarding what molecules to make, where in the body to make them, and when to make them. Epigenetic factors can cause specific genes to be expressed, not expressed or partially expressed. These epigenetic factors, triggered by envi-ronmental events, act as instructions that add markers on the genome (but are not part of the DNA itself) and can be replicated from cell to cell as cells divide over time. These molecular markers, added onto the DNA, can be passed from parents to offspring. [9]

The variables that influence biological development and maturation are typically grouped into two categories: heredity and environment, but with advancements in the study of epigenetics, it's clear that heredity and the environment interact in ways that we have only recently begun to under-stand. Whether gender identity and sexual orientation are derived from an individual's genome, epigenome, learning processes, or some combination of those three factors remains to be resolved.

Becoming a transgender person can involve one or more of three basic processes: identifying with the opposite sex and expressing behavior that is typical for that sex within society; taking hormones or hormone suppressing pharmaceuticals to augment the physiological characteristics of the oppo-site sex; or undergoing gender reassignment surgery.

Opinions about the gender identity and sexual orientation of Joan of Arc have been conveyed in theater, film, and literature. Excerpts from Joan's Rehabilitation Trial, such as those included above, have been used as a type of defense against claims that Joan was a transgender person. However, by examining the evidence that comes out of the transcripts in their entirety, one can draw the conclusion that Joan was a transgender person.

Gender dysphoria, also referred to as gender identity disorder, is a diagnosis used by physicians and psychologists to classify individuals who experience difficulties in life because their sex (female or male) is perceived to be misaligned with the way they desire to express themselves; the desire is motivated by the dysphoria, as opposed to the desire being motivated by peer pressure, other social pressures, or merely a decision to experiment. The term dysphoria is derived from a Greek word meaning "difficult to bear" or "unpleasant to experience," and the difficulty or unpleasantness can be categorized across a range from mild to intense anxiety or depression; it is the opposite of euphoria, which comes from the Greek word meaning "pleasant to experience" and which includes states that can range from mild to intense joy or elation.

Many of Joan's statements during her trial reveal an extreme level of reluctance to give up wearing men's clothes, even temporarily, so that she could attend Mass and receive Holy Communion. If her sole reason for wearing men's clothes was to help protect herself from sexual abuse at the hands of her English jailers, she would have no reason to refuse women's clothes for the purpose of going to Mass, especially considering how important Mass was for Joan, who on one occasion went to Mass three times in one day at the church of Saint Catherine de Fierbois. The transcripts of March 25 include the following:

> We told Joan that she had asked us several times, especially yesterday, due to the solemnity of these past days and of this time, if it would be permitted for her to attend Mass on Palm Sunday. That is why we asked her, if we gave her permission, whether she would abandon wearing men's clothes and put on women's clothes, as she used to do in the area of her birthplace and as the women there were usually clothed.

> Joan replied by asking us if she could attend Mass wearing men's clothes, as she was currently dressed, and if she could receive the Eucharist on Easter Sunday. So we told her that if she were to respond to our request, that is, to abandon men's clothes, permission would be given. But she replied that she did not have counsel on this matter from her Voices and therefore could not yet wear women's clothes.

Then we asked her if she would get advice from her saints regarding wearing women's clothes. She replied that it might well be permitted for her to attend Mass as she is currently dressed, which she truly desired, but with regard to changing from men's clothes to women's clothes, she could not do it and it was not in her. After the court officials had urged her, according to all the goodness and piety which she seemed to have, to wear clothes appropriate for her sex, Joan answered that it was not in her to do it; but if it was to be, it would be done soon. Then we told her to speak with her Voices to find out if she could once again wear women's clothes to receive the Eucharist at Easter. Joan replied that as far as it was in her ability, she could not receive the Eucharist by changing her clothes for women's clothes. She asked to be permitted to attend Mass in her men's clothes, adding that this attire did not burden her soul, and that wearing these clothes was not against the Church. [10]

Concerns about the accuracy of the Condemnation Trial transcripts—whether they truthfully recorded Joan's statements during the trial—were addressed by several participants during the Rehabilitation Trial who were also present during the Condemnation Trial, including the principal notary, Manchon. Witnesses who were present at both proceedings testified that the transcripts of Joan's comments were accurately recorded. Manchon's testimony during the Rehabilitation proceedings included the following:

At the beginning of the case, during the five or six days when I was writing down the Maid's answers and excuses, the judges tried to compel me to alter my words in translating them into Latin, thereby changing the meaning of her statements into something different from my understanding of them. And two men, acting under my lord of Beauvais instructions, were placed in a window near the judges seats; and there was a serge curtain in front of that window so that they should not be seen. These men wrote down and reported everything that incriminated Joan and nothing that excused her. And I believe that it was Loiseleur [who was concealed there]. And after the session, when a comparison was made with what these two had written, their account was quite different from ours and contained none of Joan's defense. My lord of Beauvais was greatly annoyed with me about this. And where

the word Nota appears in the reports of the case, that was where there were differences of opinion, and where fresh questionings were necessary; and they found that what I had written was true.
(11)

The language used by Joan regarding wearing men's clothes reinforces a belief that she experienced dysphoria regarding wearing women's clothes. Within the approximately 300-word passage referenced above, at least five excerpts appear to indicate dysphoria: 1) she "truly desired" to attend Mass wearing men's clothes even though social norms for women in the 1400s would have added considerable pressure on her to conform; 2) regarding wearing women's clothes she said "she could not do it;" 3) it was not "in her" to wear women's clothes; 4) she indicated that "as far as it was in her ability, she could not receive the Eucharist by changing her clothes for women's clothes;" and 5) she said wearing men's clothes "did not burden her soul," implying that perhaps wearing women's clothes did burden her soul.

For readers interested in the source material for this 300-word passage, the following text shows the original Latin transcripts, which were copied by Quicherat from the handwritten originals and published in 1841 under the title, *Procès de Condamnation et de Réhabilitation de Jeanne d'Arc,* and the French translation by Pierre Champion, which is in *Procès de Condamnation de Jeanne d'Arc, Texte, Traduction et Notes,* published in 1921.

Latin:

Ad quod dicta Johanna respondit requirendo quod permitteretur audire missam in habitu virili in quo erat, et quod etiam posset percipere sacramentum Eucharistiæ in festo Paschæ. Tunc eidem diximus quod ad petitum responderet, videlicet an vellet dimittere habitum virilem, si hoc sibi concederetur. Ipsa vero respondit quod de hoc non erat consulta, nec poterat adhuc recipere dictum habitum. Et nos ei diximus an vellet habere consilium cum Sanctis, utrum reciperet habitum muliebrem. Ad quod respondit quod permitti poterat in hoc statu missam audire, quod summe optabat; sed habitum mutare non poterat, nec etiam hoc erat in ipsa. Postmodum, dicti magistri exhortati sunt eam quod, pro tanto bono et devotione quem videbatur gerere, quod vellet capere habitum suo sexui congruentem. Quæ Johanna iterum respondit quod in ipsa non erat hoc facere; et, si in ipsa esset, hoc esset bene cito factum. Fuit autem sibi dictum quod loqueretur cum vocibus suis ad sciendum si resumeret habitum muliebrem, ut in Pascha posset percipere viaticum. Ad quod respondit dicta Johanna quod, quantum est de ipsa, non perciperet ipsum viaticum, mutando habitum suum in muliebrem; rogabatque quod permitteretur audire missam in habitu virili, dicens quod ille habitus non onerabat animam suam, et quod ipsum portare non erat contra Ecclesiam. [12]

French:

Et nous dîmes à ladite Jeanne que plusieurs fois, particulièrement hier, elle nous avait demandé qu'à cause de la solennité de ces jours et de ce temps il lui fût permis d'ouïr la messe, ce dimanche de la fête des Rameaux; c'est pourquoi nous lui avons demandé, si nous lui accordions cela, si elle voulait abandonner l'habit d'homme et recevoir l'habit de femme, ainsi qu'elle avait accoutumé au pays de sa naissance, et comme les femmes de son pays ont coutume de le porter. A quoi Jeanne répondit, nous requérant qu'il lui soit permis d'ouïr la messe dans cet habit d'homme où elle était, et qu'elle pût recevoir le sacrement d'eucharistie à la fête de Pâques. Or nous lui dîmes qu'elle répondît à notre demande, savoir qu'elle voulut bien abandonner l'habit d'homme, si cela lui était accordé. Mais elle répondit qu'elle n'avait point conseil sur cela, et ne pouvait encore prendre ledit habit. Et nous lui demandâmes si elle voulait avoir conseil de ses saintes pour recevoir habit de femme. A quoi elle répondit qu'il pouvait bien lui être permis d'ouïr la messe en cet état, ce qu'elle désirait souverainement; mais, changer d'habit, elle ne le pouvait, et cela n'était pas en elle. Après que les dits maîtres l'eussent exhortée, pour tout le bien et dévotion qu'elle semblait avoir, à vouloir bien prendre habit convenable à son sexe, ladite Jeanne a répondu qu'il n'était pas en elle de le faire; et que si c'était en elle, ce serait aussitôt fait. Alors il lui fut dit qu'elle parlât avec ses voix pour savoir si elle pouvait reprendre l'habit de femme pour recevoir le viatique à Pâques. A quoi Jeanne répondit que, autant qu'il était en elle, elle ne recevrait pas ledit viatique en changeant son habit contre habit de femme; et elle demandait qu'il lui soit permis d'ouïr la messe en habit d'homme, disant en outre que cet habit ne chargeait point son âme, et que de le porter, ce n'était point contre l'Église. [13]

Coming to a conclusion regarding whether Joan or any other historical figure was a transgender person is problematic because the available facts can be interpreted in different ways. We wouldn't expect to have explicit statements by Joan that she found traditional femininity "difficult to bear" or "unpleasant to experience," but she made frequent statements at the trial that can be interpreted in that light, including the following accusation and response during the March 27 session of the Condemnation Trial:

Article 16: Joan, after her capture at the castle of Beaurevoir and at Arras, was repeatedly and charitably admonished by noble and distinguished persons of both sexes to stop wearing men's clothes and to wear clothes decently appropriate for her sex. This she absolutely refused, and still obstinately persists in her refusal to do, as well as the other duties appropriate for her sex; in all things she behaves more like a man than a woman.

Joan's Response: To this sixteenth article, Joan admits that she was admonished at Arras and Beaurevoir to wear women's clothes, and that she refused and still refuses to do so. As for the other womanly duties, she says there are enough other women to do them.

Joan also indicated during the March 12 interrogations that even under circumstances where she would not be at risk of sexual assault, she would not only continue to wear men's clothes, but by doing so, she would be setting a constructive example for French society:

Asked whether she thought she was doing something wrong when she wore men's clothes, she answered no; and even at this moment, if she were back with her own party, it seemed to her that it would be to the great good of France for her to do as she did before her capture.

Also, the following is from the March 17 session, when Joan indicated that she would continue to wear men's clothes even after she was released from prison:

She said she would put on women's clothes if we let her go [from prison]. So we asked her if wearing women's clothes under those circumstances would please God, since God commanded her to wear men's clothes. She answered that if we permitted her to go because she wore women's clothes, she would do so, but then would immediately put on men's clothes and do what our Lord asked her to do.

The issues that Joan faced regarding men's clothes stem primarily from the biblical text of Deuteronomy 22:5, which states, "A woman must not wear men's clothing, nor a man wear women's clothing, for the Lord your God detests anyone who does this."

During the Rehabilitation Trial, the judges interviewed witnesses who were present when Joan arrived at Chinon wearing men's clothes. She travelled to Chinon to see the king, and she was questioned extensively by specialists in theology over a three-week period in the nearby town of Poitiers. The written record of the Poitiers inquiry has never been recovered and may have been deliberately destroyed, but the documentation was referred to at the Condemnation Trial during the March 3 session:

We asked her, regarding the first time she spoke with the king, whether the king asked her if it was by revelation that she had changed her attire from wearing women's clothes to men's clothes. She replied, "I have answered this before; I do not recall whether I was asked this specific question, but my reply was written down at Poitiers." Asked whether officials of her own party who examined her—some over the course of a month and others over the course of three weeks—had questioned her about changing her attire from wearing women's clothes to men's clothes, she answered, "I do not recall, but they asked me where it was that I began to wear men's clothes and I told them it was at Vaucouleurs."

The following testimony was given at the Rehabilitation Trial by Brother Seguin de Seguin, a Dominican Professor of Theology who was also Dean of the Faculty of Theology at Poitiers:

I saw Joan for the first time at Poitiers. The king's council was assembled in the house of the Lady La Macée, and the Archbishop of Reims, then Chancellor of France, was there. I was summoned, as were Jean Lombart, Professor of Theology of the University of Paris; Maitre Guillaume le Maire, Canon of Poitiers and Bachelor in Theology; Maitre Guillaume Aymerie, Professor of Theology and of the Order of Saint Dominic; Brother Pierre Turrelure; Maître Jacques Maledon; and many others whose names I do not remember. The members of the king's council told us that we were summoned, in the king's name, to question Joan and to provide our opinions about her. We were sent to question her at the house of Maître Jean Rabateau, where she was lodging. We went there and interrogated her.

Among other questions, Maitre Jean Lombart asked her why she had come; the king wanted to know what had motivated her to come here to see him. She answered, in a grand manner, that "there had come to her, while she was pasturing the cows, a Voice, which told her that God had great compassion for the people of France, and that she must travel through France." On hearing this, she began to cry; the Voice then told her to go to Vaucouleurs, where she would find a Captain who would conduct her safely into France and to the king, and that she must not be afraid. She had done what the Voice had ordered her to do, and she was able to travel here to see the king without encountering any obstacles.

At this point, Guillaume Aymerie asked her this question: "You assert that a Voice has told you that God has willed to deliver the people of France from the catastrophe in which they are now in; but, if it is God's will to deliver them, then why is it necessary for you to have soldiers?" Joan replied, "In God's Name! The soldiers will fight, and God will give the victory." Maître Guillaume was pleased with this answer.

Then I, in my turn, asked Joan what dialect the Voice spoke. She replied, "A better one than yours." I speak the Limousin dialect.

I then asked her, "Do you believe in God?" She replied, "In truth, more than yourself!" I said, "But God wills that you should not be believed unless there appears some sign to prove that you should be believed, and so we will not advise the king to trust in you and to risk an army based only on your simple statements. She replied, "In God's Name! I have not come to Poitiers to show signs, but send me to Orleans, where I shall show you the signs by which I have been sent." She added, "Give me men in such numbers as may seem good, and I will go to Orleans."

Then she foretold to us—to me and to all the others who were with me—that the following four things would happen, and which afterwards did occur: first, that the English would be destroyed, the siege of Orleans would be raised, and the town delivered from the English; second, that the king would be crowned at Reims; third, that Paris would be restored to his dominion; and fourth, that the Duke of Orleans would be brought back from England. I who speak, I have in truth seen these four things accomplished.

We reported all this to the council of the king, and we were of the opinion that, considering the extreme necessity and the great peril of the town, the king might make use of her help and send her to Orleans.

Besides this, we inquired into her life and morals, and found that she was a good Christian, living as a Catholic, never idle. Also, so that her manner of living might be better known, women were placed with her who were commissioned to report to the council regarding her activities and behavior.

As for me, I believed she was sent from God because, at the time when she appeared, the king and all the French people with him had lost hope, and no one thought of anything else except to save himself. [14]

Based on this and other testimony from the Rehabilitation Trial, if there were any qualms about Joan wearing men's clothes, the issue was likely addressed using criteria set by Saint Thomas Aquinas in the *Summa Theologica* (Summary of Theology), which he wrote in the thirteenth century. In the *Summa,* Aquinas indicated that it was not sinful "for a woman to wear man's clothes, or vice versa... on account of some necessity, either in order to hide oneself from enemies, or through lack of other clothes, or for some similar motive." [15] Dressing for military combat certainly would be covered by this exemption, but dressing for Mass would not apply here. The March 15 Condemnation Trial transcripts convey Joan's emotional state regarding her clothes and her desire to attend Mass: "As urgently as she could, she implored us to allow her to attend Mass in the clothes she wore, without any change." Also, Joan's decision to wear her hair cut short above her ears and, as noted in the transcripts, "styled like a vain young man," reflects a behavior and choice that goes beyond any military necessities, particularly in light of her fondness for wearing luxurious clothing, a fact noted during her canonization process as indicative of a lack of interest in asceticism.

Scientific studies investigating the basis of gender dysphoria generally search for causes related to psychological as well as biological factors, including inherited genes, prenatal exposure to various hormones, and the development and plasticity of the brain over the course of life. A review of case report literature published in 2012 found evidence to support conclusions that genetic as well as non-genetic factors may contribute to the development of gender dysphoria. In an analysis of data on monozygotic (identical) twins and dizygotic (non-identical) twins, one study looked at 561 children, all under twelve years old, who visited a clinic in Canada between 1976 and 2011 and reported gender dysphoria, including twenty-five who were twins—there were no cases where both twins had gender dysphoria. Another study reviewed data on 147 people who went to a clinic in Serbia, including two who had non-identical twin siblings; neither of the two twin siblings had gender dysphoria. A third study looked at 450 people who were treated at a Belgian clinic between 1985 and 2011, including six who were twins—only one set of identical twins had gender dysphoria, and both were female-to-male transgender. When this data from the three clinics, which does not support a conclusion of genetic factors playing a role in gender dysphoria, was combined with data from seventeen case studies, the authors did find evidence that genetic factors were likely to be one factor among other, non-genetic factors in the development of gender dysphoria: of the identified twenty-three monozygotic female and male twins, nine (39.1%) experienced gender dysphoria while none of the twenty-one same-sex dizygotic female and male twins had gender dysphoria. [16]

Many people have difficulties understanding the biological differences between gender and sex until they're confronted with direct evidence, such as a case involving a transgender student at a Chicago-area high school:

> The mother wrote that she and her husband once believed that "simple anatomy" separated a boy from a girl. But she said that

after her [male] child called herself a girl at age 4 and wanted to wear girls' clothing, they questioned their understanding. [17]

Within the Catholic Church, there are divergent opinions about the contributions that lesbian, gay, bisexual, and transgender (LGBT) persons can make with regard to the spiritual growth of the Church. Many members of the Church feel either hopeful or dismayed by the outreach Pope Francis has expressed toward the LGBT community. However, the Pope often makes statements that can be interpreted in different ways. In an article for *The New York Times,* Laurie Goodstein wrote, "Pope Francis has been sending mixed messages about his position on homosexuality, gender and same-sex marriage in the more than two years since he was elected." [18] John Allen, who covers the Vatican for *Crux,* wrote, "Parsing the words of Pope Francis is a notoriously hazardous undertaking, as he tends sometimes to say things that seem almost deliberately open to multiple interpretations." [19] While those observations are true, there are unmistakable signals being sent by the Pope that veer radically from what could have been envisioned in the Church three years ago.

In one example, on December 8, 2014, the Pope telephoned Diego Neria Lejarraga, who was born a woman but at the age of forty-eight had gender reassignment surgery. Before the phone call, Neria had written a letter to the Pope describing the issues that confront transgender people, including Neria's experiences with fellow parishioners who had rejected him at his church in Plasencia, Spain. After the call, a priest at Neria's parish reportedly referred to Neria as "the devil's daughter." After that incident, the Pope then telephoned Neria again, this time on Christmas Eve, to invite him and his fiancée to a private meeting, which occurred January 2015, at Casa Santa Marta, the Vatican City guesthouse.

In a more public event in 2015, Pope Francis solemnly washed and kissed the foot of a transsexual, Isabel Lisboa, on Holy Thursday, when the Catholic Church commemorates the Last Supper of Christ, the day before his execution on Good Friday. One of the Church's official media platforms, the Vatican Television Center, prominently featured the Pope washing and kissing Lisboa's foot, as well as her reception of Holy Communion during the Mass, leading many to believe that the Church, in its official capacity, was attempting to send a message to the faithful about how the Church should openly welcome all Catholics and all people who want to embrace the faith. The reception of Holy Communion by Lisboa, conspicuously televised, added some weight to the notion that the Church may act assertively to change its relationship with the LGBT community.

The Holy Thursday foot-washing ceremony is a re-enactment of events recorded in Chapter 13 of the Gospel of John. Jesus washes the feet of his disciples to set an example of humility, saying, "You do not realize now what I am doing, but later you will understand." After washing the disciples' feet, Jesus said, "Do you understand what I have done for you? You call me 'Teacher' and 'Lord,' and rightly so, for that is what I am. But now that I, who am your Lord and Teacher, have washed your feet, you should also wash one another's feet. I have set this example so that you should do this as I have done for you." The Holy Thursday ceremony has been contentious for Pope Francis since 2013, when he included women in the ceremony, and again in 2014, when he included Muslims. The Church has liturgical rubrics, official rules, which state that only men (presumably only Christian men) can be selected to participate in the Holy Thursday foot-washing ceremony. In his role as the Church's chief legislator, the Pope is within his prerogative to implement changes in the liturgical rubrics, but these types of changes have not yet been codified, and so the recent Holy Thursday events have caused a minor uproar among conservatives.

Two key issues confronting the Catholic Church today involve its relationship with the LGBT community and whether divorced and remarried Catholics can receive Holy Communion. From a theological perspective, the two issues are related to the extent they both deal with the Church's application of its teaching about mortal sin and how such sins preclude people from worthily receiving Holy Communion. Being in a state of mortal sin implies that individuals, should they happen to die while in a state of mortal sin, would self-exclude themselves from heaven and condemn themselves to hell by deliberately rejecting God.

Issues involving the Church's relationship with the LGBT community, and whether divorced and remarried Catholics can receive Holy Communion were debated at the Synod of Bishops held October 4-25, 2015, in Vatican City. After those discussions, a formal document was published by the Synod. Pope Francis is reviewing the report and will publish his own document, probably an Apostolic Exhortation, which will present his thoughts and decisions. The 2015 meetings served as the conclusion to a process that began in 2014, during the Church's Third Extraordinary General Assembly of the Synod of Bishops, commonly known as the Synod on the Family, which was held in October of that year in Vatican City. A draft interim document issued

October 13, 2014, prior to the final document, attracted controversy, in part, because it included the following statement:

> Homosexuals have gifts and qualities to offer to the Christian community: are we capable of welcoming these people, guaranteeing to them a fraternal space in our communities? Often they wish to encounter a Church that offers them a welcoming home. Are our communities capable of providing that, accepting and valuing their sexual orientation, without compromising Catholic doctrine on the family and matrimony? [20]

Other parts of the draft interim report addressed the "positive aspects" of non-martial cohabitation and civil [non-Catholic] marriages—a stance that would indicate an evolution, some say revolution, in the Church's pastoral approaches, which are guidelines and rules for applying doctrine in the everyday lives of Catholics.

When the October 13 draft was released, the Catholic News Service, operated by the U.S. Conference of Catholic Bishops, published an article, *Family Synod Midterm Report: Welcome Gays, Nonmarital Unions.* The article leads with the following sentence: "In strikingly conciliatory language on situations contrary to Catholic teaching, an official midterm report from the Synod of Bishops on the family emphasized calls for greater acceptance and appreciation of divorced and remarried Catholics, cohabitating couples and homosexuals." [21]

When the final report was issued on October 18, references to cohabitating couples were not as materially revised as the language related to the "gifts and qualities" of homosexuals, which was replaced by a statement that "men and women with a homosexual tendency ought to be received with respect and sensitivity." [22] Since the 2014 Synod meetings, disagreements among factions of bishops have arisen because many people perceived discordance between the Church's doctrines and the type of "pastoral applications" being envisioned.

Archbishop Vincenzo Paglia, who is President of the Pontifical Council for the Family and responsible for the Church's World Meetings of Families, stated, "Clearly, what the Catholic Church is striving for is a new, more authentic flourishing of the family, and with it all of society," and the type of family envisioned by the Church is one where "the relationship between genders is reworked with full respect for masculinity and femininity." [23] Paglia made those comments at an event held in conjunction with the U.N.'s annual Day of the Family, where he also said that differences of opinion regarding families had become "unproductively ideological" and that "it is important to realize the family is not an ideology." Afterward, in an interview broadcast May 21, 2015, Paglia expanded on those comments in his non-native English:

> Everywhere you have some signs, in the sense, I think that we are to enlarge our vision, we have to be sure that the Pope really does, in order to push a new spring of families, in the sense we have to avoid some too-ideological perspectives; we have to increase in our pastoral attitude, because now is no time only to do some theological description. The Pope wants to push the Church and the believers to see the reality of families. We have to show the mercy of God for everyone, we need families, we need all families. You know, the doctrine can be enlarged, we can go deeply. John XXIII used to say, it's not the Gospel that changes, but us, we understand, but us understand better the Gospel; this has to be during the three weeks in the discussion among bishops. [24]

Paglia was referring to a fundamental position of the Catholic Church: the Gospel (Good News) of Jesus Christ does not change, but the Church, as an institution and within each member, can and should grow over time in understanding the Gospel. [25] The growth occurs by inspiration of the Holy Spirit.

Expressing greater openness toward homosexuals in the Church as well as allowing divorced and remarried Catholics to receive Holy Communion is viewed by many as being part of a plan to change doctrine merely so that it adapts to the culture, as opposed to being part of a plan to enlarge doctrine because the Church is growing in its understanding of the Gospel due to inspiration of the Holy Spirit. Others assert that the main issues are not about doctrine but only about the language used when giving pastoral or spiritual guidance; for example, some people say it does more harm than good to refer to the use of artificial contraception as an "intrinsically evil" practice, or to say that homosexual acts are "intrinsically disordered." Still others point out that the Synod meetings were also meant to address a much larger scope of issues. Other items on the agenda included the break-up of families due to migration, which occurs for a variety of reasons; refugees fleeing war-torn areas of the world; migrants needing to search for jobs outside of their home countries while leaving other family members behind; and victims of religious persecution in the Middle East and parts of Africa. Also in Africa, polygamy is common in many areas and presents a significant issue for the Church. If a man with three wives and nine children wants to enter the Church, how does that happen? If the man must choose one wife, then what happens to the other wives and children in terms of financial and emotional support, and what should be done if all of the family members want to enter the Church?

In the United States and Europe, the two issues of greatest importance involve the Church's relationship with the LGBT community and allowing Holy Communion for divorced and remarried Catholics. The issues are perceived differently by two fundamental factions within the Synod and across the Church. The general perception of one faction is represented by the views of Cardinal Gerhard Müller, who firmly believes Catholicism is headed down a dangerous path of accommodating pagan lifestyles. [26] The other faction's position is generally reflected by the views of Archbishop Heiner Koch, who is Chairman of the German Bishops' Commission for Marriage and Family. Koch supports initiatives to have the Church recognize same-sex unions and has said, "Any bond that strengthens and holds people is in my eyes good, that applies also to same-sex relationships." [26]

Müller leads an organization within the Church, the Congregation for the Doctrine of the Faith (CDF), which "examines new teachings and new opinions in whatever way they are spread, it promotes studies in this area, and... it condemns those teachings found to be contrary to the principles of the faith, after, however, having heard the view of the Bishops." [27] Also, Müller's viewpoint is supported by Cardinal Raymond Burke, who stated the 2014 Synod report was "a gravely flawed document and does not express adequately the teaching and discipline of the Church and, in some aspects, propagates doctrinal error and a false pastoral approach."

Koch, on the other hand, supports the views of Cardinal Walter Kasper, who is the foremost proponent of revising the Church's traditional annulment process to allow divorced and remarried Catholics to receive Holy Communion. Pope Francis, after reading Kasper's book, *Mercy,* in 2013, referred to Kasper as a "superb theologian" [28], although some sources translate the Italian as "clever theologian." [29] Regardless of which interpretation is correct, Pope Francis subsequently convened an Extraordinary Consistory on the Family in February 2014 and invited Kasper to give the keynote address, which lasted most of the morning. An afternoon session of Q&A and in-depth discussions followed, and later the Pope commented that Kasper gave "a beautiful and profound presentation." [30]

Both of the primary factions, conservative and progressive, point to comments made by Pope Francis as evidence that he is of the same mind on current issues; however, the Pope has consistently appointed reform-minded individuals to leadership positions in the Church, including appointing Koch as Archbishop of Berlin in June 2015. [31] In contrast, Burke indicated on October 18, the final day of the 2014 Synod, that the Pope had informed him he would no longer be the head of the Church's top court, the Apostolic Signatura. [32]

When changes in Church teaching are being discussed, conflicts can arise about what it means to have an orthodox perspective on possible changes. "Orthodox" here is not related to the Eastern Orthodox Church or Orthodox Judaism, but simply having an orthodox perspective on canon law, doctrine, and other matters. The word orthodox comes from a combination of two Greek words, *orthos*, meaning right, true, or straight, and *dokein*, meaning to think, or *doxa*, meaning opinion or belief. In the Catholic Church, maintaining orthodoxy does not mean resisting change; it means embracing change whenever the Church augments its teaching, regardless of whether the change is preferred by various individuals and factions in the Church. If Pope Francis enlarges the Church's teaching in a way that isn't aligned with Müller's current views, then Müller, to maintain orthodoxy, would be required to support the teachings of the Pope, who is head of the CDF as well as the Church.

After Ireland's May 2015 referendum that endorsed same-sex marriage, Kasper indicated the vote would raise the prominence of the issue at the 2015 Synod meetings, saying that previously "it was only a marginal topic, but now it becomes central." [33] Koch's support for Church recognition of same-sex unions also raises the issue of Holy Communion because Catholic homosexuals in same-sex relationships—as well as divorced and remarried Catholics and cohabiting heterosexual couples—are viewed as objectively living in a state of mortal sin.

Kasper is a distinguished theologian in the Church and has explained his views on Holy Communion in light of established teaching on mortal sin: even though the Church has the authority to classify sins objectively as mortal, the Church and no member within the Church—including the Pope—can ever make a judgment regarding whether any specific individual has indeed committed a mortal sin, even if that person engages in homosexual sex, has had multiple abortions, or habitually misses Mass on Sundays. Many people in the Church expressed dismay at Pope Francis when he said, "If someone is gay and he searches for the Lord and has good will, who am I to judge?" [34] But the Pope was merely affirming a fundamental truth of Catholic doctrine stated in the *Catechism of the Catholic Church*: "Although we can judge that an act is in itself a grave offense, we must entrust judgment of persons to the justice and mercy of God." [35] Deferring to God to make these judgments is required because even though a person may appear to be engaged in mortal sin objectively, the person's actual guilt, subjectively, may be much less (venial sin) or even perfectly sinless, because only the person engaging in the activity can know whether they are guilty of mortal sin. The following text from the *Catechism* summarizes the teaching on mortal sin (the italicized words are in the source material):

> For a *sin* to be *mortal*, three conditions must together be met: "Mortal sin is sin whose object is grave matter and which is also committed with full knowledge and deliberate consent." *Grave matter* is specified by the Ten Commandments, corresponding to the answer of Jesus to the rich young man: "Do not kill, Do not commit adultery, Do not steal, Do not bear false witness, Do not defraud, Honor your father and your mother." The gravity of sins is more or less great: murder is graver than theft. One must also take into account who is wronged: violence against parents is in itself graver than violence against a stranger. Mortal sin requires *full knowledge* and *complete consent.* It presupposes knowledge of the sinful character of the act, of its opposition to God's law. It also implies a consent sufficiently deliberate to be a personal choice. Feigned ignorance and hardness of heart do not diminish, but rather increase, the voluntary character of a sin. *Unintentional ignorance* can diminish or even remove the imputability of a grave offense. But no one is deemed to be ignorant of the principles of the moral law, which are written in the conscience of every man. The promptings of feelings and passions can also diminish the voluntary and free character of the offense, as can external pressures or pathological disorders. Sin committed through malice, by deliberate choice of evil, is the gravest. [36]

All three conditions—grave or serious matter, full knowledge, and complete consent—must be met for a person to be guilty of committing a mortal sin. This means a woman who is pressured into having an abortion by a boyfriend, husband, or anyone else, is not guilty of mortal sin because the coercion restricts the freedom to choose and is therefore not complete consent. A person's ability to make a free-will decision, which is required to meet the complete consent criterion, can be compromised, and as a result, guilt of mortal sin can be completely removed by factors such as mental illness, drug addiction or "the promptings of feelings and passions."

The Church is often viewed as over-emphasizing the serious nature of sexual sins and relatively de-emphasizing the equally serious nature of non-sexual sins such as greed, envy, and pride. That over-emphasis stems from the role that free-will (complete consent) plays in deciding to commit a sin: the experience of sexual lust more quickly leads to a loss of self-control and diminished free will, or freedom, to make a rational decision not to engage in sinful behavior.

The sin of pride does not attract as much attention as the sexual sins, but the sin of pride is universally recognized by Catholic theologians as the most serious of all sins. It involves placing oneself above God and includes judging people to be guilty of mortal sin even when those people are homosexuals in same-sex relationships, women who have had abortions, or divorced and remarried Catholics who have not had an annulment of their previous marriage.

Also, the requirement to have full knowledge of whether any particular action is a mortal sin establishes a standard of culpability that is higher than most people assume. Missing Mass on Sundays is objectively a mortal sin, yet less than twenty-five percent of adult Catholics in the United States attend Mass every week. [37] It is reasonable to assume that most of these individuals receive Holy Communion when they do go to Mass even though they have not been to Confession to receive absolution from sins that are objectively mortal. In this case, it is also reasonable to assume the majority of these Catholics are not guilty of mortal sin even though they deliberately choose to skip Mass without a valid reason *and* they have a purely intellectual level of knowledge that missing Mass is a mortal sin.

Evidence that a person has *full knowledge* of whether something is a mortal sin comes from the individual's conscience, which only that person is privy to. As a result, if there is any shadow of doubt in the individual's conscience regarding whether they have committed a mortal sin, then they cannot be guilty of a mortal sin because doubt implies having less than full knowledge; the exception to this involves "hardness of heart," which means the person's conscience is no longer receptive to being informed by the Holy Spirit about how to judge their own behavior, which is a definitive sign the person is in a persistent state of mortal sin unless mitigating factors, such as mental illness or drug addiction, are present.

Archbishop Blase Cupich of Chicago linked the issues of inviolability of a person's conscience with the reception of Holy Communion—not only for divorced and remarried Catholics, but also for homosexuals in same-sex relationships. Cupich, a reform-minded progressive, spoke about counseling Catholics in second, invalid marriages as well as same-sex couples, saying, "people come to a decision in good conscience... [and] the conscience is inviolable. And we have to respect that when they make decisions, and I've always done that." [38]

Although a person's outwardly observable behavior may be judged as objectively sinful, it is still only the subjective state, which is known only to God, which determines actual sinfulness. Any person who truly cares about doing good, avoiding evil, and searching for the truth is on the path of developing a properly formed conscience, even when that conscience is at odds with the official teaching of the Church. The key role of the individual person's conscience in Catholic life was clarified during the Second Vatican Council and addressed in the *Pastoral Constitution on the Church in the Modern World.* Commenting on that document and its teaching with regard to the individual's conscience, Joseph Ratzinger, who later became Pope Benedict XVI, stated:

> Over the pope as the expression of the binding claim of ecclesiastical authority there still stands one's own conscience, which must be obeyed before all else, if necessary even against the requirement of ecclesiastical authority. Conscience confronts with a supreme and ultimate tribunal, and one which in the last resort is beyond the claim of external social groups, even of the official church. [39]

Michael Lawler and Todd Salzman summarized Catholic teaching on conscience in the Jesuit magazine, *America,* and wrote:

> Thomas Aquinas, in his book of Sentences (IV, 38, 2, 4), established the authority and inviolability of conscience in words similar to Father Ratzinger's: "Anyone upon whom the ecclesiastical authorities, in ignorance of the true facts, impose a demand that offends against his clear conscience should perish in excommunication rather than violate his conscience." For any Catholic in search of truth, no stronger statement on the authority and inviolability of personal conscience could be found, but Aquinas goes further. He

insists that even the dictate of an erroneous conscience must be followed and that to act against such a dictate is immoral. [40]

A key theme in the life of Joan of Arc involves her insistence on obeying her conscience in the face of Church authorities who threatened her, even with torture and execution. Her persistent claim that God alone, not the Church, had final authority over her actions led George Bernard Shaw, author of the play, *Saint Joan,* to refer to Joan as one of the first Protestant martyrs. But Joan did submit to the authority of the Church, except with the caveat that she served God first if her conscience informed her to do so, as noted in Article 61 of the seventy accusations made against her:

> When asked if she believes she is subject to the Church on earth, namely Our Holy Father the Pope, to the cardinals, archbishops, bishops and other prelates of the Church, she answered yes, our Lord being served first. Asked whether her Voices requested her not to submit to the Church Militant on earth or its judgment, she said that she does not merely answer us by saying anything that comes to her mind, but she answers according to the Voices' instructions, and they do not forbid her to obey the Church, our Lord being served first.

Lawler and Salzman discuss two key approaches to the development of conscience: 1) conforming one's conscience to the Church's teaching even when personal experience or science appears to be at odds, and 2) the idea that Church doctrine is an aid to conscience development, and conscience is not only at the service of doctrine. The latter of those two positions is the only approach compatible with the historical and spiritual advancement of the Church and its doctrine, which develops over time.

John Henry Newman was the foremost intellectual leader of the Oxford Movement in the 1830s, which aimed to demonstrate that the Church of England was divinely founded—not as a Protestant denomination, but as a branch of the Church founded by Christ. Newman's studies of the Early Church led him to conclude that various Catholic doctrines opposed by Protestants were not corruptions or additions to divine revelation in sacred scripture, but were genuine developments of doctrine:

> According to Newman's theory, everything essential to the faith was present embryonically in the Gospel, but many elements,

even the fundamental doctrine of the Trinity, emerged only gradually. All such development had to be an organic growth from the original seed, harmonizing with previous expressions of the faith. [41]

Newman's research into the historical events of the Early Church and its development of doctrine led him to write, "To be deep in history is to cease to be a Protestant." [42] Echoing Newman's insight that authentic doctrine develops over time via inspiration of the Holy Spirit, as opposed to merely changing to adapt to the culture, Cardinal Reinhard Marx, president of the bishops' conference of Germany, stated:

[Doctrine] doesn't depend on the spirit of time but can develop over time. ... Saying that the doctrine will never change is a restrictive view of things. ... The core of the Catholic Church remains the Gospel, but have we discovered everything? This is what I doubt. ... We cannot say that since you are homosexual, you cannot experience the Gospel. This is impossible to me. [43]

Pope Francis voiced similar views in an interview published in *America* magazine:

In Buenos Aires I used to receive letters from homosexual persons who are "socially wounded" because they tell me that they feel like the Church has always condemned them. But the Church does not want to do this. During the return flight from Rio de Janeiro I said that if a homosexual person is of good will and is in search of God, I am no one to judge. By saying this, I said what the *Catechism* says. Religion has the right to express its opinion in the service of the people, but God in creation has set us free: it is not possible to interfere spiritually in the life of a person.

A person once asked me, in a provocative manner, if I approved of homosexuality. I replied with another question: "Tell me: when God looks at a gay person, does he endorse the existence of this person with love, or reject and condemn this person?" We must always consider the person. Here we enter into the mystery of the human being. In life, God accompanies persons, and we must accompany them, starting from their situation. It is necessary to accompany them with mercy. When that happens, the Holy Spirit inspires the priest to say the right thing. [44]

In June 2015, Bishop Johan Bonny of Antwerp was appointed by the Vatican as a delegate to the October Synod on the Family. Bonny supports ecclesiastical recognition of same-sex relationships and said:

Personally, I find that in the Church more space must be given to acknowledge the actual quality of gay and lesbian couples; and such a form of shared-life should meet the same criteria as found in an ecclesiastical marriage. ... Indeed, we need to seek a formal recognition of the kind of relationship that exists between many gay and lesbian couples. [45]

Bonny's statement regarding the "actual quality of gay and lesbian couples" provides a basis for asserting the true ideal for Christian marriage is not based on biology, but on the spiritual, *agape* quality of the relationship. Comparing same-sex couples with heterosexual couples, it is evident that many gays and lesbians live the truths of Christianity to a greater quality than heterosexuals, including expressing a reverence for the Church and its sacraments in ways unseen in many heterosexuals. This example of living true Christianity is part of what was inferred in the language of the 2014 Synod interim report, which stated "homosexuals have gifts and qualities to offer to the Christian community."

Cardinal Marx, speaking of the unique opportunity enabled by Pope Francis, stated, "The doors are open, wider than they have ever been since the Second Vatican Council. The synod debates were just a starting point. Francis wants to get things moving, to push processes forward. The real work is about to begin." [46]

Pope Francis, referring to a heresy called Pelagianism, described his vision for Church reform during an address he gave at the Fifth National Ecclesial Convention in Florence, Italy:

Pelagianism, the Pope told the faithful gathered in Florence's Cathedral of Saint Mary of the Flower, "prompts the Church not to be humble, selfless and blessed. And it does so with the appearance of being a good." Such an approach, he added, "brings us confidence in structures, organizations, in perfect planning because it's abstract." But often "it leads us also to take a controlling, hard, regulatory style," he said. "The law gives to the Pelagian security to feel superior, to have a precise orientation. This is its strength, not the light of the breath of the Spirit." "In facing ills or the problems of the Church," the Pope went on, "it is useless to look for solutions in conservatism and fundamentalism, in the restoration of practices and outdated forms that aren't even able to be culturally meaningful." Christian doctrine, he added, "is not a closed system incapable of generating questions, concerns, interrogatives, but it is alive, unsettles, animates. Its face isn't rigid, its body moves and develops, it has tender flesh: that of Jesus Christ." [47]

Statements such as those by Marx and Pope Francis are often seen as attempts to open up topics for discussion that have already been settled doctrinally. Some Catholics assert that while canon law can and should be modified over time, doctrine cannot change, but that position is at odds not only with Newman's analysis of how doctrine develops over time, but also at odds with the *Catechism* and Christ's instructions to the apostles. After the last of the apostles died, nothing can be added to public revelation, "yet even if Revelation is already complete, it has not been made completely explicit; it remains for Christian faith gradually to grasp its full significance over the course of the centuries." [48] Also, Christ founded the Church and gave to Peter and the apostles as well as their legitimate successors the authority to develop doctrine over time via inspiration of the Holy Spirit. Christ, in John 16:12-15, said to the apostles:

> I have much more to say to you, more than you can now bear. But when he, the Spirit of truth, comes, he will guide you into all the truth. He will not speak on his own; he will speak only what he hears, and he will tell you what is yet to come. He will glorify me because it is from me that he will receive what he will make known to you. All that belongs to the Father is mine. That is why I said the Spirit will receive from me what he will make known to you."

A key question coming out of the Synod concerns the relationship between the Church's doctrine and its pastoral practices. This relationship poses a dilemma for Kasper's proposal regarding Holy Communion for divorced and remarried Catholics, but he maintains his proposal does not require any change in the Church's doctrine on the indissolubility of marriage.

Many in the Church, however, believe his approach is treacherous because it appears to disconnect doctrine (marriage is indissoluble) from pastoral practice (a process that would allow Holy Communion for divorced and remarried Catholics). Opponents of Kasper's proposal also believe it sets a dangerous precedent for the Church because it appears to be merely capitulating to the realities of modern culture.

Cardinal Robert Sarah, head of the organization on Divine Worship and the Discipline of the Sacraments, perceives a disconnection in the approach of Kasper, stating, "It is not possible to imagine any sort of rupture between magisterium [doctrine] and pastoral care. The idea that would consist in putting the magisterium in a pretty box, separating it from pastoral practice, which could evolve according to circumstances, fashions and passions, is a form of heresy, a dangerous schizophrenic pathology." [49]

Kasper's proposal, which has been referred to by some in the Church as a corruption of doctrine, can be seen equally as an organic development of pastoral practice based on a well-established Church teaching: guilt of mortal sin is always subjective because it involves the individual person's conscience; it implies an intentional act of free will; and it requires full knowledge of the sin's gravity. During an interview with Raymond Arroyo of EWTN News, Kasper provided an explanation in his non-native English:

Kasper: First of all, the indissolubility of marriage for me is the faith of the Church, and because it's the word of Jesus Christ you cannot create exceptions, but it's a question of how to apply the word of Jesus to concrete situations; it's a question of, and I thought the Church has the authority to bind and to loose, and the Church can in certain cases make use of this authority.

Arroyo: So you're distinguishing between doctrine and pastoral practice, are they two separate things?

Kasper: No, they are not separate; this would be doctrine; practice must be found in the doctrine, but you cannot deduce directly from a dogma to a concrete practice.

Arroyo: Right, but in this case though, when you say there is an indissoluble marriage, and someone is divorced and then found somebody else, and then they come to church and say I want the sacraments, Cardinal Sarah this week said, you have a first marriage that is ratified and consummated, now have a second union of some sort, and when these people come forth and we allow them to have Communion, he says it's a heresy, a dangerous schizophrenic pathology. You would say what?

Kasper: Well, that's a strong statement, very strong, but I, no, I cannot agree with this statement because, well, what makes impossible the access to sacraments is to live in grave sin, that's a canon law, but grave sin is not only a grave material [grave matter] but there must be the conscience and the intentionality, there must be the circumstances. The concept of grave sin is a very complex one, and therefore it needs a discernment case-by-case whether there is the situation of grave sin or not.

Arroyo: But there seems to be this dual-track though, because you're saying you want to preserve the indissolubility of marriage, but the application of Communion and how and to whom it is distributed might be another issue over here.

Kasper: No, no, it's not another issue, and when this man or this woman is not in the personal situation of grave sin, and this happens...

Arroyo (interrupting): They're not in a situation of grave sin?

Kasper: Objectively, but if there is [grave sin] subjectively, that's a problem. Grave sin implies the personal conscience, implies intentionality of the will, and therefore it needs a judgment of a priest who has the experience and...

Arroyo (interrupting): But not a tribunal; you don't like the idea of the nullity [annulment] process, the canonical process.

Kasper: No, no, no, this is a different thing. Of course this can help in certain cases, this nullity process, but the Church always distinguishes between the forum internal and the forum external, and I think the discernment, whether a person, a concrete person lives in grave sin or not, that's a question of the forum internal, not the forum external. [50]

Use of the terms "forum internal" and "forum external" is sometimes tangled up with matters of conscience regarding subjective and objective aspects of sin. In the Church's Code of Canon Law pertaining to governance, the forum describes where an ecclesiastical act occurs. Catholic marriages and annulments take place in the public, external forum, whereas going to the sacrament of Confession takes place in the private, internal forum.

So-called "internal forum solutions" were previously discussed to allow divorced and remarried Catholics to receive Communion, but they differed from Kasper's. One approach was called an internal forum solution although it did not involve the internal forum of Confession. Instead, it involved the individual's "sincere judgment of conscience that their first marriage was invalid." [51] One sharp rebuttal to that approach was expressed in the following terms: "It would be purely academic to hypothesize about the existence of cases in which moral certitude could be reached only in the internal forum, that is, in conscience; such would be so rare that they should be considered practically nonexistent." [52] Other opinions are not quite as restrictive. Archbishop Cupich seemed to allude he uses a type of internal forum solution during a press briefing at the Synod. [38] Various opinions on internal forum solutions were summarized by Father Edward McNamara, Professor of Liturgy and Dean of Theology at Regina Apostolorum University in Rome:

> Authors of this theory differ as to the definition and application of this supposed solution. In synthesis, it is a pastoral response made by a person, with the help of a priest, in which the person becomes convinced in conscience of the invalidity of a previous marriage even though an external judicial determination regarding this validity cannot be resolved. This conviction would thus allow a return to the sacraments.

> However, opinions can be quite diverse as to how to apply this proposed solution. Some authors insist that this solution is not granted by a priest but only acting under his guidance. Others explicitly say that it is a decision made by an appropriate priest made without recourse to the tribunal.

> Likewise, others sustain that before the internal forum can be invoked, it is necessary for the person to have attempted to recur to

the external forum (marriage tribunal) but with no process going forward due to procedural or other difficulties.

Others sustain that there might be cases where the person can decide even without ever contacting the tribunal if there are good reasons for not doing so. [53]

The Pope himself appeared to mediate such an internal forum solution for an Argentine woman, Jacqueline Sabetta Lisbona, who wrote a letter to the Pope in September 2013 in which she explained her situation. A Vatican spokesperson confirmed that the Pope telephoned her on April 21, 2014, and even though she was in an invalid marriage, she "spoke with the Pope, and he said she was absolved of all sins and she could go and get Holy Communion because she was not doing anything wrong." [54]

Kasper, responding to a question about why an annulment process isn't necessary to allow divorced and remarried Catholics to receive Communion, explained:

Marriage is an icon, an image of the alliance of God with his people, and notice that in holy scripture, how often the people of God abandoned him, and also Jesus was rejected by his people, then he substituted himself, went to the Cross even to give them another chance. ... He gave the Church, his apostles, the authority to forgive and not to forgive, to bind and to loose, and all this, this is all a sign of mercy, it's not only the category of human justice you can apply here, that you must, the Church must act according to the action of God and of God's mercy, and the Church is a Sacrament of Mercy, it means sign and instrument of the mercy of God, that's our Catholic understanding of the Church, and if God gives, acts in this way, the Church can do it also. [50]

Marriage is a sacrament in the Church, and it cannot be undone, but a marriage can be annulled if one or both people weren't competent to enter the marriage for one or more of several reasons. For example, even though a couple received the sacrament, it is not a valid marriage if at least one person consented to the marriage without "the intention to marry for life, to be faithful to one another and be open to children" or "intend the good of each other." [55] There are other reasons the marriage may not be valid and can be annulled, including the presence of a psychological disorder at the time of marriage. However, the annulment process is complicated and lengthy:

> Several steps are involved. The person who is asking for the declaration of nullity—the petitioner—submits written testimony about the marriage and a list of persons who are familiar with the marriage. These people must be willing to answer questions about the spouses and the marriage. The tribunal will contact the ex-spouse—the respondent—who has a right to be involved. The respondent's cooperation is welcome but not essential. In some cases the respondent does not wish to become involved; the case can still move forward. Both the petitioner and the respondent can read the testimony submitted, except that protected by civil law (for example, counseling records). Each party may appoint a Church advocate who could represent the person before the tribunal. A representative for the Church, called the defender of the bond, argues for the validity of the marriage. After the tribunal has reached a decision, it is reviewed by a second tribunal. Both parties can participate in this second review as well. [55]

Kasper's proposal would radically streamline this process in most cases by allowing a person to instead discuss their situation with a parish priest. To circumvent situations such as allowing Holy Communion for a man who has merely left his wife for a younger woman, Kasper explained:

> I am for discernment situation by situation. I never said everybody who is divorced and remarried can go to the sacraments. Every situation is different and we need a confession, fathers with experience who can speak with the people. It's a whole process; and then to come to a discernment of the situation to help also the people, to have a discernment about the situation, and then perhaps he can give the absolution. [50]

In Catholicism, same-sex marriage is typically viewed as a non-starter because of the understanding that marriage is not only an image of the relationship between God and His People, but also an image of the relationship between a Bridegroom and His Bride. In the Old Testament period, the prophets consistently described the relationship between God and the Jews in terms of the Bridegroom (God) and His Bride (the Jews). The last prophet,

John the Baptist, is not only a transitional figure between the Old and New Testaments, but he also introduced an amplification of this marriage language by proclaiming the Messiah (Jesus Christ) was also the Bridegroom. In the New Testament there's a clear continuity of this imagery; Jesus is referred to as the Bridegroom, and the Church is the Bride of Christ. The imagery also alludes to the intimacy a believer may realize by receiving Holy Communion: union with God, because Communion in the Catholic Church is literally, not symbolically, Christ's body, blood, soul, and divinity. The union takes place primarily on a spiritual level, but marital sexual love is seen as an iconic representation of the level of intimacy that is possible to have with God through the sacraments, particularly with Holy Communion.

In her autobiography, *Story of a Soul,* Saint Thérèse of Lisieux (1873 - 1897) described her First Holy Communion this way:

> I don't want to enter into detail here. There are certain things that lose their perfume as soon as they are exposed to the air; there are deep spiritual thoughts which cannot be expressed in human language without losing their intimate and heavenly meaning. ... Ah! how sweet was that first kiss of Jesus! It was a kiss of love; I felt that I was loved, and I said: "I love You, and I give myself to You forever!" There were no demands made, no struggles, no sacrifices; for a long time now Jesus and poor little Thérèse looked at and understood each other. That day, it was no longer simply a look, it was a fusion; they were no longer two, Thérèse had vanished as a drop of water is lost in the immensity of the ocean. Jesus alone remained; He was the Master, the King. Had not Thérèse asked Him to take away her liberty, for her liberty frightened her? She felt so feeble and fragile that she wanted to be united forever to the divine Strength! [56]

Similar sentiments aren't uncommon among devout Catholic women, but this imagery can't be applied to heterosexual males, which highlights the inadequacy of extending the biological basis of heterosexual marriage as a reflection of the relationship between Christ and the Church. The type of intimacy that Saint Thérèse describes isn't sexual because union with God occurs primarily on the spiritual level. Metaphors of sexual intimacy can be used as a primitive prototype or typology that points to a much deeper level of intimacy, but the locus of spiritual intimacy occurs in the soul. Saint

Teresa of Ávila (1515 - 1582) described it this way in her book on mystical prayer, *The Interior Castle:*

> I began to think of the soul as if it were a castle made of a single diamond or of very clear crystal, in which there are many rooms, just as in heaven there are many mansions. ... Let us now imagine that this castle, as I have said, contains many mansions, some above, others below, others at each side; and in the center and midst of them all is the Chiefest mansion where the most secret things pass between God and the soul. [57]

Saint Catherine of Siena (1347 - 1380) began to have mystical experiences when she was six years old and made a vow of virginity when she was seven. She was very attractive and had numerous would-be suitors, so at the age of fifteen, to discourage boyfriends and prevent her parents from arranging a marriage, she cut off her hair. For the next three years, she lived as a virtual hermit in a small room inside her parents' home. At the age of nineteen, after undergoing a period of arduous temptations, she had a mystical encounter with Christ and the Blessed Virgin Mary, during which she said she became spiritually espoused to Christ.

Saint Thérèse of Lisieux, Saint Teresa of Ávila, and Saint Catherine of Siena are Doctors of the Church—a title given only to individuals who have demonstrated an extraordinary level of theological insight through their lives and their writings. Saint Edith Stein (1891 - 1942), who may be the next woman named a Doctor of the Church, was an atheist and received a doctorate in philosophy with a dissertation under Edmund Husserl. She decided to enter the Catholic Church after reading Saint Teresa of Ávila's autobiography, *The Life of Saint Teresa of Jesus.* For readers interested in the autobiography of Saint Thérèse of Lisieux, *Story of a Soul,* many editions are available, but the most accurate translation is the version published by the Institute for Carmelite Studies (ICS) and translated by John Clarke. [56]

A fault in applying the biological basis of heterosexual marriage as a reflection of the relationship between Christ and the Church involves *eros* (erotic love) and *agape* (self-sacrificial love). It is not *eros* that defines the relationship between Christ and the Church, but *agape.* Even though *eros* or erotic love can be a significant part of spirituality, it's completely devoid of any redeeming value without *agape,* which is the type of self-sacrificial love that endures forever, regardless of circumstances that may change. Christ provides the ultimate example of *agape,* not only because his love endures forever, regardless of circumstances, but because he set an extreme example of it: the love of God is not only eternal, it is also the type of love willing to die for the beloved and willing to die in the most excruciating and humiliating way imaginable—physically tortured and executed as a common criminal, even when the beloved cares nothing for the lover. That is the model of Catholic marriage, and it is a model that very few people can live up to.

Additionally, the marital union is also meant to reflect the union and relationship that exists within the Trinity: the communion within the Trinity is perfect and complete and is marked by a giving and receiving of love, but the love is *agape,* not *eros. Paragraph 239 of the Catechism* includes the following:

> The language of faith thus draws on the human experience of parents, who are in a way the first representatives of God for man [humanity]. But this experience also tells us that human parents are fallible and can disfigure the face of fatherhood and motherhood. We ought therefore to recall that God transcends the human distinction between the sexes. He is neither man nor woman: he is God. He also transcends human fatherhood and motherhood, although he is their origin and standard. [58]

In the Creed, which is a list of core beliefs essential to the faith, the Holy Spirit is described as "proceeding from the Father and the Son," and that phrase is typically interpreted as the Holy Spirit being a manifestation of the exchange of love between the Father (God) and the Son (Christ). The word "Father" is used for God even though God the Father is neither male nor female. [59] Christ referred to God as the Father, saying, for example, "The Father and I are One." Using the term "Father" is typically viewed as merely a reflection of the male-dominated culture of the time, but in Catholicism, it is a distinction that alludes to the integral role of the Blessed Mother (Blessed Virgin Mary) in the process of redemption.

Many Catholics who are opposed to same-sex marriage assert there is a procreative dimension central to marriage, even in cases of infertility, and the procreative dimension must be affirmed in every marital act, which also precludes the use of artificial contraception. In the conception of a child, the two parents directly participate with God in the creation of a new life with an eternal soul. However, the procreative sexual love of *eros* without the eternally self-sacrificial love of *agape* is deficient in terms of reflecting the communion that occurs in the Trinity. While the procreative dimension of marriage is a strong argument to use in opposition to same-sex marriage, a stronger argument in favor of same-sex marriage is that *agape* more perfectly reflects life within the Trinity, especially because God the Father is neither male nor female.

The first Papal Encyclical of Pope Benedict XVI, *Deus Caritas Est* (*God is Love*) has one overarching theme: *Eros* is perfected by *agape*. The following is an excerpt:

> According to Friedrich Nietzsche, Christianity had poisoned *eros,* which for its part, while not completely succumbing, gradually degenerated into vice. Here the German philosopher was expressing a widely held perception: doesn't the Church, with all her commandments and prohibitions, turn to bitterness the most precious thing in life? Doesn't she blow the whistle just when the joy which is the Creator's gift offers us a happiness which is itself a certain foretaste of the Divine? But is this the case? Did Christianity really destroy *eros?* Let us take a look at the pre-Christian world. The Greeks—not unlike other cultures—considered *eros* principally as a kind of intoxication, the overpowering of reason by a "divine madness" which tears man [humans] away from his [or her] finite existence and enables him [or her], in the very process of being overwhelmed by divine power, to experience supreme happiness. All other powers in heaven and on earth thus appear secondary: *"Omnia vincit amor"* says Virgil in the *Bucolics*—love conquers all—and he adds: *"et nos cedamus amori"*—let us, too, yield to love. In the religions, this attitude found expression in fertility cults, part of which was the "sacred" prostitution which flourished in many temples. *Eros* was thus celebrated as divine power, as fellowship with the Divine. [60]

Aquinas defined sodomy as "copulation with an undue sex, male with male, or female with female" and asserted it was "contrary to right reason" and "contrary to the natural order of the venereal act [sexual activity]." [61] Merriam-Webster defines sodomy as "anal or oral copulation with a member of the same or opposite sex." In the *Summa Theologica*, Aquinas classified sodomy and other activities as *sins contra naturam* (sins contrary to nature, or sins against nature). God is seen as the author of nature, including human nature, which is a special category of nature that possesses the ability to use reason as a means to make judgments. According to Aquinas, sins against nature are the most grievous of all types of sin because, in the act of violating nature, an injury is done to God, the author of nature. [62] But in cases where same-sex attraction or gender identity is determined or predisposed by the genome or epigenome, then *not* being a homosexual or *not* being a transgender person would be the sin against nature.

During the thirteenth century, Aquinas applied logic and reason to matters of faith in a groundbreaking manner. He was often criticized by conservative Catholics during his lifetime for incorporating truths derived from purely secular or pagan sources, particularly Aristotle's logic and philosophy. For Aquinas, faith and reason could not contradict each other, even though many truths of the infinite, far-superior God were beyond the reach of a finite human mind.

Would Aquinas revise his list of behaviors that constitute sins against nature if he had indisputable proof that same-sex attraction is determined or predisposed by the genome or epigenome? Aquinas was a rigorist with regard to aligning the tenets of Catholicism with logic and reason, and he categorized his sins against nature not only based on biblical texts but also—to align faith and reason—on thirteenth century observations that have since been proven to be inaccurate, specifically, that homosexuality does not occur in animal species. He saw sexual intercourse to be an inclination that humans and animals had in common:

> There is in man an inclination to things that pertain to him more specially, according to that nature which he has in common with other animals: and in virtue of this inclination, those things are said to belong to the natural law, which nature has taught to all animals, such as sexual intercourse. [63]

Aquinas set a precedent in the Church's ever-growing understanding that there can be no incongruity between faith and reason, and his observation that humans and animals shared some behavior patterns prefigures later developments involving the theory of evolution.

Church doctrines, too, can evolve over time, and sometimes the Church develops doctrines that are at odds with the positions of its preeminent theologians. Aquinas, for example, discounted what is now a required belief of Catholicism: Mary's Immaculate Conception, which declares that Mary was the only human who was conceived without original sin.

Looming factors include the likelihood that same-sex attraction will be found to have biological determinants. If that is the case, then God can be viewed as its author. Alternative explanations to account for such a genetic determination or predisposition could also include an interpretation that same-sex attraction and gender dysphoria are based on "genetic defects" or illnesses, but that poses even greater problems for the Church because the Church does not deny access to the sacraments due to illnesses or genetic disorders.

## Science of Attraction and Repulsion

The perception of anything as attractive, repulsive, or neutral is determined primarily by three variables: 1) inherited instincts encoded in DNA at the moment of conception, 2) acquired memories, which can also modify inherited instincts, and 3) illness. Three categories of experiments illustrate the variables at work.

The first category involves a change in perception caused by illness, and the specific study referenced here is *Predator Cat Odors Activate Sexual Arousal Pathways in Brains of Toxoplasma Gondii Infected Rats* by Patrick House, Ajai Vyas, and Robert Sapolsky. [64] The findings of this study have been replicated in numerous experiments that have explored this paradoxical behavior in rats.

When rats are infected by a common parasite called *toxoplasma gondii*, the rat's perception of stimuli associated with cats, a natural predator, is modified so that what was once perceived as repulsive is later perceived as attractive. Rats typically exhibit fear and avoidance behaviors when their noses absorb odors that reveal cat urine is in the environment. However, after an infection by *toxoplasma gondii*, the rat's perception of cat urine changes from being repulsive to attractive. Instead of fleeing from the sensory information of cat urine, the rats actively pursue it and explore it.

Rats perceive different degrees of threat or danger in different cat odors because the values of those odors (repulsive or very repulsive) are encoded in the rats' DNA. After becoming infected with the toxoplasma parasite, rats still differentiate between the scent of cat urine and other odors associated with cats, and the rats will still perceive those other, non-urine cat odors, as threatening and repulsive.

The toxoplasma infection alters the rat's perception of cat urine because a change occurs in the transmission and routing of electrical signals that travel throughout various parts of the rat's brain. Electrical signals generated by the absorption of sensory information $x$ can travel along three basic paths in the brain: a) pathway that results in the perception of $x$ as attractive; b) pathway that results in the perception of $x$ as repulsive; and c) pathway that results in the perception of $x$ as neutral or meaningless. The attractive pathway and repulsive pathway can be active to varying degrees at the same time and for the same type of sensory information $x$, but typically, one pathway is much more active than the other when processing information about the meaning of non-neutral sensory information $x$.

Neutral sensory information can be perceived as either meaningless "noise" that doesn't have an attractive or repulsive value, or meaningful information that doesn't have an attractive or repulsive value.

After a rat becomes infected, toxoplasma parasites migrate to the rat's brain and form spherical cysts that are approximately 50,000 nanometers in diameter, which is about the width of a strand of hair. The infection causes microscopic cysts to form throughout the brain but with a preference for regions of the limbic system, which processes sensory information associated with the perception of a) threats or repulsive sensory information and b) opportunities or attractive sensory information.

While it's not known if the increased density or prevalence of the cysts in the limbic system (compared to other parts of the brain) is responsible for the shift in perception of cat urine from being repulsive to attractive, what is known is that within two weeks after getting infected, the cysts are prevalent in the rat's brain. Within six weeks after getting infected, the rat's perception of cat urine has changed from being repulsive to attractive.

Prior to the infection, the pattern of electrical signals that transmits the sensory information of cat urine travels along the repulsive pathway through the amygdala and into the hypothalamus; as a result, the rat will avoid, flee, and prefer to escape from areas where the odor of cat urine is present. After the infection, the pattern of electrical signals that transmits the sensory information of cat urine travels along the attractive pathway through the amygdala and into the hypothalamus; as a result, the rat will approach, explore, and prefer to be in areas where the odor of cat urine is present. The two pathways, repulsive and attractive, run parallel to each other and are in close proximity to each other, but the two pathways process two opposite types of information, repulsive and attractive.

A second category of experiments focuses on the role that genetic factors play in attraction and repulsion. The research discussed here is based on the work of Cornelia Bargmann, and a more encompassing overview of related work is discussed in *Genetic Contributions to Behavioural Diversity at the Gene-Environment interface* by Andres Bendesky and Cornelia Bargmann. [65]

This area of research involves a roundworm, a nematode, called *Caenorhabditis elegans* (or *C. elegans*). *C. elegans* is normally very attracted to the scent of diacetyl, which is a key nutrient that the worm needs to sustain its life. Diacetyl is the worm's favorite food, and it is a natural by-product of fermentation. It contributes to the smell and taste of butter, as well as some alcoholic beverages like beer and wine. When people drink chardonnay and say it has a buttery taste, it's because some winemakers promote the flavor and feel of butter in the wine, and they do it by promoting the production of diacetyl. French wine drinkers sometimes refer to these American chardonnays as *butter bombs.*

When the worms smell diacetyl, they are attracted to those diacetyl molecules. Research on the worms reveals that when they have a specific mutation in their DNA (a mutation in the gene that enables the worms to sense diacetyl), the worms can no longer detect the scent of diacetyl. As a result, an environmental stimulus that's intrinsically important to the survival and well-being of the worm can no longer be sensed and perceived when the worm has that mutation.

Even though this species of worm doesn't have a well-developed nervous system that includes anything remotely resembling a brain, it has the equivalent of an attractive pathway and repulsive pathway. However, unlike rats and other vertebrates that have a bundle of neurons (nerve cells) that make up the attractive pathway and repulsive pathway, the worm has individual neurons that function as its attractive pathway and repulsive pathway because *C. elegans* has only 302 neurons in its entire nervous system. Because of this very low number of neurons, it's "relatively" easy to manipulate the worms' genes and measure the results.

A gene in the worm called *odr-10* is responsible for making the sensory receptor that enables the worm to detect the sensory information produced by diacetyl. In a normal worm, the *odr-10* gene is expressed in a neuron that processes attractive information, but when experiments enable the *odr-10* gene to be expressed in a neuron that processes repulsive information, the worms are repulsed by the scent of diacetyl—a paradoxical response similar to the behavior of the rats that become attracted to the scent of cat urine.

A third category of experiments focuses on the role that learning and acquired memories play in the perception of stimuli as attractive or repulsive. The research discussed here is based on the classical work conducted by Ivan Pavlov. Even though Pavlov's work was done in the early

1900s, the fundamental methods he established continue to be used by neuroscientists today.

Pavlov was initially studying the physiological processes involved in the digestion of food in dogs, but he inadvertently discovered the psychological processes involved in learning and memory formation. He was awarded a Nobel Prize in 1904 for his work with the dogs, and he had just begun to publish data on learning and memory processes. From that time forward, until his death in 1936, Pavlov shifted the focus of his research from the physiological processes involved in digestion to the psychological processes involved in learning and memory formation.

To prepare the dogs for his original digestion experiments, Pavlov and his team of researchers performed surgical procedures on the dogs that enabled the scientists to collect saliva secreted in the dogs' mouths as well as other fluids generated in their stomachs. More than a hundred years ago, when cruelty to animals was not given as much thought as it is today, Pavlov thoughtfully considered the animals' well-being. He stated his researchers strictly observed "all the precautions taken by surgeons in respect to their patients" when they did the operations on the dogs. In the speech he gave when he received his Nobel Prize, he said, "our healthy and happy animals did their laboratory work with real gusto; they always eagerly moved from their cages to the laboratory and readily jumped onto the tables where our experiments and observations were conducted." [66]

The surgical procedures involved inserting metal tubes into two areas of the dogs' digestive system, one tube near the salivary glands and another tube into the stomach. The tubes enabled saliva and other fluids to be diverted from the digestive system and collected in containers that were attached to the dogs. The tube to the stomach also allowed the researchers to put food directly into the dog's stomach without first having the food go through the dog's mouth.

After each experimental session, the containers could be removed from the dogs. The researchers then measured the fluids for volume and also analyzed the chemical composition of the fluids, looking for the presence of various chemicals that facilitate the digestion process. During the intervals between experiments, when the containers were detached from the dogs, the metal tubes were sealed using removable plugs. Pavlov said the dogs lived relatively normal lives, typically more than eight years after the surgeries, "without ever showing any deviation from normal health." [66]

When the original digestion experiments began, the researchers would put various substances into the dogs' mouths—things like bread, meat, milk, salt, and mustard—and then measure and analyze the composition of the digestive fluids. Over the course of the first few experimental sessions, the dogs salivated only after food was brought into the laboratory. However, after the dogs experienced a few of the experimental sessions, saliva started to flow into the containers before any food was brought into the laboratory area to begin the sessions.

Pavlov and his research team were initially puzzled about why that would happen. However, they soon came to the conclusion that the dogs must have learned something new about the environment that they didn't know when the experiments first began: that the researchers were going to feed them. A visual stimulus, seeing people in lab coats, which previously had no special meaning for the dogs, had acquired a new meaning. The dogs began to perceive a new value in a visual stimulus that previously had no special value to the dogs. Visual sensory information that was previously perceived as relatively meaningless "visual noise" was later perceived to be important or meaningful.

Before discussing Pavlov's experiments, it's helpful to understand the difference between sensing information and perceiving information. While the dogs' eyes sensed the visual information (people in lab coats) in the same manner (by processing light waves) both before and after the initial experimental sessions, it was the dogs' perception of the people in the lab coats that changed. Perception is the flexible part of the equation while sensation is not. Sensation conforms to the physical composition of the sensory information, while perception conforms to the flexible content of memories in addition to the physical composition of sensory information and inherited instincts. DNA-based inherited instincts are malleable too, but only over generations of a species' development via natural selection. When the dogs learned that people wearing lab coats would be feeding them, a change in dogs' perception occurred because of the memories that were encoded in the dogs' brains.

The eyes and ears of animals and humans can do nothing more than process sensory information in the form of light waves and sound waves. Functionally speaking, the eyes process light waves like a video camera and the ears process sound waves like a microphone. The eyes and ears process sensory information that enters the body, and then the brain further processes that information by adding other information previously acquired via the formation of memories and the presence of inherited instincts.

Another approach to understanding the difference between sensing information and perceiving information is to consider what happens when a person is watching television and there happens to be a dog or a cat nearby. If the animal is also looking at the television screen, the person and the animal are both seeing and processing the same light waves and hearing and processing the same sound waves. The light waves act on the person's eyes and the animal's eyes in an identical fashion. The sound waves act on the person's ears and the animal's ears in an identical fashion. Both, animal and human, sense the environment identically, but each perceives the environment in radically different ways because the contents of the person's memories are radically different compared to the contents of the animal's memories. The contents of the person's memories are radically different because of the radical difference between the intellectual capabilities of humans and animals, which stems from differences in inherited DNA.

Sensation is then the process used by humans and animals to absorb sensory information in the environment, and perception is the process used by humans and animals to interpret sensory information.

Pavlov and his team of researchers were initially surprised when they saw the results of their dog psychology experiments. During the early 1900s, scientists didn't believe that psychological processes could have such a large influence on physiological and biological processes. While it seemed obvious that the physical and chemical composition of food could cause a dog to salivate when a) food was tasted by the tongue and b) food was seen by the eyes, it didn't seem logical that visual sensory information unrelated to food (merely seeing people in lab coats and with no food in the area) could cause the same physiological response as sensing and perceiving food with the tongue and the eyes. At the time of Pavlov's experiments, scientists used the term *psychical stimulation* to describe how the subjective perception of reality could influence objectively measurable physiological or biological processes.

Even more surprising than the measurements of psychical stimulation was the flexibility with which the dogs' responses could be manipulated. Working through several experimental designs, the research team began documenting many of the fundamental laws of learning and memory formation, and Pavlov later became known as one of the founding fathers of the science of psychology. Pavlov and his team clearly demonstrated how specific sensory variables could be manipulated to bring about desired psychological, physiological, biological, and behavioral responses in the dogs. Later experiments, up until the present day, confirm all of these systematic methods or manipulations, which result in learning and memory formation, work the same way in humans and animals.

In the first set of experiments, the research team established that the dogs began salivating solely in response to seeing people in lab coats, without any meat or other food present in the laboratory. During a second phase of experiments, they began "teasing" the dogs by showing them a piece of meat at a distance but not feeding the dogs. As expected, the dogs responded by producing large volumes of highly concentrated saliva.

However, after several teasing sessions, the researchers observed more unexpected results. They discovered that repeatedly teasing the dogs with the sight of meat but not feeding them resulted in salivary reactions that grew weaker and weaker over time until the volume of saliva finally dropped to zero. The dogs had now learned something completely different about the sensory information: seeing people in lab coats, as well as seeing meat itself, was no longer perceived as important or attractive.

The meaning of the sensory information "meat" had changed. What the dogs previously interpreted or categorized as meaningful, high-value information (the sight of meat) later acquired a different meaning and became to be perceived as low-value information or noise. The perception of sensory information that the dogs' DNA predefined as being important to their survival (the sight of meat) was easily manipulated by the formation of new memories. A key finding from these experiments is that a few minutes of memory formation can easily alter the perception of sensory information that had been methodically ingrained in DNA over the course of generations of a species' evolution interacting with the environment.

The researchers also found that for a given time period (for example, three hours, three days, or three weeks), if the intervals between episodes of teasing were short, the salivary response diminished rapidly (short intervals between experiences enabled rapid or more effective learning). If the intervals between teasing sessions were long, the salivary response diminished more slowly (long intervals between experiences led to slower or less effective learning). But the response always dropped to zero if the dogs weren't able to physically taste the meat during the repeated teasing sessions.

More unexpected results followed. The variable saliva response only applied to the specific type of food being shown to the dogs. For example, when the response to meat dropped to zero, teasing the dogs by showing them a piece of bread produced a strong response that generated a high volume of saliva. When the response to bread dropped to zero after repeated visual stimulation, the dogs' response to the sight of milk was very strong. The dogs clearly were able to perceive and differentiate that what was "true" for one type of food, meat, for example, was not necessarily true for other types of food, such as bread or milk.

In these experiments, the dogs (or the dogs' brains) were interpreting (or translating) patterns of light waves being absorbed by their eyes. Information that previously was interpreted as "high value" was later interpreted as "low value" or meaningless noise.

One final note about the saliva collected in the experiments with Pavlov's dogs. Saliva contains enzymes that accelerate the conversion of chemical elements within food into nutrient products, which are then more readily accessible by cells in the body. Because Pavlov's researchers had been analyzing the chemical composition of the saliva generated in response to the dogs' interactions with substances such as meat, bread, milk, and mustard, the researchers knew, for example, that dry bread caused the production of significantly larger volumes of saliva than did meat. They also knew that substances disagreeable to the dogs, such as mustard, would result in a different chemical composition of the fluid generated by the dogs' salivary glands. Unpleasant substances would promote the production of saliva that was more watery, whereas, for meat, the fluid would be thicker or have higher viscosity. They also measured and documented other qualities of the saliva such as its degree of acidity.

In a rather surprising finding of Pavlov's experiments that involved teasing the dogs by showing them food items but not feeding them, the researchers found that variations in the chemical composition of saliva produced in response to the dogs experiencing the substances in their mouths was, as Pavlov stated, "exactly duplicated in experiments using psychical stimulation, that is, in which a given object is not brought into direct contact with the mucous membrane of the mouth, but arouses the animal's attention from some distance." In other words, the animal's response to merely seeing food x was identical to the animal's response of actually tasting that specific food in its mouth.

Finally, Pavlov was able to demonstrate that all of the techniques used to change the way vertebrate animals perceived various aspects of their environment were equally applicable and effective in humans. Also, Pavlov clearly proved that intrinsically meaningless stimuli, such as the sound of a bell, could be transformed into something perceived as attractive or repulsive merely by methodically associating an inherently positive stimulus (such as food) or an inherently negative stimulus (such as an electric shock or a loud noise) with the inherently meaningless sensory information.

## Generalizations about Homosexuality in Key Biblical Texts

Homosexuals in same-sex relationships, like validly married Catholics who divorce and remarry without an annulment, are viewed by the Church to be objectively in a continual state of mortal sin. But, generally speaking, if the consciences of Catholics in such relationships do not inform them that they are guilty of mortal sin, then they are not guilty of mortal sin (subjectively) even though the Church views them to be in mortal sin (objectively). The Church teaches that these Catholics may not receive Holy Communion because:

Their state and condition of life objectively contradict that union of love between Christ and His Church which is signified and effected by the Eucharist. Besides this, there is another special pastoral reason: if these people were admitted to the Eucharist, the faithful would be led into error and confusion regarding the Church's teaching about the indissolubility of marriage. [67]

Kasper's proposal doesn't directly address the situation of same-sex couples, but the key common factor the two issues share is straightforward: Catholics who are, in reality, not guilty of mortal sin are being denied access to Holy Communion, which is "the source and summit of the Christian life." [68] The justification for this current pastoral practice involves the issue of scandal: if homosexuals in same-sex relationships as well as divorced and remarried Catholics are permitted to receive Holy Communion, then people will be scandalized, that is, they may be encouraged to engage in objectively sinful behavior because the Church would appear to be condoning objectively sinful behavior.

The issue of scandal can be traced to the words of Christ in Matthew 18:6: "If anyone causes one of these little ones—those who believe in me— to stumble, it would be better for them to have a large millstone hung around their neck and to be drowned in the depths of the sea." By "little ones," Christ is referring not only to children but to all Christians who are in the process of developing properly formed consciences. The Church has a duty to set an example regarding objectively sinful behavior, but in all matters, it is more important to set the critical example of not judging others, which involves the sin of pride.

Using Christ's teaching on scandal as a means to exclude homosexuals in same-sex relationships—as well as divorced and remarried Catholics—

from Holy Communion is a misapplication of the teaching. The context of Christ's admonishment on scandal involves a rebuke of intolerance. That particular passage in the Bible happened to coincide with the Church's lectionary for readings at Mass on September 27, 2015, the day Pope Francis celebrated the Closing Mass of the World Meeting of Families in Philadelphia. The corresponding Old Testament reading for the day was from the book of Numbers 11:25-29, which also deals with intolerance among believers who want to exclude people who don't fit their expectations. The Pope addressed the topic in his homily:

> Here is the surprise: Moses and Jesus both rebuke those closest to them for being so narrow! ... For Jesus, the truly "intolerable" scandal is everything that breaks down and destroys our trust in the working of the Spirit! ... Would that all of us could be open to miracles of love to benefit our own families and all the families of the world, and thus overcome the scandal of a narrow, petty love, closed in on itself, impatient of others! [69]

The hypocrisy of the so-called scandal created by allowing divorced and remarried Catholics as well as homosexuals to receive Holy Communion is evident when considering Christ's admonishment on judging others in Matthew 7:1-5.

> Do not judge, or you too will be judged. For in the same way you judge others, you will be judged, and with the measure you use, it will be measured to you. Why do you look at the speck of sawdust in your brother's eye and pay no attention to the plank in your own eye? How can you say to your brother, "Let me take the speck out of your eye," when all the time there is a plank in your own eye? You hypocrite, first take the plank out of your own eye, and then you will see clearly to remove the speck from your brother's eye.

In addition to rebuking people who are judgmental of others, in Luke 6:36-38, Christ spoke about the spiritual benefits available to those who refrain from being judgmental:

> Be merciful, just as your Father is merciful. Do not judge, and you will not be judged. Do not condemn, and you will not be

condemned. Forgive, and you will be forgiven. Give, and it will be given to you. A good measure, pressed down, shaken together and running over, will be poured into your lap. For with the measure you use, it will be measured to you.

It is impossible to judge others because, regardless of their outwardly observable behavior, it is impossible to know their motive or intention. Also, there are the implications of Christ's words regarding the way He will judge people, expounded on by a Franciscan Friar, Father Leo Clifford:

Christ will look into your eyes and mine, and utter these words: "Amen, amen, I say to you, what you did to those around you, you did to Me."... So, my dear friends, there is no escaping the logic that our every thought, word and deed to our neighbor is to Our Lord. And our thoughts—what a vast, thickly populated world our mind is, and what a very unkind world it can be. I so easily push God off His Judgement Seat, and I sit there pronouncing on others, though I have neither the knowledge nor the authority to judge anyone. ... And our words—oh what power we have with our tongues to bless and to curse, to make people happy and to make them miserable. How often we slash Christ far worse than the soldiers ever did at the pillar, with the haughty, unkind, sarcastic things we say. [70]

Regarding biblical texts related to the cities of Sodom and Gomorrah (the word sodomy is derived from the name of the town of Sodom), two key factors are often generalized or overlooked in a way that obscures the text in Genesis 19:1-10: the incident involved attempted rape, and the intended victims were not ordinary men, but angels, which is significant because of the special status of angels in both the Old and New Testaments, and "in some early Christian writings Jesus was Himself called an angel." [71]

The two angels arrived at Sodom in the evening, and Lot was sitting in the gateway of the city. When he saw them, he got up to meet them and bowed down with his face to the ground. "My lords," he said, "please turn aside to your servant's house. You can wash your feet and spend the night and then go on your way early in the morning." "No," they answered, "we will spend the night in the square."

But he insisted so strongly that they did go with him and entered his house. He prepared a meal for them, baking bread without yeast, and they ate. Before they had gone to bed, all the men from every part of the city of Sodom—both young and old—surrounded the house. They called to Lot, "Where are the men who came to you tonight? Bring them out to us so that we can have sex with them."

Lot went outside to meet them and shut the door behind him and said, "No, my friends. Don't do this wicked thing." ... "Get out of our way," they replied. "This fellow came here as a foreigner, and now he wants to play the judge! We'll treat you worse than them." They kept bringing pressure on Lot and moved forward to break down the door. But the men [angels] inside reached out and pulled Lot back into the house and shut the door. Then they struck the men who were at the door of the house, young and old, with blindness so that they could not find the door.

In the previous chapter of Genesis, Abraham has a dialogue with God in which God tells Abraham the city will not be destroyed if there are fifty, then forty-five, then forty, then thirty, then twenty, or even ten good people in the city. In Genesis 19, it's clear that the city was destroyed because *every* man in the city was evil or corrupted: "all the men from every part of the city of Sodom—both young and old—surrounded the house."

The city was later destroyed and the aftermath is depicted as hell-like, "dense smoke rising from the land, like smoke from a furnace," but the reason for its destruction was not homosexuality.

In explaining that the sins of Sodom were not related to homosexuality, Ezekiel, the Old Testament prophet, allegorically compares Jerusalem with Sodom and another town, Samaria, which Ezekiel refers to as two "sisters." Jerusalem is the Bride (God's chosen people), and she has become adulterous—she's turned her back on the Bridegroom (God)—by breaking the covenant between God and His chosen people. Ezekiel, speaking for God, in 16:49-50, says:

Now this was the sin of your sister Sodom: She and her daughters were arrogant, overfed and unconcerned; they did not help the poor and needy. They were haughty and did detestable things before me. Therefore I did away with them as you have seen.

Rabbi Mendy Kaminker, editor of *Beit Chabad*, the Hebrew edition of Chabad.org, provides additional background:

> Scripture is characteristically sparse when telling us of their failures, only saying that "the people of Sodom were bad, sinning to G-d very much." Talmudic and Midrashic sources give us a much fuller account of the hair-raising wickedness and godlessness that characterized these towns. The Sodomites enjoyed a relatively high standard of living. Regarding Sodom, the Torah tells us that the entire plain was "well-watered ... like the garden of G-d," and it follows that the crops were plentiful and good. The selfish Sodomites did not want to share this bounty with outsiders. To this end, they enacted laws and took great pains to repel travelers. ... Two maidens of Sodom met at the well, where they had both gone to drink and fill up their water jugs. One girl asked her friend, "Why is your face so pale?" Her friend answered, "We have nothing to eat at home, and are dying of starvation." Her compassionate friend filled her own jug with flour, and exchanged it for her friend's jug of water. When the Sodomites found out about her act, they burnt her to death. A second tale: It was announced in Sodom, "Whoever will give bread to a poor person will be burnt at the stake." [72]

Also, the following text of Genesis 18:20-21 is misinterpreted as referring to homosexuality:

> Then the Lord said, "The outcry against Sodom and Gomorrah is so great and their sin so grievous that I will go down and see if what they have done is as bad as the outcry that has reached me. If not, I will know."

Rabbi Kaminker provides this context for verse 21:

> Plotit, the daughter of Lot, who was married to a prominent Sodomite, once saw a poor man who was so hungry that he was unable to stand. She felt sorry for him. From then on, she made sure to pass him every day on her way to the well, and she would feed him some food that she had stashed in her water jug. People wondered how the man managed to live. Upon investigation, they

discovered her act and prepared to burn her. Before she died, she turned to G-d and cried, "Master of the world, carry out justice on my behalf!" Her cries pierced the heavens, and at that moment G-d said, "I will go down and see if what they have done is as bad as the outcry that has reached Me." [72]

Christ also explained the sins of Sodom in terms of not having a welcoming attitude toward strangers, particularly immigrants. The "biblical law specifically sanctified hospitality toward the *ger* ('stranger') who was to be made particularly welcome 'for you were strangers in a strange land [Egypt].'" [73] In Matthew 10:11-15, Christ said:

Whatever town or village you enter, search there for some worthy person and stay at their house until you leave. As you enter the home, give it your greeting. If the home is deserving, let your peace rest on it; if it is not, let your peace return to you. If anyone will not welcome you or listen to your words, leave that home or town and shake the dust off your feet. Truly I tell you, it will be more bearable for Sodom and Gomorrah on the day of judgment than for that town.

Those who assert the story of Sodom is fundamentally about homosexuality must also examine the words of Christ referenced above and their basis in both the Old and New Testament, first in Leviticus 19:34 and then Christ's words in Mark 12:28-31:

Leviticus 19:34: The foreigner residing among you must be treated as your native-born. Love them as yourself, for you were foreigners in Egypt. I am the Lord your God.

Mark 12:28-31: One of the teachers of the law came and heard them debating. Noticing that Jesus had given them a good answer, he asked him, "Of all the commandments, which is the most important?" "The most important one," answered Jesus, "is this: 'Hear, O Israel: The Lord our God, the Lord is one. Love the Lord your God with all your heart and with all your soul and with all your mind and with all your strength.' The second is this: 'Love your neighbor as yourself.' There is no commandment greater than these."

During the First Vatican Council of 1869-1870, the Church stated, doctrinally, that there was a harmony between faith and reason and that, by reason alone, people could come to a knowledge of the truth that God exists. Since the Second Vatican Council of 1962-1965, and increasingly articulated by all of the Popes since then, there is the clear assertion that there can be no disconnection between faith and reason. For example, reconciling the theory of evolution with biblical texts can occur because the Church uses multiple approaches for biblical analysis, including rhetorical and narrative analysis, approaches that use sociology and cultural anthropology, as well as a historical-critical method that excludes the possibility that the texts were divinely inspired.

One of the methods used by the Church is strictly literal, the fundamentalist approach, which claims that the Bible should be interpreted literally in all its details. However, relying solely on the fundamentalist approach to interpret the Bible is viewed to be seriously deficient according to the Vatican's Pontifical Biblical Commission:

Fundamentalism is right to insist on the divine inspiration of the Bible, the inerrancy of the word of God and other biblical truths included in its five fundamental points. But its way of presenting these truths is rooted in an ideology which is not biblical, whatever the proponents of this approach might say. For it demands an unshakable adherence to rigid doctrinal points of view and imposes, as the only source of teaching for Christian life and salvation, a reading of the Bible which rejects all questioning and any kind of critical research. … Fundamentalism also places undue stress upon the inerrancy of certain details in the biblical texts, especially in what concerns historical events or supposedly scientific truth. It often historicizes material which from the start never claimed to be historical. … Finally, in its attachment to the principle "Scripture alone," fundamentalism separates the interpretation of the Bible from the tradition, which, guided by the Spirit, has authentically developed in union with Scripture in the heart of the community of faith. … The fundamentalist approach is dangerous, for it is attractive to people who look to the Bible for ready answers to the problems of life. It can deceive these people, offering them interpretations that are pious but illusory, instead of telling them that the Bible does not necessarily contain an immediate answer to each and every problem. Without saying as much in so many words, fundamentalism actually invites people to a kind of intellectual suicide. It injects into life a false certitude, for it unwittingly confuses the divine substance of the biblical message with what are in fact its human limitations. [74]

Solely relying on the fundamentalist approach, which is unconcerned about reconciling faith and reason, is the root cause of maintaining a false certitude with regard to the sinful nature of homosexuality. If same-sex attraction is determined or influenced by the genome or epigenome, fundamentalists will still reject the relevance of any such scientific evidence with regard to interpreting biblical texts. Even more egregious is the tendency to interpret any biblical text in isolation, out of the context of the entire canon of scripture.

By using multiple methods for analysis of the Bible, the Church can, unlike fundamentalist denominations, more readily adapt its teaching to maintain congruity between faith and reason, as illustrated by the following comments made by Pope Benedict XVI on the theory of evolution:

Currently, I see in Germany, but also in the United States, a somewhat fierce debate raging between so-called "creationism" and evolutionism, presented as though they were mutually exclusive alternatives: those who believe in the Creator would not be able to conceive of evolution, and those who instead support evolution would have to exclude God. This antithesis is absurd because, on the one hand, there are so many scientific proofs in favour of evolution which appears to be a reality we can see and which enriches our knowledge of life and being as such. But on the other, the doctrine of evolution does not answer every query, especially the great philosophical question: where does everything come from? [75]

Perhaps the most rational argument against homosexual sex comes from the theory of evolution—because heterosexual sex is the only type of sex that enabled evolution to move forward. However, it is now the consensus among evolutionary biologists that the upward trajectory of evolution stopped with the arrival of behaviorally modern humans between 200,000 and 50,000 years ago. Anatomically modern humans evolved between 400,000 years and 200,000 years ago. If the long, 3.85 billion year history of biological evolution has reached its apex with the appearance of modern humans, then human homosexual sex can't be viewed as discordant with the overall trajectory of evolution because heterosexual sex is no longer required to move biological evolution forward.

## Was Joan of Arc a Lesbian?

Claims that Joan was a lesbian typically stem from two sections within the transcripts of her Condemnation Trial and Rehabilitation Trial. In the Condemnation Trial, Joan appears to have taken the initiative in wanting to spend two nights in bed with Catherine de La Rochelle to see the lady-in-white, whom Catherine claimed to appear as an apparition. Testimony during the Rehabilitation Trial by Marguerite la Touroulde indicated the two women shared a bed nearly every day for three weeks. First, a note about the following segment of the Condemnation Trial transcripts of March 3:

> Joan asked this Catherine if the lady-in-white who appeared to her came every night, saying that she would, to see her, sleep in the same bed with Catherine; and she went to bed with her and stayed up until midnight, but saw nothing, and then went to sleep.

> In the morning, Joan asked Catherine whether the lady-in-white had come to her. Catherine replied that she had, while Joan was sleeping, but that she had not been able to awaken Joan.

> Then Joan asked if the lady might not come another night, and Catherine answered yes; so Joan slept during the day, so that she might stay awake the whole night.

> That night she stayed in the bed with Catherine and watched all night, but saw nothing. Throughout the night Joan often asked Catherine whether the lady-in-white would come, and Catherine answered, "Yes, soon!"

The text above is translated as faithfully as possible from the French. For readers comparing this translation to W.P. Barrett's English translation of 1932, it's important to note that Barrett's translation is obfuscated to some degree. For example:

Barrett's translation—and she slept with her, and watched till midnight, saw nothing, and went to sleep.

Sanguinetti's translation—and she went to bed with her and stayed up until midnight, but saw nothing, and then went to sleep.

Quicherat's translation—et y coucha et veilla jusqu'à minuit, et ne vit rien; et puis s'endormit.

A second example regarding the use of exclamation marks:

Barrett's translation: "Yes, presently."
Sanguinetti's translation: "Yes, soon!"
Quicherat's translation: "Oui, bientôt!"

These notes are important for some critics because English translations of the source material often muddle or omit text from Quicherat's source. The following text is from the Rehabilitation Trial transcripts documenting the testimony of Marguerite la Touroulde, widow of Réné de Bouligny, advisor to the king:

> She was in my house for three weeks, sleeping, eating, and drinking there. And almost every night I slept with Joan, and I never saw or noticed anything uncanny about her. But she behaved and continued to behave like an honest and Christian woman. She confessed very often, gladly heard the Mass, and often asked me to go to Matins; and at her request I did go and took her there several times. [76]

Matins refers to Catholic liturgical prayers that end at dawn. The word *Matins* is derived from the Latin name for a Greek goddess *Leucothea*, white goddess, or goddess of the morning, also known as Aurora. [77] Although Catholic tradition eliminated any connection to the pagan origins of the word Matins—and nothing in the source text indicates otherwise—the white goddess is reminiscent of the lady-in-white, or white lady, referred to by Catherine de La Rochelle.

Regarding whether Joan had any non-orthodox beliefs or practices, according to Touroulde's testimony, she and Joan spoke about non-canonical texts that Joan perceived to be sacred but were not recognized as such by the clerics who examined her at Poitiers. Joan, according to Touroulde, responded to some of the clerics' questions by saying, "There is more in our Lord's books than in yours." [76] One unambiguously unorthodox practice of Joan involved her leadership of men, not only in the battlefield but also in religious practices. Jean de Dunois, affectionately known as "the Bastard of Orleans," testified that Joan led, not merely participated in, the daily cyclical prayers that Catholics refer to as the Divine Office or the Liturgy of the Hours:

> It was her habit every day, at Vesper time or at dusk, to retire into a church and have the bells rung for almost half an hour. Here she gathered the mendicant friars who followed the royal army, and at that hour she said her prayers and made these mendicant friars sing an anthem to the Blessed Virgin, the Mother of God. [78]

Touroulde's testimony is often used to support claims that Joan was a lesbian, and a disconcerting portion of her testimony is omitted in a popular English translation that is replicated numerous times on the web; the text that is omitted is the following:

> I saw her several times in the bath and in the hot-room, and so far as I could see I believe that she was a virgin. [76]

> Latin source text: Dicit insuper quod eam pluries vidit in balneo et stuphis, et, ut percipere potuit, credit ipsam fore virginem. [79]

> French translation: Elle déclare en outre qu'elle vit plusieurs fois Jeanne au bain et dans les étuves; elle croit, comme elle a pu le constater, qu'elle était vierge. [80]

The Latin word *stuphis* may be translated as "steam bath" or alternately as a geologic thermal spring, such as a source of hot sulfur spring water. For readers interested in the location where the omitted text should appear in Touroulde's testimony, the following material provides the context, with the omitted text in italics:

> Jeanne was very liberal in almsgiving, and willingly succored the poor and indigent, saying that she had been sent for their consolation. *And I saw her several times in the bath and in the hot-*

*room, and so far as I could see I believe that she was a virgin. I* have no doubt that she was virgin. According to my knowledge she was quite innocent, unless it be in warfare. She rode on horseback and handled the lance like the best of the knights, and the soldiers marveled. [81]

Joan's time in bed or in the baths with Marguerite la Touroulde or time in bed with Catherine de La Rochelle doesn't provide conclusive evidence that Joan was a lesbian primarily because bedding was relatively scarce in the fifteenth century and it was not uncommon for women to share a bed. However, it is reasonable to ask why Touroulde would state, "so far as I could see I believe that she was a virgin." That, too, isn't conclusive because testimony from the Rehabilitation Trial revealed that Joan not only was examined on several occasions regarding her virginity, but she sometimes challenged others to inspect her if they didn't believe it, so she may have offered to "prove" her virginity to Touroulde solely to establish the fact.

While individual historical facts are inadequate to make any definitive conclusions about Joan's sexual orientation, when viewed in their entirety, it is reasonable to make the assertion that Joan was a lesbian, particularly in light of several statements made by Joan, which are assumed to be referring to the apparitions of Saint Catherine and Saint Margaret, but instead could be referring to Catherine de La Rochelle and Marguerite la Touroulde:

March 12 Session:

We asked whether she spoke to our Lord when she promised Him to keep her virginity, and she answered that it was quite enough to promise her virginity to those who were sent from Him, namely Saint Catherine and Saint Margaret.

This statement is problematic because shortly after Joan makes this assertion, she stated, "the first time she heard her Voice she vowed to keep her virginity as long as it would please God, and that she was 13 years old or about 13 years old at the time," which is prior to the time she reports promising her virginity to Saint Catherine and Saint Margaret.

March 17 Session:

Asked why she so happily looked at this ring when she was going into battle, she answered that it was out of pleasure and in honor of her father and mother, and because, having her ring on her finger and in her hand, she touched Saint Catherine who appeared before her. Asked what part of Saint Catherine she had touched, she said, "You will get no answer from me."

Asked if she had ever kissed or touched Saint Catherine or Saint Margaret, she answered she had touched them both. We asked if Saint Catherine or Saint Margaret had a fine fragrance and she answered that it is good to know that they did. Asked whether, when embracing Saint Catherine or Saint Margaret, she felt heat or anything else, she said that she could not embrace them without feeling and touching them.

Also, Article 1 submitted to the assessors on April 5 included the following:

Moreover, the so-called Saint Catherine and Saint Margaret instructed Joan, in the name of God, to take and wear men's clothes; and Joan has worn them, and still wears them, stubbornly obeying this command to such an extent that Joan has declared that she would rather die than abandon wearing these clothes.

Karen Sullivan analyzed the Condemnation Trial transcripts, testimony from the Rehabilitation Trial and other documentation and concluded that Joan likely attributed the names of Saint Catherine and Saint Margaret to her Voices primarily because she was repeatedly asked to assign identities to Voices that were previously perceived by Joan as "Voices from God" and not specific saints. [82] Sullivan's analysis shows that, initially, Joan resisted characterizing her Voices as originating from saints until the judges in her trial led or prompted her to assign identities to the Voices. Joan's initial descriptions unmistakably assigned the origin of the Voices as coming from God. For example, on February 22, during the second session of the trial:

She said that at the age of 13 she first heard a Voice from God, to help her and to guide her. She said the first time she heard the

Voice she was very frightened. ... She said that a characteristic of the Voice was that it was admirable, and she believed it was sent from God. When she heard the Voice for the third time she said she knew that it was the Voice of an angel; she also said this Voice always protected her well, and that she understood it well.

On the same day, Joan revealed that she heard more than one distinct Voice, but she often referred to their origin in the singular, *Voice:*

She said that on her journey she passed through Auxerre and she attended Mass in the principal church there. From that time forward she said she frequently heard her Voices, including the one already mentioned. ... Joan said that there is not a day that goes by when she does not hear this Voice; and that she needs the Voice very much. She said she never asked the Voice for any final reward except only the salvation of her soul.

February 24, Third Session:

She said she firmly believes—as firmly as she believes in the Christian faith and that the Lord redeemed us from the pains of hell—that the Voice comes from God and by His command. Asked whether this Voice, which she says appears to her, comes as an angel or directly from God, or whether it is the Voice of one of the saints, she answered, "This Voice comes from God; I believe I will not tell you everything about it; and I am more afraid of failing the Voices by saying what is displeasing to them than of answering you. On this question, I beg you to grant me a delay."...

Asked if she saw anything else with the Voices, she replied, "I will not tell you everything, I do not have permission, nor does my oath touch on that. This Voice is good and worthy, and I am not bound to answer you." ... When we asked whether the Voice could see and whether the Voice had eyes, she answered, "You will not learn that yet," and she added that there was a saying among little children that "men are sometimes hanged for telling the truth."

It was during the fourth session on February 27 that Joan attributed her Voices to Saint Catherine and Saint Margaret in response to a question, "whether the Voice that spoke to her was that of an angel or a saint, a male or a female, or straight from God." Also during the fourth session:

> We asked her whether it was a long time ago that she first heard the Voice of St. Michael, and she said, "I do not speak of St. Michael's Voice, but of his great comfort."

During the fifth session on March 1, Joan provided some contradictory and nebulous statements about her Voices, revealing that she was struggling to characterize her Voices in the precise terms demanded by the judges:

> Asked how she knew whether her apparition was a man or a woman, she said she knew for certain because she recognized them by their Voices and they revealed themselves to her. ... When asked what part of them she saw, she said the face. Asked if the saints that appear to her have hair, she said, "Yes, it is very good to know that they have hair." ... We asked whether their hair was long and flowing down, and she answered, "I do not know." She added that she didn't know whether they appeared to have arms or other body parts. She said that they spoke very well and beautifully, and she understood them very well. Then we asked how they spoke if they had no other body parts, and she answered, "I leave that to God."

Sullivan noted that "it was to St. Catherine that several chroniclers compared Joan after she responded brilliantly to the clerics who examined her at Poitiers," and "Catherine of Alexandria and Margaret of Antioch resemble Joan in that they were also virgins who emerged in public life out of obedience to the Christian God and who, despite their youth, their sex, and their lack of familial or social support, became powerful in their societies." [83] Devotions to both saints were widely popular during Joan's lifetime, and although embellished stories developed surrounding the lives of the two saints, both are believed to be historical persons. It's reasonable to conclude that if Joan decided to name her Voices after two saints, then Saint Catherine and Saint Margaret would be likely choices. However, statements made by Joan indicating she not only promised her virginity to Saint Catherine and Saint Margaret, but also touched and embraced them gives credibility to the notion that Joan could have been surreptitiously referring to Catherine de La Rochelle and Marguerite la Touroulde.

Sullivan further tested her theory by examining evidence from numerous sources, including testimony from witnesses in the Rehabilitation Trial and accounts written by chroniclers, many of whom had first-hand contact with Joan. The results of the analysis fully support her theory that Joan attributed the names of Saint Catherine and Saint Margaret to her Voices because she was repeatedly asked to assign identities to Voices that Joan perceived as coming from God. A summary of her analysis in the following paragraph is based on Sullivan's chapter in *Fresh Verdicts on Joan of Arc,* edited by Bonnie Wheeler and Charles T. Wood.

The Duc d'Alençon, a close associate of Joan, recalled that Joan "declared herself sent by God." A chronicler associated with Alençon wrote that Joan said she was sent to King Charles "on the part [on behalf] of God." Marguerite la Touroulde said Joan "came on the part [on behalf] of God." Jean de Nouillompont, one of the individuals who escorted Joan from Vaucouleurs to see the king, said Joan told him that "my Lord" requested her to undertake her mission. Bertrand de Poulengy, another escort, recalled Joan saying "her Lord" requested her to travel to the king. Henri LeRoyer (who owned a house where Joan lodged on her way to see the king), Dunois (the Bastard of Orleans), Simon Charles (president of the Courts of Finance under the king), and Father John Pasquerel (Joan's confessor), all reported that Joan referred to "God, my Lord," as the source of her Voices. Gobert Thibaut, a squire in service to the king, reported that Joan said she came at the request of "the King of Heaven" to end the siege of Orleans. François Garivel, one of the king's counselors, reported that Joan said she was sent by "the King of Heaven" to help the dauphin [King Charles] as well as end the siege of Orleans and ensure the dauphin could travel to Reims for his coronation. Colette Miliet, who visited Joan in Orleans; her husband, Pierre; Guillaume Cousinot (author of *Chronique de la Pucelle* and a key historical source on the siege of Orleans); and the author of the *Journal d'un siege d'Orleans* (an anonymous account of events related to ending the siege of Orleans), all reported that Joan referred to "Messire" as the source of her inspiration; *messire* is Old French and is translated as *my sire* or *my Lord.*

During the canonization process, which the Catholic Church carries out to examine the life of an individual who is being considered for official, public recognition and honor as a saint, numerous character flaws were documented against Joan, including faults involving morality. Until 1983, the canonization process used an adversarial trial system, and the person appointed to oppose the cause for sainthood was referred to as the Devil's

Advocate (DA). The system is no longer adversarial but still involves gathering voluminous documentation about the person's life.

Henry Ansgar Kelly analyzed documentation from Joan's beatification and canonization process and referenced the following from DA Augustine Caprara, who was concerned that "she boasted of her virginity, challenging her interrogators to have her inspected." [84] Caprara also found Joan to be guilty of immodesty by not being careful enough about exposing her body around men "because the Duc d'Alençon testified that he saw her beautiful breasts at times." [84] DA John Lugari noted, "the same is true of John d'Aulon, who could glimpse her nipples when helping her to arm." [85] Other testimony from the Rehabilitation Trial noted by Lugari during the canonization process included the following anecdote provided by Jean Marcel:

> I have heard that the Duchess of Bedford had Joan examined to see whether she was a virgin or not, and that she was found to be a virgin. And I heard also from Jeannotin Simon, a tailor, that the Duchess of Bedford ordered him to make a woman's tunic for Joan, and that when he tried it on her, he softly put his hand on her breast. She was annoyed and slapped Jeannotin's face. [86]

DA Alexander Verde noted the following, as summarized by Kelly (the DA is also referred to as the Promoter of the Faith):

> Moving on to Joan's lack of humility, the Promoter cites another Consultor, who believes that not enough has been made of the objections about Joan's love of luxurious clothing, her horses [she had several horses], and so on, and the not always humble way in which she dealt with her judges. It all shows an attitude much different from that of the saints. [87]

Also, there were more serious problems discussed and documented by the DAs, including the abjuration signed by Joan to escape being burned at the stake. While signing the document under such pressure is completely understandable, it is nevertheless a clear failure in the type of *heroic virtue* that is found in people who are canonized. DA Verde also raised suspicions about her Voices, stating, "Who knows whether she did not suffer some hallucination and cultivated it as consonant with her own genius." [88]

Joan's path to canonized sainthood began in 1869 when the Bishop of Orleans sent a formal petition to Rome. Initial investigations into Joan's case began five years later due to delays caused by the Franco-Prussian War. Between 1874 and 1888, two consecutive bishops oversaw approximately ninety sessions spanning three separate investigations, after which the case was accepted by Rome's Sacred Congregation of Rites. Documentation from the first DA, Caprara, is dated 1892, and the next significant event occurred in 1894:

> The title of Venerable is first attributed to Joan in the decree of the Congregation of Rites approving of the introduction of her cause, "after the voice and writing of the Promoter of the Faith, Augustine Caprara, had been heard," [in] a decree dated January 27, 1894, and signed by the pope himself on that day. ... Later in 1894, the Sacred Congregation of Rites published a longish history of Joan of Arc in which no whisper of blame is to be heard. [89]

Two volumes of documentation were published in 1901 that address concerns raised by the second DA Lugari, who asserted "the principle obstacle to Joan's consideration for sainthood is her reliance on her own judgment in the matter of her revelations." [90] However, in Joan's defense, the "Defender Minetti spends a great deal of time showing that Joan consistently attempted to have her case removed from the prejudicial court of the bishop of Beauvais and brought to the pope." [90] *Defender* is the title given to the individual who opposes the DA.

An extraordinary event occurred in the next phase of the canonization process. The Catholic Church does not make pronouncements that a person being considered for sainthood "failed to qualify." Processes may continue for decades, and centuries may pass because the individual does not progress further from the title of Venerable. However, between April 19, 1902, when DA Verde wrote a 24-page attack on Joan's character, and February 12, 1903, when the Defender Minetti wrote a 367-page response that was supplemented by a 198-page *Expositio Virtutum* (Exposition of Virtues) document, headlines such as the following appeared in U.S. newspapers:

Will Not Be Canonized: Morals of Joan of Arc Were Not Those of a Saint [91]
Joan of Arc: Canonization Denied to Her [92]
Joan of Arc Not to Be Canonized [93]

The story published under the first headline listed above appears on page two of The Indianapolis Journal, dated November 10, 1902:

BALTIMORE, Md., Nov 9—Rome has advised ecclesiastical circles here of the decision of the Congregation of Rites that Joan of Arc, the Maid of Orleans, shall not be canonized, and in so deciding has stigmatized the name of the famous girl in a startling manner. The principal reason for which canonization is denied is the alleged discovery of facts against her moral character which precluded the possibility of according to her saintly reverence.

The congregation has also announced that Joan of Arc was guilty of the grave fault of attacking Paris on a feast of the Blessed Virgin, in signing a confession to the effect that she had no divine commission to deliver France from her enemies, and that her claims to such distinction were fraudulent and a prevarication. The confession was made, according to the English, in the hope that she might be saved thereby from the ignominious death at the stake which she afterwards suffered.

The proclamation of the reasons has caused surprise here, as it is felt that they will seriously offend religious elements in France, where Joan of Arc is regarded as a national patron saint, on the same plane with St. Patrick in Ireland and St. George in England and St. James in Spain. The practical aspersion of her character in France as a saint, it is generally believed, will prove a play into the hands of the present French Ministry, engaged as it is in suppressing the religious orders.

The Roman curia has never been partial to Joan of Arc. The agitation to have her canonized began during the later years of Napoleon III, and it is alleged that had he remained on his throne and continued to maintain an army in the eternal city for the protection of the temporal rights of the Papacy the matter would have been settled in her favor long ago. But with the overthrow of

Napoleon and the withdrawal of the French troops from Rome, which ended in the seizure of the city by the Italians and the conquest of the states of the church, the question dragged along until the accession of Pope Leo XIII, who at once saw the importance of pleasing the French Catholics and identifying French national sentiment with Catholicism.

Queen Victoria, at the head of the English nation, whose ancestors had condemned Joan of Arc at the stake, was asked if she had any objections to offer, it is said, to the Maid of Orleans being canonized, and on a negative reply being received the process of canonization was begun. Joan of Arc was accordingly "beatified," which is the first step toward canonization, and is now termed "blessed."

That the Queen of England, a Protestant, should have been consulted by the Vatican relative to the canonization of a Catholic saint, may appear extraordinary, until it is remembered that the Maid of Orleans was regarded as a witch by the English and that her "martyrdom," as the French people believed, for freedom's sake, as well as that of conscience, is the chief ground on which her canonization was asked.

The French people have now, it is said, learned for the first time that the Queen was consulted before the beatification of Joan of Arc, and indignation is felt because of it.

As far as known Joan of Arc left no descendants. She had a brother, and from him are descended the Marquises and Counts De Maleysie, one of whom is married to an American girl, Miss Sterns, of New York, who would have figured prominently at the canonization ceremonies in St. Peter's, Rome.

The following text is from *Harper's Weekly,* dated April 11, 1903, and is written in a tabloid style:

About three months ago the Congregation of Rites at Rome announced its resolution to deny canonization to Joan of Arc, giving, among its several reasons for its actions, a declaration to the effect that after a careful consideration of all evidence presented both for and against the fair Joan, it was impossible to arrive at any other conclusion but that the dame in question was not entitled to the surname of "maid" accorded to her by her admirers. ... This declaration by the Congregation of Rites that Joan of Arc was not entitled to the qualification of "maid" lends a new importance to the pretensions put forward by several French noblemen, of a more or less authentic character, to include her among their ancestors. ... It is only fair to add, however, that the general public has always been agreed that Joan of Arc left no descendants—at any rate of a legitimate character. [93]

Regarding the news reports quoted above, which relate "the discovery of facts against her moral character" and a "declaration by the Congregation of Rites that Joan of Arc was not entitled to the qualification of 'maid,'" it's clear the primary sources for the news reports implied that Joan was not a virgin. However, because there was so much evidence that Joan was, in fact, a virgin, it's possible that DA Verde and others may have concluded that Joan consummated a relationship with a woman.

Although there is no evidence Joan consummated a relationship with Robert de Baudricourt, her response to the accusation made in Article 11— as well as other comments by Joan that she was willing to give up her virginity if it was the will of God—appears to support the possibility that she had a relationship with Baudricourt that was more than friendship but which may or may not have been sexual. The charges specified in Article 11 were written by the trial judges and the story could have been embellished or entirely fabricated by Baudricourt.

Article 11:

Joan, having entered into intimate relations with Robert de Baudricourt, boasted to have told him that after having accomplished everything revealed to her by God, that she would have three sons: the first would be Pope, the second emperor, and the third king.

After hearing this, the captain said to her, "Now then, I would like to give you a child since they're going to be such powerful men, because I'm worth as much or more and I would be better off." To which Joan replied, "Gentle Robert, no, no, this is not the time; the

Holy Spirit will find a way!" Robert confirmed and repeated this conversation in many places, including in the presence of clerics, lawyers and notable persons.

Joan's response:

To this eleventh article, Joan answered by referring us to the answers she made elsewhere on this subject; and as for having three children, she never boasted about it.

Joan's statements regarding a willingness to give up her virginity if it was God's will indicates that Joan probably had heterosexual inclinations and may have been bisexual. Additionally, the following evidence indicates Joan may have been "gender fluid."

Joan's extreme reluctance to give up wearing men's clothes, even for the purpose of attending Mass, was reflected in the transcripts of the March 15 session: "As urgently as she could, she implored us to allow her to attend Mass in the clothes she wore, without any change." Yet, despite being adamant about remaining in men's clothes at all times, Joan expressed a willingness to change into women's clothes but only for specific women:

March 3 Session:

We asked her whether she was requested to stop wearing men's clothes at the castle of Beaurevoir, and she replied, "Yes, that is true, and I answered I would not stop wearing men's clothes without getting God's permission." She said the Demoiselle of Luxembourg and the Lady of Beaurevoir offered her a woman's dress, or the cloth to make one, and they told her to wear it, however, Joan replied that she did not have God's permission and it was not yet time. When asked if Messire Jean de Pressy and others at Arras did not offer her women's clothes, she said that he and many others had often asked her to wear a woman's dress. Asked whether she believed she would have done wrong or committed a mortal sin by wearing women's clothes, she replied that she did better to obey and serve her sovereign Lord, namely God. However, she said that if she had to wear a woman's dress, she would rather have done so at the request of those two ladies than of any other ladies in France, except the queen.

Joan's path to sainthood mirrors a contemporary culture that's often cited for a lack of morality and an inability to coalesce around a common set of principles that define the difference between good and bad behavior. But Joan's situation reflects the reality of many Catholics who are often referred to by Pope Francis as people on the margins—those who live on the outskirts of the Church. These individuals are striving to live a life of love but feel they are second-class members of the Church because they aren't officially permitted to receive Holy Communion even though they are not subjectively guilty of committing a mortal sin. These members of the Church include many divorced and remarried Catholics, homosexuals in same-sex relationships, and others who are in some way nonconformist but nevertheless love Christ and love the Church. Perhaps Joan of Arc will eventually be viewed as the patron saint of Catholics who were driven out of the Church by the haughtiness of holier-than-thou hypocrites.

**Origin of Joan's Voices**

Academic peer pressure typically discourages serious researchers from discussing the possibility of supernatural intervention when accounting for phenomena such as the origin of Joan's Voices. A thorough and balanced analysis is difficult because the realms of supernatural activity and divine inspiration are considered off-limits. However, undergraduate students in English composition courses are not quite so deterred, and Victoria Yuskaitis has effectively analyzed both sides of the main arguments regarding Joan's Voices—divine inspiration versus mental illness—and has written a concise report that summarizes the conclusions as well as the limitations of both arguments. It's freely available on the web under the title, *Joan of Arc: Inspired or Insane,* at the Lycoming College website. [94]

In her March 17 testimony, Joan indicated she touched and embraced Saint Catherine and Saint Margaret. Strict secularists would interpret such statements as either delusions or lies. However, it's useful to look at reports that indicate the ability or inability—to have or try to have—sensory contact with apparitions.

In one example, there are statements made by two people asserting it was impossible to touch an apparition that was reported to occur on August 21, 1879, in Knock, Ireland. Fifteen people reported seeing the Blessed Virgin Mary, Saint Joseph, and Saint John the Evangelist, who appeared in front of a gable wall at the Knock Parish church. Documentation of the event noted that "the witnesses watched the apparition in the pouring rain for two hours, reciting the Rosary. Although they themselves were saturated, not a single drop of rain fell on the gable or vision." [95] One witness, Patrick Hill, reported the following:

> I distinctly beheld the Blessed Virgin Mary, life size, standing about two feet or so above the ground clothed in white robes which were fastened at the neck. ... At times she appeared, and all the figures appeared, to move out, and again to go backwards; I saw them move; she did not speak; I went up very near; one old woman went up and embraced the Virgin's feet, and she found nothing in her arms and hands; they receded, she said, from her. [96]

The woman mentioned above, Bridget Trench, reported:

> When I arrived there I saw distinctly the three figures, I threw myself on my knees and exclaimed, "A hundred thousand thanks to God and to the glorious Virgin that has given us this manifestation." I went in immediately to kiss, as I thought, the feet of the Blessed Virgin, but I felt nothing in the embrace but the wall, and I wondered why I could not feel with my hands the figures which I had so plainly and so distinctly seen. [96]

An example of a tangible apparition was discussed by Marija Pavlovic-Lunnetti, one of six individuals who have reported seeing apparitions of the Blessed Virgin Mary since June 24, 1981. The following quote is from a talk given March 24, 2004, at Corpus Christi Basilica in Manchester, England:

> We prayed the Rosary and Our Lady appeared. The moment She appeared She said we could all get close to Her and touch Her. We said, "How is it possible, only the six of us can see you and nobody else can?" Our Lady said, "Take their hands and get them close to me." And so we did. And Our Lady allowed that everybody touched Her. Everybody felt something when they touched Our Lady. Some cold, or warm, or perfume of roses, or like an electric shock, and they all believed that Our Lady was really present. [97]

Conchita Gonzalez of Garabandal, Spain, experienced more than 2,000 apparitions of the Virgin Mary, almost all occurring between June 18, 1961, and January 20, 1963. [90] Gonzalez kept a diary of her experiences, and her diary is included in an analysis conducted by Father Joseph A. Pelletier, which is freely available on the web under the title, *Our Lady Comes to Garabandal.* Gonzalez was twelve years old when the apparitions began, and other children were sometimes involved. Pelletier wrote:

> It [kissing] was a maternal gesture that was repeated quite often in subsequent apparitions at the conclusion of the ecstasy. The children were observed placing themselves in a position to receive or give a kiss to the vision. Occasionally they lifted each other, without any effort, to reach Our Lady. This would usually take place before or after a final sign of the cross, after which the apparition would end. [98]

Natural and supernatural explanations have been offered to account for Joan's Voices and reports of apparitions. Natural explanations typically focus on hallucinations associated with conditions such as schizophrenia or epilepsy. The visible lights that Joan referred to may be indicative of epileptic seizures. Also, temporal lobe epilepsy (TLE) has been associated with reports of paranormal experiences, including visions and accurate premonitions. The Epilepsy Foundation hosts a Community Forum at epilepsy.com, which includes comments such as the following:

> While I was sitting in the waiting room I kept going into these hallucinations, they felt like I was being kissed by the Gods, as you explain it. I felt overwhelming sensations that felt like God was letting me know that he was right there next to me while I was seizing. He was telling me to not be so mad all the time, and that he was keeping an eye on me. I'm Roman Catholic, but I don't practice my faith a lot." [99]

> My first ecstatic seizure came hot on the heels of several really bad CP seizures—I couldn't seem to come out of them and then had the best experience of my life (until very recently). I'll call it my "God" moment but won't go into details other than to say I fully understand why people become convinced that God exists. [99]

> This is my first post and I do not know where to start. ... 3 months ago my 22 yr. old daughter suffered a grand mal seizure. ... Now,

here comes the strange part, last week she had a period of intense concern and after a short sleep woke up to what can only be described as a changed soul—extremely intuitive and spiritual. She has always been very in tune with people's moods/problems but now these have taken on a whole new life. She sees people's auras and accurately describes each person's colour (she has not done any research on people's auras as she had always thought this to be "hippy dippy"!!). Her descriptions so far have been 100% accurate and she also appears to know about traumas that have happened to people that she meets that have had far reaching effect and impact on their lives. I think she feels that she has become a healer of some sort and says that she feels much more relaxed now—much happier. My other daughter has been completely "freaked out" by her sister's change and feels that this is just part of her seizures and fears that her brain has been damaged. Has anyone heard of something like this? [99]

How accurate are people with TLE and their predictions? My most recent one was terribly hard on me (and those that love me) but incredibly accurate. ... I was right about things that I in no way could possibly have known. Has anybody else had predictions that were too accurate to be luck? [100]

I find it fascinating how many people who suffer from TLE also had psychic experiences from their earliest days. Hopefully one day the worlds of the paranormal and science will converge and we'll be able to understand the "why" behind such interesting phenomenon as premonitions coming true, out of body experiences, etc. [100]

I've never joined one of these talk-back things before, but I feel compelled to join this one. ... This is truly the agony and the ecstasy! Have a seizure and find religion. Who would a' thunk it. I have truly found G-d. I convinced a room full of psychiatrists that G-d was in the room and that I was talking to him and that I was neither psychotic nor grandiose. I was dying and had a near death experience that is the best thing has ever happened to me in my life. I speak to Him often and he came to me and touched me and gave me life. Yes I was seizing. [99]

It's often easy to use a natural explanation to account for something that appears to be supernatural. Natural explanations are credible insofar as they align with reported events, but some events defy any type of natural explanation. Near-death experiences (NDEs) are often dismissed as being hallucinations, however, at least one category of NDEs can't be explained away as hallucinations. These NDEs involve fully anesthetized surgery patients who are later able to report precise details about activities that occurred in the operating room. The reports are subsequently verified by physicians and other medical staff as being completely accurate. These patients typically describe the behavior of people in the operating room in rigorous detail, and can often describe the activities of people outside of the hospital—for example, indicating the routes driven by relatives traveling to the hospital during the time the patient is in surgery.

Other aspects of NDEs that defy natural explanation include reports of experiences that are consistent across a wide range of people regardless of their age, cultural background, geographic origin, religion, or lack of religion. Mona Simpson, the sister of Steve Jobs, was with him at the moment he died, and she recalled his NDE:

> Steve's final words, hours earlier, were monosyllables, repeated three times. Before embarking, he'd looked at his sister Patty, then for a long time at his children, then at his life's partner, Laurene, and then over their shoulders past them. Steve's final words were: OH WOW. OH WOW. OH WOW. [101]

The capital letters were written by Simpson and appeared in *The New York Times* in an editorial titled, "A Sister's Eulogy for Steve Jobs," in which she wrote, "Even as a feminist, my whole life I'd been waiting for a man to love, who could love me. For decades, I'd thought that man would be my father. When I was 25, I met that man and he was my brother." [101]

Also, despite skepticism on the subject of auras, there are testimonies that are difficult to discount, such as the following recollection of a survivor of a plane crash involving a flight scheduled to fly from Singapore to Los Angeles. The pilots attempted a takeoff during a typhoon and used the wrong runway. The crash killed eighty-three of the 179 people on board, and one of the survivors, an irreligious person, recounted his experience to Oprah Winfrey, who relayed it in the following words:

As he was leaving the plane, he said, all the bodies were on fire on the plane, and he looked back and he saw that auras were coming up out of the bodies, up out of the flames, and that he wasn't a religious person, but he learned in that moment that he wanted— and that some auras were brighter than others—and that he said "I want to live my life so that my aura is always bright." [102]

Throughout the history of the Church, mysticism has played a vital role in the lives of individual Catholics as well as in the Church as an institution. As defined by the *Catholic Encyclopedia*, mysticism:

Implies a relation to mystery; in philosophy, mysticism is either a religious tendency and desire of the human soul towards an intimate union with the divinity, or a system growing out of such a tendency and desire. As a philosophical system, mysticism considers as the end of philosophy the direct union of the human soul with the divinity through contemplation and love, and attempts to determine the processes and the means of realizing this end. This contemplation, according to mysticism, is not based on a merely analogical knowledge of the Infinite, but as a direct and immediate intuition of the Infinite. ... [The Church] teaches that, what man [or woman] cannot know by natural reason, he [or she] can know through revelation and faith; that what he [or she] cannot attain to by his [or her] natural power he [or she] can reach by the grace of God. God has gratuitously elevated human nature to a supernatural state. [103]

Mathilde Bertrand-Boutlè was a French mystic who wrote under the pseudonym, Lucie Christine. She described her mystical union with God in the following words:

All that can be said is that this august Majesty takes possession of the soul and ravishes her by a charm as great as the reverence with which it inspires her. And the soul, beside herself, is filled with awe at the sight of such greatness and yet feels drawn to it by an irresistible force; she finds therein her happiness, she sports in God as in a boundless universe, and she tastes in him, her first Principle and her last End, a rest to which nothing human can be compared. She feels herself penetrated by this divine nature, she feels that in it she lives and in it alone she has her being, her love is inflamed for the adorable Being who is her life, she feels that he possesses her more than she possesses her own self, and all her strength dissolving in him, like a drop of water in a boundless ocean, it appears to her that her love and her life are one! [104]

Mystical experiences in Catholicism include the types described above, which involve, to varying degrees, union with God during prayer. Other experiences such as those described by Joan involve visible phenomena perceived as apparitions, which may or may not be accompanied by audible messages. Other types of messages—interior locutions—are inaudible, not processed through the ears. Gonzalez described an interior locution she received from the Blessed Virgin Mary in her diary:

"Conchita, do not doubt that my Son will perform a miracle!" I heard it interiorly, as clearly as if through my ears and even better than if it had been through words. It left me with a peace and joy even greater than that experienced when I saw her. ... I no longer experienced any doubts about anything. ... The locutions did me so much good, so very much good, for it was as if the Blessed Virgin was within me. What happiness! ... I prefer the locution to the apparitions, because in the locution I have her within me. Oh, what happiness when I have the Blessed Virgin in me! ... I prefer to have Jesus in me, Jesus who will give me the cross to purify me, and through my crosses will permit me to do something for the world with the help of God, for by myself I can do nothing. [105]

One explanation regarding why messages received via interior locutions don't pass through the ears involves the role of the "Indwelling Trinity" in communicating those messages. [106] Similarly, the same is true for the Blessed Mother within. An essential truth or required belief (dogma) of Catholicism is that the Blessed Virgin Mary was bodily assumed into heaven in "a singular participation in her Son's Resurrection and an anticipation of the resurrection of other Christians." [107] As a result:

Pope Benedict XVI writes that "precisely because Mary is with God and in God, she is very close to each one of us. While she lived on this earth she could only be close to a few people. Being in God, who is actually 'within' all of us, Mary shares in the closeness of

God." Our Lady "knows our hearts, can hear our prayers, can help us with her motherly kindness. She always listens to us and, being Mother of the Son, participates in the power of the Son and his goodness." [108]

Gonzalez described another type of locution as "that voice of interior happiness which speaks without words." Many types of experiences in this category have been noted by mystics in the Church, and Gonzalez described a rare version accompanied by an interior force that often led her and other girls to walk—often backwards while in an ecstatic state—to a wooded area in Garabandal called The Pines, where a large number of apparitions were experienced and witnessed by others:

> When we had finished the Rosary and had failed to see her, we said: "We shouldn't be surprised or sad, as the apparition has always occurred later in the day." Since she didn't come, we went to our homes and did the things they asked us to do around the house.

> When the hour approached at which we had seen the Blessed Virgin for the first time on Sunday, our parents, because they now believed more in the apparitions, said to us: "You should go and say the Rosary at the *cuadro* [wooden frame erected at The Pines to keep crowds from disturbing the visionaries]."

> "But we haven't been called yet," we replied. They were puzzled and said: "But, how are you called?"

> We told them that it was like an interior voice, but that we did not hear it with our ears, nor did we hear ourselves called by name. It is a feeling of joy. There are three calls. The first is a weaker feeling of joy. The second is a little stronger. But the third one makes us very excited and very happy. Then the apparition occurs.

> We only depart for the site of the apparition at the second call, for, if we leave at the first, we have to wait there a long while because there is a long delay between the first and the second call. [98]

Interior locutions range across a spectrum from subtle "movements of the heart" perceived during prayer to the extraordinary example described above. At the more subtle end of the spectrum, *movements of the heart* shouldn't be misinterpreted as a reference to something purely sentimental in nature. The *Catechism* defines prayer, in part, as the "raising of one's mind and heart to God." [109] "According to Sacred Scripture, it is the heart that prays. If our heart is far from God, the words of prayer are in vain." [110] Also, from the *Catechism*:

> The heart is the dwelling-place where I am, where I live; according to the Semitic or Biblical expression, the heart is the place "to which I withdraw." The heart is our hidden center, beyond the grasp of our reason and of others; only the Spirit of God can fathom the human heart and know it fully. The heart is the place of decision, deeper than our psychic drives. It is the place of truth, where we choose life or death. It is the place of encounter, because as an image of God we live in relation: it is the place of covenant. [111]

Catholicism teaches that the *heart* is where the will or decision-making capabilities, the intellect, the body with its passions, and the soul, intersect. Pope Benedict XVI described *heart* during the twenty-sixth World Youth Day, 2011, held in Madrid, Spain. The Pope's description of the heart referenced a part of the Mass where believers are called to *lift up your hearts:*

> In the language of the Bible and the thinking of the Fathers, the heart is the centre of man [and woman], where understanding, will and feeling, body and soul, all come together. The centre where spirit becomes body and body becomes spirit, where will, feeling and understanding become one in the knowledge and love of God. This is the "heart" which must be lifted up. But to repeat: of ourselves, we are too weak to lift up our hearts to the heights of God. We cannot do it. The very pride of thinking that we are able to do it on our own drags us down and estranges us from God. God himself must draw us up, and this is what Christ began to do on the cross. He descended to the depths of our human existence in order to draw us up to himself, to the living God. [112]

Movements of the heart are typically described in terms of joy, but they can also involve negative or unpleasant feelings. Saint Ignatius of Loyola referred to movements of joy, hope, and peace as *consolations,* and movements of sadness, fear, and anxiety as *desolations.* How to interpret and respond to these movements is the subject of a book by Timothy M. Gallagher, *The Discernment of Spirits:*

> All who have preceded us in the journey of faith have experienced such movements of the heart, and they, like us have made choices in response to these movements, accepting or rejecting them. ... I realized that Ignatius here provides an unparalleled resource for overcoming what is generally the major obstacle faithful persons encounter in their efforts to grow spiritually: discouragement, fear, loss of hope, and other troubling movements of the heart. ... My aim, then, is to offer an experience-based presentation of Ignatius's rules for discernment of spirits in order to facilitate their ongoing application in the spiritual life. [113]

Discerning movements of the heart and learning how to respond to them are keys to growth in prayer, which is meant to be a dialogue as opposed to a one-way communication. Growth in prayer typically moves along a continuum throughout life, beginning with *vocal prayer* (saying or thinking about the words that form the prayer), then progressing to two types of *mental prayer.* The first type involves meditating (thinking more deeply and for longer periods of time) about, for example, the words written in sacred scripture as well as events in the life of Christ, the Blessed Mother, and holy people and angels mentioned in the Bible; this includes meditating on their roles, their activities, and the events where they appear in sacred scripture.

Unlike vocal prayer or meditative prayer, contemplative prayer involves mystical, two-way communication between the person praying and God, the Blessed Mother, a saint, or a holy angel. The Church refers to these received messages as *private revelations,* which are distinguished from *public revelation.* Public revelation includes sacred scripture and the apostolic tradition that was established prior to the time the last of the apostles died. The purpose of private revelation, which includes phenomena such as Joan's Voices, apparitions of the Blessed Virgin Mary, and interior locutions, is to provide the evidence that people need to experience the reality of the Gospel of Christ. These private revelations enable the person to move from a purely faith-based relationship with God to an experiential relationship with God.

Vocal prayers, especially when prayed silently in the mind instead of verbally, can develop into meditative and contemplative (mystical) experiences. The Rosary, for example, can be purely a vocal prayer, but it also encourages the person praying it to meditate on various events in the life of Christ and the Blessed Virgin Mary that pertain to redemption. There are five key events in each of the four overarching mysteries of the Rosary— Joyful, Luminous, Sorrowful, and Glorious—and an overview of the mysteries and of the Rosary itself is found in Saint John Paul II's Apostolic Letter titled *Rosarium Virginis Mariae* (Rosary of the Virgin Mary). Each "decade" (ten beads or ten prayers of the Hail Mary) in the five-decade Rosary is associated with an event to meditate upon, and the meditation can progress from merely thinking about the events to vividly imagining you are a witness or a participant in the events. That particular approach to prayer, which may develop into a mystical experience, is based on the writings of Saint Ignatius of Loyola, who founded the Society of Jesus (Jesuits). While placing oneself in the context of a historical event can facilitate a mystical encounter with Christ or the Virgin Mary, having such an approach to prayer isn't necessary to experience interior locutions; in fact, the approach isn't well-suited for many people.

Claims of apparitions—visual encounters with supernatural beings—are easily discounted, but some claims are strengthened by credible testimonies and objectively documented events. Randall Sullivan, a journalist who was a contributing editor at *Rolling Stone* magazine for twenty years, wrote an extensive account of Marian apparitions reported by several people in Scottsdale, Arizona. In his book, *The Miracle Detective*, Sullivan reported the Scottsdale apparitions began in September 1987 with Gianna Talone, age thirty:

> She told herself it was a dream that first time: It was after midnight and she was lying in bed when a young woman, beautiful beyond belief, appeared out of thin air and began praying over her. She could see the woman quite clearly, Gianna said, slim and of medium height, wearing a white robe and a semi-sheer veil, with long dark hair, steel-blue eyes, a porcelain complexion, ruby lips, and rosy cheeks. The fingers of the two hands pressed together in front of her were long and perfectly tapered, Gianna noticed; the

young woman did not speak, but smiled radiantly, then disappeared. [114]

Like other visionaries in the Scottsdale apparitions, Talone initially thought she "had gone mad" when, two months after seeing Mary on three consecutive nights, "she heard a voice, a male voice, quite clear and perfectly distinct, say, 'The Lord seeks favor upon you, for you have cried for the Lord.'" [114] Talone also reported a vision of the Blessed Mother in which Mary requested a prayer group of young adults aged eighteen to thirty-three be formed at Saint Maria Goretti parish:

She had been shown six young people, one of them herself, kneeling at an altar, Gianna explained. The others were Steve and Wendy Nelson, Susan Evans, plus two others, Mary Cook and Jimmy Kupanoff. Off to the side were two other young women: one standing, whom she recognized as Stephanie Staab, and another on her knees, whom she did not remember seeing before. [115]

Within weeks, each member of the core group experienced apparitions or locutions that led them to the parish church to join the prayer group, which eventually grew to more than a thousand members. A few days after Talone described her vision to Father Jack Spaulding at Saint Maria Goretti church, Spaulding recalled a visit to his office by Staab:

The first words out of Stephanie's mouth were almost the same ones Gianna had opened with, the priest recalled: "Father, I think I may be losing my mind." She had been hearing a voice, Stephanie explained, the voice of a woman who had instructed her to copy out a lengthy disquisition. When the priest read the several pages she handed him, he was visibly shaken [by] … the most moving treatise on conversion of the heart that he had ever read. [116]

A week later Spaulding received another visitor, Steve Nelson, who said, "I think I'm going crazy." "Let me finish," the priest interrupted. "You've been hearing a woman's voice." [117] Another person in the group, Evans, described her initial experience—an interior locution from Jesus:

She had been sitting with her family at a friend's wedding reception, Susan told Spaulding, when she heard a male voice ask,

"Would you give up your family for Me?" She looked around the circle of her relations, then answered, "Yes, Lord." [118]

Kupanoff, another member of the group, said, "the Virgin had spoken to him in his heart, and that he had experienced a conversion." [115]

Talone had discussed her vision with Cook, that she saw Cook in her vision, but Cook "found the whole idea really frightening, and didn't want to believe it, anyway... I didn't want it to be real, and I knew it wasn't for me." [119] Cook had had three abortions and "seemed to careen from one destructive relationship to the next, barely pausing between." [115] Two weeks later, Cook moved from Arizona to Wisconsin, but within two more weeks, she moved back to Arizona and discussed her experience with Spaulding:

Soon after arriving in Wisconsin, Mary explained to the priest when she came in that afternoon, she had heard a woman's voice. She knew it was the Blessed Mother, asking her to return to Arizona and join the prayer group, yet despite this, she had refused. The Virgin asked again though, requesting that she go back to Scottsdale and meet with Spaulding. The moment she said yes, Mary explained, a sense of peace welled up within her. [119]

The Scottsdale apparitions involving eight individuals and Talone have been investigated by the Church separately from apparitions and messages Talone reported in Emmitsburg, Maryland. The Church officially rules on apparitions to be in one of three categories: supernatural; not supernatural; or no conclusive evidence to support a ruling of supernatural or not supernatural. The Scottsdale apparitions have been designated in the third category, as inconclusive. In October 1989, Father Ernest Larkin of the Investigative Commission of the Diocese of Phoenix stated, "We don't think that these are hoaxes or that there is any attempt to deceive anybody. We simply maintain that there is not enough evidence to say that these are miracles." Father Robert Faricy, a theologian and Emeritus Professor of Spirituality at the Pontifical Gregorian University in Rome, stated, "Personally, as anyone can, we believe strongly in the authenticity of the Scottsdale apparitions and messages. Furthermore, as Roman Catholics we submit our observations and convictions in obedience to the Church and subject to official judgment." [120]

Arriving at contemplative, mystical prayer typically doesn't happen overnight, but it is possible to easily experience mystical prayer—where the person praying has a direct experience with God, the Blessed Virgin Mary, other people in heaven, as well as angels, including having conversations where the person praying asks a question and waits in contemplative silence for an answer. Faith is the catalyst that makes the experiences possible; the individual must come to the realization that they are completely inadequate to "complete the transaction" on their own.

Sacred art can play a major role in an individual's spiritual development because it can stimulate the heart in ways that words cannot. Regarding the role that statues, images, and other sacred objects can have in spiritual development, the Church teaches that such objects are *sacramentals:*

> Sacramentals do not confer the grace of the Holy Spirit in the way that the sacraments do, but by the Church's prayer, they prepare us to receive grace and dispose us to cooperate with it. For well-disposed members of the faithful, the liturgy of the sacraments and sacramentals sanctifies almost every event of their lives with the divine grace which flows from the Paschal mystery of the Passion, Death, and Resurrection of Christ. From this source all sacraments and sacramentals draw their power. There is scarcely any proper use of material things which cannot be thus directed toward the sanctification of men [and women] and the praise of God. [121]

The use of sacramentals to facilitate direct encounters with God, the Blessed Virgin Mary, saints, and angels is disparaged by many people in the Church for being akin to superstition, pure sentimentality, or perhaps even a practice best reserved for lower-class Catholics. Austen Ivereigh's biography of Pope Francis, *The Great Reformer: Francis and the Making of a Radical Pope,* includes a humorous anecdote illustrating the dichotomy that exists within the Church regarding sacramentals. In Buenos Aires, Argentina, when Pope Francis (then Jorge Bergoglio), was head of the Jesuit College, Colegio Máximo de San José, and in charge of the formation program for Jesuit seminarians and priests, many intellectuals were horrified by aspects of the program:

> He encouraged a style of popular religiosity among the students, who would go to a chapel at night and touch images! This was something the poor did, the people of the *pueblo,* something that the Society of Jesus [Jesuits] worldwide just doesn't *do.* I mean,

*touching images* ... what is that? And the older ones, praying the Rosary together in the gardens. Look, I'm not against that, but I'm not in favor either. It's just not typical of us. But it became normal at the time. [122]

There is a great deal of polarization on this issue and related activities, with perhaps a 50/50 split among the Church hierarchy as well as in the pews, with half viewing these practices as antiquated at best, and the other half—those touching the images and praying the Rosary—viewing the practices and objects as effective mediums to cross the gap between the natural and supernatural worlds.

Simply stated, "In a sacramental religion material things are doorways to the spirit." [123] The icon or the sacramental is the vehicle through which God or a saint in heaven becomes present to us. When a person prays with the intention of entering into a two-way dialogue with God or a saint and uses an icon or a sacramental object as an integral part of the prayer, the subject and the object can become united by the grace of God. The degree or level of unification between the person praying and God or a saint can range from a subtle movement of the heart to an ecstatic state where the person is oblivious to their surroundings.

Catholicism defines the soul as "intellect + will," and "intellect + will = mind." In mental prayer, the soul, the mind, is not bound by the limitations of space and time, which is why Saint Ignatius of Loyola could recommend using one's mind to vividly imagine themselves in an encounter with Christ or the Blessed Virgin. Also, prior to the death of the biological body, the soul and the body are inextricably united, so the act of *touching* an image can, by the grace of God, facilitate a connection. Discerning whether the connection is real or purely an act of one's imagination may be difficult during early stages in the development of a prayer life, but a daily practice of prayer, whether it is twenty minutes or three hours, is key to accurate discernment.

Pope Benedict XVI addressed the question of images and statues at length in his book, *The Spirit of the Liturgy,* stating:

These images, too, do not show just the "surface of the skin," the external sensible world; they, too, are intended to lead us through mere outward appearance and open our eyes to the heart of God. ... What power of inward devotion lies in the images of the Mother of God! ... Such images are an invitation to prayer, because they are permeated with prayer from within. [124]

On the topic of "praying to" statues and images, the practice was first formally addressed at the Church's Second Council of Nicaea in 787. The word *iconoclast* is typically defined as a person who attacks cherished beliefs or institutions, but the origin of the word is derived from the Greek *eikonoklastēs,* meaning to break or smash religious statues.

Iconoclasm was an eighth-century movement to rid the Church of perceived idol worship, but the Church addressed the misunderstanding at Nicaea by stating the obvious: the person who is honoring or venerating a statue or image is directing their honor and veneration to the individual represented, not the image. It is similar to the non-religious practice of viewing a picture of a loved one who has passed away, or kissing the picture; the intention is obviously directed to the person and not the image.

Sacramentals offer a way to move beyond abstract theology to develop relationships with God, the Blessed Mother, and others in heaven. Relics can also be valuable aids to developing a practice of prayer, and three types of relics are recognized:

In the Catholic Church, relics fall into one of three categories: A first-class relic is the physical bodily remains of a saint or blessed like bones, blood and hair; a second-class relic is a personal possession [of the deceased], such as clothing, devotional objects, handwritten letters or even furniture; and a third-class relic is an object that has touched a first-class relic. [125]

The power of relics, through the grace of God, has been witnessed and described innumerable times, and belief in the power of relics is biblically based in the Old and New Testaments. In 2 Kings 2:14 Elisha used the clothing of his deceased mentor Elijah to clear a path, or part the waters, of a river that he needed to cross. In Matthew 9:20-21 a woman was physically healed by touching the clothes of Christ as he passed by, and in Acts 19:11-12 parts of the clothing of Saint Paul, as well as pieces of cloth that he touched, were used to mediate physical healings and drive away evil spirits.

Relics derive their power from the grace of God, which is poorly understood because the word *grace* doesn't convey its power to modern audiences. For secularists, who don't recognize supernatural phenomena, the best translation of "grace" would be *energy.* The grace of God is seen to work through the bodies of saints, in part, because the body is a dwelling place of the Trinity, and it is that indwelling that transforms, divinizes, and glorifies the body in a manner such that it becomes a channel for the grace of God.

The potential of mystical prayer to enable two-way communications between the saints in heaven and those of us here on earth applies to non-canonized as well as canonized saints. The primary differences between a canonized and non-canonized saint are the following: all people in heaven are saints, but canonized saints are officially viewed as role models who exemplified the highest standards of holiness and divinization during their lives. As a result, they are given special honor by the Church, which allows public veneration of the particular saint, including veneration of their relics. Canonized saints are recognized as valuable intercessors, and their efficacy as intercessors is ordinarily proven during the canonization process by evidence of miraculous interventions that are rigorously documented.

Two-way dialogues with non-canonized saints are not only possible but desirable. In terms of mystical prayer, "talks" with loved ones who have passed away are sometimes easier to establish due to the saint's familiarity. Having a relationship with a saint, and deepening that relationship, is key to advancing in prayer, so the more familiar the individual is with a saint, the easier it is to establish a connection. While it would be inappropriate to venerate the relics of a non-canonized saint, those relics—a piece of clothing or other personal object handled by the deceased loved one—can predispose the person praying to receive the grace of God that enables contacts to be made. The experiences are beneficial because they remove doubts about the existence of life after death and encourage people to devote more of their time and energy to the spiritual aspects of life prior to their own death.

Regarding praying to the saints in heaven, the Latin phrase *ora pro nobis* (pray for us) is a more accurate characterization, which is in perfect alignment with the typical Protestant practice of asking a friend or loved one to pray for, or intercede for, oneself or others. However, unlike the vast majority of Protestant denominations, Catholicism teaches there is no "wall of separation" between those living on earth and the saints in heaven, as well as those in purgatory who are being purified, or divinized, in a process that strips away any vestiges of unholy attachments; in essence, stripping away any vestiges of selfishness and lack of love. This organic unity among believers across earth, heaven, and purgatory is referred to as the *communion of saints,* which is one of the core tenets of Christianity listed in the Apostle's Creed. The belief has a substantial basis in many biblical texts, including Hebrews 12:1, "Therefore, since we are surrounded by such a great cloud of witnesses, let us throw off everything that hinders and the sin that so easily entangles." The phrase *cloud of witnesses* is a reference to non-visible or supernatural beings and their ability to assist believers on their journey to heaven, which is a journey to perfection via divinization.

## Joan of Arc: Icon of Christ and the Blessed Virgin Mary?

Joan has been cast as a Christ-figure in literature and film, perhaps most prominently in the 1928 film, *The Passion of Joan of Arc,* directed by Carl Theodor Dreyer. However, information from the trial transcripts clearly presents imagery that Joan is equally, or more so, an icon of the Virgin Mary.

Catherine Le Royer, who hosted Joan during her stay in Vaucouleurs, testified during the Rehabilitation Trial that Joan firmly believed she was "the Virgin" who was prophesied to restore the kingdom of France:

> She said—I heard her say it—that she must go to the place where the Dauphin was: "Have you not heard the prophecy that France was to be ruined by a woman and restored by a virgin from the marshes of Lorraine?" I remembered having heard that, and I was flabbergasted. [126]

The woman who "ruined" France was Isabeau of Bavaria, who became Queen of France when she married King Charles VI. She acquired increasing political power as the king's mental health progressively deteriorated and stood in for him when the Treaty of Troyes was signed in May 1420. The treaty, signed during a critical period in the Hundred Years War, specified that the English king would inherit the French crown when Charles VI died, putting an end to the kingdom of France.

The prophecy that "France was to be ruined by a woman and restored by a virgin" parallels the biblical story that humanity was ruined by the first woman (Eve) through original sin, but later restored through the Blessed Virgin Mary (the New Eve). A Church tradition that began in the second century recognized the Blessed Virgin Mary as the New Eve while Jesus was seen as the New Adam: the deifying grace that was lost via original sin was again made available to humans through Jesus and Mary.

In the Bible, Genesis 3:15 contains the prophecy that a woman (Mary) and her seed (Christ) would eventually crush Satan, who was given power over humanity through original sin. The sin involved, figuratively speaking, eating an apple that was the fruit of "the tree of the knowledge of good and evil." In terms of the theory of evolution, this would be understood as the development of humans to the point of acquiring knowledge of good and evil, a state of cognitive development beyond what was possible in lesser developed forms of life. The acquisition of this type of knowledge coupled with the capacity to make free-will decisions is seen by the Church as indicative of the presence of a human soul.

Free will implies a greater level of functioning than what was described previously in the experiments involving cats, rats, worms, and dogs. Free will implies the ability to make a decision that is not solely a function of the "inputs" of inherited DNA, acquired memories, or an illness. Aligning this with evolution—acquiring greater levels of intelligence and the ability to make free-will decisions—would coincide with the appearance of behaviorally modern humans between 200,000 and 50,000 years ago. Mitochondrial Eve, genetically the most recent common ancestor of all humans, lived approximately 200,000 years ago. [127]

Durand Laxart, Joan's uncle by marriage to a cousin of Joan's mother, also testified that Joan believed she was the miraculous virgin foretold by the prophecy:

> I went myself to fetch Joan from her father's house and took her away with me, and she told me that she wanted to go to France, to the Dauphin, to have him crowned. She said, "Was it not said that France would be ruined through a woman, and afterward restored by a virgin?" [128]

The prophecy referenced here is noted in Mark Twain's book as originating with Merlin, the legendary wizard associated with stories of King Arthur, but the prophecy is legitimately attributed to the Venerable Bede, a Catholic historian and Doctor of the Church, who wrote the *Ecclesiastical History of the English People* in the eighth century.

Joan later denied being this prophesied virgin during the February 24 session of the Condemnation Trial, but her denial came immediately after the judges interrogated her about her activities at the Ladies' Tree, where sorcerers were believed to gather:

> She added that when she came to see the king, several people had asked her if there was not in her part of the country a wooded area called the Oak-Wood, because there was a prophecy that a young girl would come out of this wooded area and perform miracles. Joan said that she put no faith in that.

During her canonization process, Joan's lack of complete honesty with her judges was noted as one factor against her practice, or display, of heroic virtue. [129] However, Joan was understandably reluctant to cast herself as a participant with the non-Catholic spiritualists that her judges characterized as sorcerers. The idea that Catholics and other types of spiritualists would have gathered together at the Ladies' Tree is not unusual in the history of the Church. Catholics have always been involved in syncretistic practices, which incorporate or accommodate aspects of different spiritualties into religious practices or beliefs. The degree to which syncretistic practices are harmful can only be decided on a case-by-case basis. In a 1994 article, *Catholicism Confronts New Age Syncretism,* Bernard Green, wrote:

> This syncretistic mentality is widespread in the Church today. Witness the following description of the program of a respected Midwestern Catholic center for spirituality:

> Readings are selected every day from the sacred texts of Buddhism, Taoism, Hinduism, and Islam, as well as Christianity. On occasion, ancient festivals of the Celts or Saxons are remembered, and members dance around a maypole or fire-pit in the fields or forest. ... The Chapel is visually stimulating and instructive. ... Icons of Our Lady of Guadalupe and the Risen Christ are placed side by side with statues of Buddha, Lord Vishnu and Moses. [130]

A significant amount of Joan's spiritual formation, particularly those aspects related to her embrace of mystical experiences, probably occurred at the Spirits' Tree or Ladies' Tree. In the transcripts, the tree is sometimes called the "Ladies' Tree" and at other times it is referred to as the "Fairies' Tree." In this book, the term *Spirits' Tree* or *Ladies' Tree* is used instead of *Fairies' Tree* because there's a lack of clarity in the source material about whether the term *fairies* refers to spirits—something supernatural, preter-natural or metaphysical—or instead refers to "women who were skilled in magic." Also, the term "fairies" is not commonly understood in modern culture. The Old French *fae* or *faerie* described something "enchanted," and in Old French romance literature, "women were called Fays who had to do with enchantment and charms and knew the power and virtue of words, of stones, and of herbs." [131]

Jean Morel's deposition during the Rehabilitation Trial included the following statement about the Ladies' Tree:

As for the tree that was called the Ladies' Tree, I have sometimes heard that ladies who cast spells—*fairies* they used to call them—*used* to come in the old days and dance under that tree. But people do say that since they read the Gospel of Saint John there they do not come anymore. ... Joan the Maid and the other girls went there sometimes, and she behaved just like the others. [132]

Joan's childhood friend, Hauviette, testified:

That tree has been called the Ladies' Tree since olden times, and they say that long ago the ladies they call *fairies* went there. But I have never heard of anyone who saw one. [133]

In Joan's testimony from the February 24 session, she didn't speak of ladies or fairies but instead referred to spirits:

She said sometimes she would go playing with other young girls at the tree, making garlands for Our Lady of Domremy there. Often she heard the elderly people say, although not those of her family, that spirits frequently appeared near this tree. She heard a certain Joan—the wife of mayor Aubery of Domremy, her godmother— say that she had seen the spirits, but she herself doesn't know whether it is true or not. As far as she knew, she said, she never saw spirits at the tree. Asked if she saw them elsewhere, she said she does not know at all. She had seen young girls putting garlands on the branches of the tree, and she herself sometimes hung garlands there with the other girls; sometimes they took them away, and sometimes they left them there.

During the March 1 session of her trial, Joan said her first apparition involved an appearance of Saint Michael the archangel, who gave her the message that she must save the kingdom of France. The term *angel* refers to a *spirit* as well as a *messenger.* Later, Joan's testimony during the March 13 session, and recorded in Article 51 of the seventy articles of accusation against her, included the following:

When asked why the angel came to her rather than to another person, she answered, "It pleased God to drive back the king's enemies through a simple virgin."

That statement by Joan, whether she knew it or not, was a reference to a Catholic understanding of the role that the Blessed Virgin Mary plays in "driving back the king's enemies" as reflected in the Genesis 3:15 prophecy. The Church teaches the process of vanquishing Satan and the ability of humans to become divinized began at Calvary, site of Christ's crucifixion, and Mary was an integral part of God's plan for this redemption of humanity because God "assumed our human nature" through Mary. It is this incarnation or "enfleshment" of God in the person of Jesus Christ that is the source of redemption because it involves the transformation and divinization of human nature; and because Mary is the medium through which the incarnation takes place, Mary and Jesus, together, enable the redemptive process. Statues and images of Mary often show her standing on a globe of the earth with her bare feet crushing a serpent, which represents Satan. The *Catechism* describes the role of divinization in redemption:

> The Word [God] became flesh to make us "partakers of the divine nature." [2 Peter 1:4] "For this is why the Word became man, and the Son of God [Jesus] became the Son of man: so that man [and woman], by entering into communion with the Word and thus receiving divine sonship [or daughtership], might become a son [or daughter] of God." [Saint Irenaeus] "For the Son of God became man so that we might become God." [Saint Athanasius] "The only-begotten Son of God, wanting to make us sharers in his divinity, assumed our nature, so that he, made man, might make men [and women] gods." [Saint Thomas Aquinas] [134]

Saint Louis de Montfort, a preeminent Mariologist who lived in the eighteenth century, referred to the Blessed Virgin Mary as "Daughter of God the Father," which indicated a triune relationship between Mary and the Trinity because Mary is also seen as the Mother of God and the Spouse of the Holy Spirit (whose union with Mary resulted in the conception of God in the form of a human). Joan's remarks during the March 12 session include the following:

> Asked if her Voices called her daughter of God, daughter of the Church, or daughter great-hearted, she said that prior to the military assault on the city of Orleans and every day since, when they have spoken to her, they have often called her "Joan the Virgin, Daughter of God."

The letter Joan dictated to a scribe that was sent to the English military prior to her attack that ended the siege of Orleans included the statement, "She comes in God's name to establish the Royal Blood." The reference to Royal Blood parallels Christ's blood, which established the Kingdom of Heaven, and the letter also includes the statement, "You will not keep the Kingdom of France from God, the King of Kings and Blessed Mary's Son." In the same letter, Joan includes a reference that she, the Virgin, along with her good soldiers, will vanquish the forces that oppose the Kingdom of France:

> Know well that the King of Heaven will send a greater force to the Virgin and her good soldiers than you in all your assaults can over-come; and by these defeats shall the favor of the God of Heaven be seen.

The reference to Joan and her good soldiers parallels the role that Mary and her good soldiers have in bringing about the fulfillment of the Kingdom of Heaven by promoting devotion to Mary and her role in salvation history. The reference prefigures Marian groups such as the Militia of the Immaculata, a movement founded by Saint Maximilian Kolbe in 1917 that promotes a total consecration to Mary to facilitate spiritual renewal in believers as well as within the culture; the Blue Army, now known as the World Apostolate of Fatima, which seeks to encourage people to learn, live, and spread the messages that the Virgin Mary delivered in a series of apparitions in Fatima, Portugal; and individuals who have followed Montfort's plan for a total consecration to Mary:

> In all circumstances they will have recourse to her as their Advocate and Mediatrix with Jesus Christ. They will see clearly that she is the safest, easiest, shortest and most perfect way of approaching Jesus and will surrender themselves to her, body and soul, without reserve in order to belong entirely to Jesus. [135]

## Joan of Arc: Icon of Suppression of Women in the Church?

If Christ is the Bridegroom (male or masculine), and the Church is the Bride of Christ (female or feminine), it is ironic that the hierarchy of the Church, for all practical purposes, is made up entirely of men. In the hierarchy of the Church, it is not a requirement that Cardinals be priests, so it would seem beneficial to the Church to move to some sort of parity, at a minimum, of women Cardinals. This would not only help enable the Church to reach a higher level of perfection in terms of becoming more feminine, but it would also provide the necessary integration of the laity into the life of the entire Church, which was one of the major objectives specified by the Second Vatican Council. Also, considering that prelates would dominate all other positions in the hierarchy, it would not be unreasonable to transition to a College of Cardinals made up entirely of lay people and women religious (sisters and nuns).

The recent popes have been criticized by some for saying the question of allowing women in the priesthood is a settled issue. Individuals and groups who advocate for women in the priesthood often assume the priesthood provides access to power because priests not only manage almost all of Church governance, but also because the priesthood is the only path to the power of the Papacy. Saint Thérèse of Lisieux wrote the following about her vocation (the capital letters were written by the saint):

> To be Your Spouse, to be a Carmelite, and by my union with You to be the Mother of souls, should not this suffice me? And yet it is not so. No doubt, these three privileges sum up my true vocation: Carmelite, Spouse, Mother, and yet I feel within me other vocations. I feel the vocation of the WARRIOR, THE PRIEST, THE APOSTLE, THE DOCTOR, THE MARTYR. ...

> I feel in me the vocation of the PRIEST. With what love, O Jesus, I would carry You in my hands when, at my voice, You would come down from heaven. And with what love would I give You to souls! But alas! while desiring to be a Priest, I admire and envy the humility of St. Francis of Assisi and I feel the vocation of imitating him in refusing the sublime dignity of the Priesthood. [136]

Saint Thérèse wrote that all of her desires concerning her vocation "caused me a veritable martyrdom" because "considering the mystical body of the Church, I had not recognized myself in any of the members described by St. Paul, or rather I desired to see myself in them *all*." [137] She was then inspired to understand there is one vocation that is much more powerful than the priesthood: to become the embodiment of Christ Himself by becoming *Love—agape,* self-sacrificial *Love:*

I have found my place in the Church and it is You, O my God, who have given me this place: in the heart of the Church, my Mother, I shall be *Love*. Thus I shall be everything, and thus my dream will be realized. [138]

Thérèse's inspiration, *God is Love,* is reflected biblically in 1 John 4:7-8:

Dear friends, let us love one another, for love comes from God. Everyone who loves has been born of God [born again] and knows God. Whoever does not love does not know God, because God is love.

Saint Augustine, preaching on that biblical passage, stated:

Once for all, then, a short precept is given you: Love, and do what you will: whether you hold your peace, through love hold your peace; whether you cry out, through love cry out; whether you correct, through love correct; whether you spare, through love do you spare: let the root of love be within, of this root can nothing spring but what is good. [139]

Also, the preeminence of love is reflected in Romans 13:9-10:

The commandments, "You shall not commit adultery," "You shall not murder," "You shall not steal," "You shall not covet," and whatever other command there may be, are summed up in this one command: "Love your neighbor as yourself." Love does no harm to a neighbor. Therefore love is the fulfillment of the law.

One form of suppression of women in the Church that is overlooked involves the Virgin Mary. On the day Joan of Arc first appeared before her judges, the bailiff or usher, Jean Massieu, announced, "The woman commonly called the Virgin [is] imprisoned within the limits of this castle."

Many non-Catholics would find it absurd to believe the Catholic Church could suppress the Blessed Virgin Mary, primarily because the Church is often accused of radically over-emphasizing the role of Mary in the process of redemption. However, hesitation by the Church to dogmatically define the Blessed Virgin Mary as *Co-Redeemer* (as well as *Mediatrix* and *Advocate*) is a form of suppression of the Virgin Mary as well as a suppression of the feminine within the Church. The title *Mediatrix* means Mary distributes the graces of salvation with Jesus, and the title *Advocate* means she intercedes for people and their needs.

Recognition of Mary as Co-Redeemer is supported by Church doctrine, and Saint Pope John Paul II officially referred to Mary as Co-Redemptrix on several occasions (references are documented at FifthMarianDogma.com). Cardinal Ratzinger, prior to his papacy as Benedict XVI, also indicated that the concept of Mary being Co-Redeemer was correct, and he acknowledged that several million people had petitioned the Vatican to declare a dogma recognizing Mary as Co-Redeemer. [140] However, he believed language difficulties would lead to misinterpretation even though the prefix *co-* does not mean *equal* but instead means *with.* The suffix *-trix,* derived from Latin, means *female,* recognizing the truth that a woman was not only integral but necessary to the process of the redemption of humanity designed by God.

Catholicism is often misunderstood as promoting the worship of Mary, but the Church teaches that God alone is worthy of worship (*latria* in Latin). A distinction is made regarding the saints, such that the saints are worthy of honor and veneration (*dulia*), but Mary is worthy of a special class of honor and veneration (*hyperdulia*). The distinctions are important because they avert unorthodox practices such as characterizing Mary as a goddess to be worshipped while simultaneously recognizing her special role in salvation history. The Catholic doctrine differentiating between *latria* and *hyperdulia* implies that it would be a mortal sin, idolatry, to worship Mary. For example, the Old Testament prophet Jeremiah admonished people for worshipping an ancient sky goddess named the Queen of Heaven. Mary is not recognized as a goddess by the Catholic Church, and the Marian title *Queen of Heaven* is meant to convey Mary's unique role in the plan of redemption, not to recognize her as a goddess.

The Blessed Virgin Mary's role in redemption was addressed by Pope Pius XII in his 1954 encyclical, *Ad Caeli Reginam,* proclaiming the Queenship of Mary: [141]

> In accomplishing this work of the redemption, the Most Blessed Virgin Mary was certainly closely joined with Christ ... was associated with Jesus Christ, the very principle of salvation, by divine plan, and indeed in a way similar to that in which Eve was associated with Adam ... and if she was joined with her Son, even on Golgotha [site of the crucifixion], she offered Him, together with the

holocaust of her Mother's rights and love, like a New Eve, for all the sons of Adam … beyond doubt, it is right to conclude that just as Christ, the New Adam should be called King not only because He is the Son of God, but also because He is our Redeemer, so by a certain analogy, the most Blessed Virgin is Queen, not only because she is the Mother of God, but also because as the New Eve she was associated with the New Adam.

A passage from the liturgical *Collection of Masses of the Blessed Virgin* refers to the role that Mary's suffering had in the process of redemption:

In your divine wisdom, you planned the redemption of the human race and decreed that the new Eve should stand by the Cross of the new Adam: as she became his Mother by the power of the Holy Spirit, so, by a new gift of your love, she was to be a partner in his Passion. [142]

Saint John Paul II stated that Mary was "crucified spiritually with her crucified Son," which was the culmination of a period of suffering by Mary in union with Christ, as only a mother could understand. Mary's suffering is traditionally honored by a devotion to the Seven Sorrows of Mary, which acknowledges the integral aspect of suffering in relation to redemption.

The biblical text written by Saint Paul in Colossians 1:24, "Now I rejoice in what I am suffering for you, and I fill up in my flesh what is still lacking in regard to Christ's afflictions, for the sake of his body, which is the church," also links suffering with redemption and forms the theological basis for asserting that all believers are co-redeemers to some extent, but none more so than Mary, who was and is uniquely united with Christ.

Paul's statement doesn't imply that Christ's sacrifice was somehow lacking in making available the sanctifying graces needed for humans to become divinized, but it does mean the sufferings of individual Christians are also integral to salvation, individually and collectivity, for all of humanity.

When Paul wrote, "I rejoice in my sufferings," he was also referring to the potentially positive aspects of suffering. The Church teaches that suffering can be transformative and deifying when united to the sufferings of Christ. The potential value of suffering is typically not recognized from a strictly secular perspective, but research has shown that people who have experienced very painful or adverse events in their lives often attain a level of happiness seemingly unavailable to others. Some of the science regarding this relationship between suffering and happiness is covered by Jim Rendon in his book, *Upside: The New Science of Post-Traumatic Growth*.

When Christ is quoted as saying, "Take up your cross and follow me," he was referring to the integral role of suffering in the process of redemption, particularly for those people who wanted to be His disciples. Desiring divinization without a willingness to share in the suffering of humanity via *agape*—a willingness to endure discomfort for the sake of helping others—represents a half-hearted approach to redemption.

Biological evolution and spiritual divinization share some typological characteristics in that there is a clear relationship between the capacity to suffer and progressing up the evolutionary ladder. At every major step in the process, suffering became more perceptible and intense. Microorganisms don't feel pain. It's unclear if invertebrates such as insects and worms feel pain. However, vertebrate animals have the capacity to experience intense pain, and at the top of the list of vertebrates is the human species, which experiences suffering at a level unattainable by other species. Animals don't experience the gut-wrenching sorrow of a broken heart at a level that humans do, which is why Pope John Paul II could assert that Mary was "crucified spiritually with her crucified Son." The type of psychological suffering that only humans are capable of represents the pinnacle of suffering because, comparatively, intense physical suffering is characteristically much more bearable when the sufferer feels loved by a lover; and, alternatively, to exist in a world absent of physical suffering but devoid of love often precipitates a level of despair illustrated by many otherwise healthy and wealthy individuals who commit suicide—reflecting a level of desolation that is a foretaste of hell.

In his biblical writings, Paul referred to all Christians, collectively, as members of the Body of Christ, and united with Him, together, they form the Mystical Body of Christ on earth:

Mystical Body of Christ—in Roman Catholicism, a mystical union of all Christians into a spiritual body with Jesus Christ as their head. The concept is rooted in the New Testament and possibly reflects Christianity's roots in Judaism; St. Paul's letters to the Corinthians and Romans both use the image of a body, with a head (Christ) and many members (Christians) to describe the relationship between Christ and Christians. Later, the Church Fathers, including St. Augustine, reaffirmed and amplified Paul's assertion that the Christian church is a spiritual extension of Christ's body.

Pope Pius XII popularized the phrase in his encyclical *Mystici corporis christi* (1943). The Second Vatican Council issued the "Dogmatic Constitution on the Church," or *Lumen Gentium* (1964; "Light of the Nations"), which reflected the broader, universal nature of the mystical body by stating that all persons are members of the church, at least potentially, because Christ came to offer salvation to everyone. [143]

A supernatural union among all Christians and with Christ is reflected in scripture passages such as 1 Corinthians 12:27, "Now you are the body of Christ, and each one of you is a part of it," and John 15:5, "I am the vine; you are the branches. If you remain in me and I in you, you will bear much fruit." The *Catechism* explains Mary's unique place in the Mystical Body of Christ as arising from two key elements of her life—her relationship with Christ and the suffering she shared with Christ:

Mary's role in the Church is inseparable from her union with Christ and flows directly from it. This union of the mother with the Son in the work of salvation is made manifest from the time of Christ's virginal conception up to his death; it is made manifest above all at the hour of his Passion: Thus the Blessed Virgin advanced in her pilgrimage of faith, and faithfully persevered in her union with her Son unto the cross. There she stood, in keeping with the divine plan, enduring with her only begotten Son the intensity of his suffering, joining herself with his sacrifice in her mother's heart, and lovingly consenting to the immolation of this victim, born of her: to be given, by the same Christ Jesus dying on the cross, as a mother to his disciple, with these words: "Woman, behold your son." [144]

Saint John the Evangelist indicated he was standing next to Mary at the crucifixion, and in John 19:26-27, there is the following description of Christ instructing Mary to look at John as her spiritual son, and instructing John to look at Mary as his spiritual Mother:

When Jesus saw his mother there, and the disciple whom he loved standing nearby, he said to her, "Woman, here is your son," and to the disciple, "Here is your mother."

This passage is interpreted by Catholics as Christ establishing Mary as the spiritual mother of all believers as well as instructing all believers to look to Mary as their spiritual mother. An alternative interpretation—that Jesus was merely referring to a domestic relationship solely between Mary and Saint John—doesn't seem plausible when considering Mary's role in how sanctifying, or deifying, grace is made available and accepted by people. The enfleshment of God in the person of Jesus was made possible by Mary, and it is through Mary's saying *yes* to God's plan that humans can be redeemed and become divinized through sanctifying grace, reflecting the Virgin Mary's roles as *Co-Redeemer* and *Mediatrix*.

Regarding Mary's role as *Mediatrix* of all graces, the Church recognizes different types of graces. The sacrament of Baptism is said to impart a sanctifying, or deifying, grace that supernaturally transforms people, so they are able to commune or communicate with God on a level that's unavailable to people who haven't received Baptism. [145] The process of sanctification, deification, continues throughout a person's life if they collaborate with the action of additional graces received throughout life. [146] Other graces include *sacramental graces,* which are unique to each of the seven sacraments; *actual graces,* which impart power to conform one's life to the will of God; and *special graces,* or *charisms,* which are received to help develop the Church. [147] Participating in, and collaborating with, these various graces results in an increasingly intimate relationship with God—a relationship that isn't merely based on an intellectual understanding of various facts about Christianity, but on explicit knowledge of God through Christ. Many Christians stress the need to "have a personal relationship with Jesus Christ," and to have such a relationship requires having direct encounters with Christ that transcend abstract theology. The encounters can be through prayer or by helping others in need (Matthew 25:40). The tangible, observable evidence of whether a person is in the midst of deepening their relationship with Christ—in contrast to solely deepening one's relationship with biblical texts—involves experiencing increasing levels of love, joy, peace, patience, kindness, generosity, faithfulness, gentleness, and self-control; the manifestations of the Holy Spirit stated in Galatians 5:22-23.

Mary's role as *Mediatrix* of all graces implies she is integral to the two fundamental aspects of the journey from this life to the next: *redemption,* which restores the communion between God and humans, and *glorification,* which is a spiritual growth process that involves an ongoing process of divinization. [148] The word "divinization" is not often used, and in its place, terms such as "growth in holiness" or "growth in the spiritual life" are commonly used. Regardless of the terminology, divinization allows individuals to increasingly participate in the divine life of God. According to Catholic teaching, if the divinization process is not completed on earth, then it is completed in purgatory.

The Church's understanding of the Virgin Mary's role in redemption and divinization has evolved over time, and this growth in understanding is illustrated by four dogmas (essential truths or required beliefs) that have been declared about Mary.

First, Mary's Immaculate Conception, which is often mistakenly thought of as Christ being immaculately conceived in the womb of Mary, but instead refers to Mary being immaculately conceived in the womb of her mother, Saint Anne. Being immaculately conceived means that Mary, unlike all other humans, was conceived without the original sin of the first humans, Adam and Eve.

Second, Mary is the Mother of God because (being the only human conceived without original sin—the only human conceived and born in a state of sanctifying, deifying grace) she was able to give Jesus a flawless, or sinless, human nature; although she did not give Jesus his divine nature, she is nevertheless the Mother of God because the human nature and divine nature of Christ are inseparably united, just as every human's material body and immaterial soul are inseparably united until death of the biological body (immaterial does not imply unreal; for example, light is immaterial).

Third, Mary was a Virgin throughout her life. Despite biblical references to brothers and sisters of Jesus, "brother" and "sister" in biblical texts (the Greek is *adelphos* and *adelphe*) also refer to extended family members such as cousins and other kin; also, there are no biblical texts that indicate Mary had any children other than Jesus. Regarding the virgin birth, every year around Christmas articles are published addressing the question of whether parthenogenesis—asexual reproduction in which offspring develop from an unfertilized egg—can occur in humans. The conclusion of the articles is that it is impossible, or if it is possible, the probability is extremely low, yet theoretically possible. Over time, the science has steadily moved up the evolutionary chain of species on this question. Previously, parthenogenesis was considered to be possible only in invertebrate species. Later, it was seen in some vertebrate species, but only in captivity. Recently, it has been documented in vertebrate species in the wild. [149] In parthenogenesis, the egg cell gives rise to the embryo stages on its own. The change in our scientifically derived knowledge illustrates that it will always be incomplete, and the more we learn about the biological, chemical and physical nature of reality, the more we understand how little we currently know.

Fourth, Mary was bodily assumed into heaven in "a singular participation in her Son's Resurrection and an anticipation of the resurrection of other Christians." [107]

The fifth and final Marian dogma, yet to be declared, involves Mary's universal mediation as *Co-Redeemer, Mediatrix* of all graces, and *Advocate* for the people of God. An overview of the scriptural and traditional foundations of all the Marian dogmas is available in Mark Miravalle's book, *Meet Your Mother.*

Saint John Paul II stated that "Mary's role as Co-Redemptrix did not cease with the glorification of her Son," and her ongoing role in salvation history was described in Montfort's book, *A Treatise on The True Devotion to The Blessed Virgin,* also known as *The True Devotion to Mary:* [150]

It is by Mary that the salvation of the world has begun, and it is by Mary that it must be consummated. Mary has hardly appeared at all in the first coming of Jesus Christ, in order that men [and women], as yet but little instructed and enlightened on the Person of her Son, should not remove themselves from Him, in attaching themselves too strongly and too grossly to her. This would have apparently taken place, if she had been known, because of the admirable charms which the Most High had bestowed even upon her exterior. This is so true that St. Denys the Areopagite [the man, Dionysius, mentioned in Acts 17:34] has informed us in his writings that when he saw our Blessed Lady, he should have taken her for a Divinity, in consequence of her secret charms and incomparable beauty, had not the Faith in which he was well established taught him the contrary. But in the second coming of Jesus Christ, Mary has to be made known and revealed by the Holy Spirit, in order that by her Jesus Christ may be known, loved, and served. The reasons which moved the Holy Spirit to hide His Spouse during her life, and to reveal her but a very little since the preaching of the Gospel, subsist no longer. God, then, wishes to reveal and discover Mary, the masterpiece of His hands, in these latter times.

Saint John Paul II said that reading *The True Devotion to Mary* was a "decisive turning point" in his life and he adopted his papal motto, *Totus*

*Tuus* (Totally Yours), from the words that Montfort used to describe his total consecration to Jesus through Mary. [151]

The events prophesied by Montfort—that Mary would be increasingly revealed so that Christ may be better known and understood—are reflected and are being fulfilled by an increasing number of Marian apparitions during an era known as the *Age of Mary*, which began in 1830 and is ongoing.

Reports of Marian apparitions that get news coverage typically involve stories that are easily dismissed. However, when attempting to categorize various reports as fraudulent, mythological, delusional, or factual, many contemporary reports of apparitions cannot be easily discounted due to credible documentation and numerous witnesses.

Typically, apparitions reported prior to the 1800s are quickly dismissed as mythological because historical evidence is lacking. However, three reports appear to be particularly credible: *Our Lady of Mount Carmel*, 1251, in Aylesford, England; *Our Lady of Good Health*, 1500s, in Vailankanni, India; and *Our Lady of Guadalupe*, 1531, in an area of Mexico that is now Mexico City.

Prior to the 1900s, historical evidence is sometimes available, but imprecise and questionable. Paradoxically, since the early 1900s, when it has become increasingly fashionable to deny the existence of supernatural phenomena, it has also become increasingly difficult to discount the purported reality of a large number of Marian apparitions. Of the hundreds that have been reported, there are many events that can't be discounted as fraudulent or mythological because the evidence of their occurrence is too credible to be dismissed—especially the most modern of the apparitions that are the most extensively documented.

**1830 – Our Lady of the Immaculate Conception in Paris, France.** In 1824, at the age of eighteen, Catherine Laboure had a dream in which she was assisting at a Mass being celebrated by an old priest she didn't recognize. After the Mass the priest beckoned her to come to him but she darted out of the church frightened by the old man. During the dream, she then went to visit a woman who was ill, and when she entered the woman's room, the same priest was standing there and said, "You do well to visit the sick, my child. You flee from me now, but one day you will be glad to come to me. God has plans for you; do not forget it." [152]

Laboure later became a postulant—a candidate for admission to a religious order—on January 22, 1830, entering the house of the Sisters of Charity in Châtillon, a suburb of Paris. It was at Châtillon that Laboure noticed a portrait of an old priest, the same unknown priest who appeared in her dream. When she asked a sister at the house who the priest was, she was told it was Saint Vincent de Paul, founder of the religious order Laboure had just entered. Saint Vincent de Paul, in addition to founding the Sisters of Charity, also founded the Congregation of the Mission, which is also known as the Vincentian Fathers.

After her postulancy, which lasted three months, she was sent to the Sisters of Charity Motherhouse in Paris, at Rue du Bac, for her novitiate, which is a formation period prior to formally entering a religious order. She arrived on April 21, four days prior to the translation, or movement, of relics of Saint Vincent de Paul from Notre Dame Cathedral to the Lazarists church on the Rue de Sevres. During the evening of the movement of the relics, Laboure began having a series of visions of the heart of Saint Vincent. Two months later, she began having visons of Christ the King. Then, in July and November, Laboure experienced two apparitions of the Blessed Virgin Mary.

Under the orders of her director, Laboure wrote very detailed accounts of her visions on three different occasions, in 1841, 1856, and in 1876. Her descriptions were precise and included details such as the following:

> Our Lady wore "three rings on each of her fingers." She tells us, further, that the rings were graduated in size, "the largest one near the base of the finger, one of medium size in the middle, the smallest one at the tip." She even noticed that the rings themselves were set with stones "of proportionate size, some larger and others smaller." ... "A white veil covered her head," Catherine wrote, "falling on either side to her feet. Under the veil her hair, in coils, was bound with a fillet ornamented with lace, about three centimeters in height or of two fingers' breadth, without pleats, and resting lightly on the hair." [152]

On July 18, 1830, the day prior to a feast day celebration that honors Saint Vincent de Paul, the Directress of the convent, Mother Martha, spoke to the novices about the importance of cultivating a devotion to the saints. As a gift, Mother Martha gave each novice a relic of the saint, a small piece of cloth from a liturgical vestment worn by Saint Vincent. The plan for the following day included a walk to the church where the body of the saint was being kept, so that the sisters and novices could venerate the saint and pray at the church.

That night, Laboure tore the relic in half and swallowed one piece of the cloth. She prayed to Saint Vincent to grant her the greatest wish of her life, to see the Virgin Mary. Laboure said after sleeping approximately two hours, a small child, surrounded by a radiant light, woke her up at 11:30 p.m., telling her to go to the chapel. The child led Laboure to a chair in the chapel that was used by the Director of the religious order, and she knelt beside the chair. When the child announced the arrival of the Blessed Virgin, Laboure heard a sound that she described as the rustling of a silk dress. She turned in the direction of the sound and saw a lady descending the steps where the altar was, and then the lady sat in the chair:

> A doubt clouded the novice's mind. Was this really the Mother of God? The child reassured her: "This is the Blessed Virgin." Even this did not allay all her doubts. Was the whole thing a dream, a fancy of the night? She blushed. The lady was looking at her, waiting. The child spoke again, startling her, for now his voice was a man's voice, deep and commanding and stern. She held back no more, but threw herself at Our Lady's knee and rested her hands in Our Lady's lap. Then she lifted her head and looked up, up, into her Mother's eyes. Many years later she was to write with ecstatic remembrance of this moment, that it was the sweetest of her life. "My child," said Our Lady, "the good God wishes to charge you with a mission." [152]

On November 27, 1830, Laboure experienced another apparition of Mary, and the vision and its repercussions are seen as the start of the *Age of Mary:*

> The Virgin held in her hands a golden ball which she seemed to offer to God, for her eyes were raised heavenward. Suddenly, her hands were resplendent with rings set with precious stones that glittered and flashed in a brilliant cascade of light. So bright was the flood of glory cast upon the globe below that Catherine could no longer see Our Lady's feet.

> Mary lowered her eyes and looked full at Sister Laboure. Her lips did not move, but Catherine heard a voice. ...

"These rays symbolize the graces I shed upon those who ask for them. The gems from which rays do not fall are the graces for which souls forget to ask."

At this moment, Catherine was so lost in delight that she scarcely knew where she was, whether she lived or died. The golden ball vanished from Mary's hands; her arms swept wide in a gesture of motherly compassion, while from her jeweled fingers the rays of light streamed upon the white globe at her feet. An oval frame formed around the Blessed Virgin, and written within it in letters of gold Catherine read the words:

O Mary, conceived without sin, pray for us who have recourse to thee.

The voice spoke again:

"Have a Medal struck after this model. All who wear it will receive great graces; they should wear it around the neck. Graces will abound for persons who wear it with confidence."

The tableau revolved, and Catherine beheld the reverse of the Medal she was to have made. It contained a large M surmounted by a bar and a cross. Beneath the M were the Hearts of Jesus and Mary, the one crowned with thorns, the other pierced with a sword. Twelve stars encircled the whole.

And then the vision was gone. [152]

Laboure's confessor, Father Jean Marie Aladel, heard her account of the vision several times before he began to seriously consider the apparitions might be authentic. Regarding production of the "Immaculate Conception" medal, Laboure insisted her identity as the visionary be kept a secret. During official Church inquiries into the medal and its design, Aladel was under pressure to reveal the identity of the seer, and Laboure herself was under pressure from the Archbishop of Paris and others to come forward, but her identity remained a secret until the last months of her life, forty-six years later, in 1876.

The design of the medal wasn't seen as controversial, even though it featured a large letter *M* intertwined with, and serving as the foundation of, the cross of Christ. The front of the medal features Mary crushing the head of a serpent (reflecting the prophecy in Genesis 3:15), with the words "O Mary, conceived without sin, pray for us who have recourse to you," which indicates Mary was conceived without original sin. The front of the medal also depicts rays of light emanating from Mary's hands, portraying her as the dispenser of graces and reflecting her roles of *Mediatrix* and *Advocate*.

After approval was given for production, Aladel visited an engraver, M. Vachette, in May 1832, and placed an order for twenty thousand medals. The first two thousand were delivered in June, and by December 1836, Vachette had produced several million medals and "eleven other Parisian engravers had equaled this number, and four Lyon engravers were hard at work to meet the demand." [152] The formal name, *Medal of the Immaculate Conception,* was soon replaced by an informal name, *Miraculous Medal,* due to the number of miracles and answers to prayer that resulted from people using the medal as a sacramental.

**1846 – Our Lady of La Salette in France.** Mélanie Calvat (age fourteen) and Maximin Giraud (age eleven) experienced an apparition of the Virgin Mary in the mountains of La Salette on September 19, 1846. A lengthy description of the apparition by Calvat received an *imprimatur* by Monsignor Salvatore Luigi Zola, who was later appointed Bishop of the Diocese of Lecce, Italy. An imprimatur implies the text is free of doctrinal or moral error, but does not imply the person giving the imprimatur agrees with the content; it is a form of approval that means the text can be published. The following text includes two excerpts from Calvat's description of the apparition she experienced with Giraud: [153]

The sight of the Holy Virgin was itself a perfect paradise. She had everything needed to satisfy, for earth had been forgotten. The Holy Virgin was surrounded by two lights. The first light, the nearer to the Most Holy Virgin, reached as far as us. It shone most beautifully and scintillatingly.

The second light shone out a little around the Beautiful Lady and we found ourselves bathed in it. It was motionless (that is to say it wasn't scintillating) but much more brilliant than our poor sun on earth. All this light did not harm nor tire the eyes in any way.

In addition to all these lights, all this splendour, there shone forth concentrations or beams of light and single rays of light from the body of the Holy Virgin, from her clothes and from all over Her.

The voice of the Beautiful Lady was soft. It was enchanting, ravishing, warming to the heart. It satisfied, flattered every obstacle, it soothed and softened. It seemed to me I could never stop eating up Her beautiful voice, and my heart seemed to dance or want to go towards Her and melt inside Her.

The eyes of the most Holy Virgin, our Sweet Mother, cannot be described in human language. To speak of them, you would need a seraph, you would need more than that, you would need the language of God Himself, of the God who formed the immaculate Virgin, the masterpiece of His omnipotence. The eyes of the majestic Mary appeared thousands of times more beautiful than the rarest brilliants, diamonds and precious stones. They shone like two suns; they were soft, softness itself, as clear as a mirror. In her eyes, you could see paradise. They drew you to Her, She seemed to want to draw and give Herself.

The more I looked, the more I wanted to see; the more I saw, the more I loved Her and I loved Her with all my might.

The eyes of the beautiful Immaculate One were like the door to God's Kingdom, from which you could see all that can elate the soul. When my eyes met those of the Mother of God and of myself, I felt inside me a happy revolution of love and a declaration that I love Her and am melting with love. As we looked at each other, our eyes spoke to each other in their fashion, and I loved Her so much I could have kissed Her in the middle of Her eyes, which touched my soul and seemed to draw it towards them and make it melt into Hers. Her eyes set up a sweet trembling in all my being; and I was afraid to make the slightest movement which might cause her the smallest displeasure.

Just the sight of the eyes of the purest of Virgins would have been enough to make the Heaven of a blessed creature, enough to fill the soul with the will of the Most High amid the events which occur in the course of mortal life, enough to make the soul perform continual acts of praise, of thanksgiving, of atonement and expiation. Just this sight focuses the soul on God, and makes it like a living-death, looking upon all the things of this earth, even the things which seem the most serious, as nothing but children's playthings. The soul would want to hear no one speaking unless they spoke of God, and of that which affects His Glory. ...

In the presence of my Lady, I felt I had forgotten paradise. I thought of nothing more but to serve Her in every way possible; and I felt I could have done everything she could have asked me to do, for it seemed to me that She had a great deal of power. She looked at me with a tender kindness which drew me to Her. I could have thrown myself into Her arms with my eyes closed. She did not give me the time to do so. She rose imperceptibly from the ground to a height of around four feet or more; and, hanging thus in the air for a split second, my beautiful Lady looked up to Heaven, then down on the earth to her right and then her left, then She looked at me with Her eyes so soft, so kind and so good that I felt She was drawing me inside Her, and my heart seemed to open up to Hers.

And as my heart melted away, sweetly gladdened, the beautiful face of my good Lady disappeared little by little. It seemed to me that the light in motion was growing stronger, or rather condensing around the Most Holy Virgin, to prevent me from seeing her any longer.

And thus light took the place of the parts of Her body which were disappearing in front of my eyes, or rather it seemed to me that the body of my Lady was melting into light. Thus the sphere of light rose gently towards the right. I cannot say whether the volume of light decreased as She rose, or whether the growing distance made me see less and less light as She rose. What I do know, is that I was a long time with my head raised up, staring at the light, even after the light, which kept getting further away and decreasing in volume, [until it] had finally disappeared.

Calvat's description also includes the following report of words spoken by the Blessed Virgin Mary to Calvat:

Melanie, what I am about to tell you now will not always be a secret. You may make it public in 1858. The priests, ministers of my Son, the priests, by their wicked lives, by their irreverence and their impiety in the celebration of the holy mysteries, by their love of money, their love of honours and pleasures, the priests have become cesspools of impurity. Yes, the priests are asking vengeance, and vengeance is hanging over their heads. Woe to the priests and to those dedicated to God who by their unfaithfulness and their wicked lives are crucifying my Son again! The sins of those dedicated to God cry out towards Heaven and call for vengeance, and now vengeance is at their door, for there is no one left to beg mercy and forgiveness for the people.

References to "the priests" obviously do not call into question the behavior of priests in general but are clearly directed only to those who are guilty of the offenses described by the Virgin.

**1858 – Our Lady of Lourdes in France.** On February 8, Bernadette Soubirous (age fourteen), went with her sister and a friend to gather some wood. Soubirous stopped to remove her shoes and socks prior to crossing a stream, but the two other girls crossed immediately. Hearing a gust of wind, Soubirous turned around and experienced the first of nineteen apparitions, which occurred between February 8 and July 16. The last of her apparitions occurred on the Catholic feast day of Our Lady of Mount Carmel. The following material is a very brief description of the apparitions, as noted on the *Sanctuaire Notre-Dame de Lourdes* website. [154]

February 11 – "I saw a lady dressed in white, she wore a white dress, an equally white veil, a blue belt and a yellow rose on each foot." Bernadette made the Sign of the Cross and said the Rosary with the lady. When the prayer ended the Lady suddenly vanished.

February 14 – Bernadette felt an inner force drawing her to the Grotto in spite of the fact that she was forbidden to go there by her parents. At her insistence, her mother allowed her; after the first decade of the Rosary, she saw the same lady appearing. She sprinkled holy water at her. The lady smiled and bent her head. When the Rosary ended she disappeared.

February 18 – For the first time, the Lady spoke. Bernadette held out a pen and paper asking her to write her name. She replied, "It is not necessary" and she added, "I do not promise to make you happy in this world but in the other. Would you be kind enough to come here for a fortnight?"

February 21 – The Lady appeared to Bernadette very early in the morning. About one hundred people were present. Afterwards the Police Commissioner, Jacomet, questioned her. He wanted Bernadette to tell what she saw. Bernadette would only speak of "AQUÉRO" ("that thing" in local dialect).

February 23 – Surrounded by 150 persons, Bernadette arrived at the Grotto. The Apparition reveals to her a secret "only for her alone."

February 24 – The message of the Lady: "Penance! Penance! Penance! Pray to God for sinners. Kiss the ground as an act of penance for sinners!"

February 25 – Three hundred people were present. Bernadette relates, "She told me to go, drink of the spring. ... I only found a little muddy water. At the fourth attempt I was able to drink. She also made me eat the bitter herbs that were found near the spring, and then the vision left and went away." In front of the crowd that was asking "Do you think that she is mad doing things like that?" She replied; "It is for sinners."

February 27 – Eight hundred people were present. The Apparition was silent. Bernadette drank the water from the spring and carried out her usual acts of penance.

February 28 – Over one thousand people were present at the ecstasy. Bernadette prayed, kissed the ground and moved on her knees as a sign of penance. She was then taken to the house of Judge Ribes who threatened to put her in prison.

March 1 – Over one thousand five hundred people assembled and among them, for the first time, a priest. In the night, Catherine Latapie, a friend from Lourdes, went to the Grotto, she plunged her dislocated arm into the water of the Spring: her arm and her hand regained their movement.

March 2 – The crowd becomes larger and larger. The Lady asked her: "Go, tell the priests to come here in procession and to build a chapel here." Bernadette spoke of this to Fr. Peyramale, the Parish Priest of Lourdes. He wanted to know only one thing: the Lady's name. He demanded another test; to see the wild rose bush flower at the Grotto in the middle of winter.

March 3 – From 7 o'clock in the morning, in the presence of three thousand people, Bernadette arrived at the Grotto, but the vision did not appear. After school, she heard the inner invitation of the Lady. She went to the Grotto and asked her again for her name. The response was a smile. The Parish Priest told her again, "If the Lady really wishes that a chapel be built, then she must tell us her name and make the rose bush bloom at the Grotto."

March 4 – The ever-greater crowd (about eight thousand people) waited for a miracle at the end of the fortnight. The vision was silent. Fr. Peyramale stuck to his position. For twenty days Bernadette did not go to the Grotto, she no longer felt the irresistible invitation.

March 25 – The vision finally revealed her name, but the wild rose bush, on which she stood during the Apparitions, did not bloom. Bernadette recounted, "She lifted up her eyes to heaven, joined her hands as though in prayer, that were held out and open towards the ground and said to me: Que soy era Immaculada Concepciou (I am the Immaculate Conception)." The young visionary left and, running all the way, repeated continuously the words that she did not understand. These words troubled the brave Parish Priest. Bernadette was ignorant of the fact that this theological expression was assigned to the Blessed Virgin. Four years earlier, in 1854, Pope Pius IX declared this a truth of the Catholic Faith (a dogma).

April 7 – During this Apparition, Bernadette had to keep her candle alight. The flame licked along her hand without burning it. A medical doctor, Dr. Douzous, immediately witnessed this fact.

July 16 – Bernadette received the mysterious call to the Grotto, but her way was blocked and closed off by a barrier. She thus, arrived across from the Grotto to the other side of the Gave. "I felt that I was in front of the Grotto, at the same distance as before, I saw only the Blessed Virgin, and she was more beautiful than ever!"

Thirty years after her death, Soubirous' body was exhumed and no sign of decay was present, although her Rosary was corroded by rust, indicating a level of moisture that should have promoted decay of her body. Ten years later her body was again exhumed and still found to be without any sign of decay. Only a few relics were removed, and her body is now on display for veneration at the Convent of Saint-Gildard in Nevers, France.

**1859 – Our Lady of Good Help in Wisconsin.** While walking along a path in the wilderness, Adèle Brise (age twenty-eight) saw a luminous woman, clothed in white, standing between a maple tree and a hemlock tree. Brise said she prayed throughout the first apparition, which frightened her:

When on the next Sunday, October 9, Adèle together with her sister Isabelle and a neighbor, walked to Mass at Bay Settlement, the same Lady in white robes appeared to her a second time. Again Adèle was frightened. After a few minutes the apparition disappeared, again without speaking a word. ...

When on the return journey, with the same women and also accompanied by a man, Adèle passed the same location, the Lady appeared again, this time infused in a most fragrant incense. She was clad in a resplendent white gown, had long and golden hair, wore a yellow sash around her waist, and on her head a crown adorned with stars. Adèle immediately fell on her knees and asked her who she was. [155]

The Lady replied: "I am the Queen of Heaven who prays for the conversion of sinners, and I wish you to do the same. You received

Holy Communion this morning, and that is well. But you must do more. Make a general confession and offer up Communion for the conversion of sinners. If they do not convert and do penance, my Son will be obliged to punish them."

"Adèle, who is it?" said one of the women. "O why can't we see her as you do?" said another weeping. "Kneel," said Adèle, the Lady says she is the Queen of Heaven."

Our Blessed Lady turned, looked kindly at them, and said, "Blessed are they that believe without seeing."

"What are you doing here in idleness," continued our Lady, "while your companions are working in the vineyard of my Son?"

"What more can I do, dear Lady?" said Adèle weeping.

"Gather the children in this wild country and teach them what they should know for salvation."

"But how shall I teach them who knows so little myself?" replied Adèle.

"Teach them," replied her radiant visitor, "their catechism, how to sign themselves with the sign of the Cross, and how to approach the sacraments; that is what I wish you to do. Go and fear nothing, I will help you." Wrapped as it were in a luminous atmosphere, Our Lady lifted her hands as though she was beseeching a blessing for those at her feet. Slowly, she vanished from sight leaving Adèle overwhelmed and prostrate on the ground, and the dense woods as solemn as before. (156)

Brise devoted the rest of her life to the mission she received during the apparition. "Between 1859 and 1866 she walked as far as fifty miles to the village of Little Sturgeon in order to carry out the 'Queen of Heaven's' order. She encountered repeatedly wild animals such as bears, wolves, and deer. Soon innumerable testimonies of healings were on display in the chapel." (157)

**1871 – Our Lady of Pontmain in France.** On the evening of January 17, Eugene Barbedette (age twelve) had just finished helping his father with chores in a barn when he went outside and looked up at the stars. When the apparition began, he saw a woman dressed in a blue mantle covered with gold stars. When the boy's younger brother, father, and a neighbor came out to see what was going on, the brother, Joseph (age six) also saw the apparition, but the adults saw nothing. The boy's mother then arrived at the scene and, seeing nothing, instructed the two boys to go inside their home. The boys later went outside again and still reported seeing the apparition. So their schoolteacher, Sister Vitaline, was informed, and she arrived with three additional children.

Two girls, Francoise Richer (age eleven) and Jeanne-Marie Lebosse (age nine), said they could also see the apparition and described it exactly as the boys had done. Soon, sixty people were at the site praying the Rosary. The event lasted approximately three hours, and the apparition changed over time, which the four visionaries described to the others gathered at the site.

A blue oval formed around the Blessed Mother, and a small red cross appeared over her heart. The oval expanded to almost twice its original size, and stars appeared to become attached to the Lady's mantle. Then, letters of the alphabet in the color of gold began to appear slowly under the Lady's feet: "But pray, my children," then later, "God will soon answer you," and later, "My Son allows Himself to be moved."

The crowd began to sing a hymn, *Mother of Hope,* and the visionaries, looking at the apparition, responded animatedly, "See how she smiles! Oh, how beautiful she is!" Afterward, a large red cross with Jesus upon it appeared, and Mary's appearance changed to extreme sadness. The visionary Joseph later wrote the following description of the sadness he saw in Mary's expression: "Her sadness was more than anyone can imagine. I saw my mother overwhelmed with grief when, some months later, my father died. You know what such grief in a mother's face does to the heart of a child. But, as I remember, what instinctively came to mind was the sadness of the Most Blessed Virgin, which must have been the sadness of the Mother of Jesus at the foot of the Cross that bore her dying Son." [158]

Four unlit candles, which were in the apparition's original configuration within the blue oval, returned, two near Mary's shoulders and two near her knees. One of the stars, in motion, lit each of the four candles as the image of Christ on the cross disappeared and Mary returned to her initial posture, smiling, with arms extended downward. A white veil then appeared at her feet and gradually lifted upwards as the apparition disappeared.

**1877 – Our Lady of Gietrzwald in Poland.** Two girls reported seeing and speaking with the Blessed Virgin Mary over the course of three months beginning in June. Justyna Szafrynska (age thirteen) experienced her first apparition on June 27, followed by Barbara Samulowska (age twelve) on June 28. The Virgin instructed the girls to have a statue of the Blessed Virgin Mary as the *Immaculate Conception* placed at the site of the apparitions.

In the 1500s, an image in the church at the site—Mary with the child Jesus surrounded by angels—gained notoriety as a miraculous image. Since the 1600s, numerous cases have been reported of people being healed after praying for the intercession of Our Lady of Gietrzwald. In one of the 1877 apparitions that occurred outside the church containing the miraculous image, the two girls said they saw, appearing over a maple tree, a luminous "bright lady" sitting on a throne with the child Jesus surrounded by angels. During an apparition on June 30, the girls asked the lady what she wanted, and the Virgin Mary's reply was, "I wish you recite the Rosary every day." In a July 1 apparition, the girls asked the lady who she was, and the reply was, "I am the Blessed Virgin Mary of the Immaculate Conception." [159]

**1879 – Our Lady of Knock in Ireland.** Fifteen witnesses of the apparition ranging in age from five to seventy-four gave testimonies of what they saw, which are compiled in a 14-page PDF file available at the Knock Shrine website. Excerpts include the following: [96]

Judith Campbell – I live at Knock; I remember the evening and night of the 21 August last. Mary Byrne called at my house about eight o'clock on that evening, and asked me to come up and see the great sight at the chapel. I ran up with her to the place, and I saw outside the chapel, at the gable of the sacristy facing the south, three figures representing St. Joseph, St. John and the Blessed Virgin Mary, also an altar, and the likeness of a lamb on it, with a cross at the back of the lamb.

Patrick Hill – While at my aunt's at about eight o'clock in the evening, Dominick Byrne came into the house; he cried out: "Come up to the chapel and see the miraculous lights, and the beautiful visions that are to be seen there." I followed him; another man by the name Dominick Byrne, and John Durkan, and a small boy named John Curry, came with me; we were all together; we ran over towards the chapel. When we, running southwest, came so far from the village that on our turning, the gable came into view, we immediately beheld the lights; a clear white light, covering most of the gable, from the ground up to the window and higher. It was a kind of changing bright light, going sometimes up high and again not so high. We saw the figures—the Blessed Virgin, St. Joseph and St. John, and an altar with a Lamb on the altar, and a cross behind the lamb.

Patrick Walsh – About nine o'clock on that night I was going on some business through my land, and standing a distance of about half a mile from the chapel; I saw a very bright light on the southern gable end of the chapel; it appeared to me to be a large globe of golden light; I never saw, I thought, so brilliant a light before; it appeared high up in the air above and around the chapel gable and it was circular in its appearance; it was quite stationary, and it seemed to retain the same brilliancy all through. The following day I made inquiries in order to learn if there were any lights seen in the place that night; it was only then that I heard of the vision or apparitions that the people had seen.

**1917 – Our Lady of Fatima in Portugal.** No other private revelation has attracted as much attention from the popes and all Catholics as the apparitions reported in Fatima. The overarching *Message of Fatima* includes other apparitions experienced in subsequent years by one of the three visionaries, Lucia Santos—three apparitions in Pontevedra, Spain, in 1925, 1926 and 1927, and one in Tuy, Spain, in 1929.

Prior to the Fatima apparitions of the Virgin Mary as Our Lady of the Rosary in 1917, the three visionaries, Santos (age ten), Jacinta Marto (age seven) and Francisco Marto (age nine), reported three apparitions of an angel in 1916, who prepared them, taught them prayers, and instructed them on how to make sacrifices and become devoted to the Eucharist. During the third apparition of the angel, the children said the angel administered Holy Communion to them:

Lucia tells us in her memoirs that the three visionaries were so overwhelmed by a supernatural atmosphere that they too [with the angel] prostrated themselves and repeated the prayer three times. Lucia described the experience as so intense that the children seemed deprived of the use of their bodily senses, as they had been during the first angel apparition. [160]

The information below provides only a cursory description of how each of the 1917 apparitions began, and then is followed by several eyewitness accounts of an event on October 13 that was foretold in an apparition three months earlier. A comprehensive discussion of the events and related theology is available in Father Andrew Apostoli's book, *Fatima for Today.* Quotes from Lucia's memoirs, *Fatima, In Lucia's Own Words,* are italicized. [161]

*May 13 – Suddenly we saw what seemed to be a flash of lightning.*
*"We'd better go home," I said to my cousins, "that's lightning; we may have a thunderstorm."*
*"Yes, indeed!" they answered.*
*We began to go down the slope, hurrying the sheep along towards the road. We were more or less half-way down the slope, and almost level with a large holm-oak tree that stood there, when we saw another flash of lightning. We had only gone a few steps further when, there before us on a small holm-oak, we beheld a Lady all dressed in white. She was more brilliant than the sun, and radiated a light more clear and intense than a crystal glass filled with sparkling water when the rays of the burning sun shine through it. We stopped, astounded, before the Apparition. We were so close, just a few feet from her, that we were bathed in the light which surrounded her, or rather, which radiated from her. Then Our Lady spoke to us:*
*"Do not be afraid. I will do you no harm."*
*"Where are you from?"*
*"I am from heaven."*
*"What do you want of me?"*
*"I have come to ask you to come here for six months in succession, on the 13th day, at this same hour. Later on, I will tell you who I am and what I want."*

**June 13** *– As soon as Jacinta, Francisco and I had finished praying the Rosary with a number of other people who were present, we saw once more the flash reflecting the light which was approaching (which we called lightning). The next moment, Our Lady was there on the holm-oak, exactly the same as in May.*

**July 13** — *A few moments after arriving at the Cova da Iria, near the holm-oak, where a large number of people were praying the Rosary, we saw the flash of light once more, and a moment later Our Lady appeared on the holm-oak.*

*"What do you want of me?" I asked.*

*"I want you to come here on the 13th of the next months, to continue to pray the Rosary every day in honour of Our Lady of the Rosary, in order to obtain peace for the world and the end of the war, because only she can help you."*

*"I would like to ask you to tell us who you are, and to work a miracle so that everybody will believe that you are appearing to us."*

*"Continue to come here every month. In October, I will tell you who I am and what I want, and I will perform a miracle for all to see and believe."*

**August 13-15** – On August 13, prior to the usual time of the apparitions, the children were picked up by the head of the city council of Ourem, Portugal, which had administrative control over Fatima and the nearby village of Aljustrel. Political tensions were high in Portugal at the time because a Soviet-style revolution occurred in 1910, and anti-religious laws were enacted by the government in 1911. World War I began in 1914, and Germany declared war on Portugal in 1916. On April 4, 1917, the first Portuguese soldiers arrived at the Western Front.

By August, news of the apparitions had spread throughout Portugal, and the events were beginning to draw interest internationally. As a result, the children were picked up by Arturo de Oliveira Santos, head of the Ourem city council, on the pretense that the increasing crowds at the Cova da Iria were a threat to the stability of the area and the local government.

Lucia, Jacinta, and Francisco were taken to the Ourem city hall and intensely interrogated, and that night, they stayed at the home of Arturo de Oliveira Santos. The following day they were individually interrogated, and each child was threatened with death unless they made a statement that the apparitions were a hoax.

As each of the children refused to say the apparitions were a hoax, they were individually led (unbeknownst to each other) into an adjacent room where they were told they would be executed. When that failed to persuade the children, they were released on August 15 and dropped off on the steps of a local Catholic church. In her memoirs, Lucia stated that the August apparition took place on August 15:

*I was accompanied by Francisco and his brother John. We were with the sheep in a place called Valinhos, when we felt something supernatural approaching and enveloping us. Suspecting that Our Lady was about to appear to us, and feeling sorry lest Jacinta might miss seeing her, we asked her brother to go and call her. As he was unwilling to go, I offered him two small coins, and off he ran. Meanwhile, Francisco and I saw the flash of light, which we called lightning. Jacinta arrived, and a moment later, we saw Our Lady on the holm-oak tree.*

**September 13** – The children's imprisonment in August only served to generate more interest in the apparitions, and an estimated 25,000 people gathered at the site:

*As the hour approached, I set out with Jacinta and Francisco, but owing to the crowds around us we could only advance with difficulty. The roads were packed with people, and everyone wanted to see us and speak to us. There was no human respect whatsoever. Simple folk, and even ladies and gentlemen, struggled to break through the crowd that pressed around us. No sooner had they reached us than they threw themselves on their knees before us, begging us to place their petitions before Our Lady. … At last, we arrived at the Cova da Iria, and on reaching the holm-oak we began to say the Rosary with the people. Shortly afterwards, we saw the flash of light, and then Our Lady appeared on the holm-oak.*

**October 13** – Estimates of the number of people at the site ranged from 40,000 to 80,000, and approximately 20,000 others in the vicinity:

*We left home quite early, expecting that we would be delayed along the way. Masses of people thronged the roads. The rain fell in torrents. … Not even the muddy roads could prevent these people from kneeling in the most humble and suppliant of attitudes. We reached the holm-oak in the Cova da Iria. Once there, moved by an interior impulse, I asked the people to shut their umbrellas and say the Rosary. A little later, we saw the flash of light, and then Our Lady appeared on the holm-oak.*

The event that occurred on October 13 is referred to as the "miracle of the sun" because witnesses reported the sun appeared to move toward the earth, change colors, and whirl like a wheel. The event was visible only in a 25-mile radius of the town of Fatima, so it did not involve the sun itself. Many witnesses mistakenly believed the sun was hurtling toward the earth in a doomsday scenario. Lucia's comments in her memoirs clearly state the sun itself was not involved, but that a type of reflection of the sun occurred. Immediately before the beginning of the event, Lucia reported, speaking of Mary, "Then, opening her hands, she made them reflect on the sun, and as she ascended, the reflection of her own light continued to be projected on the sun itself." [161]

The description of Mary's appearance is reminiscent of the reference in the biblical book of Revelation 12:1, "A great sign appeared in heaven: a woman clothed with the sun, with the moon under her feet and a crown of twelve stars on her head."

Alfredo da Silva Santos, a skeptic from Lisbon, Portugal, traveled to Fatima when news began spreading that a supernatural event would occur on October 13. He reported:

We made our arrangements and went in three motorcars in the early morning of the 13th. There was a thick mist, and the car which went in front mistook the way so that we were all lost for a time and only arrived at the Cova da Iria at midday by the sun. It was absolutely full of people, but for my part I felt devoid of any religious feeling. When Lucia called out, "Look at the sun!," the whole multitude repeated, "Attention to the sun!" It was a day of incessant drizzle but a few moments before the miracle it stopped raining.

I can hardly find words to describe what followed. The sun began to move, and at a certain moment appeared to be detached from the sky and about to hurtle upon us like a wheel of flame. My wife—we had been married only a short time—fainted, and I was too upset to attend to her, and my brother-in-law ... supported her on his arm. I fell on my knees, oblivious of everything, and when I got up I don't know what I said. I think I began to cry out like the others. An old man with a white beard began to attack the atheists aloud and challenged them to say whether or not something supernatural had occurred. [162]

Avelino de Almeida, a reporter for Portugal's largest newspaper, *O Seculo*, based in Lisbon, had previously written negative articles about the apparitions occurring at Fatima. He reported the following:

> One could see the immense number of people turn toward the sun, which appeared free from clouds and in its zenith. It looked like a plaque of dull silver, and it was possible to look at it without the least discomfort.

> It might have been an eclipse which was taking place. But at that moment a great shout went up and one could hear the spectators nearest at hand shouting, "A miracle! A miracle!"... Before the astonished eyes of the crowd, whose aspect was biblical as they stood bareheaded, eagerly searching the sky, the sun trembled, made sudden incredible movements outside all cosmic laws—the sun "danced" according to the typical expression of the people.

> People began to ask each other what they had seen. The great majority admitted to having seen the trembling and the dancing of the sun; others affirmed that they saw the face of the Blessed Virgin; others, again, swore that the sun whirled on itself like a giant wheel and that it lowered itself to the earth as if to burn it in its rays. Some said they saw it change colors successively. [163]

Maria Carreira was a local resident who was among a small group of people accompanying the three children at the June 13 apparition. Later, she visited the site frequently and became known as Maria da Capelinha (Maria of the Little Chapel) because she placed flowers at the site, tied silk ribbons on the branches of the tree, removed stones, cut away thickets, and "gave the place the shape of a round threshing floor." She reported:

> The sun turned everything to different colors—yellow, blue and white. Then it shook and trembled. It looked like a wheel of fire that was going to fall on the people. They began to cry out, "We shall all be killed!" Others called to Our Lady to save them. They recited acts of contrition. One woman began to confess her sins aloud, advertising that she had done this and that. ... When at last the sun stopped leaping and moving, we all breathed our relief.

We were still alive, and the miracle which the children had foretold, had been seen by everyone. [164]

Father Ignacio Lorenco witnessed the event eleven miles from the apparition site, from the village of Alburitel, and stated:

At about midday we were surprised by the shouts and cries of some men and women who were passing in front of the school. ... Outside, the people were shouting and weeping and pointing to the sun. ... I feel incapable of describing what I saw and felt. I looked fixedly at the sun, which seemed pale and did not hurt the eyes. Looking like a ball of snow revolving on itself, it suddenly seemed to come down in a zigzag, menacing the earth. Terrified, I ran and hid myself among the people, who were weeping and expecting the end of the world at any moment.

Near us was an unbeliever who had spent the morning mocking at the simpletons who had gone off to Fatima "just to see an ordinary girl." He now seemed to be paralyzed, his eyes fixed on the sun. Afterward, he trembled from head to foot and lifting up his arms fell on his knees in the mud, crying out to Our Lady. ... During those long moments of the solar prodigy, objects around us turned all the colors of the rainbow. We saw ourselves blue, yellow, red, etc. All the strange phenomena increased the fears of the people.

After about ten minutes the sun, now dull and pallid, returned to its place. When the people realized that the danger was over, there was an explosion of joy, and everyone joined in thanksgiving and praise to Our Lady. [165]

Mary Allen testified that the miracle caused her rain-drenched clothes and the saturated earth to become dry within a ten-minute span:

As we approached the hillside upon which the appearances were supposed to have taken place, I saw a sea of people. Some newspapers said there were 70,000 people there. I didn't count, but it was more people than I have ever seen in my life, even to this day. ... We had just arrived there when suddenly my attention was drawn to a sudden bright light from the heavens, lighting up the whole countryside. Suddenly the rain ceased, the clouds separated and I saw a large sun, brighter than the sun, yet I could look at it without hurting my eyes, as if it were only the moon.

This sun began to get larger and larger, brighter and brighter until the whole heavens seemed more brilliantly lighted than I have ever seen it. Then the sun started spinning and shooting streams of light, which changed it to all colors of the rainbow. ... At the same time, it started getting bigger and bigger in the sky as though it were headed directly for us, as though it were falling on the earth. Everyone was frightened. We all thought it was the end of the world. Everyone threw themselves on their knees praying and screaming the Act of Contrition. Suddenly the sun stopped spinning and returned to its place in the sky. Everyone started shouting: "Miracle! This is a miracle!" Just then I noticed that both the ground and my clothes were bone dry. [166]

**1932 – Our Lady of Beauraing in Belgium.** Five children (ages nine to fifteen) from two families reported apparitions of Mary from November 1932 to January 1933. Approximately 15,000 people gathered at the site on December 8, the Catholic feast day of the Immaculate Conception. The crowd did not see the apparition, but they saw the children in ecstasy.

On January 2, the children reported, according to words they heard from Mary, that the following day would be their final apparition, and Mary would speak to each child individually. About 30,000 people gathered at the site on January 3:

After two decades [a decade is ten Hail Mary prayers when praying the Rosary] four of them called out and fell to their knees, leaving Fernande, the oldest, in tears because she could see nothing. ... She [Mary] then spoke to Gilberte Voisin, imparting to her what has been seen as the main promise of Beauraing, "I will convert sinners." ... To Andree she said: "I am the Mother of God, the Queen of Heaven. Pray always." ...

Fernande remained kneeling while the other children went inside for questioning, when suddenly, she, and many in the crowd, heard a loud noise like thunder and saw a "ball of fire" on the hawthorn tree. Mary appeared and spoke to Fernande, asking her if she loved her Son and herself; when Fernande replied that she did, the response was: "Then sacrifice yourself for me." At this the Blessed Virgin glowed with extraordinary brilliance, and extended her arms, so that the girl could see her golden heart, before saying, "Goodbye," and disappearing, to leave Fernande weeping. (167)

**1945 – Our Lady of All Nations in Amsterdam.** Ida Peerdeman (age forty) first reported apparitions of the Blessed Virgin Mary in 1945, and ongoing visions continued until 1959. One message from Mary on April 29, 1951, included the following:

I stand here as the Co-Redemptrix and Advocate. Everything should be concentrated on that. Repeat this after me; The new dogma will be the "dogma of the Co-Redemptrix." Notice I lay special emphasis on "Co." I have said that it will arouse much controversy. Once again I tell you that the Church, "Rome," will carry it through and silence all objections. The Church, "Rome," will incur opposition and overcome it. The Church, "Rome," will become stronger and mightier in proportion to the resistance she puts up in the struggle. My purpose and my commission to you is none other than to urge the Church, the theologians, to wage this battle. ... I know well, the struggle will be hard and bitter (and then the Lady smiles to herself and seems to gaze into the far distance), but the outcome is already assured. (168)

In May 2002, the apparitions as well as the messages were declared as authentic and of "supernatural origin" by Bishop Josef Maria Punt of the Diocese of Haarlem-Amsterdam. Peerdeman said Mary also described and provided visions of numerous future events, which Peerdeman relayed and later proved to be accurate. Many of Peerdeman's prophecies are described in a video, *Peace Through a Woman,* narrated by Martin Sheen.

On May 31, 1954, Peerdeman reported the following vision involving the Blessed Virgin Mary:

Once more I am here—the Co-Redemptrix, Mediatrix, and Advocate is now standing before you. Theologians and apostles of the Lord Jesus Christ, listen carefully: I have given you the explanation of the dogma. Work and ask for this dogma. You must petition the Holy Father for this dogma.

All of a sudden, it is as if I was standing with the Lady over the dome of a big church, and as we enter, I hear the Lady say, "I am taking you inside this. Tell others what I let you see and hear."

*We* are now in a very big church, in St. Peter's [Basilica in Vatican City]. I see lots of cardinals and bishops. The Pope enters. ... People applaud. The choir begins to sing. Now the Holy Father is announcing something, while holding up two fingers.

Then all at once the Lady is standing on the globe again and says with a smile, "In this way, my child, I have let you see what is the Will of the Lord Jesus Christ. This day will in due time be the "Coronation Day" of his Mother, the "Lady of All Nations." [169]

The tenor of some of the messages reported by Peerdeman as coming from Mary can be characterized as feisty—willfully lecturing theologians in a way reminiscent of Joan of Arc, who at times used a lecturing tone when responding to questions from ecclesiastical authorities. The forty-ninth message Peerdeman received, on April 4, 1954, included the following:

I see the Lady standing there with a very serious look on her face. She says to me, "Here I am again. Listen carefully! From the beginning, the Handmaid of the Lord was chosen to be the Co-Redemptrix. Tell your theologians that they can find everything in their books."

Now I see an old library with lots of books. The Lady points this out to me. She pauses for a moment and smiles to herself as if inwardly amused. Nearly whispering, she says, "I am not bringing a new doctrine. I am now bringing old thoughts."

The Lady pauses again and then says, "Because Mary is Co-Redemptrix, she is also Mediatrix, she is also Advocate. Not only because she is the Mother of the Lord Jesus Christ, but—and mark this well—because she is the Immaculate Conception. [170]

**1961 – Our Lady of Mount Carmel in Garabandal, Spain.** In addition to 2,000 apparitions experienced by the primary visionary, Conchita Gonzales, three other children, Mari Loli Mazon (age twelve), Jacinta Gonzales (age twelve) and Mari Cruz Gonzales (age eleven), also experienced visions. In some cases, all four girls would be in the same location, but all of them would not participate in the vision, and sometimes one or more girls would enter or exit the apparition at different times:

> When in ecstasy, the girls saw only the vision and whichever other members of their group were actually participating in the apparition with them. If one of the girls was not participating, either because she did not share in it at the start or because she was excluded or withdrawn from it at some point while it continued for the others, these others could not see her. Also, they could never see any of the spectators or bystanders, precisely because they were not participating in the vision. [171]

The apparitions lasted from a few minutes to several hours, and the girls often gave objects such as rosaries, wedding rings, and even stone pebbles to the Blessed Virgin Mary to be kissed by her. Gonzales stated:

> It was not the Blessed Virgin who told us to gather pebbles. We did it ourselves. … the Blessed Virgin touched them and kissed them and then said to us: "Give them to other people." [172]

Later, in response to questions posed to Gonzales on September 14, 1965, she stated, "The Blessed Virgin said that Jesus would perform miracles through objects kissed by her." [173]

On December 8, 1964, Gonzales reported an interior locution from the Blessed Virgin Mary, during which Mary informed Gonzales to expect an apparition of Saint Michael the archangel on June 18, 1965. Due to the advance notice of the date, crowds gathered at the site where Gonzales reported apparitions of Saint Michael and the Blessed Mother four years earlier. It was about 11:30 p.m. when Gonzales started running to the site. A Spanish news station set up cameras and flooded the area with light. Even though the lights shone directly at her, Gonzales' eyes remained wide open and didn't blink throughout the twenty-minute apparition:

Her voice which was recorded on tape had that same intense guttural whispering tone and quality that it had had in the previous apparitions. At one moment, she reached up with the approximately three-by-four-inch crucifix that she carried in her hand and touched the hem of Saint Michael's garment. Then, at the angel's bidding, she held the crucifix out for Father Pel, a French priest, to kiss. An old man of 87 with a reputation of holiness, who had spent the morning in the village church, Father Pel had followed the events of Garabandal for some time. Next, Conchita held out the crucifix to one of Father Pel's friends. Finally, she did the same for Jean Masure, a Frenchman living in Madrid. Later she told this man: "The angel says that I am to tell you that the Blessed Virgin has granted your request." [174]

On June 18, a specific message given for "the world" (as opposed to a message given only for the seer or for specific individuals) was the following:

As my message of October 18 [1961] has not been complied with and has not been made known to the world, I am advising you that this is the last one.

Before, the cup was filling up. Now it is flowing over. Many cardinals, many bishops and many priests are on the road to hell and are taking many souls with them.

Less and less importance is being given to the Eucharist. You should turn the wrath of God away from yourselves by your efforts. If you ask him for forgiveness with sincere hearts, he will pardon you.

I, your Mother, through the intercession of Saint Michael the archangel, ask you to amend your lives. You are now receiving the last warnings. I love you very much and do not want your condemnation.

Pray to us with sincerity and we will grant your requests. You should make more sacrifices. Think about the passion of Jesus. [175]

**1968 – Our Lady of Light in Zeitoun, Egypt.** The first witness was a Muslim, Farouk Mohammed Atwa, who thought he was seeing a woman attempting suicide by jumping from the top of the Church of Saint Mary in Zeitoun, which is part of Cairo. Atwa had been diagnosed with gangrene, but when he went to the hospital the next day for a scheduled operation, he was medically certified as completely healed.

Ongoing apparitions lasted approximately three years. During the first two years, the Blessed Virgin Mary appeared two or three times each week, and estimates of the number of people who witnessed the apparitions range from 250,000 to one million. About 40 million people witnessed the events on Egyptian television.

According to tradition as well as archeological evidence, Zeitoun is the site where the Blessed Virgin Mary, Saint Joseph and the child Jesus stopped after arriving in Egypt. The biblical text of Matthew 2:13 describes an incident where an angel appears to Saint Joseph in a dream: "Get up," he said, "take the child and his mother and escape to Egypt. Stay there until I tell you, for Herod is going to search for the child to kill him."

An official statement published by the Coptic Orthodox Church in Cairo on May 4, 1968, included the following:

> Since the evening of Tuesday April 2, 1968 (the 24th of Bramhat, 1684 A.M.), the apparitions of the Holy Virgin Saint Mary, Mother of Light, have continued in the Coptic Orthodox Church named after Her in Zeitoun, Cairo. The apparitions occurred on many different nights and are continuing in different forms. The Holy Virgin Saint Mary appeared sometimes in full form and sometimes in a bust, surrounded with a halo of shining light. She was seen at times on the openings of the domes on the roof of the church, and at other times outside the domes, moving and walking on the roof of the church and over the domes. When She knelt in reverence in front of the cross, the cross shone with bright light. Waving Her blessed hands and nodding Her holy head, She blessed the people who gathered to observe the miracle. She appeared sometimes in the form of a body like a very bright cloud, and sometimes as a figure of light preceded with heavenly bodies shaped like doves moving at high speeds. [176]

Wadie Shumbo, a Protestant who worked in engineering for Mobil Oil, reported:

At about 9:50 p.m. we saw lightning over the church, much stronger than one could make with a flashlight. I had a feeling something was about to happen. A thin line or edge of light appeared like the light you see when you open the door of a lighted room. Within seconds it formed itself into the shape of the Virgin. I could not speak. All who were with me said, "It's impossible." The Moslems all started to cry. This sight lasted for five minutes when the figure rose and vanished. I could distinguish only a difference in colour between the skin in the face and hands and the veil. ... When she disappeared from our side of the church, the people from the other side shouted they were seeing her, then she returned to our side for five minutes. When I returned to the car for something, I found it impossible to get back to the church because of the crowd. I could hear people shouting. Above the centre dome I saw Mary in full body, standing before the cross, I cannot describe what I felt. [177]

Wagih Rizk, a photographer who lived in Zeitoun, had suffered a severe injury to his arm from an automobile accident in February 1968. The extent of the injury was described by Dr. Hassan Sennarah:

All tissues, nerves and tendons that join your arm were cut and the bones have compound fractures and consequently you will never be able to move your left forearm and hand again. ... Your condition was severe and you have to thank God for being in such state now. [178]

Rizk then reported the experiences he had in April 1968:

On April 9, 1968, I was shaken by the news of the apparitions of the Blessed Virgin Mary at Zeitoun and so I went to see Her. That night at 2:45 a.m., I saw Her in the form of radiating light like clouds. The light was very strong, so strong that the eye couldn't bear it, and was seen near the cross over the small eastern dome. The apparition was awesome. ... Reverence and fear filled me like an electric shock.

I returned home. I couldn't control my thoughts or sleep in spite of the fact that I didn't sleep all that night to witness the apparition. I had a bizarre thought: I wanted to take photos of the Blessed Virgin and Her miraculous apparitions. Why not? ...

On April 13, I was determined not to let the opportunity escape anymore. At 3:40 am, the Blessed Virgin appeared. And very quickly, I captured the photo. ... Our Lady is still appearing in front of me. ... So I took a second photo. ... And you know, from what you have read in newspapers, the technical aspects and the way these two photos were captured ... but what you don't know is the spiritual aspect. ...

I forgot while I was looking at the apparition of the Blessed Virgin the fact that when I captured the first photo quickly, I used my left hand! Yes my left hand. ... The five hand doctors, some of them are among the most famous surgeons in Egypt, said [it] was hopeless and will never move again. ... The Blessed Virgin has miraculously healed this hand!

I started to move my left hand, up, down, to my side and to rotate and wave it in the air while extended. ... I was cured ... completely cured once the Virgin appeared. And from this day the camera never leaves me, and the camera and I never leave Zeitoun. [178]

**1973 – Our Lady of Akita in Japan.** On June 28, Sister Agnes Katsuko Sasagawa (age forty-two) felt excruciating pain and noticed a cross-shaped wound in the palm of her hand. On July 5, blood began to flow from the wound. The following day she heard an interior voice, which Sasagawa reported to be her guardian angel, saying, "The wounds of Mary are much deeper and more sorrowful than yours. Let us go to pray together in the chapel." When Sasagawa entered the chapel and walked up to a wooden statue of Mary, she later said, "I suddenly felt that the wooden statue came to life and was about to speak to me ... She was bathed in a brilliant light ... and at the same moment a voice of indescribable beauty struck my totally deaf ears." [179] The following morning, other sisters in the convent noticed blood dripping from the statue's right hand, coming out of the wood where two lines met in the form of a cross. The hand of the statue and the hand of Sasagawa bled on Fridays during the month of July. Sasagawa said her guardian angel accurately foretold the wound in her hand would disappear on July 27, but blood continued to drip from the statue's hand until September 29, when the statue emanated an intense light.

Sasagawa reported three messages from Mary, on July 6, August 3, and October 13, which is the anniversary of the Fatima "miracle of the sun." All three messages were heard by Sasagawa while she was in the presence of the statue, and she reported all three messages came "through" the statue. The October 13 message included the following: [180]

> The work of the devil will infiltrate even into the Church in such a way that one will see cardinals opposing cardinals, bishops against other bishops. The priests who venerate me will be scorned and opposed by their confreres. ... Pray very much the prayers of the Rosary. I alone am able to save you from the calamities which approach. Those who place their confidence in me will be saved.

Tears flowing from the statue on December 8, 1979, the Catholic feast day celebrating the Immaculate Conception, were recorded by a television crew in Japan and broadcast nationwide. The tears began flowing from the statue on January 4, 1975, and ended on September 15, 1981, the feast day of Our Lady of Sorrows. The sisters kept a record of the days on which the statue wept and the number of people who witnessed the tears. On all but five occasions, the number of witnesses ranged from a minimum of ten to a maximum of sixty-five. The statue wept tears 101 times, and Sasagawa said her guardian angel explained the significance in the following manner: "There is a meaning to the figure 101. This signifies that sin came into the world by a woman and it is also by a woman that salvation came into the world. The zero between the two signifies the Eternal God who is from all eternity until eternity. The first one represents Eve, and the last, the Virgin Mary."

The biblical basis for guardian angels is found in Matthew 18:10 and numerous references to the activities of angels as protectors and enablers are found in the Old and New Testament texts. The following is a description of the role of guardian angels by author Mike Aquilina:

> Our guardian angel's task is to get us to heaven—not to keep us or our loved ones from suffering or death. After all, suffering is perhaps the principal means of our spiritual growth on earth, and death is our final portal to God.

We should not be surprised when friends, or even children, die in accidents. Nor should we see it as some sort of angelic malfunction. The angel's job is to get his charge to judgement, prepared as well as possible. The angels live in the presence of God, and they know God's mind better than we do. They know when an injury or illness will draw us closer to God. They also know when another twenty-four hours on earth will merely get us another day older and deeper in debt.

God permits our suffering and even our death, always for the good of souls—for our own soul, if we correspond to the grace, for the good of others if we don't. The angels always cooperate with his perfect plan.

Judged from a human perspective, this can seem cold and even cruel. But the human perspective is limited. It takes an exceptionally talented human mind to see beyond it. ...

Nevertheless, through most of our time here, we will stand in need of much more time here—to draw still closer to God and prepare ourselves for judgement. That's the reason why our angels will sometimes go to extraordinary lengths to keep us safe. [181]

**1981 – Our Lady of Kibeho in Rwanda.** The apparitions began on November 28, 1981, and ended for the primary seer, Alphonsine Mumureke, on November 28, 1989. Seven children, six girls and one boy, claimed to see the Blessed Virgin Mary. In one of the events, Mumureke said she was told by Mary to inform her school principal that she would appear dead during one of the visions, and she indeed went into a comatose state, during which she was immovable by six men who tried to lift her from her bed. Vestine Salina informed others of her impending "death and resurrection" on Easter Sunday, which occurred as predicted. Mumureke and two others, Nathalie Mukamazimpaka and Marie-Claire Mukangango, were officially recognized by the Church as having authentic visions, including being taken on trips to heaven, where people were reported to be able to perceive colors as music, breathe water, and drink visible light.

In her book, *Our Lady of Kibeho,* Immaculée Ilibagiza described the first apparition on November 28:

At this point, the teenager's line of vision narrowed so that all she could see was a brilliantly luminous white cloud materializing in midair a few feet in front of her. ... As the beautiful figure drifted toward the girl, her feet never touched the ground. Waves of love emanated from the majestic lady, embracing Alphonsine like the loving arms of a mother. The apprehension she'd felt moments before evaporated, and her heart filled with unimaginable joy. Sensing that she was in the presence of the Divine, she fell to her knees and asked, "Who are you?" "I am the Mother of the Word." [182]

During Mumureke's next apparition on November 29:

She landed heavily on her knees and stared at the ceiling exactly as she had the day before. Her face lit up in ecstasy and she smiled peacefully, even as tears rolled down her cheeks. The transformation was so sudden and dramatic that some of the teasing students crossed themselves. But others hurled more cutting remarks at Alphonsine, who continued to smile and nod while looking upward, as though answering questions from someone she deeply loved. Many of the girls howled with laughter, waving their hands in front of Alphonsine's eyes to break her fixed gaze. When she didn't react, Marie-Claire, who had acted in amateur theater, proclaimed her classmate to be the greatest actress in all of Rwanda. Her cronies snickered and shouted in Alphonsine's ears, but Alphonsine had no reaction to them. She couldn't react because she didn't know they were there—all she was aware of was the beautiful lady hovering about her again in the same glorious light. "My child, I love you," the Virgin told Alphonsine in her soothing, lyrical voice. "Never be afraid of me; in fact, play with me! I love children who will play with me because it shows me their love and trust. Be as a little child with me, for I love to pet my children. No child should fear his or her mother, and I am your mother. You should never be afraid of me; you should always love me as I love you."
(183)

The apparitions occurred prior to the 1994 Rwanda genocide that resulted in approximately one million deaths. The Kibeho seers were shown visions of the impending massacres, which they related to more than 20,000 people who were gathered on August 15, 1982, to celebrate the feast day of the Assumption of the Blessed Virgin Mary. At one point during the apparition, Mumureke said:

The Virgin's face became etched with pain, and her eyes filled with tears of grief. After many minutes of mournful silence, the Queen of Heaven began to openly weep. "Why are you crying, darling?" Alphonsine asked Mary, frightened and concerned. "Why do you show me your tears? What do they mean, Mother? Your sadness hurts me; I should be the one crying, not you!" The Virgin Mary responded by shedding even more tears. "Mother, please!" Alphonsine begged. "Why don't you answer me? I can't bear to see you so upset ... please don't cry! Oh, Mother, I can't even reach up to console you or dry your eyes. What has happened that makes you so sad? You won't let me sing to you and you refuse to talk to me. Please, Mother, I have never seen you cry before, and it terrifies me!" At last Mary responded to the distraught teenager, asking her to sing a specific song. The 20,000 people listening to the visibly upset Alphonsine couldn't hear the Virgin's voice, but they hung on every word the visionary uttered.

Now they heard her say, "Mother, I love to sing to you, but are you sure you want me to sing that song?" The young lady apparently fulfilled Our Lady's request by singing "Naviriye ubusa mu Ijuru" ("I Came from Heaven for Nothing"): People are not grateful, They don't love me, I came from heaven for nothing, I left all the good things there for nothing. My heart is full of sadness, My child, show me the love, You love me, Come closer to my heart. "Mother, you're still weeping ... please tell me what's making you cry," Alphonsine said, abruptly ending the song. "Remember when you promised me that you'd give me anything I asked you for?

Well, I'm asking this of you now: Please don't cry!" Many minutes passed in silence as Alphonsine listened and received the message Mary wanted her to share. Then the girl said, "Yes, Mother, I will repeat it exactly as you ask me to. To the people on Earth, you say three times: You opened the door and they refused to come in. You opened the door and they refused to come in. You opened the door and they refused to come in. ...

Suddenly Alphonsine let out a gut-wrenching scream that cut through the startled crowd like a razor. "I see a river of blood! What does that mean? No, please! Why did you show me so much blood? Show me a clear stream of water, not this river of blood!" the seer cried out, as the Holy Mother revealed one horrifying vision after another. The young woman was subjected to so many images of destruction, torture, and savage human carnage that she pleaded, "Stop, stop, please stop! Why, Mother? Why are you showing me this? The trees are exploding into flames, the country is burning! Please, Mother, you're scaring me. ... Oh no! No! Why are those people killing each other? Why do they chop each other? I'm not a strong enough person to watch people killing each other." Tears gushed from Alphonsine's eyes as she trembled uncontrollably at the scenes unraveling before her.

She summoned a hymn to her lips, trying to sing the images away, but she soon fell silent, as though frozen in fear. Mary was revealing even more dreadful images to her—for example, the girl was now staring at a growing pile of severed human heads, which were still gushing blood. The grotesque sight worsened still as Our Lady expanded Alphonsine's vision until she beheld a panoramic view of a vast valley piled high with the remains of a million rotting, headless corpses, and not a single soul was left alive to bury the dead.
(184)

**1981 – Queen of Peace in Medjugorje.** The most controversial reports of Marian apparitions involve a long series that have continued since the first event occurred on June 24, 1981, in Medjugorje, Yugoslavia, in what is now Bosnia and Herzegovina. When the apparitions began, the six seers were children. An extensive analysis written from the perspective of a journalist is found in Sullivan's book, *The Miracle Detective.*

Millions of people have visited the site and several million Catholics firmly believe the visions to be authentic. However, many Catholics are vocal skeptics. Indications are that the Church will likely issue a statement on Medjugorje late 2015 or early 2016. The events began ten years prior to the start of the wars that led to the breakup of Yugoslavia, which included the Bosnian genocide and other ethnic cleansing atrocities. The Queen of Peace was reported to have come simultaneously as a warning and an opportunity for reconciliation.

Healings and miracles are commonly reported and documented in Medjugorje, but many Catholics still firmly believe the reported apparitions are a hoax perpetrated by the six visionaries, Mirjana Dragicevic, Marija Pavlovic, Vicka Ivankovic, Ivanka Ivankovic, Jakov Colo, and Ivan Dragicevic. The following is a description of events that occurred during the first twelve days of the apparitions.

**June 24** – Mirjana and Ivanka, two teenage girls from the nearby village of Bijakovici, were walking near a place known as Podbrdo hill. Ivanka saw "a bright figure" she thought was the Blessed Virgin Mary. Mirjana said she saw a very beautiful young woman who radiated light, wore a silver-gray dress, and held a baby wrapped in a blanket. The "shining woman" alternatively covered and uncovered the baby.

While Mirjana, Ivanka, and another girl who had joined them, Milka Pavlovic, were looking at the apparition, their friend, Vicka Ivankovic, arrived. Earlier, Mirjana and Ivanka had stopped by Vicka's house to see if she would join them for their walk. Upon seeing the apparition, Vicka was severely upset and ran back to Bijakovici, crying uncontrollably. As two boys, Ivan Dragicevic and Ivan Ivankovic, passed by, Vicka asked them to accompany her back to the hill.

When they arrived back at Podbrdo, Vicka turned around to ask Ivan Dragicevic what he saw, but the boy was already running away from the apparition site. Ivan Ivankovic, who left in pursuit of his friend, reported that he could only see something "white and turning."

The four girls stayed at the site, and each reported they saw the shining woman repeatedly cover and uncover the baby. At one point, Mary motioned for them to approach Her, but the four girls couldn't move. The apparition eventually faded away, but each girl remained in a state of shock. Ivanka said she was shaking. That evening, all six children described their experiences to others in Bijakovici but were met with skepticism or ridicule.

**June 25** – Thinking that the Blessed Virgin Mary might return again, Vicka, Mirjana, and Ivanka planned to go to Podbrdo at approximately the same time. As Vicka walked toward the apparition site around 6:00 p.m., she met Mirjana, and both girls then met Ivanka at the base of Podbrdo hill, where about twenty people had already gathered.

Similar to how the apparitions began at Fatima and other locations by a flash of light, the children also saw flashes of light. Vicka immediately understood that Mary was about to appear, and she ran off to get her friend,

Marija Pavlovic, who had asked Vicka to fetch her if the apparition appeared again. Marija's younger sister, Milka, was at the apparition site on June 24, but when Vicka arrived to get Marija, the girl's mother would only allow one of her daughters to go. In fact, to ensure Milka wouldn't return to the site on June 25, Mrs. Pavlovic sent Milka to work in a distant vineyard.

Vicka and Marija then returned to Podbrdo accompanied by Vicka's cousin, Jakov Colo. Shortly thereafter, Ivan Dragicevic joined the group. Ivan Ivankovic, who was twenty years old at the time, said, "This is only for children," and initially decided not to go; however, he changed his mind and arrived at the site awhile later.

From the base of the hill, the apparition became visible first to Ivanka, then Mirjana, and then Vicka. Ivan Dragicevic reported that he saw "something," and Marija and Jakov didn't see anything from the bottom of the hill. However, Ivanka, Mirjana, and Vicka reported not only that they saw the Blessed Virgin Mary, but that the brightness of the light radiating from Mary was so incredibly intense that it was beyond anything imaginable. They reported that Mary began motioning for them to approach her.

Fifteen people submitted sworn statements describing what they saw next. In the eyewitness statements, all six children were reported to ascend the hill at a speed that was humanly impossible to achieve. The terrain of the hill is covered with rocks and thorn bushes, making the hike difficult. In two minutes, the children covered a distance that would have normally taken ten minutes for an athletic, fast runner. Vicka, who was barefoot, said she felt like the ground was made out of rubber and that she was assisted by an external force.

When they reached the apparition site, all of the children except Marija could clearly see the Blessed Virgin Mary. The five who could see Mary knelt down, made the sign of the cross, and began praying. Marija then did likewise, and as she joined the other children praying the *Our Father* prayer, the apparition slowly began to appear to Marija, who initially could see only the face of Mary, then her hands, and then finally all of her.

Initially, Ivanka and Mirjana were overcome by what they saw and fainted, while Jakov was stunned and fell backward. All of the children reported they could see Mary in her entirety except for her feet, which were obscured by a cloud-like image. Mary was wearing a white veil and silver-gray dress. She smiled at the children and spoke in a voice that sounded more like singing than talking. Her first words were, "Praised be Jesus," and the children reported she spoke perfect Croatian, the children's language.

Vicka reported that the children were simultaneously praying and crying. Mary continued to smile at them, and then she began to pray the *Our Father* with the children. When the prayer ended, Ivanka, whose mother had recently passed away, was the first of the six children to speak to Mary, asking, "Where is my mother?" Mary, smiling, said, "She is with me."

At one point, Mirjana began to plead with Mary to produce some sort of "sign" that would prove to people in the village that the children weren't crazy for claiming to see and speak with the Blessed Virgin Mary. Mary's only response was to smile.

The entire apparition lasted between ten and fifteen minutes, and then Mary said to the children, "Goodbye, my angels, go in the peace of God." Mirjana asked the Blessed Virgin if she would return, and Mary nodded her head to indicate "yes." All of the children were in tears as they descended the hill.

**June 26** – When the children reached Podbrdo hill, around 6:00 p.m., there were already approximately 3,000 people gathered at the site. Vicka led the children in praying the Rosary, and others in the crowd followed. As had happened previously, flashes of light appeared at the location where the Blessed Virgin Mary was about to appear.

The flashes occurred in an area higher up Podbrdo hill, about 1,300 feet higher from where the June 25 apparition occurred. People in the crowd also witnessed the bright white light that flashed three times. However, only the six children saw Mary. Once again, the six children ascended the hill at a speed that witnesses reported as humanly impossible. One of the witnesses was a trained athlete named Jozo Ostojic, who had recently set a regional record in the 100-meter sprint. Ostojic said he was running up the hill as fast as he could, but that the six children were moving much faster.

As the six visionaries arrived at the location where the flashes of light originated, they knelt down and began to pray. Then, all six children reported that the shining young woman appeared in front of them and greeted them by saying, "Praise Jesus." Ivanka and Mirjana immediately fainted. While Marija and Vicka attended to the other two girls, the apparition briefly disappeared. After Ivanka and Mirjana were revived, the six children again knelt down and began to pray.

Someone in the crowd gave Vicka a jar of Holy Water, and she emptied the entire bottle toward the apparition, saying, "If you are Our Lady, stay with us. If you are not, be gone!" After "dousing" the Blessed Virgin with Holy Water, Vicka reported that Mary merely smiled.

The entire apparition lasted about thirty minutes. Ivanka asked the Virgin Mary why she was appearing, and Mary replied, "I have come because there are many true believers here. I wish to be with you to convert and to reconcile the whole world."

In the June 25 apparition, Mary revealed that Ivanka's mother was in heaven, so, as a follow-up question, Ivanka asked if her mother had anything to say, to which Mary replied, "Obey your grandmother and help her because she is old."

Mirjana then asked about her grandfather, who had also recently passed away, and Mary said, "He is well."

People in the crowd who could hear the children speaking with Mary prompted them to ask Mary to give everyone a sign that would prove she truly appeared to the six visionaries. Mary's reply: "Blessed are those who have not seen and who believe."

Mirjana asked, "Who are you?" The reply was, "I am the Most Blessed Virgin Mary." Mirjana then asked, "Why are you appearing to us? We are not better than others." Mary's response: "I do not necessarily choose the best."

Before the apparition ended, Mirjana asked Mary if she would return, and Mary replied, "Yes, to the same place as yesterday."

As the children descended the hill, Vicka, Mirjana, and Ivanka needed help walking, but Marija proceeded without difficulty until about halfway down when she felt that she was being restrained by an external force. When Marija stopped, the Blessed Virgin appeared to her and began to cry, saying, "Peace, peace, peace, be reconciled, only peace. Make your peace with God and among yourselves."

During the time of the first apparitions in 1981, ethnic tensions in Yugoslavia, which were previously held in check by an authoritarian communist regime, began to escalate. The death in 1980 of Josip Broz Tito, who led Yugoslavia since the 1940s, eventually led to the outbreak of numerous wars as well as the breakup of the country into various republics.

Marija remained kneeling for about ten minutes, sobbing. Then, rising to her feet, crying, she reported the Blessed Virgin Mary appeared to her, and above Mary's head was a cross that was radiating the colors of a rainbow, with particularly intense shades of blue—the color traditionally associated with the Blessed Virgin.

**June 27** – Prior to the apparition, the children were questioned by two priests from Saint James parish church in Medjugorje. Using a tape recorder, Father Cuvalo interviewed Vicka and Ivan in the morning. Father Zovko, the pastor at Saint James, listened to the tape and questioned all six children in the afternoon. He spoke with each child separately and noted that all of the children provided a consistent description of Mary's appearance and voice: young, about twenty years old, dark hair, blue eyes, wearing a silver-gray garment with a white veil, and speaking in a voice that sounded more like singing than typical speech.

Saint James parish in Medjugorje was established in 1892, and construction of the first church was completed in 1897. The current church was consecrated January 19, 1969. Improbably, the church was built with a capacity to seat five times the number of people who ordinarily attended Sunday Mass in the 1960s. The church was built by Franciscans, who have had a long history of influence in the area.

During the afternoon of June 27, local officials associated with Yugoslavia's communist regime also wanted to speak with the children. Religious gatherings outside places of worship were prohibited at the time, and the children were taken to a police station in the nearby town of Citluk. However, as it was getting late in the afternoon, the children were allowed to return to Medjugorje prior to the time of the previous apparitions. Vicka said, "We would have gone even if we had been told that we would be shot."

Approximately 5,000 people were at Podbrdo hill that evening and the children decided to split into two groups. Mirjana, Vicka, and Ivanka were in one group, and Marija, Jakov, and Ivan were in the second group. The plan was for those in the group who saw the pre-apparition flashes of light to call out to the other group. However, both groups saw the flashes and began shouting to alert the others.

Once again, eyewitnesses claimed the children ascended the hill at an unbelievable speed. Father Kosir, a young and athletic priest, said the children moved at a pace that was at least twice as fast as he could have climbed the hill.

When the children reached their destination on the hill, they saw the Blessed Virgin Mary, but there was a crush of people pressing on them from all sides. The group of six children got separated in the mayhem, and the apparition temporarily disappeared. When they were able to regroup, they began to pray the Rosary. Simultaneously, all six children became silent and began staring at a point above them. Immediately, people began to rush forward, and the children shouted that some people in the crowd were stepping on the Virgin Mary's long veil. The apparition once again temporarily disappeared.

Some men from the village then intervened and managed to get the crowd under control by demanding that people clear out a circle of space that would give the children some breathing room. The Blessed Virgin Mary then reappeared as the men held back the crowd. "Praised be Jesus," were the first words spoken by Mary.

This time, Jakov asked the first question, "What do you expect of our Franciscans?" Mary replied, "Have them persevere in the faith and protect the faith of others."

Jakov then asked the Virgin Mary for "a sign because the people treat us as liars," and Mirjana also asked for a sign because "people say we are drug users and epileptics." Mary replied, "My angels, do not be afraid of injustice. It has always existed."

The children asked how they should pray, and Mary instructed them to pray the *Our Father,* the *Hail Mary,* and the *Glory Be* prayer seven times.

The apparition ended after Mary said, "Goodbye, my angels. Go in the peace of God."

As the children descended the hill, a local resident, Jozo Vasilj, who previously refused to go to the apparition site, scrutinized the visionaries to try to discern the truth about their claims to see the Blessed Virgin Mary. He said he saw Mirjana walking down the hill as if she was "half drunk," and then approximately thirty feet behind Mirjana, he saw Vicka walking with Jakov.

Vasilj said he could eavesdrop on the children unnoticed because of the large number of people wandering around on the hill. He heard Jakov quietly say to Vicka, "Look, now Our Lady is helping Mirjana," and Vasilj reported that Mirjana immediately began to walk properly, adding that it was impossible for Mirjana to have heard Jakov due to the distance between the children and the low voice in which Jakov spoke to Vicka.

Vasilj then followed behind Vicka and Jakov for at least sixty feet as they all descended the hill looking at Mirjana. As soon as Vasilj heard Vicka say, *"Ode!"* (Croatian for "She's going!"), Mirjana gazed upward and then sat down on a large stone. Vasilj once again reported that it was impossible for Mirjana to have heard Vicka due to the distance between them and the ambient noise of the crowd.

Prior to arriving at the apparition site on June 27, Vasilj said he "felt nothing" and was "against it," thinking the claims were "crazy." After eavesdropping on the children and witnessing what occurred with Mirjana, Vicka, and Jakov, Vasilj said he burst into tears, ran off into nearby bushes so nobody would see him crying, and then wept for more than an hour before returning to his house.

**June 28** – Between 10,000 and 15,000 people gathered at Podbrdo hill, and for the first time, someone brought a tape recorder to document the apparition. Grgo Kozina was close enough to the six children to be able to ask the visionaries questions while they were interacting with the Blessed Virgin Mary.

The first words heard on the tape are those of Kozina, who says, "It's Sunday, 6:29, 6:30. The wind is blowing and the bushes are moving. The six of them were kneeling and are now getting up. Now they are kneeling again." He asks the children, "Did she come?" And the reply is "Yes, yes, she came."

On the tape you can hear the children talking to each other about what questions they should ask Mary. One of the girls says, "Let's ask Our Lady what she wants from us," and then the others repeat, as a confirmation among themselves, "Our Lady, what do you want from us? Let's all ask, what do you want from us?"

Kozina asks, "Where is she?" Jakov responds, "Here." And then, after Mary answers the first question regarding what she wants, Jakov and the other children repeat the answer they heard from Mary: "People should pray, believe, and persist in their faith."

Earlier, during conversations between the children and Father Zovko, he instructed the children to ask Mary what she wanted from the priests. On the tape, you can hear the children repeat the question three times, "Our Lady, what do you want from our priests?," before Mary answers: "Let the priests remain strong in faith and help you."

The children then can be heard on the tape discussing with each other about what the next question should be. Ivanka says, "Let's ask, as Father Jozo was wondering, why she is appearing here and not appearing to everyone in the church." The children ask, "Our Lady, why don't you appear in the church so that everyone can see you there?" Mary's reply: "Blessed are they who believe without having seen."

The children then asked Mary, "Will you come back to see us again?" After a brief pause, you can hear the children on the tape saying, "Yes, she will return at the same place, she will come again here at the same place."

At this point, the apparition appears to be fading away, but then Vicka can be heard on the tape saying, "Look, there she is!" Kozina asks, "Where is she, on the bush or on the rock?" Vicka replies: "Here, here. She is slowly disappearing. She is slowly disappearing. She's gone! She's gone! Let's pray again." You can then hear Kozina's voice on the tape saying, "Nineteen minutes before seven." Marija and Vicka then start to sing a hymn, encouraging people in the crowd to join in.

Later, you can hear the children say, "Here she is! She is here!" And Kozina's voice can be heard saying, "Seven. They have seen her again."

Vicka asks Mary, "Dear Madonna, what do you want from the people who are gathered here?" Mary's reply is, "Let those who do not see believe as those who do see."

Vicka then asks, "Will you leave us a sign so that people believe that we are not liars or comedians?" Mary's response was only a smile, and then as she disappeared from sight, she said, "Go in the peace of God."

**June 29** – Because the crowd had grown to over 10,000 on the previous day, officials associated with Yugoslavia's communist government became concerned that political unrest might stem from—or be the cause of—the gatherings on Podbrdo hill.

Yugoslavia was an amalgam of at least eighteen ethnic groups, including Slovenes, Macedonians, Montenegrins, Jews, Hungarians and Albanians, and at least fourteen languages were spoken across the territory of Yugoslavia. The most diverse area of the country, and where ethnic tensions grew in the greatest intensity, was the area now known as Bosnia and Herzegovina, where Medjugorje is located.

Conflicts among ethnic groups in the region had been going on for hundreds, if not thousands, of years. World War I began on June 28, 1914, when a Bosnian Serb assassinated Archduke Franz Ferdinand of Austria as part of a revolutionary movement to attempt to unite southern Slavic provinces of Austria-Hungary into Yugoslavia.

In the afternoon hours of June 29, the children were picked up and put into an ambulance by government officials under the ruse they needed medical attention. However, their first stop was a police station in the town of Citluk, where they were harshly interrogated.

After being questioned at the police station, they were taken to a nearby hospital and examined. They were then driven to the city of Mostar, about 35 miles from Citluk. There at the local hospital, in an attempt to frighten the children, they were led to a morgue to view corpses that were undergoing autopsies.

To add to this form of "shock therapy," the children were placed in a hallway in the hospital's psychiatric ward for about an hour to witness the comings and goings of insane people who were residents at the hospital. Then, the children were taken to see a doctor who suggested they were drug addicts and could be confined to the mental hospital if they continued to cause turmoil in Medjugorje. After that, they were taken back to Citluk for another medical examination, which ended around 5:30 p.m. when Vicka confronted the doctor about continuing the charade of ongoing tests. The children were then released, and they took a taxi to their homes in Bijakovici before heading to Podbrdo hill.

Following the children to the site of the apparition was Dr. Darinka Glamuzina, a pediatrics specialist who examined the children earlier in the day. Dr. Glamuzina, an ardent communist, had boasted to the children that she was an atheist and that when her parents forced her to attend Mass when she was a child, she refused to take Holy Communion. In addition to Dr. Glamuzina, members of Yugoslavia's secret police were making their presence known by stationing themselves outside the homes of the seers.

As the children walked from their homes in Bijakovici to Medjugorje, a distance of less than a mile, they were met by more than 15,000 people gathered at Podbrdo hill. Grgo Kozina was there once again to document the apparition with his tape recorder. The children began by singing hymns and saying prayers, encouraging the crowd to join in. Kozina spoke into his tape recorder, saying the children fell to their knees and went silent at 6:26 p.m.

The next voices to be heard on the tape are those of the children, saying, "Dear Madonna, are you happy to see so many people here today?" Mary's response: "More than happy."

The children then say, "Dear Madonna, how many days will you be with us?" Mary's reply: "As long as you want me to, my angels."

"What do you expect of the people who have come in spite of the brambles and the heat?" Mary replies, "There is only one God, one faith. People should believe firmly and not fear anything."

"What do you expect of us?" Mary replies: "That you have a solid faith and you maintain confidence."

The children then ask, "Will we be able to endure these persecutions? Many people persecute us because we 'see.'" Mary replied, "You will be able to endure, my angels. Do not fear. You will be able to endure everything. You must believe and have confidence in me."

Standing near the children was Dr. Glamuzina, and Vicka made a startling request of the Blessed Virgin Mary. Pointing at Dr. Glamuzina, Vicka asked Mary, "Could this lady touch you?"

Mary's reply: "There have always been unfaithful Judases, but let her come."

Vicka then directed Dr. Glamuzina where to place her hand to touch the Virgin Mary's long veil. On the tape made by Kozina, the children can be heard saying, "She is touching her!"

Dr. Glamuzina described what she felt, saying she "trembled" and was momentarily shocked. She then staggered down the hill, where she met the accompanying police. Dr. Glamuzina told the police she would no longer participate in the investigation, and she would not provide any further comments about her experience.

After Dr. Glamuzina placed her hand on the apparition, the children can be heard on Kozina's tape, saying, "She's gone! She's gone!" After a brief period of silence, the children begin to sing, and then people in the crowd begin to sing also. After several minutes pass by, the children's voices can be heard on the tape, shouting: "The light! The light! She's here!"

On June 28, the parents of a very ill three-year-old boy, Daniel Setka, asked Vicka to intercede for him. Daniel could not speak, walk, or hold his head up, and was diagnosed with epilepsy. The sick child's father carried Daniel up Podbrdo hill on June 29, and it was at this point in the apparition that Vicka presented Daniel to Mary, saying, "Dear Madonna, will little Daniel speak someday? Please provide a miracle so that everyone will believe us. These people love you very much, dear Madonna, perform a miracle!"

The next voices on the tape are those of the visionaries, saying, "She is looking at him! Dear Madonna, say something!"

Then Kozina's voice is heard on the tape, saying, "Is she still looking at the boy?"

The children say, "She is still looking! Dear Madonna, say something, we ask you! Say something, we ask you! Say something, dear Madonna!"

Approximately one minute passes by on the tape, and then the children can be heard saying, "Have them firmly believe that he will be healed."

Moments later, Mary says, "Go in God's peace," and the children can be heard on the tape saying, "She's gone! Look, the light!"

Daniel Setka's illness began when he was four days old. By the time he was one month old, doctors said he wouldn't live a year. After his encounter with the Blessed Virgin Mary on Podbrdo, something changed. Several witnesses corroborated what took place on the evening of June 29.

Daniel's parents stopped at a café near Saint James church in Medjugorje, and moments after ordering dinner, the child spoke the first words in his life, saying, "Give me a drink!" Daniel's mother and grandmother immediately started shouting and crying, while his father exclaimed, "It's a healing!"

The following day, Daniel and his parents ascended Podbrdo. At first, Daniel could only walk a few steps and hold his head up for a few seconds. His parents would stop about every sixty feet to allow Daniel to test his legs.

About halfway up the hill, Daniel started to walk easily and spoke the first words since the previous evening in the restaurant. At first, witnesses said his words were incomprehensible. But then, suddenly, Daniel spoke clearly, saying, "Mama, look, I'm walking!" Daniel was not only walking, but climbing over the rocky terrain of Podbrdo. Within twenty-four hours, local television crews and international media outlets were reporting the story.

**June 30** – As evening approached about 20,000 people had gathered at Podbrdo, which now was being referred to as "Apparition Hill," but the children were nowhere to be found. Earlier in the afternoon, two young social workers affiliated with Yugoslavia's communist government arrived in Bijakovici and requested that the children and their families meet at Vicka's house. There, they were informed that government authorities wanted to question the children, and that the children had the option of accompanying the social workers on a "sightseeing tour" to discuss their experiences or be questioned by members of Yugoslavia's secret police, who were on their way to Medjugorje from Citluk.

The children agreed to accompany the social workers and were treated to a tourist-like experience. They enjoyed a meal at an expensive restaurant and a stop for ice cream in the town of Cerno. The social workers even suggested a drive to visit resort areas along the Dalmatian Coast as a means to keep the children away from the apparition site that evening.

The children were about six miles from Medjugorje when they began to see crowds of people streaming toward Podbrdo. When they realized the social workers had no intention of driving them to the apparition site, the children demanded to be released. The social workers complied, knowing it would be impossible for the children to reach Podbrdo by the usual time of the apparitions.

As the children ran from the car and into a field, they instinctively knelt down and began to pray. Shortly thereafter, they saw a light-filled cloud begin to form above the crowd gathered at Podbrdo. They all began to cry, thinking they would miss seeing the Blessed Virgin that evening. However, all six children later reported they witnessed the same phenomenon: Mary moving through the sky toward the children. It was at this moment that the two social workers later reported a "display of light" before they quickly got back into their car and sped away.

The children said the first words spoken by the Blessed Virgin Mary were, "Praised be Jesus," and then Mary joined with the children in praying the *Our Father* prayer. Mirjana was the first to ask Mary a question, "Are you angry that we are not on the hill?" Mary replied that it didn't matter where the children were.

During the morning of June 30, before the children were picked up by the social workers, Father Zovko of Saint James Parish urged the children to ask Mary if the location of the apparitions could be moved from Podbrdo to the church. Knowing that communist officials were increasingly concerned about the number of people gathering at Podbrdo, Father Zovko sought to avoid a confrontation with state authorities. His fears were realized that afternoon. While the children were being driven around by the social workers, the local chairman of the communist party demanded that Father Zovko appear in Citluk to answer questions about the events occurring in Medjugorje.

Mirjana's second question for Mary was, "Would you be angry if we did not return any longer to the hill but we waited in the church?" Mary replied, "Always at the same time."

Mirjana also asked Mary when the visits would end. Later, when speaking about Mary's reply, Mirjana said, "Something told me, 'three days,'" but none of the other children heard Mary provide an answer.

Before the apparition ended, the children once again asked Mary to please "leave a sign" so that people would believe they were telling the truth. As Mary began to depart, she said, "Go in the peace of God," and a bright light illuminated the people gathered at Podbrdo before Mary disappeared from sight.

**July 1** – The two young social workers who attempted to prevent the children from reaching the apparition site the previous day submitted their resignations to communist authorities. After describing what they witnessed to government officials, the social workers said they could no longer be involved in the investigation of the children. Further complicating matters for local government administrators were news reports of Daniel Setka's miraculous healing, which led to a large increase in the number of people traveling to Medjugorje, including more journalists.

As a result, the number of militia officers sent to Medjugorje was greatly increased. Security police arrived in the morning and requested that the families of the visionaries meet at the local elementary school to discuss the gravity of the situation. The families were told the children would be committed to a mental hospital or sent to prison if the gatherings didn't stop. The parents then asked Father Zovko for help, who in turn asked God for help. Entering the sanctuary in Saint James Church, Father Zovko knelt down at the altar and began to pray.

Shortly thereafter, two militia officers offered four of the six children a ride in a police van from their homes in Bijakovici to Medjugorje. It was a short distance of less than a mile, but the crowds had become huge, and Ivanka, Marija, and Vicka accepted the offer thinking it was a safe way to get through the crowds. Seemingly, the police merely wanted to keep the children away from Podbrdo, and since the children were on their way to Saint James Church in Medjugorje—not Podbrdo—it seemed like a prudent choice. However, when the officers sped past the church on their way to the police station in Citluk, the children started to scream for help and bang on the windows.

At that moment, Ivanka, Marija, and Vicka reported that the Blessed Virgin Mary instantaneously appeared to them in the police van, but the apparition burst forth so unexpectedly that it frightened them. Combined with the trauma of being kidnapped by the militia for what they thought might be a trip to prison or to a psychiatric hospital, the three children reacted hysterically. The officers, dumbfounded by the girls' screams and the expressions on their faces, shouted at them saying they were witches and immediately stopped the vehicle. The three girls bolted out of the van and started running back toward Medjugorje.

While these events were unfolding, Father Zovko was still kneeling at the altar in Saint James Church, pleading for divine intervention. Suddenly, the priest reported that he distinctly heard a voice say, "Come out and protect the children." Without delaying, he quickly went to the main door at Saint James, opened it, and saw Ivanka, Marija, and Vicka running toward the church. The girls told Father Zovko they were being chased by police, and the priest immediately took them to an interior room and locked them inside. Moments later, the police arrived asking Father Zovko if he saw the children, to which the priest replied, "I did." The police just nodded their heads and ran off toward Bijakovici.

Later, around 4:00 p.m., the other three visionaries arrived at Saint James church. There was no prior announcement made to the public that the children would no longer be returning to Podbrdo for the apparitions, but word spread that there would be a special service at Saint James that evening. At 5:00 p.m., Father Cuvalo began to lead people in praying the Rosary, and then at 6:00 p.m. Father Zovko began the Mass. There were so many people packed inside the church that Father Zovko said, "I found it impossible to extend my hands."

During Mass, the six children remained in the interior room, and the Virgin Mary appeared to them while Father Zovko preached his homily, or sermon. That evening, Mary appeared only briefly, smiled at the children, and then disappeared.

**July 2 to July 5** – On July 2, the apparition once again took place inside the church, and afterward Father Zovko presented the children to the people. Addressing the crowd that was gathered, Jakov Colo said Mary spoke only three words that evening, "Praised be Jesus."

On July 3, the children were under the impression that this evening's apparition would be the last. On June 25 or June 26, one of Vicka's cousins gave Mirjana a book about Bernadette Soubirous, who experienced the apparitions involving the Blessed Virgin Mary in Lourdes, France, between February 11 and July 16, 1858. Before receiving the book, none of the visionaries were aware of Saint Bernadette or her apparitions.

By June 27, the children began reading the book out loud to each other, trying to discern if the events involving Saint Bernadette at Lourdes could help them understand what was happening at Medjugorje. Without any prior knowledge of Marian apparitions, when the children learned that Mary appeared to Saint Bernadette a total of nineteen times, they began to think that Mary would appear to them a total of nineteen times.

After adding up all of the occasions when Mary appeared to them, as a group as well as individually, the children felt as though July 3 would mark the date of the last apparition at Medjugorje. Also, Mirjana had asked Mary during the June 30 apparition when the visits would end, and Mirjana said, "Something told me, 'three days,'" but none of the other children heard a reply.

Estimates of the crowds converging on Medjugorje July 3 ranged from a low of 25,000 to more than 50,000 people. Mirjana, thinking this day would be her last encounter with the Blessed Virgin Mary, left Medjugorje to return to Sarajevo, where she was a high school student. She was in Medjugorje on summer break, staying at her uncle's home in Bijakovici, and she wanted to have her final apparition with Mary at her home in Sarajevo. The remaining five children gathered at the church in the same small room as on the previous evenings.

After the apparition in Saint James church that evening, the five children stood with Father Zovko near the altar, but only Jakov and Vicka addressed the crowd. Jakov said, "The Madonna truly appears to us. It is a fact. I swear it on my life. I asked for a sign, and she lowered her head as if she approved. Then she disappeared." Vicka reported, "This evening the Madonna gave messages for us, and not for the world. When she appeared for the last time this evening, she said, 'My angels! I bless you, you will be happy, and you will go into the bosom of your Father. Keep your faith.'"

On July 4, all six visionaries assumed the apparitions at Medjugorje were over. However, at 6:25 p.m., the Blessed Virgin Mary appeared to Vicka while she was out in a garden with some friends picking flowers. Vicka reported that her fingers became numb, she fell to her knees, and then Mary suddenly appeared to her.

All of the other children had similar reports. Marija said Mary appeared to her in her bedroom that evening. Ivan said Mary appeared to him while he was washing up after a day working on the family farm.

Mirjana said Mary appeared to her during an intense police interrogation in Sarajevo that began early in the morning and lasted until late into the night. It was on July 4, 1981, that the events in Medjugorje were officially declared "counterrevolutionary" by the communist regime.

On July 5, and on subsequent evenings, the five visionaries who lived in Bijakovici went to Saint James church, where Mary continued to appear to them.

Later, on August 17, Father Zovko was arrested on charges of sedition, primarily for refusing orders from the government to stop the evening Mass at Saint James Church and for failing to prevent crowds from gathering at Podbrdo. On October 21, Father Zovko was convicted of crimes against the state and sentenced to three and a half years in prison. The sentence was later commuted, and he was released after eighteen months.

The visionaries continue to receive messages from Mary periodically, and their ongoing activities serve to increase a general awareness of, and devotion to, the Blessed Virgin Mary.

There are claims by some theologians that the messages received by the visionaries are too simplistic and too repetitive to be authentic, and that there is not enough theological depth in the communications. Additionally, there have been accusations that some of the messages contradict Catholic doctrine or are otherwise very controversial, including the following from an apparition on October 1, 1981, during which the visionaries asked the Virgin Mary questions, and she replied with answers.

Question: Are all religions good?

Mary's response: Members of all faiths are equal before God. God rules over each faith just like a sovereign over his kingdom. In the world, all religions are not the same because all people have not complied with the commandments of God. They reject and disparage them.

The statement that "members of all faiths are equal before God" is in alignment with the teachings of the Second Vatican Council. A major change occurred with regard to how the Church interprets the phrase "outside the Church there is no salvation." Today, the Church interprets this to mean anyone, regardless of their religion, or even lack of religion, can be saved and enter heaven because the salvific graces of Christ and the inspiration of the Holy Spirt work outside of Catholicism and Christianity:

Those who have not yet received the Gospel are related in various ways to the people of God. In the first place we must recall the people to whom the testament and the promises were given and from whom Christ was born according to the flesh. On account of their fathers this people remains most dear to God, for God does not repent of the gifts He makes nor of the calls He issues. But the plan of salvation also includes those who acknowledge the Creator. In the first place amongst these there are the Muslims, who, professing to hold the faith of Abraham, along with us adore the one and merciful God, who on the last day will judge mankind. Nor is God far distant from those who in shadows and images seek the unknown God, for it is He who gives to all men [and women] life and breath and all things, and as Saviour, wills that all men [and women] be saved. Those also can attain to salvation who through no fault of their own do not know the Gospel of Christ or His Church, yet sincerely seek God and moved by grace strive by their deeds to do His will as it is known to them through the dictates of conscience. Nor does Divine Providence deny the helps necessary for salvation to those who, without blame on their part, have not yet arrived at an explicit knowledge of God and with His grace strive to live a good life. [185]

After this teaching was promulgated in 1964 with the publication of the Dogmatic Constitution of the Church, *Lumen Gentium,* many Catholics left missionary work, thinking it was no longer important to evangelize non-Catholics to enter the Church. Others interpreted this teaching to mean that Protestant forms of Christianity were equivalent to Catholicism and, as a result, offered an easier path to salvation because the "once saved, always saved" doctrine provides more leeway for error. Others, like divorced and remarried Catholics who were effectively barred from Communion, felt a more satisfying experience in Protestant churches. However, those interpretations overlook or minimize the value of the sacraments, not only for salvation after death, but for the benefits they offer in the present life, particularly the ability of the Eucharist to facilitate divinization if people are predisposed and open to receiving the graces.

The text of the Dogmatic Constitution of the Church clearly states the grace of God is not only active outside of Christianity, but that the action of that grace can bring people to salvation even though they may never become Christians and may adhere to no religion whatsoever. The Virgin Mary's role as the *Mediatrix* of all graces clearly places Mary as the "Lady of All Nations" and the Spiritual Mother of All Peoples, regardless of their connection to the institutional Church. In her apparitions, the Virgin Mary often appears with different facial features that reflect the characteristics of people of the local culture. Her clothing also sometimes reflects the local culture, and the symbolism in her clothing is sometimes extraordinary, as in the case of her appearance as the Virgin of Guadalupe.

The Virgin Mary's first reported appearance in Medjugorje occurred on June 24, the Catholic feast day that celebrates the birthday of Saint John the Baptist. As John the Baptist was a transitional figure between the Old and New Testaments, Mary's apparitions since 1830 mark an intervention that represents a turning point in salvation history—not a turning point in the process of salvation, but a turning point in the recognition of the role that the Blessed Virgin Mary has in redemption and divinization.

"Medjugorje" literally means "between two mountains," and the name reflects the beginning of an ascent up a spiritual mountain—an ascent to the climax of the *Age of Mary,* when, as she stated at Fatima, "In the end, my Immaculate Heart will triumph." [186]

**Using Symbols and Typologies to Interpret Patterns in Information**

Mountains are mentioned in the Bible hundreds of times, not only due to their presence in biblical geography, but for their symbolism. Ascending up a mountain is interpreted as getting closer to God.

God often interacted with biblical figures on mountaintops. Moses received the Ten Commandments on Mount Sinai, and Elijah communicated with God on a mountaintop. Christ's Transfiguration, which included a vision of Moses (representing the Law) and Elijah (representing the prophets), occurred on a mountaintop.

Gaining insight into how to discern the difference between myths and historical events requires an ability to view events and some mythologies as typologies that accurately prefigure future events. Unlike historical events, myths are stories or legends that have been purposely developed to explain history or natural phenomena. Mythological stories, symbols, and historical events can be categorized according to how they are typologies or prototypes that accurately prefigured the future unfolding of historical events.

Using this framework, many events recorded in the Old Testament are viewed as typologies that prefigured events recorded in the New Testament and beyond. Also, physical aspects of reality can be viewed as prototypical or typological precursors of spiritual aspects of reality.

Saint Paul refers to typologies several times in the Bible. He wrote that the Adam described in the book of Genesis is a typology, a prototype, or pattern (τύπος in Greek) of Christ, the New Adam; in Romans 5:14, "Adam, who is a pattern of the one to come." Paul also described ancient religious practices as typological precursors that were "a shadow of the things that were to come; the reality, however, is found in Christ." (Colossians 2:17).

The Old Testament story of Jonah and the whale, or big fish, prefigures historical events of the New Testament or New Covenant of Christ. In the first part of the book of Jonah, God is demanding and full of wrath; in the second part, God is loving and merciful. While encountering a severe storm at sea, Jonah instructs his shipmates to throw him into the water (sacrifice him) so that God's wrath would cease and the storm would subside. Jonah was then swallowed by the whale, and he stayed in the stomach of the whale for three days (Christ in the tomb), and on the third day, after Jonah begged God for mercy, Jonah was ejected from the fish onto dry land. In the New Testament, an incident is recorded in Luke 11:29 where a crowd of people asked Jesus to give them "a sign," and Jesus replied, "This is a wicked generation. It asks for a sign, but none will be given it except the sign of

Jonah." The "sign" of Jonah is described by Christ as a symbol or typology that prefigures the historical events that involved Christ's sacrifice, His three days in the tomb, and His Resurrection.

The requirement to sacrifice an unblemished Passover lamb so the Jews could be saved or redeemed from slavery in Egypt is a prototype of Christ's sacrifice so that all people could be redeemed from sin (physical slavery in Egypt is a typology of spiritual slavery to sin), and Christ is referred to as the Passover Lamb many times, such as in 1 Corinthians 5:7.

The Old Testament necessity for a blood sacrifice is described in Leviticus 17:11, "For the life of a creature is in the blood, and I have given it to you to make atonement for yourselves on the altar; it is the blood that makes atonement for one's life," and this is a prototype of the once-and-for-all sacrifice of Christ.

Abraham is asked by God to sacrifice his son Isaac, which prefigured Christ's crucifixion. Isaac said to his father, "The fire and wood are here, but where is the lamb for the burnt offering?" Abraham replied, "God will provide for Himself the lamb for the burnt offering, my son." When Abraham was about to sacrifice Isaac, an angel informed Abraham, "Do not lay a hand on the boy … do not do anything to him. Now I know that you fear God, because you have not withheld from me your son, your only son."

In the Old Testament book of Numbers 21:8, "The Lord [God] said to Moses, 'Make a snake and put it up on a pole; anyone who is bitten can look at it and live.'" In the New Testament book of John 3:14, Jesus says, "Just as Moses lifted up the snake in the wilderness, so the Son of Man must be lifted up [on the cross], so that everyone who believes may have eternal life in him."

The Jewish Feast of Tabernacles, which commemorates the Israelites' journey through the wilderness to the geographical Promised Land, prefigures all believers' journey to the spiritual Promised Land, which is heaven. The Tabernacle was a tent the Jews carried throughout their journey to the Promised Land, which housed the Ark of the Covenant and contained not only the Ten Commandments, but the presence of God. In Catholicism, the Ark of the Covenant in the Old Testament is seen as a typology of the Ark of the New Covenant, the Virgin Mary, who carried the presence of God in her womb.

The approach of using typologies to search for patterns in information to better understand current and future events is the same process used in "big data" analytics, which uses artificial intelligence and other types of software to analyze data and identify patterns that can be used to solve problems and gain competitive advantages in business.

Understanding the process of redemption, or salvation, involves understanding the limitations of humanity and searching for answers to solve the riddle: what is the meaning of life? The answer is simple. The meaning of life is evolution. But there are two types of evolution, biological and spiritual. Biological evolution advanced along a path of a completely amoral, selfish competition among various species and individual members of the species to consume resources and have sex. Spiritual evolution advances along the completely moral and self-sacrificial approach of *agape* love, which is the antithesis of biological evolution: it involves spending increasing amounts of time and energy helping other people, and spending decreasing amounts of time and energy on behaviors that benefit one's own selfish interests.

In terms of physical typologies that point to spiritual realities, sex is a prototype or typology that prefigures union with God. Sex, which is often an obsession with people, is merely a somewhat laughable, primitive prototype for what can occur during mystical prayer, and what will occur in heaven.

Subjective bias against the theory of evolution prevents many religious believers from seeing the history of biological evolution as a typological pattern that prefigures spiritual evolution or divinization, the process whereby people become increasingly like God.

Evolution is a multi-faceted phenomenon that isn't limited to biology. The evolution of matter—the development of molecules, atoms, and subatomic particles—occurred over time. When our universe was in its embryonic stage, molecules, atoms and subatomic particles didn't exist. The universe itself evolved from a state of nothingness; before 13.8 billion years ago, the universe didn't exist. Stars and galaxies didn't exist when the universe was in its infancy. After the Big Bang, about 500,000 years passed before stars and galaxies developed.

The sun evolved. Like all stars, the sun developed over a period of 100,000 years or more. Our local star, the sun, didn't exist five billion years ago. The earth began its evolution about 4.5 billion years ago when dust and rocks circling the sun formed an accretion disk, which later "got rounded" into a ball-like shape as gravity pulled it all together from a central core of mass.

Life—animated matter—arose on earth out of inorganic matter about 3.85 billion years ago. Animals evolved out of microorganisms about 580 million years ago. Land-based plants arose between 600 million and 500 million years ago. Mammals, which have a specialized part of the brain that other animals don't have, arose approximately 230 million years ago. Primates (prime, first-rank animals), which have brains that are larger than other mammals, arose from predecessor animals about 65 million years ago.

An early type of human life arose between seven million and five million years ago. A more evolved type of human life developed about 2.5 million years ago. Anatomically modern humans evolved between 400,000 and 200,000 years ago, and behaviorally modern humans evolved between 200,000 years and 50,000 years ago.

Each individual human life evolves from an embryonic stage, and the culmination of each individual's evolution is not death, but eternal life.

All of evolution is a prototype, a typology, a fundamental repeating pattern, that prefigures a much larger phenomenon: an evolution, or ascent, into heaven, which involves humans as well as non-human elements of creation.

The process of redemption, how it specifically occurs in the life of each individual believer, was explained by Pope Benedict XVI in an Easter Vigil homily given on April 15, 2006. The following is a compilation of excerpts from that homily. [187]

> Jesus is not a character from the past. He lives, and he walks before us as one who is alive. At Easter we rejoice because Christ did not remain in the tomb, his body did not see corruption; he belongs to the world of the living, not to the world of the dead.

> But somehow the Resurrection is situated so far beyond our horizon, so far outside all our experience that, returning to ourselves, we find ourselves continuing the argument of the disciples: Of what exactly does this "rising" consist? What does it mean for us, for the whole world and the whole of history?

> The point is that Christ's Resurrection is something more, something different. If we may borrow the language of the theory of evolution, it is the greatest "mutation," absolutely the most crucial leap into a totally new dimension that there has ever been in the long history of life and its development: a leap into a completely new order which does concern us, and concerns the whole of history.

The discussion that began with the disciples would therefore include the following questions: What happened there? What does it mean for us, for the whole world and for me personally? Above all: what happened? Jesus is no longer in the tomb. He is in a totally new life. But how could this happen? What forces were in operation?

The crucial point is that this man Jesus was not alone, he was not an "I" closed in upon itself. He was one single reality with the living God, so closely united with him as to form one person with him. He found himself, so to speak, in an embrace with him who is life itself, an embrace not just on the emotional level, but one which included and permeated his being. His own life was not just his own, it was an existential communion with God, a "being taken up" into God, and hence it could not in reality be taken away from him. Out of love, he could allow himself to be killed, but precisely by doing so he broke the definitiveness of death, because in him the definitiveness of life was present. He was one single reality with indestructible life, in such a way that it burst forth anew through death.

Let us express the same thing once again from another angle. His death was an act of love. At the Last Supper he anticipated death and transformed it into self-giving. His existential communion with God was concretely an existential communion with God's love, and this love is the real power against death, it is stronger than death. The Resurrection was like an explosion of light, an explosion of love which dissolved the hitherto indissoluble compenetration of "dying and becoming." It ushered in a new dimension of being, a new dimension of life in which, in a transformed way, matter too was integrated and through which a new world emerges.

It is clear that this event is not just some miracle from the past, the occurrence of which could be ultimately a matter of indifference to us. It is a qualitative leap in the history of "evolution" and of life in general towards a new future life, towards a new world which, starting from Christ, already continuously permeates this world of ours, transforms it and draws it to itself. But how does this happen? How can this event effectively reach me and draw my life upwards towards itself? The answer, perhaps surprising at first but totally real, is: this event comes to me through faith and Baptism.

Baptism means precisely this, that we are not dealing with an event in the past, but that a qualitative leap in world history comes to me, seizing hold of me in order to draw me on.

Baptism is something quite different from an act of ecclesial socialization, from a slightly old-fashioned and complicated rite for receiving people into the Church. It is also more than a simple washing, more than a kind of purification and beautification of the soul. It is truly death and resurrection, rebirth, transformation to a new life.

How can we understand this? I think that what happens in Baptism can be more easily explained for us if we consider the final part of the short spiritual autobiography that Saint Paul gave us in his Letter to the Galatians. Its concluding words contain the heart of this biography: "It is no longer I who live, but Christ who lives in me."

The Resurrection is not a thing of the past, the Resurrection has reached us and seized us. We grasp hold of it, we grasp hold of the risen Lord, and we know that he holds us firmly even when our hands grow weak. We grasp hold of his hand, and thus we also hold on to one another's hands, and we become one single subject, not just one thing.

I, but no longer I: this is the formula of Christian life rooted in Baptism, the formula of the Resurrection within time.

I, but no longer I: if we live in this way, we transform the world. It is a formula contrary to all ideologies of violence, it is a program opposed to corruption and to the desire for power and possession.

Eternal life, blessed immortality, we have not by ourselves or in ourselves, but through a relation—through existential communion with him who is Truth and Love and is therefore eternal: God himself.

The Resurrection is a cosmic event, which includes heaven and earth and links them together.

### The Resurrection of Christ: Myth or Historical Fact?

The Resurrection is an event that people often claim to be a myth, but historical evidence supporting the Resurrection significantly outweighs the claims of mythology. N.T. Wright's book, *The Resurrection of the Son of God,* is an academic analysis of historical events relevant to the Resurrection as well as a study of myths related to life after death. An 800-page book may be perceived as either intimidating or boring, but Wright's writing style and subject matter make the book entertaining, such as the following excerpt from a section titled, "Becoming a God (or at least a Star)?"

It was not only heroes and emperors who, in some accounts, could go to live with the gods. The virtuous, the philosophers (they were, after all, making up the rules at this point) might attain to the stars as well. This latter theme (often under the label "astral immortality") has been important in the study of ancient Jewish as well as pagan beliefs, and we must briefly set out its main features. The idea that after death humans (or some of them—it can be thought of as a reward for special virtue) actually become stars goes back behind the Socratic period to Pythagorean philosophy and Orphic religion, and is found also in Babylonian and Egyptian sources. It is already found in the fifth-century playwright Aristophanes, and finds classic early expression in Plato's Timaeus. ...

Even here, we note, Plato does not say that the virtuous souls become stars, merely that the individual stars are their homes, to which they will return—unless they fail the moral test, in which case they return to one body or another, according to the theory of transmigration. But the idea of the soul going off to where the stars are, and in some way almost being identified with the stars, became popular across the hellenistic world. [188]

In Pope Benedict XVI's explanation above, he claims the power or energy of the Resurrection transcends space and time, and that it is this characteristic of the Resurrection that enables each believer to "latch onto" this power or energy through faith and Baptism. While the claim may seem ludicrous to many scientifically minded individuals, one only has to look at developments in physics such as string theory, M-theory, and quantum mechanics, to name a few, to see that the supernatural activities recognized by Catholicism appear downright pedestrian in comparison. Serious researchers claim: our universe is only one small bubble in the metauniverse; reality is made up of 10 dimensions, 11, or more; laws of physics across the metauniverse may be such that what is viewed as miraculous by humans is ordinary in other universes; and activity in other universes may, or may not, influence events in our universe.

One small example: researchers claim they have addressed all possible loopholes and have proven that objects separated by long distances—from one end of the universe to the other—can instantaneously affect each other, communicating information faster than the speed of light and implying that time can run backward as well as forward. [189]

### Role of the Laity in the Catholic Church

The Church doesn't change the Gospel, but on its journey to perfection, it regularly changes or enlarges doctrines as a result of better understanding the Gospel in the light of inspiration by the Holy Spirit. Lay people, those members of the church who aren't ordained, play an integral role in this process:

Never before in the history of the Church has the absolutely essential role of the layperson been so dramatically emphasized as it is now. Particularly since Vatican II, the Church has called for a renewal in the life and role of the laity. Yet among the faithful, there remains a fundamental lack of understanding of the lay vocation and its role in the Church's mission. For many, there is a notion that the only real vocation in the Church is the ordained or vowed priesthood and religious. They believe "the Church" is the ordained office and only people in habits or collars are called to serve. Many think that the role of the laity is to help out around the parish and that they are not called to play an integral part in the mission of the Church. ... The Church teaches that in dignity laypeople are absolutely equal to those in ordained and religious life. In mission, the work of the laity is the crucial means by which the world is to encounter Christ. [190]

The following text is from the Code of Canon Law:

The Christian faithful are free to make known to the pastors of the Church their needs, especially spiritual ones, and their desires. According to the knowledge, competence, and prestige which they possess, they have the right and even at times the duty to manifest to the sacred pastors their opinion on matters which pertain to the good of the Church and to make their opinion known to the rest of the Christian faithful, without prejudice to the integrity of faith and morals, with reverence toward their pastors, and attentive to common advantage and the dignity of persons. The Christian faithful have the right to receive assistance from the sacred pastors out of the spiritual goods of the Church, especially the word of God and the sacraments. [191]

It's important for all Catholic laypeople to be engaged with the mission of their Church, to speak with priests and bishops, and if one is so inclined, to speak to the Pope by sending a letter. Papal staff read all letters and decide which letters are forwarded to the Pope. Letters from the U.S. require three first-class postage stamps, and the address is:

Pope Francis
00120 Vatican City

Thank you, Saint Joseph, for answering my novena prayer according to the will of God and for your service to the Church.

*E.P. Sanguinetti*
*June 13, 2016*

# JOAN OF ARC

## REFERENCES

1. Quicherat, Jules-Étienne-Joseph, [ed.]. *Procès de Condamnation et de Réhabilitation de Jeanne d'Arc.* [trans.] E.P. Sanguinetti. Paris : Chez Jules Renouard, 1844. p. 5. Vol. 2.

2. —. *Procès de Condamnation et de Réhabilitation de Jeanne d'Arc.* [trans.] E.P. Sanguinetti. s.l. : Chez Jules Renouard, 1844. p. 18. Vol. 2.

3. —. *Procès de Condamnation et de Réhabilitation de Jeanne d'Arc.* [trans.] E.P. Sanguinetti. Paris : Chez Jules Renouard, 1844. p. 298. Vol. 2.

4. —. *Procès de Condamnation et de Réhabilitation de Jeanne d'Arc.* [trans.] E.P. Sanguinetti. Paris : Chez Jules Renouard, 1845. pp. 193-194. Vol. 3.

5. —. *Procès de Condamnation et de Réhabilitation de Jeanne d'Arc.* [trans.] E.P. Sanguinetti. Paris : Chez Jules Renouard, 1845. pp. 147-148. Vol. 3.

6. —. *Procès de Condamnation et de Réhabilitation de Jeanne d'Arc.* [trans.] E.P. Sanguinetti. Paris : Chez Jules Renouard, 1845. pp. 148-149. Vol. 3.

7. —. *Procès de Condamnation et de Réhabilitation de Jeanne d'Arc.* [trans.] E.P. Sanguinetti. Paris : Chez Jules Renouard, 1845. pp. 157-158. Vol. 3.

8. —. *Procès de Condamnation et de Réhabilitation de Jeanne d'Arc.* [trans.] E.P. Sanguinetti. Paris : Chez Jules Renouard, 1845. p. 168. Vol. 3.

9. Carey, Nessa. *The Epigenetics Revolution: How Modern Biology Is Rewriting Our Understanding of Genetics, Disease, and Inheritance.* New York : Columbia University Press, 2013.

10. Quicherat, Jules-Étienne-Joseph, [ed.]. *Procès de Condamnation et de Réhabilitation de Jeanne d'Arc.* [trans.] E.P. Sanguinetti. Paris : Chez Jules Renouard, 1841. pp. 192-193. Vol. 1.

11. Pernoud, Régine. *The Retrial of Joan of Arc: The Evidence for her Vindication.* San Francisco : Ignatius Press, 2007. pp. 50-51.

12. Quicherat, Jules-Étienne-Joseph, [ed.]. *Procès de Condamnation et de Réhabilitation de Jeanne d'Arc.* Paris : Chez Jules Renouard, 1841. pp. 192-193. Vol. 1.

13. Champion, Pierre. *Procès de Condamnation de Jeanne d'Arc, Texte, Traduction et Notes.* Paris : Edouard Champion, 1921. p. 111.

14. Ayroles, Jean-Baptiste-Joseph. *La Vraie Jeanne D'Arc, Tome IV, La Vierge-Guerriere.* [trans.] E.P. Sanguinetti. Paris : Rondelet, 1898. pp. 156-157.

15. Aquinas, St. Thomas. *Summa Theologica.* [trans.] Fathers-of-the-English-Dominican-Province. Second and Revised Edition 1920. s.l. : Online Edition by Kevin Knight 2008. pp. Second Part of Part 2, Question 169, Article 2, Reply to Objection 3.

16. Heylens G, De Cuypere G, Zucker KJ, Schelfaut C, Elaut E, Vanden Bossche H, De Baere E, and T'Sjoen G. *Gender Identity Disorder in Twins: A Review of the Case Report Literature.* s.l. : The Journal of Sexual Medicine, March 2012. pp. 751-757. Vol. 9; Issue 3.

17. Associated Press. Mom of Transgender Teen Denied Locker Room Access Speaks Out. November 14, 2015.

18. Goodstein, Laurie. Gay and Transgender Catholics Urge Pope Francis to Take a Stand. *The New York Times.* July 28, 2015.

19. Allen, John L. What do the pope's words mean for the Communion debate? *Crux.* August 5, 2015.

20. *Relatio Post Disceptationem of the General Rapporteur, Cardinal Péter Erdő.* Vatican City : Holy See Press Office, October 13, 2014.

21. Rocca, Francis X. *Family Synod Midterm Report: Welcome Gays, Nonmarital Unions.* Vatican City : Catholic News Service, October 13, 2014.

22. *Pastoral Challenges of the Family in the Context of Evangelization.* Vatican City : Synod of Bishops, October 18, 2014.

23. Martín, Inés San. Vatican Official Praises "Modern Family" for Raising Family Issues. *Crux, Boston Globe Media.* May 14, 2015.

24. Paglia, Vincenzo. President, Pontifical Council for the Family. [interv.] Raymond Arroyo. *The World Over.* May 21, 2015.

25. The Holy See. *Catechism of the Catholic Church, Second Edition.* Washington, DC : United States Catholic Conference of Bishops, 2000. Paragraphs 94 and 99.

26. Pentin, Edward. Cardinal Müller Warns Against Adapting the Church to Today's Often Pagan Lifestyles. *National Catholic Register.* June 8, 2015.

27. *Integrae Servandae, Apostolic Letter Given Motu Proprio.* The Holy See. Vatican City : s.n., December 7, 1965.

28. Rocca, Francis X. At First Angelus, Pope Francis Says God Never Tires of Forgiving. *Catholic News Service.* March 17, 2013.

29. Mena, Adelaide. Don't Claim Pope Francis for Your Own Agenda, Kasper Says Amid Controversy. *Catholic News Agency.* November 6, 2014.

30. Pope-Francis. *Transcript: Pope Francis' March 5 Interview with Corriere Della Sera.* [interv.] Ferruccio de Bortoli. [trans.] Estefania Aguirre and Alan Holdren. s.l. : Corriere Della Sera, March 5, 2014.

31. Catholic News Agency. *Bishop Heiner Koch, a German Delegate to Family Synod, Appointed Berlin Archbishop.* June 8, 2015.

32. Burke, Cardinal Raymond. *Cardinal Burke to CWR: Confirms Transfer, Praises Pushback.* [interv.] Carl E. Olson. s.l. : Catholic World Report, October 18, 2014.

33. Hickson, Maike. *Cardinal Kasper Defends Ireland's Gay Marriage Decision.* s.l. : LifeSiteNews, May 29, 2015.

34. Catholic Herald. *'If a Gay Person Seeks God, Who am I to Judge Him?' says Pope Francis.* July 13, 2013.

35. The Holy See. *Catechism of the Caholic Church, Second Edition.* Washington, DC : United States Catholic Conference of Bishops, 2000. Paragraph 1861.

36. —. *Catechism of the Caholic Church, Second Edition.* Washington, DC : United States Catholic Conference of Bishops, 2000. Paragraphs 1857-1860.

37. Center for Applied Research in the Apostolate, Georgetown University. *CARA Report, Mass Attendance.* 2014.

38. McElwee, Joshua J. Chicago's Cupich on Divorce: Pastor Guides Decisions, but Person's Conscience Inviolable. *National Catholic Reporter.* October 16, 2015.

39. Vorgrimler, Herbert, [ed.]. *Commentary on the Documents of Vatican II.* s.l. : Herder and Herder, 1968. Gaudium et Spes, Part 1, Chapter 1.

40. Salzman, Michael G. and Lawler,Todd A. Following Faithfully. *America Magazine.* February 2, 2015.

41. Hitchcock, James. *History of the Catholic Church.* San Francisco : Ignatius Press, 2012. p. 363.

42. Newman, John Henry Cardinal. *An Essay on the Development of Christian Doctrine.* London : Longmans, Green and Company, 1878.

43. McElwee, Joshua J. *Cardinal Marx: Doctrine Can Develop, Change.* s.l. : National Catholic Reporter, October 28, 2014.

44. Pope-Francis. A Big Heart Open to God. [interv.] S.J. Antonio Spadaro. s.l. : America Magazine, September 30, 2013.

45. Dick, John A. *Belgian Bishop Advocates Church Recognition of Gay Relationships.* December 30, 2014. National Catholic Reporter.

46. Pongratz-Lippitt, Christa. *Cardinal Marx: Pope Francis has Pushed Open the Doors of the Church.* s.l. : National Catholic Reporter, National Catholic Reporter, October 28, 2014.

47. Pentin, Edward. Pope Francis on Keys to Authentic Christian Humanism. *National Catholic Register.* November 10, 2015.

48. The Holy See. *Catechism of the Caholic Church, Second Edition.* Washington, DC : United States Catholic Conference of Bishops, 2000. Paragraph 66.

49. Sarah, Cardinal Robert and Diat, Nicolas. *Dieu ou Rien.* [trans.] Matthew Sherry. Quoted in Chiesa News, Gruppo Editoriale L'Espresso. Paris : Fayard, 2015.

50. Kasper, Cardinal Walter. [interv.] Raymond Arroyo. *World Over Live.* Washington, DC : EWTN, May 21, 2015.

51. Pennsylvania Bishops. In Truth and Love. *Pastoral Letter.* July 29, 1994.

52. Pompedda, Monsignor Mario F. Noted Rotal Auditor Explains Canonical Status of Catholics Who are Divorced and Civilly Remarried. *L'Osservatore Romano, English Edition.* September 16, 1992.

53. McNamara, Father Edward. Communion and the Divorced and Remarried. *Zenit.* February 11, 2014.

54. Burke, Daniel. *Pope Stirs Communion Debate with Call to Woman.* s.l. : CNN, April 21, 2014.

55. United States Catholic Conference of Bishops. *Church Teachings - Annulments.* [www.foryourmarriage.org] 2015.

56. Lisieux, Saint Thérèse of. *Story of a Soul, Third Edition.* [trans.] O.C.D. John Clarke. Washington, DC : ICS Publications, 1996. p. 77.

57. Avila, Saint Teresa of. *Interior Castle.* [ed.] E. Allison Peers. [trans.] E. Allison Peers. 1577.

58. The Holy See. *Catechism of the Caholic Church, Second Edition.* Washington, DC : United States Catholic Conference of Bishops, 2000. Paragraph 239.

59. —. *Catechism of the Caholic Church, Second Edition.* Washington, DC : United States Catholic Conference of Bishops, 2000. Paragraph 370.

60. Pope-Benedict-XVI. *Deus Caritas Est.* Vatican City : The Holy See, 2005. Paragraphs 3-4.

61. Aquinas, Thomas. Second Part of Part Two, Question 154. *Summa Theologica.* 1274.

62. Aquinas, St. Thomas. *Summa Theologica.* [trans.] Fathers-of-the-English-Dominican-Province. Second and Revised Edition 1920. s.l. : Online Edition by Kevin Knight 2008. pp. Second Part of Part 2, Question 154, Article 12, Reply to Objection 1, Whether the Unnatural Vice is the Greatest Sin Among the Species of Lust?

63. —. *Summa Theologica.* [trans.] Fathers-of-the-English-Dominican-Province. Second and Revised Edition 1920 . s.l. : Online Edition by Kevin Knight 2008. pp. First Part of the Second Part, Question 94, The Natural Law; Article 2. Whether the natural law contains several precepts, or only one?

64. House, Patrick, Vyas, Ajai and Sapolsky, Robert. Predator Cat Odors Activate Sexual Arousal Pathways in Brains of Toxoplasma Gondii Infected Rats. *PLOS ONE.* August 17, 2011.

65. Bendesky, Andres and Bargmann, Cornelia I. Genetic Contributions to Behavioural Diversity at the Gene-Environment Interface. *Nature Reviews - Genetics.* December 2011, Vol. 12, pp. 809-820.

66. Pavlov, Ivan. Physiology of Digestion. [Online] 1904. nobelprize.org/nobel_prizes/medicine/laureates/1904/pavlov-lecture.html.

67. Congregation for the Doctrine of the Faith. *Letter to the Bishops of the Catholic Church Concerning the Reception of Holy Communion by the Divorced and Remarried Members of the Faithful.* September 14, 1994.

68. The Holy See. *Catechism of the Caholic Church, Second Edition.* Washington, DC : United States Catholic Conference of Bishops, 2000. Paragraph 1324.

69. *Homily of the Closing Mass of the Eight World Meeting of Families.* Pope-Francis. s.l. : Vatican Publishing House, September 27, 2015.

70. Clifford, Leo. *Reflections.* Irondale : EWTN Catholic Publishing, 2015. pp. 26-27.

71. Hitchcock, James. *History of the Catholic Church.* San Francisco : Ignatius Press, 2012. p. 38.

72. Kaminker, Rabbi Mendy. Parshah Study: What Was Wrong with Sodom? *Chabad.org.* October 2012.

73. Skolnik, Fred (ed.). *Encyclopaedia Judaica.* Farmington Hills : Macmillan Reference USA in association with the Keter Publishing House, 2007. p. 561.

74. Pontifical Biblical Commission. *The Interpretation of the Bible in the Church.* Washington, DC : United States Catholic Conference of Bishops, 1993. p. 19.

75. *Meeting of the Holy Father Benedict XVI with the Clergy of the Dioceses of Belluno-Feltre and Treviso.* Pope Benedict XVI. Auronzo di Cadore : The Holy See, 2007.

76. Pernoud, Régine. *The Retrial of Joan of Arc: The Evidence for Her Vindication.* [trans.] J.M. Cohen. San Francisco : Ignatius Press, 2007. p. 125.

77. Herbermann, Charles G., et al., et al., [ed.]. *The Catholic Encyclopedia.* New York : Robert Appleton Company, 1911. Vol. 10.

78. Pernoud, Régine. *The Retrial of Joan of Arc: The Evidence for her Vindication.* [trans.] J.M. Cohen. San Francisco : Ignatius Press, 2007. p. 143.

79. Quicherat, Jules-Étienne-Joseph, [ed.]. *Procès de Condamnation et de Réhabilitation de Jeanne d'Arc.* Paris : Chez Jules Renouard, 1845. p. 88. Vol. 3.

80. Duparc, Pierre, [ed.]. *Procès en Nullité de la Condamnation de Jeanne d'Arc.* Paris : Klincksieck, 1977-88.

81. Murray, T. Douglas, [ed.]. *Jeanne D'Arc, Maid of Orleans, Deliverer of France.* New York : McClure, Phillips & Co., 1902.

82. Sullivan, Karen. "I Do Not Name to You the Voice of St. Michael:" The Identification of Joan of Arc's Voices. [ed.] Bonnie Wheeler and Charles T. Wood. *Fresh Verdicts on Joan of Arc.* New York : Garland Publishing, 1996, p. 88.

83. —. "I Do Not Name to You the Voice of St. Michael:" The Identification of Joan of Arc's Voices. [ed.] Bonnie Wheeler and Charles T. Wood. *Fresh Verdicts on Joan of Arc.* s.l. : Garland Publishing, 1996, p. 103.

84. Kelly, Henry Ansgar. Joan of Arc's Last Trial: The Attack of the Devil's Advocates. [ed.] Bonnie Wheeler and Charles T. Wood. *Fresh Verdicts on Joan of Arc.* New York : Garland Publishing, 1996, p. 210.

85. Kelly, Henry Angsar. Joan of Arc's Last Trial: The Attack of the Devil's Advocates. [ed.] Bonnie Wheeler and Charles T. Wood. *Fresh Verdicts on Joan of Arc.* New York : Garland Publishing, 1996, p. 218.

86. Pernoud, Régine. *The Retrial of Joan of Arc: The Evidence for her Vindication.* [trans.] J.M. Cohen. San Francisco : Ignatius Press, 2007. p. 234.

87. Kelly, Henry Angsar. Joan of Arc's Last Trial: The Attack of the Devil's Advocates. [ed.] Bonnie Wheeler and Charles T. Wood. *Fresh Verdicts on Joan of Arc.* New York : Garland Publishing, 1996, p. 224.

88. —. Joan of Arc's Last Trial: The Attack of the Devil's Advocates. [ed.] Bonnie Wheeler and Charles T. Wood. *Fresh Verdicts on Joan of Arc.* New York : Garland Publishing, 1996, p. 221.

89. —. Joan of Arc's Last Trial: The Attack of the Devil's Advocates. [ed.] Bonnie Wheeler and Charles T. Wood. *Fresh Verdicts on Joan of Arc.* New York : Garland Publishing, 1996, p. 215.

90. —. Joan of Arc's Last Trial: The Attack of the Devil's Advocates. [ed.] Bonnie Wheeler and Charles T. Wood. *Fresh Verdicts on Joan of Arc.* New York : Garland Publishing, 1996, p. 218.

91. The Indianapolis Journal. Will Not Be Canonized: Morals of Joan of Arc Were Not Those of a Saint. November 10, 1902, p. 2.

92. Minneapolis Journal. Joan of Arc; Canonization Denied to Her. *The Minneapolis Journal.* August 4, 1902.

93. Harper's Weekly. Joan of Arc Not to be Canonized. April 11, 1903, p. 610; Vol. 43.

94. Yuskaitis, Victoria. Joan of Arc: Inspired or Insane? *Schemata: Student Essays Across the Curriculum.* [Online] November 15, 2010. [Cited: September 27, 2015.] lycoming.edu/schemata/docs/FWRPrizeWinner_Yuskaitis_ENGL107.pdf.

95. Knock Museum. History. *Knock Shrine.* [Online] [Cited: September 27, 2015.] knockshrine.ie/history.

96. —. Witness Accounts. *Knock Shrine.* [Online] [Cited: September 27, 2015.] knockshrine.ie/history/witnesses-accounts.

97. Klins, June, [ed.]. *I Have Come to Tell the World that God Exists.* Bloomington : AuthorHouse, 2011. p. 28.

98. Pelletier, Father Joseph A. and Gonzalez, Conchita. *Our Lady Comes to Garabandal: Including Conchita's Diary.* Lindenhurst : Workers of Our Lady of Mount Carmel de Garabandal, 1971. p. 87.

99. Epilepsy Foundation. *Community Forum.* [Online] [Cited: September 27, 2015.] epilepsy.com/connect/forums/living-epilepsy-adults/ecstatic-seizures.

100. —. *Community Forum.* [Online] [Cited: September 27, 2015.] epilepsy.com/connect/forums/epilepsycom-help/left-temporal-lobe-epilepsy-and-premonitions.

101. Simpson, Mona. A Sister's Eulogy for Steve Jobs. *The New York Times.* October 30, 2011.

102. Winfrey, Oprah. *CNN Transcripts.* [Online] May 1, 2007. cnn.com/TRANSCRIPTS/0705/01/lkl.01.html.

103. Sauvage, George. Mysticism. *The Catholic Encyclopedia.* New York : Robert Appleton Company, 1911.

104. Christine, Lucie. *How Mary Responded to Jesus.* [ed.] Pierre-Marie Dumont. Yonkers : MAGNIFICAT, October 2015. pp. 97-98. Vol. 17.

105. Pelletier, Father Joseph A. and Gonzalez, Conchita. *Our Lady Come to Garabandal: Including Conchita's Diary.* s.l. : Workers of Our Lady of Mount Carmel de Garabandal, 1971. pp. 119-120.

106. Garrigou-Lagrange, Reginald, O.P. The Indwelling of the Blessed Trinity. *The Summa & Other Matters.* [Online] thesumma.info/reality/reality22.php.

107. The Holy See. *Catechism of the Caholic Church, Second Edition.* Washington, DC : United States Catholic Conference of Bishops, 2000. Paragraph 966.

108. Pope-Benedict-XVI. *The Solemnity of the Assumption of the Blessed Virgin Mary.* [ed.] Pierre-Marie Dumont. Yonkers : MAGNIFICAT, August 2012. Vol. 14.

109. The Holy See. *Catechism of the Caholic Church, Second Edition.* Washington, DC : United States Catholic Conference of Bishops, 2000. Paragraph 2559.

110. —. *Catechism of the Caholic Church, Second Edition.* Washington, DC : s.n., 2000. Paragraph 2562.

111. —. *Catechism of the Caholic Church, Second Edition.* Washington, DC : s.n., 2000. Paragraph 2563.

112. *Homily of Benedict XVI.* Pope Benedict XVI. 2011. 26th World Youth Day.

113. Gallagher, Timothy M. *The Discernment of Spirits.* New York : Crossroad Publishing, 2005. pp. 2-4.

114. Sullivan, Randall. *The Miracle Detective.* New York : Grove Press, 2004. p. 311.

115. —. *The Miracle Detective.* New York : Grove Press, 2004. p. 315.

116. —. *The Miracle Detective.* New York : Grove Press, 2004. p. 313.

117. —. *The Miracle Detective.* New York : Grove Press, 2004. pp. 313-314.

118. —. *The Miracle Detective.* New York : Grove Press, 2004. p. 314.

119. —. *The Miracle Detective.* New York : Grove Press, 2004. p. 316.

120. Faricy, Robert. *Our Lady Comes to Scottsdale: Is it Authentic?* Milford : The Riehle Foundation, 1991. p. viii.

121. The Holy See. *Catechism of the Caholic Church, Second Edition.* Washington, Dc : United States Catholic Conference of Bishops, 2000. Paragraph 1670.

122. Ivereigh, Austen. *The Great Reformer; Francis and the Making of a Radical Pope.* New York, NY : Henry Holt and Company, 2014. p. 193.

123. Hitchcock, James. *History of the Catholic Church.* San Francisco : Ignatius Press, 2012. p. 493.

124. Ratzinger, Joseph Cardinal. *The Spirit of the Liturgy.* San Francisco : Ignatius Press, 2000. p. 128.

125. Tracy, Tom. Venerating Relic a Chance for Youths to Reflect on John Paul's Papacy. *Catholic News Services.* November 7, 2013.

126. Pernoud, Régine. *The Retrial of Joan of Arc: The Evidence for her Vindication.* [trans.] J.M. Cohen. San Francisco : Ignatius Press, 2007. p. 99.

127. *Alternatives to the Wright-Fisher Model: The Robustness of Mitochondrial Eve Dating.* Krzysztof, Cyran and Kimmel, Marek. 3, June 19, 2010, Theoretical Population Biology, Vol. 78, pp. 165-172. doi: 10.1016/j.tpb.2010.06.00.

128. Pernoud, Régine. *The Retrial of Joan of Arc: The Evidence for her Vindication.* [trans.] J.M. Cohen. San Francisco : Ignatius Press, 2007. p. 86.

129. Kelly, Henry Ansgar. Joan of Arc's Last Trial: The Attack of the Devil's Advocates. [ed.] Bonnie Wheeler and Charles T. Wood. *Fresh Verdicts on Joan of Arc.* New York : Garland Publishing, 1996, p. 219.

130. Green, Bernard D. Catholicism Confronts New Age Syncretism. *New Oxford Review.* April 1994.

131. Kready, Laura. *A Study of Fairy Tales.* Boston : Houghton Mifflin - Riverside Press, 1916. p. 160.

132. Pernoud, Régine. *The Retrial of Joan of Arc: The Evidence for her Vindication.* [trans.] J.M. Cohen. San Francisco : Ignatius Press, 2007. p. 72.

133. —. *The Retrial of Joan of Arc: The Evidence for her Vindication.* [trans.] J.M. Cohen. San Francisco : Ignatius Press, 2007. p. 81.

134. The Holy See. *Catechism of the Caholic Church, Second Edition.* Washington, DC : United States Catholic Conference of Bishops, 2000. Paragraph 460.

135. Montfort, Louis-Marie Grignon De. A Treatise on the True Devotion to the Blessed Virgin. *ewtn.com.* [Online] ewtn.com/library/Montfort/TRUEDEVO.HTM. Paragraph 55.

136. Lisieux, Saint Thérèse of. *Story of a Soul, Third Edition.* [trans.] O.C.D. John Clarke. Washington, DC : ICS Publications, 1996. p. 192.

137. —. *Story of a Soul, Third Edition.* [trans.] O.C.D. John Clarke. Washington DC : ICS Publications, 1996. pp. 193-194.

138. —. *Story of a Soul, Third Edition.* [trans.] O.C.D. John Clarke. Washington DC : ICS Publications, 1996. p. 194.

139. Augustine, Saint. Homily 7 on the First Epistle of John. [ed.] Philip Schaff and online edition edited by Kevin Knight 2009. *Nicene and Post-Nicene Fathers, First Series, Vol. 7.* Buffalo : Christian Literature Publishing Company, 1888.

140. Ratzinger, Joseph Cardinal and Seewald, Peter. *God and the World: A Conversation with Peter Seewald.* San Francisco : Ignatius Press, 2002. p. 306.

141. Pope-Pius-XII. *Ad Caeli Reginam: Encyclical Proclaiming the Queenship of Mary.* s.l. : Vatican Library, 1954.

142. Congregation of Divine Worship. Preface of Mary at the Foot of the Cross II. *Collection of Masses of the Virgin Mary: Missal.* Collegeville : The Liturgical Press, 2012, p. 94.

143. Encyclopedia Britannica. Mystical Body of Christ . [Online] October 20, 2009. britannica.com/topic/mystical-body-of-Christ.

144. The Holy See. *Catechism of the Caholic Church, Second Edition.* Washington DC : United States Catholic Conference of Bishops, 2000. Paragraph 964.

145. —. *Catechism of the Caholic Church, Second Edition.* Washington, DC : United States Catholic Conference of Bishops, 2000. Paragraphs 1999 and 2000.

146. —. *Catechism of the Caholic Church, Second Edition.* Washington, DC : United States Catholic Conference of Bishops, 2000. Paragraphs 2001 and 2002.

147. —. *Catechism of the Caholic Church, Second Edition.* Washington, DC : United States Catholic Conference of Bishops, 2000. Paragraphs 2000 and 2003.

148. Gaitley, Michael E. *The One Thing is Three.* Stockbridge, MA : Marian Fathers of the Immaculate Conception, 2012. p. 43.

149. Booth, Warren, et al., et al. Facultative Parthenogenesis Discovered in Wild Vertebrates. *Biology Letters.* September 12, 2012.

150. Montfort, Louis-Marie Grignon De. *A Treatise on The True Devotion to The Blessed Virgin.* [trans.] Frederick William Faber. London : Burns and Lambert, 1863. pp. 27-28.

151. Apostoli, Andrew. *Fatima for Today.* San Francisco : Ignatius Press, 2010. p. 183.

152. Dirvin, Joseph I. *Saint Catherine Labouré of the Miraculous Medal.* Charlotte : TAN Books, 1984.

153. Calvat, Melanie. Apparition of the Blessed Virgin on the Mountain of La Salette 19 September 1846. *Fordham Univeristy Modern History Sourcebook.* [Online]

154. Sanctuaire Notre-Dame de Lourdes. The Apparitions in 1858. [Online] en.lourdes-france.org/deepen/bernadette-soubirous/the-apparitions.

155. Gaál, Emery de. *On a Criteriology for Mariophanies: The Marian Apparitions in Robinsonville/Champion in the Diocese of Green Bay (Wisconsin).* University of St. Mary of the Lake. Mundelein, IL : s.n.

156. Dominica, Sister Mary. *The Chapel, Our Lady of Good Help: A Shrine of Mary on the Green Bay Peninsula.* Green Bay : The Sisters of St. Francis of Bay Settlement, 1955. p. 8.

157. Gaál, Emery de. *On a Criteriology for Mariophanies: The Marian Apparitions in Robinsonville/Champion in the Diocese of Green Bay (Wisconsin).* University of St. Mary of the Lake. Mundelein, Illinois : s.n. p. 7.

158. Barbedette, Joseph. Pontmain, France, 1871, Our Lady of Hope. *ewtn.com.* [Online] https://www.ewtn.com/Devotionals/novena/hopepontmain.htm.

159. O'Neill, Michael. Gietrzwald, Poland (1877). *The Miracle Hunter.* [Online] miraclehunter.com/marian_apparitions/approved_apparitions/gietrzwald/index.html.

160. Apostoli, Andrew. *Fatima for Today.* San Francisco, CA : Ignatius Press, 2010.

161. Santos, Lucia. *Fatima In Lucia's Own Words.* [ed.] Louis Kondor. [trans.] Dominican-Nuns-of-Perpetual-Rosary. 16. Fatima : Secretariado Dos Pastorinhos, 2007. p. 182.

162. DeMarchi, John. *Fatima: From the Beginning.* [trans.] I.M. Kingsbury. Fatima : Missões Consolata, 2006. p. 140.

163. —. *Fatima: From the Beginning.* [trans.] I.M. Kingsbury. Fatima : Missões Consolata, 2006. p. 137.

164. —. *Fatima: From the Beginning.* [trans.] I.M. Kingsbury. Fatima : Missões Consolata, 2006. p. 136.

165. —. *141-Fatima: From the Beginning.* [trans.] I.M. Kingsbury. Fatima : Missões Consolata, 2006. p. 141.

166. Message of Fatima: Part III. *Soul.* Winter 2009, p. 7.

167. Sharkey, Don. *A Woman Clothed with the Sun.* pp. 226-227.

168. Miravalle, Mark. *Meet Your Mother.* Stockbridge, MA : Marian Press and Lighthouse Catholic Media, 2014. pp. 79-80.

169. —. *Meet Your Mother.* Stockbridge : Marian Press and Lighthouse Catholic Media, 2014. pp. 80-81.

170. Peerdeman, Ida. Our Lady of All Nations. *Fifth Marian Dogma.* [Online] fifthmariandogma.com.

171. Pelletier, Father Joseph A. and Gonzalez, Conchita. *Our Lady Comes to Garabandal: Including Conchita's Diary.* Lindenhurst : Workers of Our Lady of Mount Carmel de Garabandel, 1971. p. 70.

172. —. *Our Lady Comes to Garabandal: Including Conchita's Diary.* Lindenhurst : Workers of Our Lady of Mount Carmel de Garabandal, 1971. p. 44.

173. —. *Our Lady Comes to Garabandal: Including Conchita's Diary.* Lindenhurst : Workers of Our Lady of Mount Carmel de Garabandal, 1971. p. 45.

174. —. *Our Lady Comes to Garabandal: Including Conchita's Diary.* Lindenhurst : Workers of Our Lady of Mount Carmel de Garabandal, 1971. p. 174.

175. —. *Our Lady Comes to Garabandal: Including Conchita's Diary.* Lindenhurst : Workers of Our Lady of Mount Caramel de Garabandal, 1971. p. 176.

176. Coptic Orthodox Church, Cairo, Egypt. The Apparitions Of The Blessed Holy Virgin Mary. *zeitun-eg.org/zeitoun1.htm.* [Online]

177. Johnston, Francis. *When Millions Saw Mary.* Chulmleigh : Augustine Publishing, 1980. p. 23.

178. Rizk, Wagih. Mr. Wagih Rizk Collection Of Photos. *zeitun-eg.org/zeitngal.htm.* [Online]

179. Cruz, Joan Carroll. *Miraculous Images of Our Lady.* Charlotte : TAN Books, 1993. p. 269.

180. —. *Miraculous Images of Our Lady.* Charlotte : TAN Books, 1993. pp. 271-272.

181. Aquilina, Mike. *Our Guardian Angel.* [ed.] Pierre-Marie Dumont. Yonkers : MAGNIFICAT, October 2015. Vol. 17.

182. Ilibagiza, Immaculée and Erwin, Steve. *Our Lady of Kibeho: Mary Speaks to the World from the Heart of Africa.* Carlsbad : Hay House, 2008. pp. 35-36.

183. —. *Our Lady of Kibeho: Mary Speaks to the World from the Heart of Africa.* Carlsbad : Hay House, 2008. pp. 40-41.

184. —. *Our Lady of Kibeho: Mary Speaks to the World from the Heart of Africa.* Carlsbad : Hay House, 2008. pp. 146-149.

185. The Holy See. *Lumen Gentium, Dogmatic Constitution of the Church.* Vatican City : s.n., 1964. Paragraph 16.

186. Santos, Lucia. *Fatima In Lucia's Own Words.* [ed.] Louis Kondor. [trans.] Dominican-Nuns-of-Perpetual-Rosary. 16. Fatima : Secretariado Dos Pastorinhos, 2007. p. 124.

187. Pope-Benedict-XVI. *Easter Vigil Homily.* s.l. : Vatican, April 15, 2006.

188. Wright, N.T. *The Resurrection of the Son of God.* Minneapolis : Fortress Press, 2003. pp. 57-59.

189. *Loophole-Free Bell Inequality Violation Using Electron Spins Separated by 1.3 Kilometres.* B. Hensen, H. Bernien, A. E. Dréau, A. Reiserer, N. Kalb, M. S. Blok, J. Ruitenberg, R. F. L. Vermeulen, R. N. Schouten, C. Abellán, W. Amaya, V. Pruneri, M. W. Mitchell, M. Markham, D. J. Twitchen, D. Elkouss, S. Wehner, T. H. Taminiau & R. Hanson. London : Nature Publishing Group/Macmillan, October 21, 2015, Nature. doi:10.1038.

190. Ignatius Press. *Essential Role of the Laity.* s.l. : Ignatius Press, 2006. p. 1.

191. The Holy See. *Code of Canon Law.* s.l. : Vatican Library. Canon 212-213.

Made in the USA
San Bernardino, CA
22 January 2017